PREACHERS VS. PORN

PREACHERS VS. PORN

EXPOSING CHRISTIANITY'S WAR ON SEXXX

MARK KERNES

Charleston, SC
www.PalmettoPublishing.com

Preachers Vs. Porn

Hardcover ISBN: 979-8-8229-0960-1
Paperback ISBN: 979-8-8229-0961-8

TABLE OF CONTENTS

INTRODUCTION

Most of you have never heard of me (unless you watched the AOL Build panel on the "documentary" (yeah, right) *Hot Girls Wanted*, read the chapters I authored in the *International Encyclopedia of Human Sexuality*, or read *Adult Video News* or its website for the past 35 years).

But over the course of my employment with *Adult Video News* (*AVN*), I'd become very interested in the politics of the adult industry, and perhaps more importantly, how national/world politics affects the adult industry—particularly the intersection of politics and religion as they affect that industry. I just may be one of the country's foremost authorities on that subject. The current volume is a compendium of some of my more interesting reporting on that subject, and serves as a history of the interactions, political and social, between porn, politics, the clergy and religious right activists.

For me, it all began on that fateful day in February 1983 when I walked into Movies Unlimited, a major videotape(!) renter/retailer in Northeast Philadelphia, looking to rent a XXX-rated tape or two, and when I found a couple that I thought would get me off, I took them to the front counter to be checked out. The cashier was a fairly young guy, and when he saw I was renting XXX tapes, he pointed me to a small pile of black-and-white magazines that were sitting on the counter. That was my introduction to *Adult Video News*, and it turned out that the cashier was also the magazine's publisher, Paul Fishbein. We got to talking, and I think he saw in me a budding writer, and asked if I'd like to review a few tapes, which reviews would be published in his magazine.

"Maybe," I replied. "What does it pay?"

"$15 apiece, and you get to keep the tape," came the answer.

"Sold!" I said.

And so began my 38-year association with *AVN*, its three (main) owners during that period, and my entré into what I still think is the most fascinating industry on the planet, the adult entertainment industry.

Though the magazine began and was originally based in Philly, with Fishbein occasionally heading up to New York City to read reviews of XXX movies on *The Howard Stern Show*, Fish (as most called him) realized that although there was a thriving adult production industry in Manhattan, the real "motherlode" of adult activity was in Los Angeles, and in mid-1991, he announced that the magazine would be moving to LA... and would I like a full-time job on its staff?

At the time, I was a court reporter—not the journalistic kind; the guy who sits behind a small piano-like gadget and types on its keys to record what witnesses are saying in court or in depositions—and while it made me very nervous to give up that fairly lucrative job, the siren call of people having sex on camera seemed worth taking a chance on—and after all, if it didn't work out, I could always go back to court reporting.

So I became *AVN*'s Managing Editor for a time (in the process, introducing the term "gonzo video" as a genre in the adult mix because I've long been an avid Hunter Thompson fan), and eventually segued into becoming its Legal Affairs Editor, thanks to my legal background. In that capacity, I got Fish to send me to Senate hearings in Washington, D.C. that were targeting porn; Supreme Court arguments regarding obscenity cases and other legal attacks on "the industry" (as everyone who's in it calls it), and even conventions put on by conservatives, fundamentalists or some combination of both, like the Conservative Political Action Conferences (CPAC) and the Values Voter Summits (VVS), several of which reports are contained in this volume.

Incidentally, you'll see lots of "statistics" quoted by the speakers at the conferences I've attended and written about, and the stats drawn from the articles these ultra-religious types have authored. My advice: Don't take any of them at face value; do your own research if you must.

But this is largely a history book, and I should probably note in passing that readers will see a couple of themes repeated throughout, in large part because as I continued to cover the anti-porn scene, certain themes like so-called "porn addiction" and the idea that just about any woman who would perform sex on camera had to be trafficked into it continued (continue!) to be claimed in religious/conservative mailings and e-mailings. Moreover, of late, the fundies have decided that any form of prostitution—and the vast majority of it is consensual, a simple transaction between pro and client—is "sex trafficking," an accusation meant to tar the profession with the claim that most prostitution is *not* consensual. Since The Faithful have continued to harp on those themes, and for *AVN* readers who might have missed earlier articles covering those topics, they bore repeating a couple of times.

Anyway, in the course of my news-gathering, I wound up subscribed to an awful lot of Religious Right and conservative "news" feeds—I'm guessing these groups frequently trade or buy email lists from one another—and I've got to say, it's still a joy (in a nausea-inducing way) to read them, so as I'm writing this, here are a few "gems" gleaned from the past few weeks' offerings:

•Thomas More Society: "Cake designer Cathy Miller has been vindicated in the California courts for practicing her Christian principles on the job. On October 21, 2022, attorneys from the Thomas More Society brought home a First Amendment victory for the cake shop owner of Tastries, a popular Bakersfield, California bakery that was targeted by gay activists. The ruling, handed down by Judge Eric Bradshaw of the Superior Court of California in Kern County, decided for Miller in a lawsuit brought against her by the Department of Fair Housing and Employment."

•Mat Staver, Liberty Counsel: "Imagine ropes restraining your body as you struggle to break the surface of the water to suck in another gasp of air. A nearby person wants to help you, but the rescuer is being physically restrained. This frantic fight for life is how our counselors and their clients feel in the face of horrible laws that ban lifesaving counsel for people caught in the bondage of UNWANTED same-sex attractions, behavior or gender confusion. Believe me, this is a struggle for life and death."

•American Family Association: "In the wake of the high court rulings in June in favor of religious liberty and the rights of states to limit or end abortion, a Heartland Institute poll found that:

> **"53% of Democrats and 54% of people ages 19 to 39 said they support abolishing the Supreme Court and replacing it with justices elected directly by the people. The high court is fundamentally a racist and sexist institution, according to these people.**

"Even more stunning, the poll found that almost half of the young people surveyed (48%) were in favor of allowing the United Nations to overrule the U.S. Supreme Court." [Emphasis in original]

•Stephen Moore, Townhall.com: "It was about eight to 10 years ago that the Left made a unilateral decision to shut down all opposition and any skepticism about climate change by pronouncing that the debate was over.

"The 'scientific consensus' had been reached, as if sent down on tablets from God, that mankind was causing the rapid warming of the planet. Period. End of argument. Doubters will be denounced as science deniers and stripped of their science credentials and muzzled by the speech police."

One of the major anti-adult memes making the rounds these days is that the adult industry is a haven for sex traffickers, and that many of the female performers are trafficked women. Don't believe it. I know a fair number of people in what I think of as the "official" adult industry, based in L.A., San Francisco and New York City, and they're there because they want to be, or at least because they see the money that can be made as a successful actress or movie producer—and frankly, from what I've read and the people I've spoken to, trafficked women just aren't good enough actresses to fool people into thinking they really like what they're doing if they actually don't.

Not all the "preachers" herein are clergy; some are just blathering "believers" with little or no scientific/research backgrounds but who nonetheless feel they have a right to comment on a subject about which most have near-total ignorance.

Interestingly, but perhaps not too surprisingly, most of the articles quoted in this volume that appeared on conservative/Religious Right websites are no longer available on the Web. After all, the "facts" contained in many of them have since been proven so appallingly wrong, it's no wonder the purveyors of same don't want their acolytes to be able to see (and research) them.

But if I had to say one thing that most attracted (attracts!) me to the adult industry, it's the open-mindedness that so many of my industry friends and acquaintances have, and which led me to think in new pathways myself.

Anyone remember *Pleasantville*? It was a 1998 movie about a kid who gets magically transported into a town whose name was the title for a *Leave It To Beaver/Father Knows Best* black-and-white '50s TV show, and how his presence transforms the entire community and all its inhabitants from colorless to multihuedness. But the thing that struck me most about the movie was the early scene where the protagonist's TV mother, played by Joan Allen, begins to masturbate as she's taking a bath, noticing that as she becomes more aroused, things around her begin to show their colors—and when she reaches orgasm, a tree just outside her window bursts into flames—the town's first actual fire *ever*—and Allen herself becomes the show's first "colored" citizen.

Mainstream Hollywood rarely gets so subtly graphic in how it depicts sex, in part from worry that they'll somehow be charged with obscenity, as were the owners of a video store in Oklahoma City that rented *The Tin Drum* to some people. (Of course, the case was thrown out.)

But while *The Tin Drum* case was essentially a child porn bust—the young-looking male protagonist gets to stare at a naked woman—it's almost funny that one of the "definitions" of obscenity contained in the Supreme Court's *Miller* decision is that the alleged obscene content makes you horny, and that it has no "redeeming social value." Guess what? Making people horny IS a redeeming social value!

Of all the activities that human beings engage in, *the* most important one is sex. That should be self-evident: Without sex, there *are* no human beings. Sadly, however, somewhere below sex but still in the Top 10 list of human activities is religion; many humans seem to have brain chemistry that makes them susceptible to the fantasy that there's some overriding entity that created everything and/or cares intimately what human beings do with their lives—and that one of the things that humans do that the entity cares very deeply about is how, when, where and with whom they have sex.

Think about this for a second: According to the Bible, Eve was created by God by forming her from one of Adam's ribs—sort of the ultimate male power trip, when you think about it—but after that single instance of creating a new life, women have done all the heavy lifting (so to speak) since. And let's not forget the significance of the tempting "snake"—an obvious stand-in for a male penis—which tempts Eve and led to the downfall of humankind until rescued by—you guessed it—another guy. And let's not forget that the most likely reason why the Bible has nothing good to say about gays is that gay people, at least back in the Olden Days, didn't have kids, and if there's one thing a church needs, it's congregants, and gays don't supply those, so fuck 'em, right?

And let's not forget, the Catholic church is the largest aggregation of pedophiles—priests!—in the world, and who knows how many more pedophile clergy are being hidden by other religions. The Freedom From Religion Foundation publishes lists of clergy busted for pedophilia and other crimes in its monthly newsletter.

About the format of this volume: Most of the articles are presented in chronological order—that is, by the date (or month, in the case of articles that only showed up in *AVN* magazine) on which they were published—but some have been strung together because it made sense to keep discussions of a single topic in one close space, especially regarding the two main anti-adult congressional bills *cum* court cases, the Child Pornography Prevention Act (CPPA) and the Child Online Protection Act (COPA). I've added prefaces to some of the articles either to clarify some terms used and/or identify and give background to some of the "characters" mentioned.

About the quotes: I spent 20 years as a court reporter and so by training, in quoting someone, I always use the exact words a person has said—and sometimes, they don't speak very clearly or grammatically, which necessitates the use of a dash when the sentence goes off-track. I also use ellipses to indicate words that were left out because they weren't germane to the quoted material and/or didn't change the meaning of the quote.

The internet (formerly Internet) was in its infancy back in 1994, so gathering information on religion's war on sex was tougher to come by—unless one went to church on a regular basis, and the "right" church at that. Fortunately, AVN employed a clipping service that would physically(!) send us porn-related articles from newspapers across the country. My interest in the connection between religion and sex began fairly early, and the following is one of the first pieces I wrote that directly tackled the subject.

THE GREATEST ROADBLOCK TO SEXUAL SANITY

January 1994

I remember that a cold chill went down my spine upon reading, once again, about a monastery in Southern California, a dozen of whose priests admitted that over the last 30 or so years, they had molested 34 young boys. That clerical practice is nowhere near as rare as everyone from the Pope on down would have us citizens believe, and just about every level of clergyman from Chicago's Cardinal Bernardin down to the lowliest deacon has been accused at one time or another of illegally fiddling around with America's youth.

We at *AVN* are probably more familiar with this problem than most, because our clipping service has supplied us, over the past five years, with literally scores of newspaper articles detailing accusations against and convictions of priests, ministers, etc. (as well as cops, schools teachers, etc.) in child sexual molestation cases.

Now, supposedly, these child molesters were, to all outward appearances, normal, upstanding citizens, and many of the clergymen in particular had taken vows of celibacy which would seem to preclude fooling around with the altar boys. That they did so anyway makes them hypocrites—but moreover, it calls into question churches' teachings about sex.

Let's talk for a moment about how society views sex, and how that philosophy manifests itself in concrete examples.

How many of you have *ever* told your parents that you masturbate? If you did, how old were you when you did? (Your parents walking in on you while you were doing it doesn't count.) In this day and age, why are people still writing to advice columnists like *Dear Abby*, asking whether they should "lose their virginity"? (Her sister Ann Landers has actually recommended masturbation as the preferred sexual release for horny folks without partners—and has gotten a ration of shit for it from the Truly Uptight.)

Let's go a little deeper. Why is a young girl's "loss of virginity" (an interesting phrase in itself; no one gives a second thought to cutting hair or fingernails) any bigger of a deal than her joining the school softball team? Would *Dear Abby* find worth printing in her column letters from men and women who are 25 or 30 years old who actually boast of never having had sex? Paying any respect to such a twisted outlook simply supports the concept that ignorance is a virtue!

And deeper still! How many women would find it repulsive to give their husbands or boyfriends a blowjob? How many men find it distasteful to lick a pussy? How many more people would ever even consider licking their partner's ass, much less engaging in anal intercourse?

The answer to these questions is a big complex, but fundamentally, all of these sex-related quirks are the result of American culture being so steeped in the Judeo-Christian biblical view of sex that one need never go to services or ever read a religious tract to have absorbed the Church's lessons. Not even self-proclaimed atheists (nor the quiet, practical, unofficial kind) are immune.

It starts with one's earliest training, when little Johnny has stuck a hand down his trousers and is fiddling with his cock, and mommy screams, "Don't touch that!" It starts when daddy warns his little girl not to lift her dress in public, even if she's wearing underpants. The Message is constantly droned in, hammered in, wormed in, snuck in undercover, secretly, stealthily, clandestinely, furtively, *ignorantly* from every direction and in every context—and The Message is that sex and anything to do with sex is somehow special and certainly not be considered rationally or objectively, because... sex is dirty and sex is just plain WRONG except under very special circumstances.

And guess what, folks? This is the biggest problem facing the adult entertainment industry today, and when all other objections to the industry's work are eliminated, this one will remain, as long as the Great American

Electorate doesn't realize (or refuses to realize) that nearly every single legal barrier imposed on the sex act—rape excluded, of course—is a direct result of the influence of Judeo-Christian theology.

Now, this is specifically not an attack on the many life-affirming teachings of the Christian, Jewish and even Islamic religions, but their views on sex have become the basis for every sex law on the books. Take the legal definition of "obscenity," for example. The dictionary defines the term as "material arousing a morbid or prurient interest in sex." Well, "morbid," at least as understood by any potential jury member, might apply to having a fetish for dead bodies or rotting garbage or such-like, but it could hardly be applied to any consensual sex act—unless the juror has a pretty fucked-up idea of sex in the first place. And as for "prurient," my dictionary defines it as "impure, immoral, dirty, unclean"—and again, none of these apply to consensual sex acts... except possibly "immoral"—but in our culture, "morality" is only susceptible to definition in *religious* terms, and our Constitution supposedly prevents its citizens from being persecuted for their *religious* beliefs.

The problem is, as I've said before, that adult entertainers deal with sex differently (dare I say "more rationally"?) than their outside cousins—and the Judeo-Christian American culture demands that the performers be persecuted for being saner about sex than their fellow citizens. Americans must learn to look at Sex rationally and objectively, free of biblical influence, if our children are to have any hope of becoming truly "normal".

The genesis (if you'll pardon the expression) for this article was something I read in my all-time-favorite magazine, Paul Krassner's The Realist, *whose issue #16 featured an interview*[1] *with a famous psychologist Dr. Albert Ellis, who, after being asked, "Isn't the apparently inconsistent use of the word fuck due to the fact that it actually has two meanings? ... How about the famous Army saying, 'Fuck all of them but six and save them for pallbearers'. There, fuck means kill." Ellis responded, "Yes, and it is wrongly used. It should be 'Unfuck all of them but six.'" Also, for "some reason," I'm reminded of these lyrics from one of my favorite songs by The Tubes:*

> *The smell of burning leather*
> *As we hold each other tight*
> *As our rivets rub together*
> *Flashing sparks into the night*
> *At this moment of surrender, darling*
> *If you really care*
> *Don't touch me There*

TAKING BACK THE LANGUAGE OF SEX

September 1995

"Fuck you!" Hard to think of a nastier insult one person can throw at another, isn't it? But think about it: "Fuck" means "to have sex with." When said by one male to another, the phrase could be interpreted as an attempt to exercise control. (Historically, the male leader of a tribe gets to have sex with anybody he wants.) But when said by a male to a female, or vice-versa, the issue is slightly different. Certainly, in our society, nobody thinks that one is trying to exercise control over another when the phrase is used. Yet "fuck," when used in any other context than as an insult, is meant to convey a reasonably pleasurable experience. In adult videos, people fuck each other every day, and often have a pretty good time doing it. So how did the phrase that means "I (or somebody else) want(s) to have sex with you" become an insult?

There's probably a scholarly answer to that question, which, even if I knew it, would no doubt be much too long to print here. But that's not the point. The point is, when Americans want to insult each other, they talk about having sex. And when we realize that the expletive is often accompanied by a gesture of a raised fist with the middle finger sticking upward, a fair representation of an erect cock and balls, the carnal picture is complete.

To someone who thinks that having sex is a beautiful, fun thing to do, the idea of insulting another person by saying "fuck you" has got to sound crazy, yet nearly every one of us does it just about daily. And on some unconscious level, we all know what the phrase really means—and that realization has got to play havoc, again on an unconscious level, with our attitudes towards sex.

Anyone who's ever watched a major movie on commercial TV knows there are a few words that were in the original version that you'll never hear: "tits," "cock," "pussy," "ass" and a few others. Infinity Broadcasting, which syndicates the *Howard Stern Show*, recently paid more than $1 million in fines because Stern said some of those words on the air. Why?

In "polite society," a woman who has sex with a number of different men is termed a "tramp." "Tramp" is also a slightly archaic word for a bum, an indigent person who doesn't work, and begs for food and shelter. The male equivalent, "stud," doesn't have anywhere near the same negative connotation—but if certain so-called feminists have their way, it will. If sex is fun, and there are no exclusivity agreements to interfere, what's wrong with this picture?

Before answering, we have to add one more "fact": Just about everything everyone in the adult entertainment industry does is "immoral." Why? Because for the vast majority of Americans, what's "moral" and, more importantly, what isn't, are defined by the tenets of the two major western religions, Christianity and Judaism—with Islam a close third. Sex within marriage is good, they say; sex outside isn't. Sex with multiple partners is also a "sin," and if you get paid for doing it, that's even worse. And if you find yourself attracted to someone of the same sex, those good Judeo-Christians would just as soon you stay in your closet.

The problem is, we, as sexual creatures, have allowed those who fear and want to control sex to define our sexual experiences for us. Their definitions, which we have unthinkingly adopted, have so colored our attitudes about sex that most Americans can no longer consider the subject dispassionately. Worse, most of these wacky religious opinions have become incorporated into law. Hence, anyone who practices prostitution, anyone who transports a woman across state lines for "immoral purposes," anyone who walks down a public street (in most cities) without wearing clothes, any farm or frat boy who's thinking about fucking a heifer—and on and on and on—could easily find him- or herself behind bars for no rational reason.

Fighters for sexual freedom have two very hard jobs ahead of them. Not only must they redefine "morality" to include an intelligent, commonsensical, realistic view of interpersonal (especially sexual) relationships, but they must rid the culture of everyday expressions that portray a negative view of sex. Why do I think that this latter project may be the harder one?

Ah, the "good old days" when nobody talked about pedophile priests... And I may have been wrong about sex not being mentioned in the Founding Documents; some theorize that the phrase "pursuit of Happiness" in the Declaration of Independence actually refers to it being OK to have sex. (Note: This was written prior to the Supreme Court's decision in Lawrence v. Texas, which legalized consensual sodomy.)

WORDS TO LIVE BY

November 1996

Leafing through *The New York Times* in late September, I came across an article[1] extolling the virtues of the Norman Vincent Peale Center for Christian Living, where apparently at least some of the employees (or possibly they're just volunteers) sit around all day praying.

"Downstairs, in a room the size of a large closet, Jackie King squeezes her eyes shut, leans forward into a speakerphone, and lets the words roll out in a torrent: 'Heavenly Father, we come to you on behalf of Bob's nephew Fred, who's been going through some serious problems in the area of his heart. Father, the doctors have tried all that they thought they could, and now they feel they have to open him up and have surgery, and we pray that you would be in the midst of everything that is done, that you would heal his body, completely heal his heart.'"

Now, those of us who find it unbelievable that there's some omnipresent, omnipotent, omnibenevolent entity running the universe think that talking to the air like this is seriously delusional. Not to mention a complete waste of time.

But in (as I write this) the waning days of the presidential campaigns, there seems to be some attempt on the part of the media to bring us all "closer to God"—some sort of building-upon (or cashing–in-on) both major candidates' "I'm holier than thou in a secular sort of way" stance, and a more vicious threat I haven't seen in quite a while.

For instance, a couple of weeks ago, the *Los Angeles Times* ran a piece which said, essentially, that science is (or at least a bunch of the scientists they interviewed are) a little bit religious, and believe it or not, religion is a little bit scientific. (Eeeennnnhhh—wrong!)

And then, building on the success of last season's *Touched By An Angel*, the fall '96 TV season is delivering up such smash-hit new shows as *Seventh Heaven*, about a family where dad (Stephen Collins) is a preacher who, according to one review, "knows better than *Father Knows Best*," and flashes toothy smiles like Dudley Do-Right.

There are other examples of this sort of rampant religiosity, and have been through the length of recorded history, but what it all boils down to, for anyone who's interested in sexual sanity, is that "the church" (or "synagogue" or "mosque" or whatever) pretty much has everybody by the balls—figuratively, of course, but a bit closer to "literally" than I care to think about too much.

You see, sex is a primary human instinct. Valerie Solanas, the assassin (assassinatrix?) of Andy Warhol, once wrote that men would "swim through a river of snot, wade nostril-deep through a mile of vomit" to get laid by "any snaggle-toothed hag," and though that statement certainly doesn't apply to anyone reading this (hee-hee), at least it conveys the urgency of the sexual urge. I'm pretty sure the urge to eat and the urge to fuck are vying neck-and-neck for top honors.

So it should be clear that any person or organization that can put any sort of controls on a person's urge to fuck has gone a long way to putting controls on a person's thought processes—dare I say "entire life?"

Those are the battle lines, and for most people, the enemy has already invaded the front; people are indoctrinated with religious views of sex since their first contacts with society at large, and in most cases, merely through what they "learned at their mother's knee." Even atheists are affected, because sexual taboos can be conveyed by a simple gesture or expression of shock or surprise, and after one sees enough of these over a course of years, something sinks in.

All the laws about prostitution, sodomy, public nudity, pornography and the myriad other sexually-related activities in which adult humans (no pedophiles, please) engage every day are based on religious beliefs... and are contrary to logic, reason, common sense and the U.S. Constitution. We know about this last part because sex (the act, not the gender) isn't even mentioned in that great document. What *are* mentioned are the Ninth and Tenth Amendments, which read, respectively, "The enumeration in the Constitution, of certain rights, shall not be construed to deny or disparage others retained by the people," and "The powers not delegated to the United States by the Constitution, nor prohibited by it to the states, are reserved to the states respectively, or to the people."

While it's likely that the Founding Fathers expected sexual morés to be taken care of by social acceptance or approbation, the fact that they didn't write anything about sex into the Constitution suggests strongly that they didn't think the government should have any role in it. Perhaps, in that light, readers will be able to use the following quotes from the Founding Dads when some idiot tries to tell you, "*Of course* the government should legislate morality":

> "Government is not eloquence, it is not reason, it is force. Like fire it is a dangerous servant and a fearful master."—*George Washington*

> "Question with boldness even the existence of God; because if there be one, He must approve the homage of Reason rather than that of blindfolded Fear."—*Thomas Jefferson*

> "Whenever we read the obscene stories, the voluptuous debaucheries, the cruel and tortuous executions, the unrelenting vindictiveness with which more than half of the Bible is filled, it would be more consistent that we call it the word of a demon rather than the word of God. It is a history of wickedness that has served to corrupt and brutalize mankind."—*Thomas Paine*

> "During almost fifteen centuries has the legal establishment of Christianity been on trial. What has been its fruits? More or less, in all places pride and indolence of the clergy;

ignorance and servility in the laity; in both superstition, bigotry and persecution."—*James Madison*

"When a religion is good, I conceive it will support itself; and when it does not support itself, and God does not take care to support it so that its professors are obliged to call for help of the civil power, 'tis a sign, I apprehend, of its being a bad one."—*Benjamin Franklin*

And maybe just one more, from *The Federalist Papers* #10 (circa 1790), as we start the first of our quadrennial "four more years": "Enlightened statesmen will not always be at the helm."—*James Madison*

I wish I could remember where I first saw the phrase that's the title of this first piece, but I think it refers to adults not taking responsibility for properly educating their kids about sex—so of course, they're afraid that in their ignorance, those kids will start exploring their sexuality at too young an age—and maybe even trying to make sexy videos of themselves. Fortunately, the legitimate adult industry has an answer for that, and it wasn't the one Congress in its "infinite wisdom" came up with. A "humorous" aside: Rep. Mark Foley (R-FL) who in the wake of CPPA's defeat wanted to introduce more anti-child-porn legislation, sent sexually explicit messages to his congressional pages and was forced to resign because of it[1]. This also predates, by more than two decades, the findings of a Pennsylvania grand jury that uncovered 300 pedophile priests in that state alone who had molested more than 1,000 kids.

PASSING THE BUCK TO BABIES[2]

December, 1996

All right, look: we're against having minors perform in sexually explicit videos just like any good Christian Coalition member, and we have even less use for pedophiles than the Diocese of Chicago (which had plenty—39 priests at last count[3]), but this new Child Pornography Prevention Act of 1996 is pure horseshit.

For one thing, it doesn't even deal with real people, but with computerized trick photography, where some unscrupulous artists have apparently taken kids' heads and electronically grafted them onto the bodies of people having sex—and that's not counting the animated stuff where no one real is involved at all! Second, it doesn't even deal with "real" acts! Showing a minor having sex on video has long been illegal. No, what this law deals with is people who "appear to be" (but aren't) minors having either what is or "appears to be" (but isn't) sex on video. Just to spell it out for you, THERE ARE NO KIDS INVOLVED IN SEXUAL ACTS IN ANY ADULT INDUSTRY TAPE!!!

But that isn't the point, is it? Oh, sure, the Congressional Record is replete with anecdotes from Sen. Orrin Hatch and his ilk about how pedophiles use this computer-generated, teeny-looking stuff to convince kids that having sex with old perverts is okay—kids whose parents have been too afraid to consider the concept that someone might lust after their teen or pre-teen bodies, and that if the kids ever come across such a loser, how to deal with the situation. So they make laws so they don't have to deal with the subject—they wish!

The real target of the law, however, is adults... admittedly, adults who are made up to look younger than their actual age, and the people who market such tapes. But once one catches sight of the tits on, say, Brittany O'Connell, or even Alex Dane, nobody's going to mistake either for a 12-year-old. It's sort of the Traci Lords situation[4] in reverse: most people that saw her tits assumed she couldn't be a teen. Maybe we ought to simply teach a course in how not to assume, which as my boss, a Quentin Tarantino fan, frequently points out, "makes an *ass* of *u* and *me*."

It's the whittling-away aspect that really gets to me, though. As Dr. Willis Ware, a computer security analyst with the RAND Corporation in Santa Monica, recently wrote in the NorthStar online newszine[5], "If the country ever finds itself in an uncomfortable position with respect to privacy, it will not be the result of a grand collusion executing a master plan. Rather, it will be the end point of a series of decisions, each made by a bureaucrat; and each having been seen, at the time, as a valuable thing to have done and serving a commendable social cause."

So what if they take some tape called *Teeny Teens* off the shelves because its older-than-18 players look younger? So what if they arrest a mother at an art exhibit featuring Van Gogh nudes for bringing along her two-year-old son? So what if they require magazines with sexy covers to be wrapped in opaque plastic? So what if they adopt a rating system for television that effectively insures that anything even remotely sexually controversial will never darken the electromagnetic spectrum, much as movie studios now require that sexy new films get at least an "R" rating from the MPAA? So what if some video box cover printers will no longer handle art that depicts anyone who might look under 18? So what if some video company someday "forfeits" all its assets because it's lacking a paper that says a particular performer is over 18—even though she is? And let's not forget that the part of the Justice Department that prosecutes "obscenity" is the *Child Exploitation* and Obscenity Section. What's in a name, eh?

Well, maybe it's time to stand up for kids. I doubt that any of us out there had a childhood that was all sweetness and light. We pretty much all got banged around a bit, if not by our parents, then by the bully in the schoolyard. We all had disappointments that we assumed meant the world was coming to an end, but it didn't, and we went on to bigger and better disappointments later. Most of our parents never gave us the lowdown on this "sex" thing until after we'd already formed a few ideas about it through conversations with our friends on the playground. A few of us—very few, judging by the scientific literature on the subject—got molested by a weird parent or uncle (or aunt!), but since we were reasonably sane, we eventually figured out that it was him/her and not us that had the problem. But we didn't talk about it because everything around us, like covered magazines and barricaded art exhibits and restricted movie theaters, suggested to us that talking about it was somehow dirty.

Kids are a lot tougher than the common wisdom would have you believe, and you *know* that because, chances are, you were once a kid yourself, and *you* got through it all. But more importantly, there is no credible scientific evidence that teens who see erotic art or even actual sucking, licking or fucking are harmed by the experience (assuming, of course, that their parents haven't predisposed them to being screwed up by it in the first place.) There have, however, been numerous studies of monkeys which show that if a young one doesn't see its mother or other relatives take part in various sexual and pre-sexual acts, the "kid" won't be able to learn such behaviors later in life[6]. Come to think of it, this very enforced ignorance may just be the cause of many of the sexual "perversions" some adults get into when they're finally pushed out of the nest.

So what's the bottom line? Well, we can't say it too often: NOBODY IN THE ADULT INDUSTRY WANTS MINORS HAVING SEX IN FRONT OF THE CAMERA. And the industry realizes that the "line in the sand" (and that's just what it is) for a minor is that 18th birthday, and has no desire to challenge that common wisdom.

BUT... there is no valid reason for using kids' ignorance (the religious would say "innocence") as a weapon to restrict adults' freedom of speech simply because some anal-retentive types want to keep the children from seeing, for as long as possible, what they eventually, inevitably *will* see.

Go after the predators of children, sure, but leave adults' sexual privacy and speech rights alone.

✡✡✡

NEW "KID PORN" LAW SURVIVES FIRST CHALLENGE

Free Speech Coalition Vows to Appeal

September, 1997

SAN FRANCISCO — On August 13, U.S. District Court Judge Samuel Conti ruled that a law ostensibly outlawing tapes containing adults who play minors engaged in real or simulated sexually-explicit conduct is constitutional. That same day, the Free Speech Coalition (FSC) announced that it had filed a notice of appeal with the Ninth Circuit Court of Appeals, seeking to overturn Conti's ruling.

The Child Pornography Prevention Act (CPPA)[7], which was surreptitiously added to the 1997 federal budget bill and signed into law by President Clinton, is the subject of a lawsuit[8] filed by the Coalition and other plaintiffs. The Coalition argued that the law was so broadly worded that it could cover any image in which an adult portrays a minor engaged in sexual activity.

In its Motion for Summary Judgment, the government argued, and Judge Conti agreed, that the CPPA provides adequate defenses for anyone charged with kid porn under the law. 18 U.S.C. §2252A(c) provides an affirmative defense if someone charged with violations under the act can prove that a) it was a real person, not a computer image, that engaged in the sexually explicit conduct; b) such person was an adult at the time; and c) that the defendant did not "advertise, promote, present, describe or distribute the material in such a manner as to convey the impression that it is or contains a visual depiction of a minor engaging in sexually explicit conduct."

"It is highly unlikely that the types of valuable works plaintiffs fear will be outlawed under the CPPA—depictions used by the medical profession to treat adolescent disorders, adaptations of sexual works like *Romeo and Juliet*, and artistically-valued drawings and sketches of young adults engaging in passionate behavior—will be treated as 'criminal contraband,'" Conti wrote in his Order[9]. "In addition '[n]o government official is vested with authority to permit or deny plaintiffs the right to produce these works, and thus the [CPPA] imposes no unconstitutional prior restraint on speech.'"

"Although there may be a degree of ambiguity in the phrase 'appears to be a minor,'" Conti later admitted, "any ambiguity regarding whether a particular person depicted in a particular work appears to be over the age of eighteen can be resolved by examining whether the work was marketed and advertised as child pornography." Conti did not deal with the issues of the cost and public ignominy connected with such "examination."

"We have a lot of trouble with the language of the law, which contains such vague terms as 'appears to be' and 'convey[s] the impression,'" said Jeffrey Douglas, executive director of the FSC. "Who's to decide who 'appears to be' under 18? The same FBI and other federal agents who determined that 'children were at risk' at the Branch Davidian compound in Waco, Texas?"

Indeed, the recent direction by Oklahoma Federal Judge Richard Freeman that local police seize copies of *The Tin Drum* from local video stores[10], according to Douglas, can be traced directly to the CPPA.

"Personal possession of this new form of 'child pornography,' even as stock in a video store, is a very serious felony, even though the material contains only images of people over 18," Douglas warned. "If you possess copies of videotapes such as *Fast Times at Ridgemont High, The Last Picture Show, Midnight Cowboy, The People Vs. Larry Flynt, Sleepers, Ripe* or hundreds of other movies, you possess child pornography, legally indistinguishable from real child pornography, involving the sexual molestation of children."

On the issue of the CPPA's "chilling effect" on certain forms of protected speech, Conti wrote, "Plaintiffs also contend that the CPPA places unbridled discretion in the hands of government officials and deals an unnecessarily severe punishment for an incorrect determination of whether or not an adult appears to be a minor. The Court agrees with defendants that the CPPA neither completely bans depictions of adults who appear to be minors nor punishes producers or distributors who create works in which adults appear who might be mistaken as minors. Indeed, the affirmative defense laid out in 18 U.S.C. §2252A(c) clearly permits the use of adults, even if they look like minors, as long as the works in which they appear are not marketed as child pornography."

"One of the purposes of our Constitution is to take such 'evaluation' power out of the hands of the government and its employees," Douglas answered. "Following this ruling, however, the federal government now has a 'green light' to prosecute drawings, photographs, paintings and computer-generated images of adults portraying characters which may 'appear to be' under 18."

"This ruling resolves nothing of consequence," said Eric Freedman, a constitutional law professor at Hofstra Law School. "The judge never reached the real problems of the statute. That'll have to wait for another lawsuit."

"There is no question," wrote attorney Lawrence Stanley in a *Cardozo Law Journal* article, "but that the propaganda concerning child pornography has been and continues to be used by law enforcement officials and politicians, religious leaders, and the media to create confusion, feelings of powerlessness, and fear among the populace. This manipulation makes curtailment of First Amendment freedoms and expansion of police powers easier. The moral panic over child pornography can then be viewed as part of a larger trend in American society toward greater government and police intrusion into private lives."

"This is no longer simply a nightmare scenario," Douglas concluded. "The First Amendment's wall against governmental intrusion into free and protected speech has been breached. In the name of 'protecting children', the entire arena of visual communication regarding teenage sexuality is banned in the United States."

"Judge Conti appears to have clarified the obvious," *AVN* legal commentator Clyde DeWitt analyzed, "that the CPPA does not punish depictions of adults who are advertised as adults, regardless of the fact that they may look younger. When all of the performers are adults, problems would arise, one would think, only where the adults look like minors or play characters who are minors, and where the video or photograph is not associated with a prominent disclosure that the performers were all really adults. Thus, an accurate *and conspicuous* disclosure that all of the performers appearing in the video and related graphical materials were at least 18 years of age at the time of the photography should suffice, particularly if it includes a statement that all of the *characters* also are adult characters. (There is debate as to whether the latter is necessary, and the author believes that it is not.)"

✲✲✲

FREE SPEECH COALITION HOPEFUL AFTER SUPREME COURT ARGUMENT

December, 2001

WASHINGTON, D.C. — "Oral argument went much better than I had hoped for," said Free Speech Coalition (FSC) board chairman Jeffrey Douglas, who observed the oral argument that took place before the U.S. Supreme Court on Oct. 30 in the case of *Ashcroft v. Free Speech Coalition*. "The members of the court that we assumed we would not have a prayer of getting—[Antonin] Scalia and [William] Rehnquist—essentially showed true colors. The court showed a sensitivity to some of the more subtle and complex issues. That was very encouraging. The lack of affirmative defense for possession; the interplay of the language of 'sexually explicit' and 'indistinguishable from' — all those things showed a level of sophistication and understanding that's terrific. Traditionally, I've been told by people that live in this environment that the best you can hope for is four or five of the justices that are really knowledgeable and really involved and then they're trying to carry the others. I would say that at least six or seven of the justices were very knowledgeable and very concerned about the matter. It was an outstanding oral argument on both sides. I leave the court with substantially more optimism than I expected to."

On the other hand, the man on the spot—H. Louis Sirkin, representing the FSC and three other respondents in his first-ever high court argument—was a bit more guarded in his assessment.

"I don't like to make predictions," Sirkin told *AVN* in an exclusive interview. "My feeling is that I always wait until I see what a jury does or a court does on an appellate argument before I start to talk. I thought the questions were good questions. Certainly, as I've experienced in everything that I've seen in the past in the court hearings and arguments that I've watched in the past, they were certainly well prepared [but] I don't know; I'll wait till I get their opinion."

The FSC case was the first one before the court that Tuesday morning, with the Court sitting at the E. Barrett Prettyman United States Courthouse while its usual chambers were being examined for possible anthrax infection. The Justices entered the courtroom promptly at 10 a.m., and invited Assistant Solicitor General Paul D. Clement to the rostrum to begin his argument.

Clement justified the act in question, the Child Pornography Prevention Act (CPPA), by asserting that the criminalization of "virtual child pornography"—computer-generated depictions of minors engaged in sexually explicit conduct—was necessary largely due to the amazing strides that had been made in computer graphics capabilities over the past few years.

"Congress has updated the child pornography law to keep pace with technology," Clement said.

Clement went on to cite the 5th Circuit case of *U.S. v. Fox*, where he noted that the government's own expert witness had testified that he wasn't sure whether some of the child porn images which had been introduced as evidence were of real children, or were computer simulations.

"But let me ask you," interrupted Justice Stephen Breyer, "has any case been lost on that ground?"

No, replied Clement, but without the CPPA, it would have been more difficult to obtain a conviction in that case.

Justice Ruth Bader Ginsburg was the next to question, and her initial concerns revolved around whether a computer artist would have the same affirmative defenses available as would the producer of an adult video, where it could be proved that all the actors were over 18? Clement admitted that the artists probably would not, noting that, "Age is uniquely subject to verification."

Following on that line of questioning, Justice Sandra Day O'Connor stated that as the law was written, there appeared to be no defense for simple possession of "virtual child pornographic" materials, since the law itself provided no defense for a possessor, only a producer, and the Court had previously held, in the case of *U.S. v. Osborne*, that mere possession of child pornography was a crime.

Clement responded that a possessor's defense could easily be that the government could not prove "scienter," or knowledge of the nature of the material, and that in any case, the marketing of the materials could make it clear that everyone involved were adults.

"Let's say I go to a video store and I buy three movies, *Traffic*, *Lolita* and *Titanic*," Justice Breyer asked, echoing a similar query from Justice O'Connor. "Each contains simulated sexual activity by someone who is 17... The question is, why am I not guilty of [possessing child pornography] under your interpretation?"

Clement didn't get a chance to answer the question directly, having been interrupted by further questions from the Court, but he later suggested that the mainstream films would probably not be prosecuted, and that in any case, they "involve only a tiny fraction" of the material targeted by the CPPA.

Justice Ginsburg was concerned that the government would have the Court create yet another category of prohibited speech, noting that "There is a vast difference between an actual child [being] violated and a simulated picture."

Clement argued at several points that the point of the law was not simply to protect a child that may have been directly involved in the production of pornography, but to protect children in general from being seduced by pedophiles perhaps using simulated child porn in the seduction.

Both Justices Breyer and O'Connor were concerned that in the 1982 case of *New York v. Ferber*, the high court had already recommended, where it was necessary to portray adolescent sexuality, that young-looking adults be used, and that the government was apparently asking the Court to reverse that ruling.

Clement responded that the advances in technology over the past 20 years had essentially made *Ferber* outmoded, and he reasserted his point that, in contradistinction to *Ferber's* dictum that the purpose of the decision was to prevent real children from coming to harm, the CPPA was designed to protect children as a class of citizens, rather than individuals.

Clement was also asked why the *Miller* decision didn't work just as well in prosecuting child pornography, since the use of a child in sexual situations would undoubtedly offend community standards, but Clement, citing *Osborne*, noted that the *Miller* test didn't apply to child porn, which the Court had ruled could not have redeeming value.

"It seems to me that this is a big step away from harm to an actual child," Justice Ginsburg opined.

When it was Sirkin's turn at the podium, he barely got out his first point—that because of the law, all visual messages involving child sexuality would be banned—before Justice Antonin Scalia hit him with, "Such as what? I'm trying to think what great works of art would be taken away from us if we were unable to see minors copulating."

Sirkin, appearing before the Court for the first time, seemed momentarily flustered, but answered that movies like *Lolita* could probably not be made at all under the CPPA, and Justice John Paul Stevens helped by recalling *Romeo and Juliet*. Scalia replied that no filmed version of the Shakespearean play that he'd seen involved minors having sex, to which Stevens retorted to the effect, "You just haven't seen the right movie."

Sirkin managed to point out that the CPPA was overbroad, in that there were many other materials in society, such as Sears catalogs, that could be used by pedophiles to seduce children, so that banning this form of expression, which didn't involve actual children, did not serve the government's purposes.

Sirkin also noted that even without the CPPA, the government's conviction rate in child porn cases was over 97 percent, so the CPPA was hardly as vital as Clement claimed it to be.

Chief Justice William Rehnquist asked what the effect would be if the Court limited the definition of "appears to be" to "virtually indistinguishable from," as the government and *amici* had urged in their briefs? Sirkin responded that some cartoons would still fall afoul of the law, and that in any case, the CPPA created a slippery slope that would lead to more and more forms of speech being banned.

Justice O'Connor, apparently concerned about the use of the *Miller* test in child porn situations, asked if the CPPA covered more than obscenity? Sirkin pointed out that the law covers all "simulated sexual activity" involving those who "appear to be" minors as well, referring once again to mainstream movies such as the Oscar-winning *Tin Drum*. When asked by Justice Scalia if the law could be read not to cover simulated-sex situations, Sirkin reminded the Justice that the law specifically referred to those acts.

Apparently playing devil's advocate, Justice Breyer queried whether the problems with the law to which Sirkin referred weren't "so few and far between" that trial courts couldn't proceed on a case-by-case basis? Sirkin pointed out that the existence of the prohibitions against simulated children having simulated sex created a "chilling effect" which would cause creators wishing to portray messages about child sexuality to abandon projects for fear of being accused of being child pornographers under the CPPA. He also stated his belief that, despite the government's assertions regarding the *Fox* case, a true expert could tell whether any particular image was that of a real child or a computer-generated one.

However, when Justice Scalia pointed out that in the Congressional findings, witnesses had asserted that such indistinguishable virtual images could be produced, Sirkin reminded the Justice that no such examples had been shown to Congress, and that if the purpose of the law were merely to make it easier for the courts to convict alleged child pornographers, getting rid of the entire Bill of Rights would make it even easier.

Justice Stevens then asked whether the affirmative defenses in the law couldn't be tailored so as to make them constitutional? Sirkin replied that they could not.

After Sirkin noted that, considering the *Osborne* and *Miller* decisions, very few child pornographers would be acquitted for lack of the CPPA,

Chief Justice Rehnquist analogized that though very few people commit murders, it was still a good idea to have the murder statutes on the books.

"But there's no *virtual* murder statute," Sirkin replied. "If there's a murder that looks real on the screen, we don't go out and charge anyone with murder."

Shortly before Sirkin's 30-minute time limit was up, the Justices appeared to run out of questions, so Sirkin returned to his prepared remarks to reiterate that the law provides no defense for someone who simply possesses "virtual child porn"; that the statute isn't sufficiently narrowly tailored to accomplish the government's purpose without infringing essential rights, and that the law contains no exceptions for "virtual child porn" that may have literary, artistic, political or scientific value, particularly in the area of medical research. He also noted that the decisions in *Ferber* and *Osborne* were based upon real harm done to real children, and that the CPPA was a giant leap beyond that standard.

The entire argument process lasted precisely one hour, leaving all the non-judicial participants apparently exhausted, and when it was over, the majority of press and public attendees filed out. In the audience were such ACLU luminaries as chief counsel Ann Beeson, who will likely argue the COPA case—*ACLU v. Ashcroft*—at the end of November, and about a half-dozen associates. Also on hand to cheer on the government were Bruce Taylor, president of the National Law Center for Children and Families; Jan LaRue, attorney for the Family Research Council—and someone who looked much like Victor Cline, one of the researchers who had testified before Congress in the pre-CPPA hearings.

"I was very pleasantly surprised at the way the judges seemed to line up during the oral argument," observed First Amendment attorney Al Gelbard, who was also in the audience. "I thought we were facing a 4-5 or a 3-6 [split among the Justices] against us, and I'm flipping that over in my head now. I'm very pleased that Justice O'Connor—I was sure she wasn't going to help us with this, but she understood and she excoriated the government lawyer for quoting a footnote when the body of *Ferber* said something else. I think that was pretty impressive, and she reminded him that she was there [on that Court] for the opinion."

The Court will now spend several months considering the arguments that were made, and will probably render its opinion sometime in the late spring. The entire adult and artistic community will be waiting... nervously.

☆☆☆

PIGTAILS, MINI-SKIRTS IN; KIDS' HEADS ON ADULT BODIES STILL OUT

Free Speech Coalition Wins Major Victory In U.S. Supreme Court
April, 2002

LOS ANGELES — In what can only be described as a landmark First Amendment decision, the U.S. Supreme Court ruled[11] on April 16 that in order for material to be considered child pornography, it has to have (surprise!) children in it.

Specifically, the high court in a 6-3 decision struck down Sections 2256(8)(B) and 2256(8)(D) of the Child Pornography Prevention Act (CPPA), which made it a crime punishable by 15 years in federal prison to include someone who "appears to be" a minor in a real or simulated sexually-explicit role, or if such work were advertised so as to "convey the impression" that there were minors therein involved in sexual situations.

According to FSC Executive Director William Lyon, "This is the most important victory for free speech and for the adult industry in over a decade. FSC must take care in picking cases. Our funds are limited so we only choose cases that will have an impact on the *entire* adult industry. In this case, not only would the vague language in the CPPA affect parts of the adult entertainment world, but much of mainstream entertainment as well."

Indeed; though the case was brought to the court by the Free Speech Coalition (FSC) and three other plaintiffs—Bold Type, Inc., the publisher of a book advocating a nudist lifestyle; painter Jim Gingerich and photographer Ron Raffaelli—the real winner in the long run will be mainstream Hollywood.

"We congratulate the producers of *Traffic*, *Fast Times At Ridgemont High*, *American Beauty*, *Midnight Cowboy*, *The Tin Drum* and many other films on not having to recall and destroy these important cinematic works of art," said FSC Board Chairman Jeffrey Douglas.

However, the six-year struggle, which was ably helmed by First Amendment attorneys H. Louis Sirkin, Laura Abrams and John Feldmeier, was uphill all the way for the poorly-funded Coalition, which got no financial support from any mainstream companies, though Hollywood was quick to applaud the decision when it was announced.

"The Directors Guild of America[12] lauds today's Supreme Court ruling which overturned the misguided Child Pornography Prevention Act of 1996," said Directors Guild of America (DGA) president Martha Coolidge. "The Supreme Court correctly analyzed the impact of this law restricting the creative rights of filmmakers and other artists, and supported the position of the DGA that this legislation encroached upon First Amendment rights to free speech. We can all thank the Supreme Court for once again defending the First Amendment freedoms central to our free society, and preserving the creative freedoms that all Americans treasure."

The DGA, however, never mentioned the FSC in its post-opinion press release, and though they signed on to an *amicus* brief in support of the lawsuit, contributed no funding to it.

The Video Software Dealers Association[13], on the other hand, congratulated the Coalition on winning, noting in their press release, "It's never easy to argue against a law that claims to be aimed at something as vile as child pornography. This discomfort is one reason we have trade associations—to argue in favor of unpopular but protected speech. But the issue here was not whether those who argued the Children [sic] Pornography Prevention Act was unconstitutional were defending child pornography—we weren't and we condemn it. The question was whether VSDA would defend the rights of video stores and others to offer products that explore human nature in a way that is not obscene and does not harm children. Therefore, VSDA is pleased to have contributed to the overturning of this unconstitutionally vague and overly expansive law."

Few others in Hollywood took a public position on the suit, at least partly, in Douglas' opinion, due to their fear of being identified with anything which challenged the government's position on child porn.

"When people hear the words 'child pornography,' they become fearful and go into a sort of brain-freeze," Douglas observed. "But we at the Coalition recognized that the CPPA wasn't about children at all; it was about the suppression of ideas. Worse, in trying to suppress adult material made by adults for adults, the government appears almost to be trivializing the real harm done to real children by pedophiles and child rapists."

One of those who failed to get that point is Jan LaRue, Senior Director of Legal Studies for the conservative Family Research Council (FRC)[14].

"The Court's speculation about movies like these [*Traffic*, *American Beauty*] and paintings being prosecuted is abject nonsense," claimed LaRue in an FRC press release, and reiterated during a debate with Douglas on MSNBC. "Such films do not contain the kind of conduct prohibited by the statute, and even if they did, they aren't pandered as child pornography. Congress made clear that the law should not be construed to apply to such material. All of the other circuit courts understood that. All the Court needed to do is determine the reach of the statute and exclude the kinds of images to which it could not apply. That's the Court's job."

LaRue apparently missed reading Chief Justice William Rehnquist's dissent, where he made it clear that such material was *exactly* what the CPPA covered.

"The CPPA's definition of sexually explicit conduct is quite explicit in this regard," wrote Rehnquist, joined by Associate Justice Antonin Scalia. "It makes clear that the statute only reaches 'visual depictions' of: '[A]ctual or simulated... sexual intercourse, including genital-genital, oral-genital, anal-genital, or oral-anal, whether between persons of the same or opposite sex;... bestiality;... masturbation;... sadistic or masochistic abuse;... or lascivious exhibition of the genitals or pubic area of any person.'"

Other factions of the Religious Right's legal talent were equally misinformed.

"The Supreme Court's decision, in my estimation, went out of its way (as it does frequently) to protect pornography, thereby leaving the purveyors of child pornography and those who would prey upon children unregulated and... free to continue in their moral depravity," said Brian Fahling, of the American Family Association (AFA)[15] Center for Law & Policy, to AgapePress's Rusty Pugh and Jody Brown. "The court's willingness to shield child pornography from legitimate governmental regulation makes it almost impossible to protect children from those who would sexually abuse them."

In fact, all child pornography laws that involve actual children remain intact, but as First Amendment attorney Paul Cambria points out, that doesn't mean that sexually-explicit material, whether involving adults playing minors or computer-generated material, is necessarily safe from legal action.

"As long as the video contains explicit sex, it can be prosecuted under *Miller*," Cambria told *AVN*, referring to the three-prong "test" for obscenity contained in the Supreme Court's *Miller v. California* decision. "Producers must still realize that prosecutors are free to argue that depictions of people having sex as being under age may exceed the level of toleration of the average adult in the community. So while this is a very sound victory for the First Amendment, producers still have to be mindful of the obscenity laws and the reaction that a jury may have to a video where adults are made to look like children having sex."

Other Religious Right supporters attacked the opinion as harmful to children in general, even though the material contained no actual children.

"We're extremely disappointed with this decision," said Jay Sekulow, Chief Counsel of Pat Robertson's American Center for Law and Justice (ACLJ)[16], which filed a brief in support of the law. "The Supreme Court clears the way for pornographers to use the First Amendment as a shield and gives them a green light to engage in this kind of Internet activity. The court failed to close a legal loophole that can only diminish efforts to protect children and punish pornographers. The decision sadly will make the job of law enforcement that much more difficult in the pursuit of porn operators who target children."

But were Sekulow more familiar with the Supreme Court's opinion, he would have known that that claim was shot down by the opinion's author, Justice Anthony M. Kennedy, writing for the majority.

"The Government seeks to justify its prohibitions in other ways," wrote Kennedy. "It argues that the CPPA is necessary because pedophiles may use virtual child pornography to seduce children. There are many things innocent in themselves, however, such as cartoons, video games, and candy, that might be used for immoral purposes, yet we would not expect those to be prohibited because they can be misused. The Government, of course, may punish adults who provide unsuitable materials to children... and it may enforce criminal penalties for unlawful solicitation. The precedents establish, however, that speech within the rights of adults to hear may not be silenced completely in an attempt to shield children from it."

Kennedy's words struck a chord with *AVN* legal columnist, attorney Clyde DeWitt.

"To me, the opinion is reminiscent of two of Justice Kennedy's comparably well-reasoned opinions," DeWitt told *AVN*. "The first was his blistering dissent to the 1993 *Alexander v. United States* decision, where he rejected the majority's hyper-technical, result-driven analysis, and so eloquently explained why seizing an entire expressive business enterprise in response to a couple of obscenity findings was certainly a prior restraint. The second was his opinion in the 1989 *Texas v. Johnson* case, where he concurred with the Court's striking down of Texas' anti-flag-burning statute, reminding judges that, "The hard fact is that sometimes we must make decisions we do not like. We make them because they are right, right in the sense that the law and the Constitution, as we see them, compel the result."

Certainly Kennedy's rationale in this case was four-square in line with the high court's previous decisions, most notably *New York v. Ferber*[17]. In that case, the court held that, "[I]f it were necessary for literary or artistic value, a person over the statutory age who perhaps looked younger could be utilized. Simulation outside of the prohibition of the statute could provide another alternative." Kennedy noted in the instant opinion that, "*Ferber*, then, not only referred to the distinction between actual and virtual child pornography, it relied on it as a reason supporting its holding. *Ferber* provides no support for a statute that eliminates the distinction and makes the alternative mode criminal as well."

Kennedy also attacked the so-called "affirmative defenses" offered by the CPPA as essentially 'too little, too late.'

"It [CPPA] allows persons to be convicted in some instances where they can prove children were not exploited in the production," Kennedy observed. "A defendant charged with possessing, as opposed to distributing, proscribed works may not defend on the ground that the film depicts only adult actors. So while the affirmative defense may protect a movie producer from prosecution for the act of distribution, that same producer, and all other persons in the subsequent distribution chain, could be liable for possessing the prohibited work. Furthermore, the affirmative defense provides no protection to persons who produce speech by using computer imaging, or through other means that do not involve the use of adult actors who appear to be minors. In these cases, the defendant can demonstrate no children were harmed in producing the images, yet the affirmative defense would not bar the prosecution. For this reason, the affirmative defense cannot save the statute, for it leaves unprotected a substantial amount of speech not tied to the Government's interest in distinguishing images produced using real children from virtual ones."

Another aspect, which Kennedy could not properly consider, is the fact that the affirmative defenses would only kick in during trial, after an arrest had been made—and after many thousands of dollars had already been expended on a legal defense to what Kennedy has affirmed would be constitutionally-protected speech.

Kennedy found Section 2256(8)(D) of the statute equally unconstitutional, since its prohibition on advertising that "conveys the impression" that the material contained sexual depictions of minors was so vague, it didn't necessarily even relate to the actual content of the material at issue.

"As a consequence," Kennedy wrote, "the CPPA does more than prohibit pandering. It prohibits possession of material described, or pandered, as child pornography by someone earlier in the distribution chain. The provision prohibits a sexually explicit film containing no youthful actors, just because it is placed in a box suggesting a prohibited movie. Possession is a crime even when the possessor knows the movie was mislabeled. The First Amendment requires a more precise restriction."

Most surprising to court observers was the concurring opinion by Justice Clarence Thomas, a conservative justice who almost always votes with Chief Justice William H. Rehnquist and Associate Justice Antonin M. Scalia.

Thomas noted that so far, not one defendant accused of trafficking in child porn had been acquitted based on the defense's claim that the images it possessed were computer-generated rather than actual children.

"At this time, however, the Government asserts only that defendants raise such defenses, not that they have done so successfully," Thomas pointed out. "In fact, the Government points to no case in which a defendant has been acquitted based on a 'computer-generated images' defense. While this speculative interest cannot support the broad reach of the CPPA, technology may evolve to the point where it becomes impossible to enforce actual child pornography laws because the Government cannot prove that certain pornographic images are of real children. In the event this occurs, the Government should not be foreclosed from enacting a regulation of virtual child pornography that contains an appropriate affirmative defense or some other narrowly drawn restriction," Thomas cautioned.

And in fact, at least one legislator appears ready to do so. Florida Congressman Mark Foley[1] announced to AgapePress that he will re-introduce anti-child porn legislation, and will "work with the Justice Department and others to ensure the wording addressed the concerns of the court over the 1996 law being too broad."

Even sex-positive activists opined that the conflict on the issue is far from over.

"The 'virtual child' question is not entirely settled," said John Wirenius, the New York attorney representing the National Coalition for Sexual Freedom (NCSF)[18]. "The court left the door open for Congress to regulate this type of imagery, and it's likely that they'll try to address it again. We've had 'son of CDA,' and now it's likely we'll have 'son of CPPA.'"

Wirenius is representing the NCSF in its fight to overturn the remaining sections of 1995's Communications Decency Act (CDA), which attempt to apply local "community standards" to nationwide or worldwide communication media like the Internet. "Son of CPPA" refers to the Child Online Protection Act (COPA), which is currently under Supreme Court consideration, and an opinion in the case may be handed down before this article sees print.

Meanwhile, the Christian Coalition[19] has called on Congress to enact a constitutional amendment that would keep the CPPA as the law of the land. The exact wording of such an amendment, which would be a direct attack on the First Amendment, was not available at press time.

Virtually the entire adult industry, as expected, was very happy with the result.

Perhaps most affected is Max Hardcore, who at press time still faced child porn charges in Los Angeles under what his attorney, Jeffrey Douglas, described as a "tortured interpretation" of the California penal code. Douglas has filed a motion to dismiss the charges based on the CPPA decision.

Hardcore told *AVN* the ruling will not change how he shoots, though he's "very pleased with the decision."

"We're going to continue to produce our movies using girls that are young, fresh and excited," Hardcore added. "It's never my intention to the American market to lead a viewer to believe that a girl is underage. What we try to do is to portray a young lady's innocence to the experience of sex for the first time... My experience has been that a lot of the girls we work with enjoy role playing and acting as if it's the first time for them."

"We're selling a fantasy that's 18 and over," said Scott Taylor, president of New Sensations, producer of such series as *Naughty College School Girls* and *Young as They Cum*, which depict young-looking women. "In no way are we going to cater to something that seems underage, but girls 18 and above are a tremendous attraction to our audience."

Allan MacDonell, editorial director for Larry Flynt Productions (LFP), expects to relax what he termed "ridiculous" standards for what his company could show in its *Barely Legal* magazine.

"The only effect that law had on us was if there was something like a teddy bear in a shot, we wouldn't use that shot," he told *AVN*. "It got so that you couldn't even have a girl with a lollipop, or if she was wearing pigtails."

But perhaps those most happy with the decision were the board members of the Free Speech Coalition, which will recoup the attorneys' fees it paid out to win the case.

"As President of the Free Speech Coalition, I am very pleased with the ruling by the Supreme Court this morning," said FSC (and Topco) president Scott Tucker. "The Free Speech Coalition does not condone the use of minors in the adult industry, and its members do not employ any minors in movies or videos. Additionally, all performers are required to provide proof of their age, and these records are maintained by the company employing the particular person.

"The FSC brought this case because it saw that the law being challenged was overly broad and that it inhibited free speech and artistic expression," Tucker added. "The Supreme Court agreed that the law, as written, was violative of the constitutional protections afforded to all citizens. It's a great victory."

"We are absolutely delighted that the Court made this very fine ruling, and we're glad that they supported the Ninth Circuit," commented Coalition Executive Director William Lyon. "I hope that everybody in the industry will realize that this is the kind of thing that Free Speech Coalition was really designed to do. This is not just a victory for the adult industry, but for free speech in general, because once again, it comes down to saying that adult American citizens have the right to choose what they read, view and discuss. Individual freedom was the big winner today."

Guess AT&T has learned its lesson about being a source for sexy fare on its video channels; guess that's why they had one of their people start the reactionary One America News Network (OANN). Guessing all these pastors love AT&T now... And isn't it great how the Mormon Church has come out in favor of defining marriage as "the exclusive union between a man and a woman." Seems to me I read somewhere that that church didn't always feel that way...

"PORNOGRAPHY AWARENESS WEEK" (IN CASE YOU MISSED IT) AND OTHER QUACK NOSTRUMS FROM THE RELIGIOUS RIGHT

November, 2000

The period from October 29 to November 5 may not have seemed special to most of *AVN*'s readers, but the American Family Association (AFA), the Citizens for Community Values (CCV), Morality In Media (MIM) and most of the other Religious Right (RR) censorship groups spent that time getting themselves all in a lather, because those eight days constituted "Pornography Awareness Week 2000[1]."

However, rather than use the time as an information-sharing experience to help citizens find the best XXX material available in their local areas, the religious groups rededicated themselves to "work toward eliminating the devastating effects of pornography on communities"... and toward putting adult retailers, e-tailers and manufacturers out of business.

"This year... we've... tried to focus on a few of the most prevalent areas where we are being invaded," said the AFA's National Field Director David Miller, who clearly doesn't know what "invaded" means, "and we think that's on the Internet. And where our society is most vulnerable would be in our libraries, where children have access, often in the presence of adults, or children who have access to the Internet in their schools. In fact, taxpayer dollars help provide access to the $10 billion per year industry in an alarming manner—through public libraries. Even more disturbing is that the ACLU and the American Library Association (ALA) rabidly condemn libraries attempting to stop the flow of smut to patrons, especially children.

Yet, most citizens are shocked to learn how much control and influence these radical groups actually have over city, county and state libraries."

Miller also said that many parents may not be aware that their local video store could be the source of hardcore porn. (Shock me, shock me, *shock me*!) An AFA bulletin said Miller believes parents frequent those stores, "... not knowing that that same store has a back room full of hardcore X-rated videos, and they're also distributing that kind of porn in their community. And those back rooms can often contain illegal material that is being disseminated."

The "week" also gave the fundamentalists another excuse to engage in one of their favorite activities—Clinton/Gore bashing—and the AFA's daily e-screeds (called "AgapePress News Summaries"[2]) were filled with snipes at Gore's presidential candidacy, and at Democrats in general.

"With Pornography Awareness Week preceding the presidential election by only a few days," warned AFA Director of Web Development Paul Chaney, "it seemed prudent to compare the positions of George W. Bush and Al Gore on pornography. It is important that Christian citizens have a clear understanding of where each of these men stand, and to know their records on the issue."

But apparently, in order to get that "clear understanding," the AFA felt it necessary for churches and other religious organizations to distribute "voter guides"—even though the practice led to a Supreme Court decision in which Pat Robertson's Christian Coalition lost its tax exempt status. The AFA seemed particularly miffed at a "pastoral letter" from Rev. Barry Lynn, an attorney and director of Americans United for Separation of Church and State, to religious leaders across the country, warning of the dangers of candidate advocacy in a religious setting.

Terming Lynn's letter "propaganda," the AFA described the missive as having "the purpose of confusing our pastors and silencing our pulpits on political issues." The AFA's e-mail quoted Lynn's letter, as well as "the reply of one pastor who has responded by exposing Lynn's political agenda along with a solid refutation of the many glaring untruths contained in the letter."

The "solid refutation," however, consisted of the boilerplate the RR usually serves up.

"Who anointed you to be America's guardian of civil rights?" asked Pastor Raymond J. Rooney, of Verona, Miss, of Lynn. "You are quick to point out in your letter the relationship that exists between a non-profit organization and the IRS tax code. I understand that relationship. Obviously, you think I do not. The IRS is already empowered to take appropriate legal action should an infraction of the law occur. Therefore, since Americans are already protected concerning this issue, your reasons for writing this letter become pretty clear. You and your liberal organization are making a blatant political statement to America's pastors."

As any impartial observer can see, the IRS has been lax in failing to revoke the tax-exempt status of churches engaging in politicking—but try to imagine the high dudgeon Pastor Rooney would be in if, after handing out his voter guides, they tried to do it to his parish!

The religionists also got bent out of shape at finding out, through a *New York Times* article, that major corporations like General Motors, AT&T, Time-Warner and others are making millions through subsidiaries with softcore pay-per-view offering systems like The Hot Network and DirecTV.

"GM and AT&T might just as well be selling heroin on the street corner and thumping their chests because it's profitable," said AFA president Donald Wildmon. "These companies are helping to corrupt our culture, and hastening God's judgment on our nation."

And speaking of "God's judgment," unless you read AgapePress, you probably didn't know that a "Torah Court" in New York had already excommunicated Senator Joseph Lieberman for "supporting views that go against the teachings of Orthodox Judaism." The "court" ruled, apparently without a trial of any sort, that Lieberman had caused "grave scandal" (which the AFA interpreted as "the desecration of God's name") by claiming to be an observant Jew but "misrepresenting and falsifying" the teachings of the Torah. AgapePress quoted Rabbi Joseph Friedman as saying that Lieberman's stances on gay rights, partial-birth abortion, and intermarriage are "shameful."

Yes, the RR have been hitting the "homosexual panic" button so regularly over the past few months that it's a wonder their fingers aren't sore and blistered.

The Citizens for Community Values[3] newsletter, for instance, ran a headline in its Summer, 2000 issue, "P&G Joins Homosexual Activists Attacking Dr. Laura." Seems Procter & Gamble has angered the CCV by refusing to advertise on the physical therapist's new TV show—so along with an extensive definitions list of "Sexual Orientations," the CCV listed some examples of P&G's "Anti-Christian/Anti-Family Bias":

"*That '70s Show*, Fox...: Eric, 17, streaks naked through the auditorium when the President comes to town; Eric and friends strike a mock 'Last Supper' pose in the school cafeteria; prevalent message: parents are stupid dolts."

"*Friends*, NBC...: Of the 26 profanities in this program, 21 were the use of God's name in vain."

They actually sat there and counted the number of profanities in a half-hour TV show! Right-Wing Religious Nutcases—ya gotta love 'em!

And because knowledge is power, some selected quotes from Agape-Press:

• "The re-election of Howard Dean in Vermont has put up a serious roadblock in the efforts to overturn the controversial civil unions bill. But Republicans are still going to try."

• "The people of Nebraska have sent a strong message to Vermont that says, 'Your civil unions are not welcome here.' The constitutional amendment not only bans same-sex 'marriage', but civil unions as well."

• "The United Methodist Committee of the Institute on Religion and Democracy is not happy with the appointment of a pro-homosexual to the United Methodist Church's lobbying agency."

• "Nevada approved an initiative that gives constitutional status to the state's statutory definition of marriage as the exclusive union between a man and a woman. Supporters included the Coalition for the Protection of Marriage, an umbrella group of conservative Christian organizations. The Mormon Church was the single largest supporter of the initiative, raising more than $750,000 for the campaign."

And those are all from just November 8! But the best bit had arrived on October 31:

"Ministry Helping Porn Addicts Realize Jesus Christ Is Only Source Of Hope

"A former pornography addict says many Christian men are battling sexual sin and temptation. He now runs a ministry that walks along with men in their battle to overcome their own addiction to porn. Steve Gallagher founded Pure Life Ministries in the mid-1980s, after a long struggle with sexual addiction. Gallagher says true repentance and full surrender to the Lord is the only way to break free from pornography."

Right-Wing Religious Nutcases—ya gotta love 'em!

Or do ya?

I'd been going to comic book and science fiction conventions since the early '70s, so I sort of knew what to expect at the National Pro-Family Conference—and now you'll know what I found. For those not familiar with Reuben Sturman, he was an early adult retailer/distributor, and one of his claims to fame was, when he'd hear of a store being busted for obscenity somewhere, he'd restock that store free of charge. Unable to make obscenity charges against Sturman stick, they finally got him on tax evasion. BTW, "SOB"=Sexually Oriented Business.

ASSIGNMENT: UNDERCOVER AT THE ANTI-PORN CONFERENCE

May, 2000

FT. MITCHELL, KY. — I don't know what impelled me to bring to Paul Fishbein's attention the e-mailed flyer I'd gotten from the American Family Association in mid-March, announcing the 'National Pro-Family Conference on Pornography, Sexually Oriented Businesses and Material Harmful to Children.' It was to be held Friday and Saturday, April 14 and 15, at the Drawbridge Inn in Ft. Mitchell, Kentucky, about five miles south of downtown Cincinnati, Ohio... and the impish thought occurred to me, "Why not find out what the anti-porn people say to each other when they're not talking for media consumption and putting a nice (dare I say 'sane'?) face on their madness?

So I walked into Fish's office, handed him a print-out of the flyer, and asked, "So? Can I go?"

"This is great!" He exclaimed. "You should go undercover. Bring back as much information as you can."

Fast-forward one month to Yours Truly checking into the Cross-Country Inn, just across the parking lot from the Drawbridge. The Cross-Country had two advantages: Its rooms were half the price of the Drawbridge, and perhaps more importantly, I *wouldn't* be staying in the same hotel as the leaders and members of Citizens for Community Values (CCV), the American Family Association (AFA), the Community Defense Counsel [sic] (CDC), the Family Research Council (FRC), Focus on the Family

(FotF), Enough Is Enough, Christian Alliance for Sexual Recovery, the American Decency Association, and "Victims of Pornography" (no, not the real thing; just a group of that name, run by Vicki Burress, the wife of CCV head Phil Burress)—just in case anybody figured out who I was during the conference.

I arrived Thursday night in order to be well-rested, but the beds at the Cross-Country didn't exactly seem designed for sleeping, so I spent most of the night watching television. Interestingly, besides nine recent Hollywood movies, the Cross-Country's cable system also offered a small selection of "adult" movies, including the classic *Torrid Without A Cause*[1], and several obvious compilations whose titles didn't ring any bells.

Apparently, the Drawbridge had similar offerings, and that became an irritant to some of the conference attendees, who asked Burress (any reference to Phil is him, unless otherwise noted) why CCV couldn't have found a hotel in which to hold the conference that didn't offer porn on TV? Burress replied that he'd tried to find one, but all of them had it... except the Omni in downtown Cincinnati, which they couldn't afford to rent. However, by Saturday afternoon, the Drawbridge was no longer offering its adult fare, having apparently been prevailed upon to suspend that choice for the few remaining hours of the conference.

The first "general session" was scheduled to begin at 9:45 Friday morning, so I arrived a little after 9:30 to pick up my registration materials and check out the conference headquarters in the hotel. All the meeting rooms had Medieval and Elizabethan names, and the large auditorium where the general sessions took place was dubbed "House of Stuart." As I approached it, I passed a "hucksters room" with booths trumpeting the good works of about 15 organizations, including the ones named above, but I decided not to enter there until later, just in case someone might, upon close contact, recognize either my name or my face. It was my intention to blend into the background as colorlessly as possible—and it turned out that several of my associates at *AVN* had been right: Not responding to some of the horseshit that passed for fact during the conference was the hardest thing I did during those two days. (Well, that, and trying to get some sleep.)

As it turned out, I needn't have worried about being recognized; the conference leaders knew who I was from the get-go, since at least one of them—Burress—apparently reads *AVN* regularly. But more on that later.

According to Burress, the idea for the National Pro-Family Conference (NPFC) started about three years ago at a meeting of activists in Washington, D.C., though it took till now to get the idea off the ground. The NPFC was supposed to be the biggest gathering of anti-porn activists in the country, if not the world, but though Burress said he expected at least 250-300 people to attend one or both days of the conference, my count put the total at 150 or less, with most of those showing up for Saturday's general session being holdovers from Friday. (That didn't stop the anti-porn media from reporting the 300 attendance figure, though.)

But though Burress claimed that the attendees represented 30 million families, it led me to suspect that perhaps there are fewer anti-porn activists out there than these groups would have us—and the general public—believe.

Burress started out with an overview of the "problem" of pornography, stating that the present situation "is basically out of control, mostly because of the Internet." He reminisced about the good ol' days in Cincinnati, circa 20 years ago, when he claimed there were no adult stores in town... after local law enforcement drove out 11 bookstores.

But, he said, "Porn loves a vacuum. If you turn your back, it's gonna be here."

And who would be the chief culprit? Former local citizen Larry Flynt; who else? He was continually mentioned, and pretty much everyone at the conference had (if you'll pardon the expression) a hard-on for Flynt, since he made no apologies for his promotion of sexual freedom through tapes and literature. In fact, one of the groups—I think the Community Defense Counsel, but I'm not sure which table I picked it up from—distributed a cartoon reflecting their idea of Flynt's intentions... and those of his helper, who got a big charge out of the drawing when I showed it to him the following evening as he was accepting an award from the ACLU.

Burress laid out his plan for a two-pronged assault: Community-based action, and getting the right people into elective office.

Referring, for example, to Morality In Media's condemnation of supermarkets displaying magazines like *Cosmopolitan* and *Ladies Home Journal* with headlined articles like "How to Please Your Man in That Special Way," he remarked, "It's about people saying 'I'm not going to shop at your store if you sell pornographic materials.'"

"But," he added, "if you don't work to get the right people in office, you're wasting your time."

"Pornographic materials" turned out to be a sticky phrase throughout the conference, and few of the speakers even tried to draw a distinction between hardcore porn and obscenity—no wonder; most of them think they're the same thing—and some (including Burress) would add softcore porn to the same hopper. After all, "Softcore pornography... is where most children get started," he stated.

But I had to wonder if statements like, "The difference between softcore and hardcore pornography is that softcore pornography is protected by the First Amendment; hardcore pornography is not," were the result of simple ignorance on Burress's part, or willful deception? As far as he and several other speakers were concerned, if they can see a dick going into a pussy, mouth or ass—what they kept referring to as "Penetration Clearly Visible," or "PCV"—the material is prosecutable. The U.S. Supreme Court, of course, differs.

(It occurred to me that Burress's obsession with "PCV" might be some sort of transposed Freudian holdover from his previous profession as a plumber, where he'd have had to work with PVC pipe.)

It was about at this point that Burress made his first mention of *Adult Video News*, "which is the trade publication for the pornographers"; something about his having read in *AVN* that VCX's *Taboo* had sold over 1 million units over the years. (A later speaker would suggest that porn with an incest theme, as the *Taboo* series is, should be eminently prosecutable.)

Burress then launched into another concept that was touted throughout the conference: The "porn addict."

"You can't just look at someone and tell whether or not they're into pornography or addicted to pornography," he stated, and later added, "If you feel uncomfortable about the way a man is looking at you, trust your instincts, because a person who is addicted to pornography cannot look at a woman other than sexually."

That last, apparently, referred to what Burress described as the five steps of porn addiction: 1) Exposure; 2) Addiction; 3) Desensitization; 4) Escalation; and 5) Acting out—which, according to Burress, often means rape or sexual assault.

Burress then flashed on the projection screen a copy of lobbyist Kat Sunlove's column "Are You Ready?" from the March, 2000 *AVN*, which he'd apparently downloaded from the *AVN* Website.

Quoting Kat, he read, "How likely is it, would you say, that we [who, Burress explained, meant "the pornographers"] are going to continue to enjoy the same benevolent neglect that the industry has enjoyed under Janet Reno? Regardless of who is elected, our fortunes are going to change." He then commented, "Seven years, they have refused to enforce obscenity laws, and you wonder why we have it so bad today?"

"'We have experienced the lull before the storm'," Burress continued to read, "'the false confidence that "times have changed," only to be hit with multiple, well-coordinated attacks against our industry by federal authorities'."

"There is no coordinated attack against the industry," Burress claimed. "They are basically free to do anything they want, and the feds are not going to anything about it and many of the local prosecutors will do nothing about it."

He bolstered his statement by noting that although both George W. Bush and Al Gore had been asked to sign pledges stating that, if elected, they would uphold the existing laws against pornography, neither candidate would sign.

Burress then introduced Bruce Taylor, currently President and Chief Counsel for the National Law Center for Children and Families, and formerly a "senior trial attorney" for the Justice Department's National Obscenity Enforcement Unit. But his chief claim to fame was his involvement in the prosecutions of early porn mogul Reuben Sturman.

In one of his first jobs, as an assistant prosecutor in Cleveland, Taylor was responsible for analyzing the then-new *Miller* set of decisions for his boss, and later, the creation of boilerplate forms that local law enforcement could use to simplify the arrest and prosecution of pornographers and adult retailers.

Taylor expressed his frustration with the Supreme Court's refusal to come up with a clear definition of pornography—a position echoed by many free speech advocates as well.

Referring to the late Justice Potter Stewart's invocation[2] that "I can't define it but I know it when I see it," Taylor said, "I think that's the dumbest thing I ever heard. A Supreme Court Justice is not entitled to sit up on the Supreme Court and say 'I can't define it.' Well, then, quit! Your job is to define it so we know what it is." (Damn straight!)

Taylor was also unhappy with the Hal Freeman decision[3] in California, which established that adult performers are not prostitutes, and producers not panderers.

"I just want to bring one of those producers into court and ask him if he paid actors to have sex," Taylor stated.

He had no better things to say about adult retailers, charging that most if not all are involved with organized crime.

"Bookstores are only here for two purposes," he condemned. "They're not to show people First Amendment material. They either launder money from some other stores or your friends' activities, or you skim the money that you do make... If you look at the bottom line, they're just a little bit higher than break-even, so they pay a little bit of income tax, then they steal all the money that comes through the door. If you make money, you make it. If you don't make, you add some from someplace else."

Later, Taylor charged, "Here's John Gotti, who's had three trials that they couldn't convict him on. They finally convicted him of racketeering for ordering a hit on the guy he had in charge of being the muscle for the porn industry."[4]

Burress then reacquired the podium and attempted to summarize some of Taylor's major points.

"You cannot just clean up hardcore pornography and expect your community standards to rise when you have proliferation of softcore pornography," Burress told the audience. "If you go after just the hardcore pornography, and you don't have the firepower sitting in the prosecutor's office or in the police department, you are wasting your time, because you cannot win the battle against hardcore pornography without rapid prosecutions. Let's start with the video stores. Back rooms in the video stores, adult videotapes, X-rated tapes—clearly prosecutable; clearly violate your obscenity laws."

(Clearly horseshit.)

"From my perspective," he continued, "clearly the videotapes that are being shown in the hotels and motels today are prosecutable... What's the difference between what's on cable, what's in the hotels and motels and what's in the X-rated videotapes in the video stores? Penetration is not very visible in the hotel, motel and cable [versions]. They shoot these films from different angles and they don't show the penetration clearly visible, and they think that that somehow makes it protected speech? No. It's simulated, and there is a lot of touching, and it is actual. So clearly, even the hotels and motels today that have gotten into the pornography business and specialty tapes, that is prosecutable material, and we need to do something about that."

Burress made it clear that he takes lack of porn prosecution very seriously.

"The jury decides whether or not the video presented in the court case violates the community standards or not," he stated. "If it never gets to a jury to judge the material in your community—in other words, if a prosecutor never prosecutes, so that it can get to a jury, [so that] the jury of peers in your community decides whether or not it violates community standards or not—*you're* being denied your day in court. This is outrageous, the fact that across America today, prosecutors are refusing to prosecute porn."

Burress then enlisted his wife and another activist in role-playing how to approach three types of local prosecutors: Those that are gung-ho to prosecute porn; those who are interested but ineffectual; and the ones who are openly hostile to the would-be censors.

But although Burress claimed that he would be using "actual statements that have been told to citizens who go in to meet with the local prosecutor," he has the weak prosecutor say to the anti-porn protesters, "I set the community standards"—which seemed an obvious lie, and something any prosecutor would know better than to try to foist on even a semi-aware public.

Burress did say, however, "I can't blame a prosecutor for not enforcing obscenity laws when none of the citizenry has written letters or made phone calls or even talked to the man. He's got to know that you care about the issue."

He summarized the role-playing by noting that sometimes the only thing that works on a reluctant prosecutor is the threat of turning his constituency.

"There's a lot of prosecutors out there that have three questions: 'How is this going to help me get reelected? How is this going to help me get reelected? How is this going to help me get reelected?'"

As I later sat through the various lectures and workshops presented at the conference, I began to realize that the entire structure of their argument was based on The Big Lie—or, rather, Two Big Lies: that all adult businesses create adverse secondary effects in the (undefined) community where the business is located, and that sexually explicit material is in some way intrinsically harmful to the average person's psyche.

Nowhere was The Big Lie concept more succinctly demonstrated than in Friday's after-lunch session, where the first order of business was to screen the American Family Association's "porn addict" 30-second television "public service" spot, featuring a series of images including the one that "graced" the convention's guidebook: "You're addicted, and sometimes it's all you can think about." Yeah, right...

Family Research Council lawyer Jan LaRue[5] was the afternoon's first speaker, and she wasted little time getting to her version of The Big Lie.

"Cities and counties across this country have a duty, a responsibility and a right to regulate these businesses as effectively and judiciously as they can under the law because of the adverse secondary effects that these businesses bring to a community," LaRue declared. "I'll list some of them now for you, and there's a host of them, including increased crime, decreased property values and decreased tax revenues, spread of sexually transmitted diseases, sexual harassment, urban blight, littering of pornographic materials, used hypodermic needles, used condoms, increased traffic and noise and cruising."

Apparently LaRue has never visited places like the Fairvilla Superstore in Florida, or some of the other upscale adult businesses that daily undercut her Big Lie.

"I've met people that live around these kinds of businesses," LaRue continued. "Let me tell you about one I met in Garden Grove, California. Garden Grove is in Orange County, California, and it has seven of these SOBs within a mile, mile-and-a-half of each other on one boulevard. I met a family that lives directly behind one of the businesses. There's just a little alley in-between them, and there was a five-year-old girl going outside, into her front yard; comes into the house carrying a used hypodermic needle and a used condom and said, 'Mommy, what is this?' Now, I submit to you that no five-year-old, no child should have that kind of experience. And the parents showing me hardcore video box covers with explicit sex acts on the cover, and people go into these businesses and purchase these materials or rent them and rip the cover off and throw them into the neighboring residential yards around these kinds of businesses. Men sit on the curb in front of these businesses, masturbating in the middle of the afternoon. Garden Grove Boulevard is the boulevard of male prostitutes and Beach Boulevard, which are both major thoroughfares in southern California—it's the boulevard for female prostitutes. Why are they there? Because there are seven of these businesses strung together on that boulevard."

Certainly enough of LaRue's charges here would be laughable if she weren't so serious about them—for instance, you don't get box covers with video rentals—but men masturbating on the curb in front of adult businesses on a major thoroughfare in Orange County? Is she crazy?

LaRue also claimed to have debated, likewise in Orange County, "an ACLU attorney; he teaches Constitutional Law at the largest law school in the country, and in his private practice, he defends sex businesses." When supposedly confronted by a questioner from the audience, who (she said) asked, "Do you have anything to refute what Jan LaRue said about SOBs causing increased crime?", LaRue stated, "You know what he said, without blinking an eye? He said, 'There's no dispute. They very definitely'—now, I wrote it down—'They very definitely cause increased crime in the area.'"

Fortunately, I know all the attorneys in Southern California who specialize in defending adult businesses, so I called around, trying to track down LaRue's elusive debater. Thanks to John Weston, I discovered that his name is Ron Talmo, and when I spoke to him, he remembered facing off against LaRue before a group of high school students, in a debate sponsored by the Constitutional Rights Foundation of Orange County.

When I asked Talmo if he'd said what LaRue claims to have written down, he replied, "Absolutely not!"

However, what Talmo *does* recall saying is that adult businesses do have an impact on the valuation of other businesses in the areas where the adult venues are located—"But that doesn't necessarily mean the value goes down," Talmo added.

However, with LaRue, one outlandish tale follows another. She spoke of a "liberal" who served with her on an "ad hoc citizens group" that was trying to come up with an ordinance to regulate the two adult bookstores operating in one (unnamed) Santa Barbara County community.

"There was one woman on the committee who happened to be very liberal, and she just didn't see the need for all these regulations, and wasn't this all a First Amendment issue?" LaRue began. "Well, she came in to the next meeting, and boy, was she hot. It seems that one of the patrons of the business right near her home, about 2 o'clock in the afternoon, he made a purchase in one of the businesses; happened to be one of those blow-up dolls? How can I put this delicately? He parked in a residential neighborhood near her home, buck naked, trying to have a meaningful encounter with this doll. She became a conservative overnight."

For the puritan she appears to be, LaRue certainly seems to find sex just about everywhere she looks, as she made evident throughout the conference.

LaRue claimed that the main opposition to an adult ordinance came from the assistant city attorney, who was so opposed to any form of regulation that LaRue suspected the worst.

"Finally, I took the vice cop [who had testified before the committee] aside, and confidentially, I said, 'Are we dealing with corruption here?' And he said, 'This is off the record, but yes.'" (Guess it's *on* the record now...)

"Organized crime has pretty much gotten out of the obscenity business today," she half-heartedly admitted, "and a lot of the SOBs are owned by people that live in the community and so forth, [but] a lot of them are just shell corporations and are operated by criminals. The two bookstores in this town, I looked at their licensing applications and, you know, they had those innocuous names. The owners are listed on the application... A lawyer for the businessmen started talking to the media, and [in] one article, he gave the name of the corporation that owned the businesses as Hall Avenue Books. That's not anywhere on the application. Where did this come from?

"Well, we ran the name through the Secretary of State of California, and lo and behold, we found out that the two guys listed on the application for licensing were not the owners of the businesses after all. The owner of the businesses was a guy named Eddie Wedelstedt.[6] If you don't know who Eddie Wedelstedt is, he's the guy who took over Reuben Sturman's operation when Reuben went to prison. And so there was an organized crime element behind it, so it's very important, in the licensing of these businesses, that you get all the information you can about who's really behind the business."

And I sat there thinking, *I sure hope Jan's libel insurance is paid up...*

But LaRue was on a roll, and there was no stopping her.

"In Phoenix, Arizona," she claimed, "the land use study there indicated that in the areas where these businesses were located, sex offenses were 506 percent higher; in some areas, a thousand percent higher. In Garden Grove, California, where I told you that the seven businesses are, those seven businesses accounted for 36 percent of all of the crime in the city. And people talk about this as a harmless pastime; it's a bunch of baloney. These businesses are not part of the Better Business Bureau. They are the worst enemy of good business in these cities, and you need to make sure that your community is protected from them as much as possible....

"A question I'm frequently asked is how these businesses generally are trading in material that meets the definition of obscenity, and because we know of all these adverse effects that they bring to a community, why can't we just set all these standards and ban them outright, and would it be all right to do that? Well, there's a website you should visit if you want to know why you can't. It's www.ussupremecourt.gov... So that's why you can't ban them outright, but you can do the next best thing and you regulate them to death. And it has to be a constitutional ordinance, but you should have a regulation in that ordinance. The CDC [Community Defense Counsel] and the National Law Center has a manual with a model ordinance[7] and a memorandum of law to back it up."

Yes, it's that nasty old First Amendment again that's keeping LaRue and her shrinking audience—the count for this session was down about 25 percent from the day's beginning—awash in pornography, defined as broadly as they could manage.

The above-mentioned book, by the way, was titled "Protecting Communities From Sexually Oriented Businesses,"[8] and was given out to all attendees by the CDC. It's full of "boilerplate" ordinances and regulations that cities can supposedly adopt without having to change a word, and just about every ordinance passed these days has some of this book's verbiage in it. The text can be found in the Law Library section of the CDC's website, www.communitydefense.org—as well as "testimony" of families that have been harmed by pornography.

After LaRue concluded, the CDC's Scott Bergthold spoke, but he added little information to the mix. He did admit, however, that "I think one of the main things that our movement suffers from around the country is credibility. And that's because of sometimes the way that we approach this issue." (Don't know if he was referring to anything beyond being loud and obnoxious...)

Friday afternoon, we had a choice of "workshops" we could attend. The first "breakout session" included the possibilities "Internet Pornography at Home & Business"; "How One Person or a Small Group Can Make a Difference" ("Today, society is finally recognizing that sexual exploitation victimizes women. More people are speaking out on this issue to change the way Americans think about the real harm of pornography.... This workshop will provide some insightful ways one person, or a small group of concerned people, can impact their community and the nation."); "Holding Accountable Those Who Promote Public Indecency"; "An Inside Look at Sexually Oriented Businesses and Stopping Public Advertising of SOBs"; and "Mobilizing & Activating the Faith Community" ("This workshop will give you practical ideas and action steps to mobilize your community to action. We will walk step-by-step through several proven working 'action-step' models, and discuss many successful examples you can incorporate in your own community").

I chose "Holding Accountable... " partly because I wanted to avoid any session led by Phil Burress or Bruce Taylor, both of whom, I feared, might know who I was and have me thrown out. (I'd met Taylor briefly only two weeks before at a Pepperdine Law School Seminar on porn and the Internet and as noted before, Burress apparently is well familiar with *AVN*.) I planned to attend their workshops the second day, but as I found out later, only half my fear was justified.

The "public indecency" of the title, as one might guess, involved "ladies magazines" commonly found at supermarket checkout counters, on roadside billboards and—who else?—"King of All Media" Howard Stern. Robin Whitehead, an attorney for Morality In Media (MIM), spoke on the first two topics, quoting some of the titillating material to be found in *Vogue*, *Redbook* and other point-of-purchase publications.

"First of all," Whitehead began, "we feel that these promos [on billboards and magazine covers] send the wrong messages to children, vulnerable teenagers, young adults, but on top of that... even though the focus is on the group I just mentioned, a lot of adult men and women also find these headlines extremely offensive, the content to be immoral and demeaning to women in what they say.

"Secondly, the material, the content in these magazines, are pornographic. You might say, 'Ohmigod, we're talking *Cosmo*, *Glamour*, *Mademoiselle*, what have you; how bad can it be?'... Cover headline, August, 1999, *Cosmopolitan* magazine: 'Your Man Unzipped; How To Be a Genius With His You-Know-What.' Excerpt: 'Kiss his inner thigh, butterfly kisses by fluttering your eyelashes, and slowly make your way toward his penis. Then up the amplification by showering it with little kisses and tongue flicks. The sexy trick is to use your own hair. Just wrap it around his rod, making twisting motions as you work your tresses up and down the length of his penis.'

"I didn't know that stuff was in there!" she exclaimed.

MIM's solution to the "problem" is to target supermarkets, urging them not to carry the publications, or to hide the headlines behind blinders, but so far, their only real success story has been the Kroger chain.

But that's not all. MIM is just as upset by highway and urban billboards, with Whitehead charging that some "exploit women as sex objects." She explained MIM's billboard campaign.

"Pro-family leaders... representing 30 million U.S. families, met with the executive board of the Outdoor Advertising Association of America, OAAA, and their members own 90 percent of all billboards in the U.S. The leaders presented the following code of ethical conduct... to the OAAA and requesting their members to make this part of their corporate policy. The code of conduct states, 'That because advertising is an influential medium with a high profile in our urban, suburban and rural environments, and thus has a major impact on the standards, lifestyles and quality of life of our communities, the members of the association will not display ads that present children in sexual situations, show contours of the male genitals pressing against underwear or other tight clothing, focus on or emphasize the genital or pubic area, buttocks or female breasts, show the appearance of, describe or suggest urination, excretory activities or explicit sexual conduct. In addition, because of the urban blight, increased crime [and] decreased property values caused by sexually oriented businesses such as adult bookstores, gentlemen's clubs and/or striptease shows, we will not accept ads from such businesses.'"

The claim that the leaders of the NPFC represent "30 million families" was repeated several times during the two-day gathering, but considering the low attendance at the conference and the penchant for these leaders to play fast and loose with the facts, any legislator who challenged these folks to "put up [the 30 million] or shut up" would likely quickly find out how extensively the horseshit was flying here.

Also note that the above "code of ethical conduct," if adopted, would wipe out, besides the adult ads, virtually all clothing advertisements, from Calvin Klein to Levi's to FUBU, not to mention just about everything depicting people having fun in the sun, including the Coppertone kid. Who knows whether even a "Got Milk?" mustache would survive? And forget Los Angeles billboard staple Angelyne[9]!

But in any case, several pro-censorship groups have jumped on this bandwagon, with MIM being joined by the American Family Association, Concerned Women for America and the National Coalition for the Protection of Children and Families (NCPCF) in fighting the supermarket magazine blight. In fact, Rev. Jerry Kirk, CEO of the NCPCF (formerly the National Coalition Against Pornography—these people aren't *too* sneaky), who attended the session, claimed to be able to produce a protest letter on the subject signed by "22 religious leaders including three Muslim leaders [and] the senior rabbi in America."

Discussion at the workshop then turned to the "Howard Stern Project," which began in 1996 in Grand Rapids, Michigan and has since spread to all 24 Stern markets. Seems volunteers tape the *Howard Stern Show* every day, five hours' worth, in every market, and therefore have libraries of the material going back nearly five years, "so if a company ever calls and says, 'We're not advertising on the Stern show,' we can go back to August 1998 [or] such-and-such a date and pull that tape and get verification," said Bill Johnson of the American Decency Association.

"We were very, very troubled by the filth... the whole desensitization, about how the tentacles of this kind of filth can reach and impact our community and become something that little by little becomes acceptable and is followed by similar types of programs," Johnson added. "You really have to count the costs, initially, whatever program you're considering, whether it's a Jerry Springer or that variety of kind of program... and as Christians, as I'm sure many of you here are, it's important to really get a real sense of God's direction for your life. Is this what God would have you to do?"

Perhaps more revealing was Johnson's rationale for targeting Stern.

"We felt that Howard Stern needed to be addressed because for one thing, he's so aggressive. He's so much a person that has pushed the envelope. He's been so arrogant. He's been desirous of basically making a mockery of the Federal Communications Commission, of our airwaves, of life itself, just day after day after day."

Johnson claimed that Stern has lost 90 percent of his advertisers over the years, though Johnson was quick to note that "It doesn't mean that it's because of the letters that we've done; we can't say that." But they've decided to be low-key about the whole thing: "We don't go and do press conferences or anything of that nature. We just go about our work, day after day."

Yeah; God's little censors.

The next workshop, "Who Are the Victims of Pornography and Can They Be Helped?", featured Gene McConnell, who's been doing the lecture circuit (as have several others) for 12 years, claiming to have once been addicted to porn.

"I was a man in church," McConnell stated. "I was a pastor, and I was consuming pornography behind closed doors when no one was watching, and that pornography habit I knew was not going to help me; I knew it was harmful, and I prayed that this would break in my life. I prayed that it would go away. But I kept finding myself back there again and again and again.

"My wife became bulimic, anorexic; she was cutting her wrists; she was suicidal; she was in and out of the hospital, and what it caused in her was a tremendous amount of pain, because she felt like she never could measure up; she never was enough.

"The product is toxic, in and of itself," he concluded. "It would be no different than someone selling pills in a drugstore that are causing harm."

One would think that if this were actually so, reputable medical and/or psychological practitioners would have noticed it by now, but...

"Be aware... that the DSM IV[10], which is the bible of diagnoses sponsored by the American Psychiatric Association, they do not consider sex addiction a diagnosis; it is not yet recognized," warned Rob Jackson, one of the founders of the Christian Alliance for Sexual Recovery. (No, they have nothing to do with Viagra.)

"It almost sounds as if God can restore and save others, but he's got to work a little bit harder to restore the [porn] addict," Jackson intoned. "The [porn] addict is just worse."

I began to wonder how I had survived in the adult business for so long... and I wondered if these folks had any idea of what role the repression of their own sexual thoughts, feelings and fantasies, and the lack of interpersonal communication engendered thereby, had played in the breakup of their relationships?

After the workshops, the assemblage reconvened in the main hall for the afternoon General Session. The topic was porn on the Internet, presided over by Enough Is Enough's Donna Rice Hughes[11], with a panel that included Jack Samad of the National Coalition for the Protection of Children and Families, Steve Watters of Focus on the Family and Karen Jo Gounaud of Family-Friendly Libraries.

The bulk of this group's presentation was a PowerPoint program Hughes and others had compiled, called "Protecting Children and Families in Cyberspace," with each of the panelists explaining the section that best corresponded with their "expertise."

And, of course, all the speakers were good for a few laughs.

"Cybersex is... the crack cocaine of sexual addiction," Samad assured. "Think about that. Crack cocaine, smoked through a pipe, is probably the most addictive drug out on the marketplace, and when you view cybersex or adult material on the Internet at that speed, you're going from one site to another to another, and before you know it, time leaves you and before you know it, you're addicted to the images and the fantasies you see on the Internet."

Wonder if Samad knows he's stealing Dr. Judith Reisman's thunder? "Images bypassing the cognitive process," a hypothesis she touted at a March Pepperdine Law School seminar, has been her schtick for nearly 20 years.

Apparently, Gounaud had accepted a similar fallacy.

"The research [shows] that children who are exposed to extreme visual images of sexuality were reacting—especially the younger children—much the same way as a child who had actually been molested," Gounaud claimed, "and they were surprised to find the similarity. They thought that you had to actually go through a sexual experience to have those reactions, and they found out visual experience was enough."

Watters unwittingly threw in a small dose of reality when he noted, "At least 20 percent of the estimated 50 million Americans who are now online are visiting sex sites," adding that 63 percent of male churchgoers have visited those sites. However, he also claimed that "As many as 40,000 individual websites contain child pornography, pedophilia and pro-pedophilia content."

The day's events ended at 6 p.m., and I got a chance to find out that there are no decent restaurants in Ft. Mitchell, save perhaps the Outback Steakhouse.

My inability to sleep in the Cross-Country Inn's bed caused me to be late for Saturday morning's opening session. When I walked in, ad man Clint Cline was already into his talk titled "Changing How a Community Thinks about Pornography, Sexually-Oriented Businesses and Material Harmful to Minors."

"Adolf Hitler used the media very, very effectively to seduce an entire culture," Cline claimed—not the first time at the conference that freedom-loving adult businesspeople had been compared with Fascist dictators. "He used films and he used printed media; he used... radio, and the interesting thing about Germany at the time, they had no experience with media. They didn't have a television set in every home; they just had movie theaters... They didn't see it coming. They were seduced without even knowing they were seduced... Pornographers have a very clear understanding of their future... so they use the entertainment media to break down even principled opposition."

Cline was apparently referring to principles other than those found in the Bill of Rights.

He did, however, make an important point regarding how to motivate people to get involved in an issue. It begins with making them aware of the subject; piquing their interest in it; providing knowledge about the debate; maybe inspiring some wishful thinking about what they might like the result of the discussion to be; getting them involved in bringing about that result; and finally, getting them to make a commitment to the cause—really working to push what has now become their agenda. It's a formula that sex-positive activists might want to take to heart.

Anyway, with Saturday morning's first workshop session, I was ready to take the plunge and attend one where my name might be recognized. I chose "An Inside Look at Sexually Oriented Businesses and Stopping Public Advertising of SOBs," which was being led by conference organizer Phil Burress and FRC's Jan LaRue.

Before the workshop actually began, though, Burress engaged in a short discussion with one attendee who was complaining about the "pornography" that could be found on the Drawbridge Inn's cable system—a discussion which capsulized the Religious Right's entire game plan.

"There's two reasons why someone would get out of the pornography business," Burress explained. "One would be a moral reason, and the other would be economic, so what we have found is, for the most part, the moral reason doesn't work with most people; otherwise they wouldn't have gotten into it in the first place. So what we had to do is, we had to persuade people why it's economically right to not be involved in the porn business."

And there it was: The (if you'll pardon the expression) *fundamental* reasoning behind zoning ordinances, *Renton*'s time-place-manner restrictions[12], boycotts, letter-writing campaigns, media blitzes—the whole thing, all geared to make adult businesses so unprofitable that owners throw up their hands and find another line of work, and the Constitution be damned!

It was a sobering realization.

The workshop itself began with a discussion of outdoor advertising, with Burress noting that a billboard owner in northern Indiana had given Citizens for Community Values 200 billboards that said, "Strip Bars And Pornography Victimize Women And Children," which, Burress claimed, "turned the battle upside down in northern Indiana.

"The problem is," he continued, "there's a lot of privately owned billboards that are owned by the porn industry [or] strip bars... because no one would sell them space."

And then he dropped his bombshell.

"I think Nancy Fletcher [President of the Outdoor Advertisers Association of America] is on our side," he opined. "*I don't think everyone in the room is on our side; quite the contrary*, but the point is that they're in business to make money. We're not anti-outdoor advertising. What we want is, we don't want to get offended when we're driving down the highway."

Burress' thoughts about his supposed right not to be offended aside, it was at that point that I knew the jig was up. He was looking right at me when he said the above words, but I just gulped once and sat there smiling... and thinking, *Is this the point where they bring out the tar and feathers?*

But no; the workshop simply continued, leaving me to wonder why Burress hadn't "outed" me to the multitudes. It was only later that I divined what I think is the reason.

Burress had several advertising-related ideas on how to defeat the adult entertainment industry.

"We think it's absolutely critical that if you do have sexually oriented businesses in your community, cut off the mainstream advertising. Don't [let] them use your radio or television or outdoor advertising; they pollute the community enough... This is content-neutral. We're not talking about what's going on inside that place. We're not talking about the First Amendment-protected dancing that's going on... We're talking about the conclusive proof that you get in *Renton v. Playtime [Theaters] Inc.*, the court case in 1986 that says these places cause increased crime and decrease property values. So why should anyone be engaged in business in advertising that's going to hurt the community?"

The claim that restricting adult advertising is "content-neutral" is laughable enough, but the assertion that the rhetoric filed in Supreme Court briefs is "conclusive proof" of *anything* is simply ignorant... not to mention wrong.

Burress also averred that he had an article written by David Sherman, "a former manager of Déjà Vu strip bars in the Midwest. David just finished speaking before the legislature in Michigan. They're moving forward to pass a statewide law. That's what all the groups are working on right now. We're going state by state now. We want to pass state-by-state legislation that does two things: Restricts the hours of operation and also distances the dancers from the patrons. That will kill the industry, and it will also help reduce crime."

Notice which objective he put first. Yeah, *he's* worried about content neutrality!

Then it was time, once again, for my favorite nutcase, Jan LaRue, to speak.

"I was helping a city in California enact an SOB ordinance. I had to drive up there, make a number of trips to attend meetings, and one day, my husband went along with me; it's a lovely drive up there... So we got there early, and I said—and there were two adult businesses in this town, and so, going in, we decided to ride past one. I said, 'Pull in here. I want to check this place out a little bit.' We went around the back, went in the parking lot. I said, 'I just want to sit here and watch for a while, see what goes on.' My husband said, 'Do you want me to go inside for you; check it out?' I said, 'Sure.' I said, 'but don't touch anything.' Now, I'm dead serious. This business had peepshow booths with doors on them, and I said, 'Don't touch it.' He said, 'Okay.' Well, I don't think seven minutes passed—it might have been five minutes—my husband came out and he was about the color of the lilies. I mean, the blood was drained from his face. He got into the car, and he was almost speechless, and he was mad. He said, 'I can't believe what I saw in there.' I said, 'What did you see?' He said, 'Well, the stuff on the wall,' he said. 'The videos, the magazines, that's all obscene!' He said, 'Why isn't somebody doing something? What happened to the cops?' My husband's a retired vice cop. When you can shock one of those guys, that's how bad it is in this place... The sexual paraphernalia that he saw and the kinds of the videotapes—he just couldn't believe it. And then he saw a guy was going back to these peep booths back there. I said, 'That's why I told you not to touch it.'... It's a very serious public health and safety concern, besides the prostitution that goes on. Every guy I've talked to that's walked into one of these businesses was propositioned within 30 seconds of going in the place, either by a woman or a guy, and so you're talking about very serious crime going on.

"Another day of driving in this city, I went by myself and got there a little early; went in and parked, and used to watch what was going on, and it was about 3:15 in the afternoon, and all of a sudden, cars started streaming around the corner, streaming into the parking lot and guys jumping out of the car, running in, and I'm watching. They run in, they come out; they've got no bag, meaning they haven't rented anything; they haven't purchased anything, and they're going in for about 10, 15 minutes and coming back out. And there's a string around the corner, and I noticed that these are all blue-collar workers; they get off at 3 o'clock in the afternoon and they stream into this business, and what do they do? They're going into those peepshow booths, one after another after another after another after another... Did you ever see this happen outside of Barnes & Noble?"

LaRue went on in that vein for several minutes, railing against everything from "sex supermarkets" (multi-use adult businesses) to stores without booths that are take-out only (she cited the 10th Circuit's decision that such stores should still be zoned adult, even if no secondary effects have been shown), and she lauded the Supreme Court's decision in *Pap's A.M.*[13] that she hoped would spell the end of nude dancing everywhere.

That workshop was the end of my personal involvement with the conference, since I fully expected to be attacked by these religionists if I showed my face again. (I do, however, have tapes of all the sessions I couldn't attend.)

But later, I began to think, why *didn't* Burress out me to the workshop audience? Some have suggested that he didn't want to have a riot on his hands had the attendees found out who I was, but I think the more likely explanation is simpler: Burress just didn't want to have to explain how a member of the porn industry could have walked and chatted among them for two days without the attendees noticing that he was a pawn of Satan. After all, I wasn't wearing a soiled t-shirt, had no gold chains or pinky rings nor was I smoking a cigar—in other words, I was the exact opposite of what they expected a pornographer to look like.

The problem is, however, that even leaving aside the anti-adult propaganda found in these people's religious teachings, there was still little chance that any of them would sit down with any of the better-spoken ones of us to listen to the facts of how adult businesses are run and what sort of people work in them.

And that left me with a great sadness—and a renewed commitment to prevent these people from making the laws that control my industry.

Freedom *isn't* free, as long as those who should be counted on to preserve it have no idea what it is.

And *that* makes me *angry.*

✲✲✲

I also wrote an editorial about the conference to go along with my conference report for AVN after I got back. The opening quote may seem familiar (like as the frontispiece of this volume) but it's just so "on point" that I thought it was important enough to use it to "set the stage" for this volume:

"Our time has come
Age of the Hammerheads
This is our mission
To be the Daleks of God...
Shout! Push! Hammerheads
Bold and resolute...
We are big and clever
And we don't know anything
—*from "Hammerheads" by Shriekback*

And that, of course, was the main problem with the attendees at the National Pro-Family Conference on Pornography, Sexually Oriented Businesses and Material Harmful to Children, and to a lesser extent, even the leaders. These good Christian folks (I suppose I may have missed one or two Jewish attendees, but I wouldn't put any money on their having been there—not to mention Muslims, Buddhists, Hindus, etc.) are not dumb, but they are abysmally ignorant... and thanks to their almost-to-a-person strong religious beliefs, are likely to stay so. As Larry Flynt pointed out elsewhere, there aren't any churches in America publicly supporting the decriminalization of prostitution, and the same goes for access to sexually explicit materials.

The leaders, on the other hand, who presumably have been exposed to porn even more than the masses (but who, for some reason, are immune to its effects, though a couple of them did admit to viewing the stuff on a regular basis before they Saw The Light), should not be able to hide behind the ignorance excuse. So I think one can only assume that, starting from what may have been a vague anti-free-expression (or at least, anti-sexual-expression) position, they've figured out that there's a golden tit of anti-pornism out there that they can suckle (if you'll pardon the image), which will lead them to "power and glory," in all their religious implications... and perhaps a few bucks in the bank as well.

For all their talk about being "pro-family" (which, apparently, these days, means anti-Constitution) and supporting "community values," enough of their number have made the news by being exactly the opposite. Their poster boy should be Charles Keating,[14] founder of Citizens for Decent Literature, who was convicted of bilking thousands of bank customers out of their life savings. Or how about Peter Popoff,[15] who used a concealed radio receiver to "divine" who in his audience needed healing, and why? Or maybe Oral Roberts,[16] who announced in 1986 that the Lord would "call him home" if the flock didn't contribute $8 million to his church by March 31. And how many times has Jimmy Swaggart[17] been busted for engaging the services of prostitutes?

But then again, I'm not sure what you can expect from a state (Ohio, where Citizens for Community Values, the conference sponsor, is based) whose attorneys seriously argued before the U.S. Supreme Court in April that the state motto, "With God, All Things Are Possible," "would not have a religious connotation" to some people, according to a news story[18] in *The New York Times*?

They're also woefully ignorant of some of the principles upon which America was founded, or they haven't thought about them with any insight. It doesn't make any more sense today to assume the sanction against suppressing speech only applies to speech (and books and movies and dance acts) that everyone agrees with, than it did in 1791 when the Bill of Rights was added to the Constitution.

And then there's the question of "how many lives have been lost to pornography," when far and away the most prolific social killer in the history of the world has been religion. Whether it's the Crusades or the

Spanish Inquisition (which most don't realize lasted over six centuries) or the Holocaust or beating and burning a guy to death in Wyoming because he was gay[19]—homosexuality being "an abomination," according to some Biblical scholars (not unlike eating shellfish or wearing two types of fabric)—God's body count is still growing.

But once these would-be censors get into the discussion of "lives lost," the term "porn addiction" is bound to arise—as if human beings can't make choices for themselves as to what material they will look at, even if some of us (even some of us in the porn industry) deem such decisions, in our wisdom, unwise.

But if we grant the concept of mental "addiction"—which, incidentally, many psychiatrists and psychologists do *not*—religionists may want to consider the concept of the pot calling the kettle black. After all, how would one describe a person who prays every day; reads from the Bible every day (perhaps several times in a day); goes to church at least once a week for several hours; gives over 10 percent of his income to said church; accepts the interpretations of Biblical passages from a priest or minister, even though to follow said interpretations would require the listener to discriminate against gays, women or other identifiable segments of society, and to deny others their constitutional rights—most especially free speech?

But for some reason, our society does not coalesce this behavior into the term "religion addict."

Fortunately, ignorance can be cured. It simply requires knowledge, the use of reason, and the refusal to accept as fact anything that can't be proved. So there's hope for the poor burghers who attended the Pro-Family Conference, and even the religion addicts.

But they have to *want* to change.

☆☆☆

But the 2000 conference was only the first of a string of such conferences, and when I tried to register for the one in 2001, I was refused—so I wrote the following "open letter" in April of 2001:

Dear Delegates To The 2001 National Pro-Family Conference On Pornography, Sexually-Oriented Businesses And Material Harmful To Children,

I almost wish I could stand among you today much as I stood among you, incognito, last year at this time, just so I could observe how much more militant you've become, how much more strident in your beliefs after only one year of ceaseless propaganda from websites and organizations like AgapePress, Morality In Media and even your own Citizens For Community Values, plus a lot of Republicans elected to national office.

But after countless broken windows at adult stores, several dead abortion doctors and bombed family planning clinics, and the fact that you now know who I am, wiser (if not older) heads prevailed upon me, and so I address you from a distance.

I had, however, considered returning to you, probably wearing an *AVN* t-shirt this time so I could be easily recognized, but bringing with me several very nice, reasonably wholesome-looking ladies like Tina Tyler, Christi Lake or maybe even Tricia Devereaux... only this time, *they'd* be undercover. For the first day of the conference, the ladies would appear and mingle, *sans* much makeup and dressed in their best business suits—yes, I know you'll find it hard to believe, but each of them owns at least one—and they and I wouldn't even exchange so much as a knowing glance. They'd chat you up, discuss your beliefs and probably fake a few of their own to draw you out in conversation. Not to worry; I'd only bring bright gals who could easily hold their own in debating the finer points of "God's holy ordinance" (or is that "ordnance"?) with you. (Did you know that a lot of atheists are more familiar with the Bible than most of you? That's why they became atheists in the first place!) Heck, maybe the ladies would even sign up for a shift on the next picket line in front of Cincinnati's *Hustler* store!

But the *next* day... well, I'd encourage them to dress and paint themselves like the Whores of Babylon you know they really are, and you can try to figure out how you could have been fooled by what appeared to be "such nice young girls." (Surely, you didn't recognize them? After all, none of you read *AVN*, watch adult videos or visit porn websites, right?) And they (and I) would be available to answer any questions you might have about sexually-explicit videos; the people that make them—both before and behind the cameras; gay people ("Threat or Menace?" We've got the answer!); health and/or slavery (just kidding) in the industry; sex-positivism; the First Amendment (apparently you and the Supreme Court have had a little trouble understanding those 45 words)—whatever.

And we might have a few questions for you, as well!

Like, f'r'instance, what's this about women writing to Dear Abby that they get undressed in closets, and that their husbands have never seen them naked? And we hear that most of you actually turn the lights out before you fuck! What's with that?

We'd also like to meet some of these people who claim to have been "addicted" to pornography to find out just what kind of repressed, non-communicative families they grew up in. Or do you think it could be a genetic defect? (You'll be happy to know, doctors are doing wonderful work with gene therapy these days.)

And do you really think it's possible that a 40-year-old virgin could impartially discharge her duties as an "Obscenity and Pornography Complaints Ombudsman"? (By the way, "ombudsman" means "one who investigates complaints and mediates grievances and disputes"—but that Utah woman[20] is going to do her best to bust adult store owners and put them in jail, or at least out of business, so that's kind of stretching the definition a bit, wouldn't you say?)

Incidentally, we've decided to take back the word "pornography." After all, it's not yours; you don't even know what it means. You think *Buttman* and Vivid tapes are the same. Hell, you think Tom Zupko[21] and *Playboy Playmate* videos are the same! So I'm sorry; you just can't use that word anymore. Perhaps you could simply go back to calling it "filth"? We could live with that.

Now, about this "homosexual" thing: I know the thought of one warm, naked body lying next to, and even penetrating, another of the same sex has you all in a bit of a lather. That's probably why not a day goes by in the *AgapePress News Summary* that somebody doesn't have some comment on some aspect of the vast and powerful "homosexual conspiracy," whether it's forcing you to hire one of these butt buddies when you'd rather employ a more-or-less-nearly-as-qualified Aryan Nations militiaman, or decrying the ACLU for trying to figure out how to force your cub scout son to go on overnights with somebody like Big Gay Al from *South Park*.

But I feel I must tell you, people are born straight, gay, or something inbetween, all as your God must have intended, and this crap about "curing" homosexuals like John Paulk[22] probably means the poor fellows have just stopped having sex altogether—unless, of course, they were bi to begin with—which, of course, is itself an "abomination."

But considering all the *other* abominations listed in the Bible that you folks *don't* give a shit about—like eating shellfish, whale blubber, snakes and rabbits, or wearing clothes made of two different types of fibers—you sound like hypocrites when you single out gays for your figurative (and occasionally literal) rack. (And have you read all that stuff in Leviticus about how to recognize and deal with leprosy? That's plain *nasty*!)

But cheer up, 'cause Supreme Court Justice Clarence Thomas is on your side. Why, just the other day (2/13/01), he said that people shouldn't shy away from stating their views, no matter how controversial—or, dare one add, fucked-up and/or simple-minded?

"We are required to wade into those things that matter to our country and our culture, no matter what the disincentives are or the personal cost," said the *other* Supreme Court Justice that Duh!bya admires[23].

In closing, let me just remind you that it's been said that the insane become adept at reading the minds of their keepers—and since anybody who'd work in porn has to be at least a little crazy, remember: We know *exactly* what you're thinking.

✡✡✡

Finally, this topic was much discussed among the attendees at the 2000 conference, and it was (and probably still is) clearly a fetish for Phil Burress... so I wrote something about that in February of 2003:

Ohio Activists Target Two More Hotels' Adult Pay-Per-View

CINCINNATI — Citizens for Community Values, the Cincinnati-based pro-censorship group which succeeded in getting three hotels in southern

Ohio and northern Kentucky to jettison their adult pay-per-view choices, was on the attack again in early December.

This time, the targets were the Red Roof Inn in Clermont County's Union Township, where CCV president Phil Burress used to live, and the Marriott at Union Center Boulevard in Butler County's West Chester Township, where Burress currently lives.

"We're going on the offensive, and we're going to stay on the offensive," said Burress, who, with his wife Vicki, pulls down over $115,000 per year plus benefits by targeting adult material—which he claims he no longer looks at, even to vilify.

According to Cincinnati-based First Amendment attorney H. Louis Sirkin, Vickie Burress is the one who watches the X-rated material in order to report on its contents to her husband, who claims to have been addicted to the material until attending a Billy Graham revival meeting in 1977.

"Isn't it interesting to have a censor who is censoring based upon not his personal viewing or knowledge?" Sirkin said of Burress' latest crusade. "And isn't it interesting that the censor who's conveying the information, she's not censored from what she watches... Nobody censors the censor, but the censor wants to censor us. It's okay for their eyes but not for ours, because apparently we don't have the same ability to be able to absorb the material in the same healthy fashion that she does."

CCV's tactic is to rent a room at a hotel, set up a camcorder in front of the TV, order an adult pay-per-view movie... and leave. Later, someone comes to retrieve the tape, which is then sent to the local prosecutor.

"It's hardcore sex," said Clermont County prosecutor Daniel Breyer, whose staff reviewed one such tape consisting of three or four vignettes.

However, On Command, the company which provides the adult material for the Red Roof Inn's PPV system, stated in August that the movies it supplies show, at most, some barely discernable hardcore shots seen only from a distance, not the "penetration clearly visible" that, for instance, former Justice Department prosecutor Bruce Taylor considers the hallmark of hardcore.

Breyer said he plans to present the video to a grand jury for possible criminal charges against the hotel.

"Hardcore porn is not protected by the First Amendment," Burress told the *Cincinnati Enquirer*. "I don't care if you're Larry Flynt or Bill Marriott, you should be held to the same standard. Just because you're selling this material in a fancy hotel instead of a XXX-rated bookstore does not change the law."

In fact, all sexually explicit material *is* protected by the First Amendment unless and until it is found to be obscene by a jury of local citizens, or by a judge sitting as trier of fact if a jury trial is waived.

More cautious than Breyer is Butler County Prosecutor Robin Piper, who said he had reviewed the videotape from the West Chester Marriott and would be writing to the hotel's owners, Winegardner & Hammons, who also own the Marriott Northeast in Warren County, a previous CCV target.

While Piper did not disclose what the content of his letter to the hotel would be, he affirmed that his office was "committed to the prosecution of obscenity." A letter sent last August from Campbell County, Ky. prosecutor Justin D. Verst to the Comfort Suites in Newport, Ky., contained several outright fabrications about his own county's commitment to the prosecution of obscenity. (See "Censornatti," Nov., 2002 *AVN*.)

"[The hotels] are just basically intimidated," said Sirkin. "They make decisions out of emotion, and God forbid they should stand up for something. In this region of the country, it's not very honorable to stand up and take a pro-active constitutional stand in opposition to what I call the vigilante groups."

CCV, however, plans to use the ignorance of the hotels' corporate counsels regarding First Amendment matters to further its anti-porn agenda—and to increase its bank account. The organization has started a website, cleanhotels.com[24], which claims it will rate hotels around the country on whether they offer adult fare on their pay-per-view systems, and post the names of the "clean" ones on the site, together with contact information.

"The first phase of CleanHotels.com encompasses only hotels in the Greater Cincinnati Area," reads the site's home page. "This site will be expanded nationwide as research is completed."

However, the site warns in a "disclaimer," "Despite this rating, please be aware that some of these hotels may still offer other premium channels such as HBO®, Showtime®, or Cinemax® which may from time to time offer programming that includes sexually explicit scenes."

The site also notes that its listings have not been verified by on-site inspections of the hotels, and warns, "If you find a listed hotel that is offering sexually explicit adult pay-per-view movies, please notify CleanHotels.com through our Report a Hotel page and it will be investigated. As well, if you find a clean hotel that is not listed here, please notify CleanHotels.Com so that they can be added."

But, the site admits, "Approximately 40% of hotels in America are pandering hardcore sexually explicit pornography (dirty movies) in their rooms through pay-per-view services under categories such as 'adult movies' or 'adult desires.'"

Sirkin opined that the site might actually be beneficial to travelers looking for adult fare.

"In some sense, it'll become a national directory for people to be able to know where adult movies are available and probably what type," he noted.

Religious Right Watch was a long-running series on AVN.com, and the following are excerpts from some of those articles, generally in chronological order, with each section dated for easy comparison. As I began writing about religious groups' influence on the adult industry, I realized that some of their opposition presented itself in subtle ways, not worth an entire long article but worth commenting on nonetheless, in part because some of those "little" actions could possibly grow into larger movements—and sure enough, some of them did.

RELIGIOUS RIGHT WATCH: A COMPENDIUM

June, 2001:

What Adult Businesses Are Up Against, Part 1

From the National Coalition for the Protection of Children and Families (NCPCF) website:

"NCPCF and the initial Citizens for Community Values (CCVs) of Atlanta, Memphis, South Bend, Long Island and San Diego invite you to join a cadre of giants—giants of character, giants of vision and giants of fortitude. The CCVs of America campaign works to accomplish the following objectives in cities across the country.

"•Increase public awareness of the harm and availability of exploitive and abusive pornography as it relates to sex oriented businesses, including, but not limited to, 'adult' bookstores, strip clubs and massage parlors.

"•Develop zoning ordinances for cities where they do not exist; and maintain and enforce existing zoning ordinances.

"•Support the enactment and enforcement, within the Constitution, of limitations on pornography; and;

"•Offer assistance to people whose lives pornography has harmed."

What Adult Businesses Are Up Against, Part 2

Religious-fanatical "Dr." Laura Schlessinger,[1] the radio advice purveyor whose doctorate is in physical therapy, urged religious broadcasters to use the airwaves to galvanize support for such initiatives as battling online pornography.

"We can have an impact," Schlessinger told a breakfast meeting of the National Religious Broadcasters on April 25.

What Adult Consumers Are Up Against

Adelphia Communications Corp., which is the exclusive cable TV provider in, among other places, California's Inland Empire, Lancaster, Palmdale, Oxnard, Simi Valley and other areas from the Pacific Palisades to coastal communities in Orange County, may be violating the rules of its cable monopoly by refusing to carry any sexually-oriented programming.

Last fall, the company, run by rural Pennsylvania resident John Rigas, dropped the Spice Channel, its only adult service, and more recently has refused to carry five L.A.-based public access programs, including *Colin's Sleazy Friends* and the *Dr. Susan Block Show*, all because they conflict with Rigas' "moral code."[2]

"The early pioneers made a conscious decision that we didn't need that product," Rigas said. "In the last five years, as cable has embraced more adult programming, we've never spent time thinking about reversing our decision... We've had letters from all over the country thanking us for taking that kind of stand."

"What Adelphia is doing is illegal," said Peter Eliasberg, a staff attorney for the ACLU of Southern California. "Just because something has sexual content doesn't mean it's obscene."

Eliasberg said the ACLU is researching the situation to see if a lawsuit against the cable company is warranted.

Separation Of Religion And State

"As the mayor of the City of Fayette and as a Christian, we are opposed to any business coming into our city with hard-core pornography," said Fayette, Ala. mayor Ray Nelson. "We have high moral values in our community [and] in Fayette County, and we have a [grass roots] effort going here in our city... our pastors and churches... that are opposed to this type of immorality. We're going to stand up against it and we're going to do everything we can to keep this out of our city."

Nelson's ire was directed at the Movie Gallery, the nation's third-largest video retailer, which plans to open a store in town, which likely will have an adult section.

"What we find is, in small towns, the mayors and city council and the people and the churches and pastors say, 'We've never had this problem. It will never happen here,'" analyzed Randy Sharp, the AFA's Director of Special Projects.

Apparently, the Movie Gallery's hometown newspaper, *The Dothan Eagle*, is part of the "conspiracy," since it refused to run an AFA ad describing Movie Gallery as "one of the largest distributors of hard-core pornography in America."

"This is reverse censorship on the part of a newspaper," Sharp charged. "They don't like the message that we have, and so they're trying to squelch our First Amendment right by refusing the ad. Censorship is one-sided."

(*AVN* readers are encouraged to send pro-adult articles to AgapePress to see how one-sided the "censorship" is.)

But sadly, according to Sharp, "Once a company peddling porn comes into a community, it is almost impossible to stop it."

January 30, 2002:

Speaking of porn...

"Pure Life Ministries," it says here, "has launched a new service to inform more Americans that they can be freed from the grip of pornography and sexual sin through the saving grace and love of Jesus Christ.

"PLM's inaugural edition of *Unchained!* magazine was mailed to some 50,000 readers and ministry supporters in November. The magazine initially will be published quarterly.

"Founded by Steve Gallagher, PLM is a Kentucky-based organization that helps men break free from the restraints of pornography and sexual sin. Through its live-in program, PLM has helped hundreds of men who have sought to turn their lives around and, in many cases, restore marriages devastated by sexual sin."

Hmmm... wonder how many "civil unions" were created by *that* arrangement?

BTW, I sent away for my free copy of *Unchained!* I'll be reviewing when it arrives. Somehow, I don't think it'll be jack-off material. [UPDATE: It never arrived.]

And speaking of...

The Justice Department has just spent $8,000 on blue draperies to hide the naughty bits of two partially nude statues that have been standing in the Great Hall of the Department of Justice since the 1930s. The department used to rent the drapes, but has now purchased them and left them hanging. Attorney General John Ashcroft ordered the statues covered because he didn't like being photographed in front of the female one, the "Spirit of Justice," which features an exposed tit.[3] Apparently, Ashcroft has been pictured in front of it several times while making announcements about terrorist attacks.

And this is the guy from whom the adult industry can expect a fair shake when it comes to the government's dealing with sexually explicit materials???

And speaking of the government dealing with sexually explicit materials, the Armed Forces Radio and Television Service (AFRTS), which distributes broadcast programming to American military personnel worldwide, has apparently decided not to broadcast the greetings from porn stars which were recorded by Sin City, *AVN* and The Erotic Network at the Adult Entertainment Expo earlier this month.

At least, that's what the Cybercast (formerly Christian) News Service (CNSNews) says. They quote Larry Sichter, affiliate relations director for the AFRTS, as saying, "We carry over the air broadcasts primarily from the top programs in America. Since we don't carry any [adult] programs, those stars really aren't anybody that our audience would have been interested in."

I'm gonna go out on a limb here and say, "You're fuckin' nuts, Larry."

Scott Stein, who handled the videotaping for Sin City, said he was in the process of editing out the naughty bits for AFRTS broadcast, but Sichter responded, "[T]he chances of airing anything from him are very, very low."

Almost needless to say, Wendy Wright of Concerned Women for America agrees, and goes a bit further.

"The Armed Forces have had a terrible time with sexual harassment and they go through extensive training of the men to not sexually harass the women and this would undermine their own efforts in that area," Wright said. "You would have to wonder what's next. What about all the women in the Armed Forces?"

Okay, Wendy; we'll make sure to include a few shots of Dillion Day, Mark Davis, Dale DaBone, Bobby Vitale... hell, we'll even throw in Jeff Stryker.

But that might not be good enough. According to CNSNews, "Wright added that any message from the adult entertainment industry would be unacceptable.

"'Even if they are wearing turtlenecks and burkas, it is going to be presented to the servicemen as a service provided by an erotic network. It is an attempt to legitimize the porn industry,' she said."

And that's a problem because...?

March, 2002:

"Saving" The Masses From Porn

"We're not here to judge anyone or to picket the show. What good would that do?" asked Craig Gross, one of two unaffiliated ministers manning the xxxchurch.com[4] booth at the Adult Entertainment Expo. "We decided the best thing to do was to actually be in the show and try to talk to the people in the industry in a professional and respectful manner and not be confrontational."

Trouble is, the philosophical position of Gross and fellow minister Mike Foster is that unless "saved" by faith in Jesus Christ, everyone attending the convention, with the possible exceptions of themselves, is going to hell—and the only way not to be confrontational about that concept is simply not to talk about it.

"Will people in porn have a greater difficulty getting into heaven?" *AVN* asked Foster.

"Here's what I say: It's that we all have issues," Foster replied. "Christians, people in the porn industry— we all have issues, and the Bible says that it's our faith in Jesus Christ that saves us, and so that's the message that we're preaching. We as individuals, we're all going to have to stand before God one day and give account for what we did, right or wrong; we're responsible for our actions."

"Would God judge someone who had sex outside of marriage and on videotape more harshly than another person?" we pressed.

"No," came the reply. "Actually, the Bible's pretty clear on that, that sin is sin, and God judges it all the same, whether you tell a little lie or you're the biggest porn queen in the world; it doesn't matter. We're all humans; we've all made mistakes; we've all fallen short of what God really intended for our lives, but the great thing is that he sends grace to us and mercy to us and love and compassion, and that's the great thing about God and that's the great thing about having a relationship with him."

It doesn't take too much reading between the lines to see that whether one has sex in a XXX video, or even watches one, or one takes an Uzi and sprays the crowd at the local McDonald's, unless "saved" in the approved fashion, all of those "sinners" have reserved seats in The Cold Place (or The Hot Place; projections differ)... for eternity.

But if there's one thing mainstream Christianity does these days, it aims, as the song lyric goes, to "accentuate the positive," leaving the fire and brimstone for the fundamentalists. Thus it behooves the casual observer to pay close attention to what's being said and written.

For instance, check out xxxchurch.com, and find a home page with a button titled "Vegas Video Shoot." Click it, and be taken to a page with two recorded Quicktime sermons; nothing to do with Vegas and nothing to do with video (the sermons are audio only), and certainly nothing directly to do with porn.

Or try the "say no to the bunny" section and find, "It is No Accident that you have arrived at this website! By reading this article you are opening yourself to the possibility of a real life change. True freedom awaits you, if you'll have it. Thousands of others have found what they need to live a self-controlled lifestyle again... One that is no longer dominated by sexual and pornographic imagery.

"Think for a moment what has led you here? Consider the series of events that have caused you to discover xxxchurch.com and admit that there might be a reason and purpose for that which you are reading."

Leaving aside the attempt to use synchronicity ("It is No Accident" and "what has led you here") to con people into thinking that "God" directed them to the site, the fact is, if a person's life is "dominated by sexual and pornographic imagery," that's an obsession, and it's time to see a *psychologist*, not a clergyman.

And later, another writes, "You and I are out of our league when it comes to temptations like this. We have a crafty adversary who presents the deception as something good, and godly by design. We fail to realize that what we do affects many other areas of life. Actually, it leads to a sort of death. Oh, but our adversary convinces us 'its [sic] not that big of a deal'."

And there you have it: Porn is the work of the Devil.

Bottom line on xxxchurch.com: Same old shit. And sadly, they kept buying booth space at the Adult Entertainment Expo until *AVN*'s bosses finally wised up.

May, 2003:

Porn-Bashing The Family Planners

The Religious Right has finally twigged to the fact that Philip D. Harvey,[5] founder of Population Services International Inc. (PSI), a nonprofit corporation that supplies condoms and birth control info to the Third World, is the same Philip D. Harvey who founded Adam & Eve, the adult mail-order giant whose original purpose was to supply condoms to U.S. citizens who couldn't buy them locally—and the RRs are definitely not happy about it.

In fact, Rev. Sun Myung Moon's *Washington Times* did a smear story on the fact that USAID has awarded $170 million in contracts to manage health programs, including those designed to curb STDs, to PSI—which brought immediate promises from USAID officials that Andrew S. Natsios, the agency's administrator, would order "an immediate review of the PSI contract." Dr. James Dobson's CitizenLink e-zine went even further, and urged readers to contact the White House to get PSI's funding pulled.

Though Harvey receives no salary from his PSI work, and though PSI and Adam & Eve share no funds or staff, that didn't stop the *Times* from raking up Adam & Eve's decade-old legal troubles, when the Justice Department illegally targeted the company as part of its multi-jurisdictional prosecution strategy designed to drive it out of business.[6]

That, of course, wasn't how the *Washington Times* saw it. Instead, they quoted a former Justice Department prosecutor—likely one of the several who now work for censorship organizations like Pat Trueman of the American Family Assn.—as saying, "He knows how to use the system, how to delay the process and when he brought a lawsuit against the Justice Department in our case in 1993, [Attorney General Janet] Reno dropped the case in exchange for him dropping the suit. That's what happened, pure and simple."

August, 2003:
Fundies Vs. Comic Books

The American Family Assn. (AFA) has targeted donations made by the hosts of comic book conventions in Pittsburgh and Detroit to such charities as Make-A-Wish and the Muscular Dystrophy Assn. Why? Well, here's part of a report from AFA chapter president Diane Gramley:

"Heather and I walked down the first aisle a little further and immediately began encountering blatant pornographic material—*Playboy* magazines on the bottom shelf and right at eye level of young children... On down aisle one brought us to Playboy Playmates Mandy Fisher, Jennifer Lavoie and Julie Cialini. The tables were covered with their albums of nude and semi-nude photos. Right across from Fisher and Lavoie was 'artist' Stacey E. Walker with her very 'revealing' drawings and photos...

"As we 'visited' with the men who were representing the [Comic Book Legal Defense Fund[7]], we noticed that the table right across from them had pornographic videos. The jacket covers were not X-rated, but the titles included *Girls Gone Wild*, *Girls Gone Wild II*, and *Janene* [sic] *and Vince Neil—Uncut/Uncensored*. As we stood a short distance away, we saw a young man who had been following his father take a quick look at the videos as his father turned his back. How poignant the lesson to parents and dangers to their children when they turn their backs in such a 'comic book convention' as this!!"

February, 2007:
Anti-porn religionists are getting more dangerous, as evidenced by an incident which occurred in Florida in December.

The Café Risque Adult Super Center had been the target of protests since early 2006, well before it was scheduled to open, but on Dec. 5, police in Gainesville arrested Thomas C. Magyari on charges of having pumped hazardous materials into the store by means of a homemade rig consisting of two gallon-sized jugs and a pair of hoses.[8]

Apparently, Magyari filled the jugs with a mixture of swamp water, yeast, laundry soap and rotten eggs that he had allowed to ferment for about a week, set the jugs on the roof of the business near its air conditioning system, and arranged for the liquid to be pushed into the store by water pressure. What Magyari missed, however, was the videotape surveillance system that caught him doing it.

The complaint, for "criminal mischief," said Magyari had intended to cause water and mold damage that might delay the business from opening. Cops called Magyari's concoction and delivery system a "weapon of mass destruction."

March, 2007:
Hope you didn't miss getting your copy of Bishop Paul Loverde's newest pastoral letter, "Bought with a Price: Pornography and the Attack on the Living Temple of God,"[9] wherein he describes porn as "an evil plague that is ravaging society."

"This plague stalks the souls of men, women and children, ravages the bonds of marriage and victimizes the most innocent among us," the Bishop wrote. "It obscures and destroys people's ability to see one another as unique and beautiful expressions of God's creation, instead darkening their vision, causing them to view others as objects to be used and manipulated."

Ken Henderson, a self-described "porn addict" for 25 years, agreed, and traces the "problem" to the greater acceptance by society of sexual immorality, which in turn has led to a much greater acceptance of pornographic imagery.

"Things on prime time television today would have been R-rated or X-rated in the 1950s," Henderson charged.

"The threat of pornography is always a necessary and timely issue. It is pervasive and constant in our society," Bishop Loverde said.

And Catholics are rising to the challenge! The Diocese of Austin, Texas, has formed an Anti-Pornography Task Force and launched a website titled "Pornography Isn't Pretty" that posts news reports and studies to make the case that "pornography is not a harmless product but a tumor that needs to be removed in its entirety from the face of the human community."

But Bishop Loverde has some ideas on how to fight the scourge: "Young people are urged to dress with modesty and to avoid impure speech and entertainment. Husbands are directed to honor their wedding vows. Parents are cautioned to strictly monitor their children's use of the Internet and other media, and priests are directed to engage in frequent and open spiritual direction and to seek assistance from fellow priests as needed." (Like helping them cover up when they diddle little boys? Classic!)

May 7, 2010:

The Past As Prologue

Dan Coats has just won the Republican primary in Indiana and might retake his former seat in the U.S. Senate.

Now, where have we heard that name before?

"The senator who vowed to protect children from indecent material on the Net[10] has spawned a son of the now-defunct Communications Decency Act," wrote CNET News' Courtney Macavinta in 1997. "In June, the Supreme Court ruled that a controversial part of the Dan Coats CDA unconstitutionally censored protected speech because it prohibited transmitting or displaying indecent material to minors via the Net. The high court said the law was too broad and could have criminalized simply posting Web pages about safe sex, art, or medical issues, for example."

So what did Coats do in response to the Supreme Court's ruling? He introduced "CDA II"—but *AVN* readers probably know it better as the Child Online Protection Act: COPA.[11]

The Child Online Protection Act (COPA) was passed by Congress in 1998, but was immediately challenged in court because it required all commercial distributors of material that was claimed to be "harmful to minors" to prevent minors from accessing those materials on the internet. Trouble was, the law, which never went into effect, would have prevented high schoolers from accessing information on breast cancer, sex education and myriad other non-explicit content. The following recounts that legal battle.

INTERNET FREEDOM AT ISSUE BEFORE U.S. SUPREME COURT

January, 2002

WASHINGTON, D.C. — Listening to the government's argument in the case of *ACLU v. Ashcroft* could easily give a free speech advocate the feeling of having passed through Alice's looking glass.

For instance, when Justice Anthony Kennedy asked Solicitor General Theodore Olson whether, under the Child Online Protection Act at issue in the proceedings, local or national "community standards" would apply to material on the Internet, Olson replied that he would not object to national standards, and said that Congress, in adopting the law, had decided that there were "relatively constant standards" regarding acceptance of sexual materials throughout the country.

Wha'?!?

This from a government that, for decades, engaged in postal sting operations wherein it tricked adult video producers into sending sexually explicit videos from relatively liberal parts of the country like Los Angeles to relatively conservative parts like Dallas or Oklahoma City, then brought obscenity charges in those areas against the senders!

"The [Third Circuit] court of appeals rested its condemnation of community standards on a finding that Web businesses cannot prevent material from reaching particular geographic areas, effectively forcing those businesses to conform to the standards of the most puritan community," Olson had argued in the government's Supreme Court brief.

One of the best challenges to that government theory came, interestingly, from Justice Antonin Scalia, not someone who has generally been friendly to adult community interests.

"Doesn't any jury necessarily apply the standards of its own community?" Scalia asked. "What does someone who was raised his whole life in North Carolina know about Las Vegas?"

The concept continued to trouble Justice Kennedy.

"I have a California jury," Kennedy said, framing the issue. "Is it proper or is it necessary for that jury to consider what the standards are in other parts of the country before it renders its verdict?"

"Yes, that would be possible," Olson replied, but seemed to undercut his own argument when he continued, "Jurors are allowed to draw from their experience, which necessarily comes from the community in which they reside."

The problem of how to apply the Court's settled *Miller* obscenity standards to the Web obviously concerned the justices greatly, especially since it was Chief Justice William Rehnquist who had authored the decision in *Hamling vs. United States*, wherein he stated that "juror[s] sitting in obscenity cases [should] draw on knowledge of the community... from which [they come]."

"I don't see how we could reach a different conclusion for obscenity," Justice Scalia opined from the bench.

"Whether [material] was obscenity or not depended on community standards," Rehnquist stated. "Why should it be different for [harmful-to-minors] pornography than for obscenity?"

Rehnquist later claimed that it's "no problem to subject a publisher to different standards throughout the country."

This is a particularly important issue for adult retailers as well as Webmasters, since "community standards" implicate two prongs of the three-prong *Miller* test.

"There are ways for Web businesses to limit their material to particular geographic areas," Olson had agreed in the brief, claiming that Webmasters could require passwords to be mailed to those wishing to access sexually explicit sites, with certain zip codes ineligible for access. Adult website operators, however, would find amusing Olson's naivete in expecting those seeking passwords to adult sites from "forbidden" geographic areas to provide legitimate mailing addresses.

Olson also stressed the "limited amount of material" found on the 'Net that would be affected by upholding COPA.

"COPA applies primarily to pornographic teasers that appear on the Web sites of commercial pornographers," Olson wrote in the government's brief. "Thus, if COPA requires vast amounts of material on the Web to be placed behind screens, it is only because commercial pornographers display so many pornographic teasers."

Ann Beeson, a staff attorney for the ACLU, who argued the case for several plaintiffs including Salon.com and PlanetOut, tore most of the government's arguments to shreds.

"A national standard would be an exercise in futility," she told the justices, because in the real world, "The least tolerant community would get to set the standards on the Web."

Beeson also made short work of COPA's "affirmative defenses," which would require that websites obtain from a prospective site-surfer a credit card or debit account number, adult access code, personal identification number, a digital certificate that verifies age, or "any other reasonable measures [of age verification] that are feasible under available technology."

"The district court found, and the government does not dispute, that there is no 'authority that will issue a digital certificate that verifies a user's age,'" Beeson wrote in the ACLU's brief. "Further, there are 'no other reasonable measures' available to restrict access to minors. Thus, the only technologies currently available for compliance with COPA are credit cards and adult access codes. Either option would require users to register and provide a credit card or other proof of identity before gaining access to restricted content."

Trouble is, Beeson argued, many people would not want to do that because of embarrassment, privacy considerations or simply laziness, and thus, their access to sexually explicit but constitutionally-protected material would be cut off. Moreover, "Plaintiffs testified, without contradiction, that their users would not want to be associated with the 'adult' access code industry, and would instead forego accessing the plaintiffs' content," Beeson wrote.

"Many of the plaintiffs' readers and other Web users are even more reluctant to identify themselves because the information they seek is intensely personal, sensitive, or controversial," the brief said. "Mr. Tepper of the Sexual Health Network, for example, testified that some of his readers would simply not go to his site if they had to identify themselves. His site aims to provide information about sexuality to disabled persons who will only seek it anonymously. Similarly, many gay or lesbian people who are 'closeted' rely on a Web site such as PlanetOut 'because it allows closeted people access to this information while preserving their anonymity.'"

Setting up access systems also are an expensive undertaking, she said, and most of her clients would not be able to afford to do so.

Beeson also took issue with the idea that only a few porn teaser screens would be affected.

"Instead of limiting its reach to commercial pornographers, COPA broadly applies to all speech on the Web—even speech provided for free—if the speaker is engaging in some business through which she merely hopes to make a profit through advertising or other means," Beeson noted. "Plaintiff BlackStripe, for example, provides Web users with a free Web-based forum to obtain and discuss information pertaining to same-gender-loving individuals of African descent, and is funded, in part, by selling space on the Web site to advertisers."

That small amount of "commerce," Beeson argued, would bring BlackStripe under COPA's prohibitions.

Therefore, she wrote, "Web speakers are faced with two strong incentives to self-censor: financial burdens and the risk of criminal penalties."

Further, Beeson argued that COPA could not accomplish what its proponents intended.

"The law would also fail to protect minors from the 40 percent of Web content that originates abroad," she wrote.

In her argument before the Court, Beeson said that a better alternative would be the use of net-filtering software, and that Congress had set up a commission which had already concluded that that would be a better solution than COPA required.

The Court will now consider the arguments, and a ruling will be issued before the end of the Court's term in June, 2002.

☆☆☆

COPA Back Before The Supremes

May, 2004

WASHINGTON, D.C. — It wasn't exactly 'déjà vu all over again,' but on Mar. 2, the U.S. Supreme Court again heard argument in *Ashcroft v. ACLU*, better known as the *Child Online Protection Act*, or *COPA*, case.[1]

COPA I, as it's now known, was argued in 2001, with a decision coming from the high court in mid-2002 that essentially said that the decision by the Third Circuit U.S. Court of Appeals gave insufficient grounds to throw the law out, and so the Supremes sent it back to the lower body for reconsideration.[2]

Writing for a plurality of the Court, Justice Clarence Thomas wrote, "After our decision in *Reno v. American Civil Liberties Union*, Congress explored other avenues for restricting Minors' access to pornographic material on the Internet. In particular, Congress passed and the President signed into law the Child Online Protection Act, 112 Stat. 2681 §736 (codified in 47 U. S. C. §231 (1994 ed., Supp. V)). COPA prohibits any person from 'knowingly and with knowledge of the character of the material, in interstate or foreign commerce by means of the World Wide Web, mak[ing] any communication for commercial purposes that is available to any minor and that includes any material that is harmful to minors.'"

Trouble is, "material harmful to minors" has its own court-approved definition, and that definition relies heavily on a reworking of the three criteria for obscenity under *Miller v. California*—and one of those criteria is "community standards." In its original opinion in *COPA I*, the Third Circuit seized on the question of community standards and said that since the Internet is worldwide in character, the "community" to be considered for Web-based speech was worldwide as well, thereby making the *Miller* definition of community standards at least unconstitutionally vague, and at worst totally inapplicable to Internet speech.

Complicating matters is that there's been a hell of a lot of legislation dealing with Internet speech since the *COPA I* decision came down, not the least of which was the *Child Internet Protection Act*, or *CIPA*, case,[3] whose outcome was an affirmation of Congress' plan to cut off funding to libraries that refused to install filtering software on any publicly-accessible computers that could connect to the Internet.

Also impacting the situation is that the American Civil Liberties Union put on an excellent case before the trial court, and it's that evidence, plus certain common facts that the law allows "judicial notice" to be taken of, that all of the higher courts are required to rely upon in assessing the outcome of the case. But things move so fast in the online world that much of what was true during trial is no longer true today. For instance, it was testified in 1998 when *COPA I* came to trial that there were approximately 28,000 adult Websites on the Internet. A search today would find millions—a fact that caused Justice Sandra Day O'Connor to suggest, during the *COPA II* argument, that "part of the problem is that the pornography laws that would apply to adult [Internet] viewers don't seem to be enforced very well, the obscenity laws." Solicitor General Theodore Olson responded that there have been 21 federal obscenity indictments over the past two years, 17 of which involved the Internet, but court-watchers know that all of those indictments are from a handful of cases, including several from the still-to-be-tried *Extreme* case.

From the Justices' questioning of Olson, it would be easy to draw the inference that they were less concerned about the constitutionality of the law and more about the proliferation of sexual material on the 'Net. Olson, of course, helped by providing testimony *cum* argument that "11 million children visit these porn sites every week, and that between the ages of 15 and 17, 70 percent of the children, according to the statistics that we cite, visited porn sites inadvertently. It is very difficult to avoid."

Justice Kennedy tried his best to bring the argument back to the actual issues in the case, which now included not only the unconstitutionality of applying local community standards to the Worldwide Web, but the additional issue of "whether [the] statute encroaches upon speech in a constitutionally overinclusive manner." Part of that last issue has to do with the high court's mandate that material accused of being "obscene," or in this case "harmful to minors," must be judged as a whole, and there was much discussion of whether a single page or image on a website could be considered by itself, or must the entire site—indeed, the entire Web itself—be considered? Also, Justice Antonin Scalia brought up the question of whether what might be deemed harmful for a 5-year-old would be acceptable for a 16-year-old.

When the ACLU's turn came, their case was argued by Ann Beeson, the organization's general counsel.

"COPA violates the First Amendment for two independent reasons," she stated. "First, it is a criminal statute that suppresses a wide range of protected speech between adults on the Web, and second, the Government has a range of more effective, less restrictive tools available to protect minors. The Government's attempt to narrow the range of speech that is affected by this statute defy the law's plain language, the record, and plain common sense. Even under the Government's interpretation, COPA criminalizes speech that under any definition adults have the right to access. It criminalizes a depiction or even a description of nudity or even a description or depiction of the female breast. It does not just cover sexual conduct."

The Justices dove right in with questioning what material produced by Beeson's clients, which included a variety of artists, Internet retailers and service organizations, had "serious scientific value," one attribute that would exempt it from the court's idea of obscenity. Beeson responded that if the court refused to make a distinction between clearly non-obscene material that was deemed harmful to minors and material that was considered obscene for adults, it was in effect preventing the Web from carrying any information of a sexual nature that in any other forum would be, for adult viewers, protected speech. (Author and sometime-*AVN* contributor Susie Bright will be heartened to know that Beeson used Bright's sex therapy writings as examples of protected speech that would be banned under COPA.)

"[A]s a society," Beeson argued, "we have defined a wide range of material as having value for adults and lacking value for even older minors. A 16-year-old cannot get into an R-rated movie. If you're a speaker on the Web and you communicate material that's like Bertolucci films, for example, or *Sex and the City*, you are going to be very, very worried. The Government has made your speech a crime and you have only three options under the statute. All of those options violate the First Amendment.

"The first option is that you can take a risk and leave your speech up there, Justice Breyer, as you're saying, you know, leave it up there. You're Susie Bright and you think that your... speech is not covered. What happens? You can go to jail, not because you made that column deliberately available to a minor, but because you merely displayed the column to the general public. That is a pure violation of this Court's rule in *Butler v. Michigan* that you cannot make it a crime to display material to adults in the name of protecting children.

"The second option. You're worried, you don't want to go to jail, you self-censor. Everything that you have self-censored, adults had the right to access. It violates the First Amendment for the Government to do this through the statute.

"The third option is that you can set up costly screens, which the record shows drive away your users."

Beeson was quite eloquent when the Justices allowed her to get a word in edgewise, and from their comments and questions, it was obvious that the Justices were heavily divided over what to do about the law. At least one felt that the existence of filtering software was a valid reason to rule against the Act, and Beeson, who had taken a stand against forced filtering in the *CIPA* case, agreed that it would be useful here, and added that "all of the major Internet service providers provide these parental controls as a... default for parents."

It's impossible to predict from the argument which side the Supreme Court will favor in this twice-fought case—but the court will make its decision known by early summer.

✡✡✡

Supreme Court Passes The Buck... Again

COPA Remanded To District Court For Trial

August, 2004

WASHINGTON, D.C. – The Child Online Protection Act is gone... for the moment. The good news is, the U.S. Supreme Court, after hearing argument on the merits of the preliminary injunction against the 1998 law for the second time, ruled that the statute is likely unconstitutional, and ordered that it not be enforced.

The bad news is, while the Court could have struck the law down in its entirety, it didn't. Instead, it ordered that the injunction remain in place while a trial is held on the merits of the case in the United States District Court for the Eastern District of Pennsylvania in Philadelphia.

So why didn't the Court just strike down the law?

"Because it's too controversial," opined Paul Cambria, one of the country's foremost First Amendment attorneys. "They're giving the government a chance to try to make it right. They're giving them this bullshit, 'You know, maybe things have changed in five years; we'll give you another chance to factually make this thing happen,' and by then, most of us will be retired and we won't have to deal with it."

In a sense, a trial of sorts has already been held. Immediately after COPA was passed, the American Civil Liberties Union (ACLU) sued the government on behalf of various Webmasters, retailers and others who either did business on the Web or posted information of a sexual nature that would be prohibited under COPA, and the ACLU asked for a preliminary injunction against enforcement of the new law. After days of testimony by both plaintiff and government expert witnesses, that injunction was granted. The case is now called *American Civil Liberties Union v. Ashcroft*.

"The court first noted that the statute would place a burden on some protected speech," wrote Justice Anthony M. Kennedy for the majority. "The court then concluded that respondents were likely to prevail on their argument that there were less restrictive alternatives to the statute: 'On the record to date, it is not apparent ... that [petitioner] can meet its burden to prove that COPA is the least restrictive means available to achieve the goal of restricting the access of minors' to harmful material." [Citations redacted throughout]

The preliminary injunction was appealed to the Third Circuit Court of Appeals, which deemed the law both vague and too far-reaching. Of particular interest in that opinion was the finding that, for purposes of deciding whether any particular speech was harmful to children, the law essentially adopted the obscenity standards set in *Miller v. California*—the so-called "*Miller* test"—and questioned whether the third prong, "community standards," could possibly be defined as it applied to the aptly-named World Wide Web.

It was that finding which the Supreme Court considered when COPA was first argued in 2001, and the Court's conclusion at that time was that the community standards overbreadth was insufficient to force a striking of the law altogether, and it remanded the case to the Third Circuit for reconsideration.

The Third Circuit came back swinging.[4]

"On remand, the Court of Appeals again affirmed the District Court," Kennedy wrote. "The Court of Appeals concluded that the statute was not narrowly tailored to serve a compelling Government interest, was overbroad, and was not the least restrictive means available for the Government to serve the interest of preventing minors from using the Internet to gain access to materials that are harmful to them."

However, in this second consideration of the law, the high court essentially side-stepped the entire second Third Circuit opinion and opted to concentrate on the original findings of the District Court.

"Because we affirm the District Court's decision to grant the preliminary injunction for the reasons relied on by the District Court, we decline to consider the correctness of the other arguments relied on by the Court of Appeals," Kennedy stated.

What the Court majority found most impressive in the District Court opinion, authored by Judge Lowell A. Reed, Jr., was the concept that "there are plausible, less restrictive alternatives to COPA. A statute that 'effectively suppresses a large amount of speech that adults have a constitutional right to receive and to address to one another ... is unacceptable if less restrictive alternatives would be at least as effective in achieving the legitimate purpose that the statute was enacted to serve'," wrote Kennedy, quoting from Judge Reed's decision.

"In considering this question, a court assumes that certain protected speech may be regulated, and then asks what is the least restrictive alternative that can be used to achieve that goal?" Kennedy explained. "The purpose of the test is not to consider whether the challenged restriction has some effect in achieving Congress' goal, regardless of the restriction it imposes. The purpose of the test is to ensure that speech is restricted no further than necessary to achieve the goal, for it is important to assure that legitimate speech is not chilled or punished. For that reason, the test does not begin with the status quo of existing regulations, then ask whether the challenged restriction has some additional ability to achieve Congress' legitimate interest. Any restriction on speech could be justified under that analysis. Instead, the court should ask whether the challenged regulation is the least restrictive means among available, effective alternatives... It is not an answer to say that COPA reaches some amount of materials that are harmful to minors; the question is whether it would reach more of them than less restrictive alternatives."

For the majority, the answer appeared to be filters.

"Filters are less restrictive than COPA," Kennedy wrote. "They impose selective restrictions on speech at the receiving end, not universal restrictions at the source. Under a filtering regime, adults without children may gain access to speech they have a right to see without having to identify themselves or provide their credit card information. Even adults with children may obtain access to the same speech on the same terms simply by turning off the filter on their home computers. Above all, promoting the use of filters does not condemn as criminal any category of speech, and so the potential chilling effect is eliminated, or at least much diminished. All of these things are true, moreover, regardless of how broadly or narrowly the definitions in COPA are construed."

Justice John Paul Stevens went even further on that path in his concurring opinion, joined by Justice Ruth Bader Ginsburg.

"COPA's use of community standards is not the statute's only constitutional defect," Stevens opined. "Today's decision points to another: that, as far as the record reveals, encouraging deployment of user-based controls, such as filtering software, would serve Congress' interest in protecting minors from sexually explicit Internet materials as well or better than attempting to regulate the vast content of the World Wide Web at its source, and at a far less significant cost to First Amendment values."

It's an argument with which Justice Steven Breyer, writing in dissent for himself, Chief Justice William Rehnquist and Justice Sandra Day O'Connor, completely disagrees.

"I cannot accept its conclusion that Congress could have accomplished its statutory objective—protecting children from commercial pornography on the Internet—in other, less restrictive ways," Breyer wrote.

The high court opinion goes into some depth as to why filtering would be more successful than a law which criminalizes certain Internet speech, but in doing so, it's hard to see why the Court didn't simply strike down COPA in its entirety.

"It is not enough for the Government to show that COPA has some effect," said Kennedy, presaging the arguments likely to be made at trial. "Nor do respondents bear a burden to introduce, or offer to introduce, evidence that their proposed alternatives are more effective. The Government has the burden to show they are less so. The Government having failed to carry its burden, it was not an abuse of discretion for the District Court to grant the preliminary injunction."

And later:

"The closest precedent on the general point is our decision in *Playboy Entertainment Group*,[5]" the opinion says. "*Playboy Entertainment Group*, like this case, involved a content-based restriction designed to protect minors from viewing harmful materials. The choice was between a blanket speech restriction and a more specific technological solution that was available to parents who chose to implement it. Absent a showing that the proposed less restrictive alternative would not be as effective, we concluded, the more restrictive option preferred by Congress could not survive strict scrutiny...

In the instant case, too, the Government has failed to show, at this point, that the proposed less restrictive alternative will be less effective."

Apparently, one of just two things that prevented the Court from striking down the law was a perceived lack of an evidentiary base to do so.

"[T]here is a serious gap in the evidence as to the effectiveness of filtering software," Kennedy noted. "For us to assume, without proof, that filters are less effective than COPA would usurp the District Court's fact-finding role... and on a related point, the factual record does not reflect current technological reality—a serious flaw in any case involving the Internet. The technology of the Internet evolves at a rapid pace. Yet the fact findings of the District Court were entered in February 1999, over five years ago. Since then, certain facts about the Internet are known to have changed."

Undoubtedly, however, the ACLU will be happy that the Supreme Court is making many of the plaintiffs' trial arguments for them.

"One argument to the contrary is worth mentioning—the argument that filtering software is not an available alternative because Congress may not require it to be used," Kennedy noted. "That argument carries little weight, because Congress undoubtedly may act to encourage the use of filters. We have held that Congress can give strong incentives to schools and libraries to use them."

One particularly encouraging aspect of this decision is the high court's placing the burden of protecting children directly on their parents.

"COPA presumes that parents lack the ability, not the will, to monitor what their children see. By enacting programs to promote use of filtering software, Congress could give parents that ability without subjecting protected speech to severe penalties," Kennedy analyzed, referring to the high court's decision declaring that the Children's Internet Protection Act (CIPA), which required libraries receiving federal funds to install filtering software, was not unconstitutional.

Fortunately, Justice Kennedy, the author of several pro-speech and pro-personal freedom decisions in the past three years, recognized the enormous burden the activation of COPA would place on free expression.

"There are also important practical reasons to let the injunction stand pending a full trial on the merits," he wrote. "First, the potential harms from reversing the injunction outweigh those of leaving it in place by mistake. Where a prosecution is a likely possibility, yet only an affirmative defense is available, speakers may self-censor rather than risk the perils of trial. There is a potential for extraordinary harm and a serious chill upon protected speech.

"Content-based prohibitions, enforced by severe criminal penalties, have the constant potential to be a repressive force in the lives and thoughts of a free people. To guard against that threat the Constitution demands that content-based restrictions on speech be presumed invalid, and that the Government bear the burden of showing their constitutionality. This is true even when Congress twice has attempted to find a constitutional means to restrict, and punish, the speech in question."

As expected, however, Justice Stevens could be counted on to go even further in his defense of speech and in setting forth the dangers of this law.

"In registering my agreement with the Court's less-restrictive-means analysis, I wish to underscore just how restrictive COPA is," Stevens analyzed. "COPA is a content-based restraint on the dissemination of constitutionally protected speech. It enforces its prohibitions by way of the criminal law, threatening noncompliant Web speakers with a fine of as much as $50,000, and a term of imprisonment as long as six months, for each offense. Speakers who 'intentionally' violate COPA are punishable by a fine of up to $50,000 for each day of the violation. And because implementation of the various adult verification mechanisms described in the statute provides only an affirmative defense, even full compliance with COPA cannot guarantee freedom from prosecution. Speakers who dutifully place their content behind age screens may nevertheless find themselves in court, forced to prove the lawfulness of their speech on pain of criminal conviction."

As unsurprising as Stevens' support of free speech is the vehemence with which Justice Breyer defended the COPA statute.

"After eight years of legislative effort, two statutes, and three Supreme Court cases the Court sends this case back to the District Court for further proceedings. What proceedings?" Breyer wanted to know. "I have found no offer by either party to present more relevant evidence. What remains to be litigated? I know the Court says that the parties may 'introduce further evidence' as to the 'relative restrictiveness and effectiveness of alternatives to the statute.' But I do not understand what that new evidence might consist of."

"Moreover," he continued, "Congress passed the current statute '[i]n response to the Court's decision in *Reno*' striking down an earlier statutory effort to deal with the same problem. Congress read *Reno* with care. It dedicated itself to the task of drafting a statute that would meet each and every criticism of the predecessor statute that this Court set forth in *Reno*. It incorporated language from the Court's precedents, particularly the *Miller* standard, virtually verbatim... And it created what it believed was a statute that would protect children from exposure to obscene professional pornography without obstructing adult access to material that the First Amendment protects... What else was Congress supposed to do?"

"I recognize that some Members of the Court, now or in the past, have taken the view that the First Amendment simply does not permit Congress to legislate in this area," Breyer ranted. "... Others believe that the Amendment does not permit Congress to legislate in certain ways, e.g., through the imposition of criminal penalties for obscenity... There are strong constitutional arguments favoring these views. But the Court itself does not adopt those views. Instead, it finds that the Government has not proved the nonexistence of "less restrictive alternatives." That finding, if appropriate here, is universally appropriate. And if universally appropriate, it denies to Congress, in practice, the legislative leeway that the Court's language seem to promise. If this statute does not pass the Court's 'less restrictive alternative' test, what does? If nothing does, then the Court should say so clearly."

Sadly, Breyer falls into the trap set by would-be censors since time immemorial: That *some* censorship isn't really censorship; that in fact it actually *enhances* free speech.

"The Court's decision removes an important weapon from the prosecutorial arsenal," Breyer claims. "That weapon would have given the Government a choice—a choice other than 'ban totally or do nothing at all.' The Act tells the Government that, instead of prosecuting bans on obscenity to the maximum extent possible (as respondents have urged as yet another 'alternative'), it can insist that those who make available material that is obscene or close to obscene keep that material under wraps, making it readily available to adults who wish to see it, while restricting access to children. By providing this third option—a 'middle way'—the Act avoids the need for potentially speech-suppressing prosecutions. That matters in a world where the obscene and the nonobscene do not come tied neatly into separate, easily distinguishable, packages. In that real world, this middle way might well have furthered First Amendment interests by tempering the prosecutorial instinct in borderline cases. At least, Congress might have so believed. And this likelihood, from a First Amendment perspective, might ultimately have proved more protective of the rights of viewers to retain access to expression than the all-or-nothing choice available to prosecutors in the wake of the majority's opinion."

"What was perhaps most surprising was the switch in predicted positions, with Justice Thomas in the majority and Justice Breyer in the dissent," commented *AVN* columnist and First Amendment attorney Clyde DeWitt. "It also looks as though Justices Stevens and Ginsburg are ready to can the *Miller* decision entirely."

DeWitt refers to the section of Stevens' dissent which reads, "I continue to believe that the Government may not penalize speakers for making available to the general World Wide Web audience that which the least tolerant communities in America deem unfit for their children's consumption, and consider that principle a sufficient basis for deciding this case."

"The majority of the Court sidestepped the real issue by simply holding that the trial court did not abuse its discretion in granting a preliminary injunction," DeWitt analyzed. "But this was an extremely rare situation because the Court granted review of a case that wasn't finished. And, on an appeal from a grant or denial of a preliminary injunction, the basic issue is never more than simply whether the trial court abused its discretion."

But Cambria was less than satisfied by the narrowness of the opinion.

"The big thing for me was the community standard; what is the standard, because that really would have had an impact on Lou's case, and I wanted to see that issue resolved," said Cambria, referring to H. Louis

Sirkin's representation of Extreme Associates, currently under indictment for interstate transportation of obscenity in the Western District of Pennsylvania. "Now Lou is stuck with whatever district court judge he has deciding that issue, and if it's bad, that could ripple to the rest of us. I wish they would have decided that or at least commented that, 'Yes, you're right; it can't be a local standard.' That's my disappointment. I didn't think they were going to find the statute constitutional but I was hoping that they would get involved in the standard. That was very important, but it didn't happen.

"It's still good from our standpoint," Cambria continued. "It's not a defeat, and it shows that the court is still recognizing that the First Amendment's alive and well as it relates to adult content, and they're not pulling back from that, as some people like Scalia would like to have them do. They're recognizing that there is an overbreadth doctrine that there's a danger of when it comes to the Internet. This is all good stuff, and especially in the Internet; they're realizing that it's different, and that's important for us, to have them realize that it's different and be treated differently. So we have adult content still being protected; we have them deciding that the Internet should be treated differently and we have them, although they're giving the government a second bite at the apple, they still haven't let the government win. So those things are extremely important. It's still a good day as far as freedom fighters are concerned."

But the fact that the case is being returned to the District Court for trial means that the resolution of this issue is far in the future. It's unlikely that the trial would start before the beginning of next year, and no matter which side wins, the other is likely to appeal, which will take several more years.

Of interest is that the government and its supporters, all of whom argued in the CIPA case that filtering technology was useful and reliable enough to require that it be installed in public library computers across the country, will now have to reverse that position to argue that the technology isn't good enough; that an outright ban on adult material on the Web is the only reliable solution to keep such content out of the hands (and eyes) of minors. Moreover, the "community standards" issue which the Supreme Court didn't deal with in this opinion is likely to be a key issue at trial.

"Assuming that, after the trial, this case again returns to the Supreme Court—a pretty safe assumption—that will be four trips on this single issue, which must be some kind of a record," DeWitt noted.

The fact that the appeals from that verdict, whatever it is, will be several years in the future, points up another important issue, which is, what will be the make-up of the Third Circuit Court of Appeals, or even the U.S. Supreme Court, when the COPA case gets to them? There are still several vacancies on the Third Circuit bench, and although no Supreme Court justices announced their retirement at the end of this term, as many as four may retire before the presidential election of 2008, so the philosophies of the resident of the White House during that period will be crucial.

✲✲✲

Third Circuit Strikes Down COPA
July 22, 2008

PHILADELPHIA – It's always comforting when a federal court, sitting less than a mile from the building where the Declaration of Independence was signed, once again affirms Americans' constitutional right to free speech—this time over the World Wide Web. That's exactly what a panel of the Third Circuit U.S. Court of Appeals did today in affirming[6] Judge Lowell A. Reed, Jr.'s opinion that the Child Online Protection Act (COPA) is "impermissibly overbroad and vague."

This represents the third time COPA has come before the Third Circuit—twice before on preliminary injunctions against the law taking effect, and now after Judge Reed found at trial that his fellow judges on the Circuit were right all along: COPA is simply bad law, and not the least restrictive means by which the government could accomplish its (alleged) goal of protecting minors from exposure to sexually explicit content.

"[T]his time the Supreme Court affirmed our decision though it remanded the case to the District Court for a trial on the merits," wrote Senior Judge Morton I. Greenberg for the three-judge panel which included Thomas L. Ambro and Michael A. Chagares. "The Court contemplated that the record would be updated on the remand to reflect the then current technological developments and to account for any changes in the legal landscape. The Court further directed that the District Court determine whether Internet content filters are more effective than enforcement of the COPA restrictions or whether other possible alternatives are less restrictive and more effective than COPA to effectuate Congress's intention."

COPA was the "fix" to the 1996 Communications Decency Act,[7] which banned all "indecent" and "obscene" speech from the Internet—and which was quickly found by the U.S. Supreme Court to be unconstitutionally vague. COPA, on the other hand, limited the banned speech to "material that is harmful to minors" posted only "for commercial purposes," and incorporated a definition of "material harmful to minors"—"minors" here meaning anyone under 17—that has been widely copied by state legislatures attempting to craft anti-adult zoning and other censorious measures aimed at restricting adults' access to adult sexual speech:

"(A) the average person, applying contemporary community standards, would find, taking the material as a whole and with respect to minors, is designed to appeal to, or is designed to pander to, the prurient interest; (B) depicts, describes, or represents, in a manner patently offensive with respect to minors, an actual or simulated sexual act or sexual contact, an actual or simulated normal or perverted sexual act, or a lewd exhibition of the genitals or post-pubescent female breast; and (C) taken as a whole, lacks serious literary, artistic, political, or scientific value for minors."

COPA's idea of "commercial purposes" was equally unworkable:

"A person makes a communication 'for commercial purposes' only if the person when making the communication 'is engaged in the business of making such communications'," Judge Greenberg reported. "A person is 'engaged in the business' when the person: 'devotes time, attention, or labor to such activities, as a regular course of such person's trade or business, with the objective of earning a profit as a result of such activities . . . . [and] only if the person knowingly causes [or solicits] the material that is harmful to minors to be posted on the World Wide Web'."

Hence, the American Civil Liberties Union, acting for a number of actual or putatively "commercial" individuals and businesses including Salon

Media Group, the Center for Democracy and Technology, and a coalition of writers, artists and health educators, sued the government to prevent their sites from being banned.

When trial on the issues was finally held in early 2007, Judge Reed concluded that "COPA facially violates the First and Fifth Amendment rights of the plaintiffs because: (1) COPA is not narrowly tailored to the compelling interest of Congress; (2) defendant has failed to meet his burden of showing that COPA is the least restrictive and most effective alternative in achieving the compelling interest; and (3) COPA is impermissibly vague and overbroad."

Judge Greenberg spends some time in his opinion discussing the "law-of-the-case" doctrine, which essentially says that once the issues in a particular case have been framed, courts at each succeeding stage of the proceedings are generally bound to consider those same issues, unless "extraordinary circumstances" are present. For the most part, such circumstances didn't occur here.

However, since the current opinion is a post-trial opinion rather than one involving a preliminary injunction, both the trial court, and therefore also the appeals court, have taken fresh looks at some issues that have been attendant to the case all along, not the least of which was whether COPA can survive the "strict scrutiny" doctrine that is applied to all cases involving content-based restrictions on speech.

Strict scrutiny requires that a law restricting expression must both serve a compelling government interest in accomplishing a particular goal, and must also be narrowly tailored so that it does not draw in speech that has little or nothing to do with that stated goal. Among the problems the Third Circuit found with COPA, both in its prior opinion and the current one, were that the statute's language, requiring that the "material harmful to minors" be "taken as a whole," would in practice "appl[y] in a literal sense to an infant, a five-year old, or a person just shy of age seventeen," causing "Web publishers [to] face great uncertainty in deciding what minor could be exposed to its publication, so that a publisher could predict, and guard against, potential liability... Under the plain language of COPA, a

Web publisher will be subjected to liability if even a small part of his or her Web site displays material 'harmful to minors."

"In its decision made after the trial on the merits now on appeal before us," Judge Greenburg wrote, "the District Court concluded that COPA is not narrowly tailored because it is both overinclusive and underinclusive ... because it 'prohibits much more speech than is necessary to further Congress' compelling interest,' [and] because it 'applies to speech that is obscene as to all minors from newborns to age sixteen, and not just to speech that is obscene as to older minors....'"

Since the Third Circuit did not deal with underinclusiveness in its prior decision, it was free to address that concept based on the findings at trial, and it noted that Judge Reed found that, "[T]here is a significant amount of sexually explicit material on the Internet which originates from outside of the United States.... [U]nlike Internet content filters which are able to block from view unsuitable material regardless of its origin, COPA has no extra-territorial application. As a result, ... COPA is not applicable to a large amount of material that is unsuitable for children which originates overseas but is nevertheless available to children in the United States .... COPA's lack of extraterritorial application renders it underinclusive."

This is, of course, a fact that adult Webmasters—and attorneys—have long been familiar with, but the Third Circuit concluded, despite ample evidence adduced at trial regarding COPA's lack of jurisdiction over foreign material, that "if we had to pass on the issue we might conclude that COPA is not unconstitutionally underinclusive." But nonetheless, the panel stated, "We note, however, that our possible disagreement with the District Court on this one point would not change our ultimate decision to affirm its order granting a permanent injunction, as there are numerous other grounds that require us to find that COPA is not narrowly tailored and is unconstitutional. Accordingly, we will refrain from deciding the matter."

The court also found that age verification services and obtaining credit card numbers on sites are virtually useless in preventing minors from accessing explicit material since they "can easily be circumvented by children who generally know the first and last name, street address and zip codes of their parents or another adult." For that and a few other reasons, the Third

Circuit agreed that these "affirmative defense" mechanisms failed to cure COPA's failure to be narrowly tailored in the amount of speech it restricts.

Finally, "In addition to failing the strict scrutiny test because it is not narrowly tailored, COPA does not employ the least restrictive alternative to advance the Government's compelling interest in its purpose, the third prong of the three-prong strict scrutiny test," the panel concluded.

The answer? Blocking and filtering software, of course!

"The District Court discussed Internet content filters at length in its Findings of Fact," Judge Greenburg stated. "We will review these findings in detail, as the need to determine whether filters are more effective than COPA to effectuate Congress's purpose in enacting that statute was the primary reason the Supreme Court remanded the case."

A major part of that remand was to consider the advances in technology since COPA was first considered back in 1999, and sure enough, the district court found that, "[f]iltering products have improved over time and are now more effective than ever before. This is because, as with all software, the filtering companies have addressed problems with the earlier versions of the products in an attempt to make their products better. Another reason the effectiveness of filtering products has improved is that many products now provide multiple layers of filtering. Whereas many filters once only relied on black lists or white lists, many of today's products utilize black lists, white lists, and real-time, dynamic filtering to catch any inappropriate sites that have not previously been classified by the product."

Judge Reed also found that filtering programs are now harder for children to bypass; that filters will block foreign sexually-oriented sites that COPA can't; and also that the government had failed to show that COPA would be less restrictive than filtering because, "unlike COPA there are no fines or prison sentences associated with filters which would chill speech. Also unlike COPA, ... filters are fully customizable and may be set for different ages and for different categories of speech or may be disabled altogether for adult use."

And besides, the Supreme Court has already given instruction on how the government could promote and support the use of filters, noting most importantly that, "The need for parental cooperation does not automatically disqualify a proposed less restrictive alternative." (Now, if only the high court would apply that same logic to zoning-mandated setbacks for adult businesses!)

The Third Circuit also perceptively noted, "the circumstance that some parents choose not to use filters does not mean that filters are not an effective alternative to COPA. Though we recognize that some of those parents may be indifferent to what their children see, others may have decided to use other methods to protect their children—such as by placing the family computer in the living room, instead of their children's bedroom—or trust that their children will voluntarily avoid harmful material on the Internet. Studies have shown that the primary reason that parents do not use filters is that they think they are unnecessary because they trust their children and do not see a need to block content." Let's hear it for Freedom of Choice!

"Given the vast quantity of speech that COPA does not cover but that filters do cover, it is apparent that filters are more effective in advancing Congress's interest, as it made plain it is in COPA," the panel concluded. "Moreover, filters are more flexible than COPA because parents can tailor them to their own values and needs and to the age and maturity of their children and thus use an appropriate flexible approach differing from COPA's 'one size fits all' approach. Finally, the evidence makes clear that, although not flawless, with proper use filters are highly effective in preventing minors from accessing sexually explicit material on the Web."

Finally, the appeals court found that COPA is filled with terms that, when it comes to speech restrictions, are impermissibly vague:

"We are bound by our conclusion in *ACLU II* [the Third Circuit's last opinion on the preliminary injunction dispute] that COPA's definition of 'minor' renders the statute vague," the Court said. "Furthermore we agree with the District Court's conclusion that COPA's use of the phrases and terms 'communication for commercial purposes,' 'as a whole,' 'intentional,' and 'knowing' renders it vague, for the reasons the District Court stated in its opinion."

And with vagueness almost invariably comes overbreadth, because if a statute isn't clear about what speech it covers, it certainly would, in practice, take in more speech that it permissibly may.

"Thus, we explained," the Court said, referring to *ACLU II*, "an isolated item located somewhere on a Web site that meets the 'harmful to minors' definition can subject the publisher of the site to liability under COPA, even though the entire Web page (or Web site) that provides the context for the item would be constitutionally protected for adults (and indeed, may be protected as to minors)."

"In sum, COPA cannot withstand a strict scrutiny, vagueness, or overbreadth analysis and thus is unconstitutional," Judge Greenburg summarized. "We reach our result both through the application of the law-of-the-case doctrine to our determination in *ACLU II* and on the basis of our independent analysis of COPA and would reach the same result on either basis standing alone. For the foregoing reasons, we will affirm the District Court's March 22, 2007 order."

It seems almost a foregone conclusion that the Justice Department's next stop will be a *cert* petition to the U.S. Supreme Court ... but with this excellent analysis by the Third Circuit, and with the Bush administration out the door by Jan. 20, 2009, and a likely concomitant sea change in the Justice Department's policies toward speech, it's hardly a slam dunk that that petition will be filed, or that the Supreme Court will look favorably upon it. However, only time will tell.

UPDATE: On January 21, 2009, the United States Supreme Court refused to hear appeals of the lower court decision, effectively shutting down the law.

Believe it or not, there are a lot of people out there who don't like adult entertainment; in fact, they absolutely hate it, and they show that hatred in various ways. Below, I've identified some of the main players and the tactics they use to harass adult retailers, supporters and industry members. Note: As of this printing, some of those described below are either dead or inactive—but too many are still around.

THE ENEMIES LIST: THESE ARE THE FOLKS WHO WANT TO PUT YOU OUT OF BUSINESS

Posted March 1, 2002

There's a war going on. Everyone who produces adult entertainment in any form knows it, as do most of those who sell it and consume it, but it's a war about which a large portion of the general public is as yet unaware.

It's a war between the forces of sexual liberation, represented by the adult video, Internet, cabaret, and magazine industries, and those of sexual repression. That latter group is represented by dozens of censorship organizations and porn-hating individuals, all of which "spread the word" through churches and synagogues, through seminars—you can read about one such meeting which this author attended undercover in 1999 on AVN's Website—through public demonstrations outside adult bookstores and nightclubs, occasionally through testimony before Congress, and in an increasingly significant way through their Websites and e-newsletters. A good rule of thumb for recognizing censorship organizations is that their titles will have some mix of two or more of the following buzz-words in them: "Children," "Family" or "Families," "Research," "Concerned," "Values," and "Moral."

So who are the "bad guys"? Well, there are plenty of them, some of whose names are very familiar, while others operate deep behind the scenes and don't get much press unless they surface at local demonstrations or as witnesses in a Congressional hearing. But their supporters know who they are; most of them are mentioned at least a couple of times a month in emailed "AgapePress News Summaries" (more on those later), while others have no problem quoting themselves and their cohorts in "press releases" that go out over Internet news feeds, which in turn lead to these same commentators being described as "experts" by national news media.

Several once-known names have fallen by the wayside. Few any longer mention Andrea Dworkin and Catharine MacKinnon of Women Against Pornography, who worked to enact laws that would allow women "victims" of porn to sue for the "pain and suffering" the material had caused them. Their star fell quickly when the press began quoting their more extreme utterances, and the fact that they refused to debate anti-censorship activists in public kept them out of the national limelight. Likewise, Charles H. Keating, Jr., owner of Lincoln Savings Bank, member of the original President's Commission on Obscenity and Pornography (1968) and founder of Citizens for Decent Literature (later renamed Citizens for Decency Through Law), is no longer prominent in anti-porn circles since his conviction for having bilked hundreds of depositors out of their life savings. (His organization, however, survives, though it has no Website.)

So who are the current bad guys?

The Attorneys:

Ayn Rand, in *Atlas Shrugged*, said of some of the characters she depicts that if they could get real jobs, they wouldn't be working for the government. Whether there's any validity to that concept is open for debate, but the fact is that some of the more visible legal personalities in the censorship movement arrived on the scene fresh from government service.

U.S. Department of Justice (DOJ) veterans **Bruce A. Taylor** and **J. Robert Flores**, for example, were both prosecutors during the Reagan/Bush years in the National Obscenity Enforcement Unit (NOEU), which changed its name in the early '90s to the more euphemistic Child Exploitation and Obscenity Section (CEOS).

Best known for having been the main prosecutor of early porn mogul Reuben Sturman, Taylor began his public career as an assistant prosecutor in Cleveland, Ohio, where one of his first assignments was to digest what have become known as the U.S. Supreme Court's *Miller* decisions on obscenity, and to formulate a plan to prosecute purveyors of sexually explicit material that would withstand Supreme Court scrutiny. It may have been his anti-porn zeal that earned him his Justice Department position, but it certainly led him, after leaving the DOJ, to form the National Law Center for Children and Families, of which he is currently president and chief counsel.

Though the National Law Center (NLC) claims to be a "specialized resource to those who enforce state and federal obscenity and child exploitation laws," Taylor himself has often been ineffective when it comes to the nitty-gritty. Last November, after the city of South Bend, Ind. brought Taylor in as a special prosecutor for the first of three scheduled bookstore trials, a 12-person jury took just six hours to find Little Denmark owner Robert Henderson not guilty on all counts of trafficking obscenity, money laundering, and conspiracy. Several attorneys who actively defend adult businesses have expressed the opinion that Taylor is both a lackluster legal writer and an unimpressive advocate in the courtroom. Nevertheless, Taylor is a favored speaker at anti-porn events, and a commentator on various newscasts regarding the adult industry.

Flores is still listed as vice-president and senior counsel for the National Law Center, but his current full-time job is as head of the federal Office of Juvenile Justice and Delinquency Prevention, in which position he will likely have a lot to say about porn on the Internet and its (presumed) effect on minors. Flores was Acting Deputy Chief of CEOS during the first Bush presidency, was appointed to the Child Online Protection Act (COPA) Commission, and has been an active opponent of free sexual speech on the Internet. For example, his Nov./Dec. 2000 article for the Concerned Women for America (CWA), "Blind to the Law," is still available online. An excerpt: "Despite connections with organized crime, today the pornography industry feels free to hire lobbyists to influence politicians. We must tell the truth about this dirty 'business.' We must make sure that pornographers, sex club operators, pimps—and the criminal organizations they control—do not write the final chapter of this sordid story.... The new president must lead the battle by appointing law-respecting U.S. attorneys and judges. It's time to wipe the smirk off the porn industry's face."

One of the National Law Center's ex-affiliates is worth mentioning: **Janet M. "Jan" LaRue**, now senior director of legal studies for the Family

Research Council, used to be a senior counsel with the NLC. Author of "A Constitutional and Effective Sexually Oriented Business Ordinance," LaRue played a significant role at 1999's National Pro-Family Conference On Pornography, Sexually Oriented Businesses and Material Harmful to Children, speaking at one of the group's general sessions and leading several seminars.

LaRue gave the conference the following account of some parents' "experiences" in Garden Grove, Calif.: "The parents showed me hardcore video box covers with explicit sex acts on the cover, and people go into these businesses and purchase these materials or rent them and rip the cover off and throw them into the neighboring residential yards around these kinds of businesses. *Men sit on the curb in front of these businesses, masturbating in the middle of the afternoon.* Garden Grove Boulevard is the boulevard of male prostitutes and Beach Boulevard, which are both major thoroughfares in Southern California—it's the boulevard for female prostitutes. Why are they there? Because there are seven of these [adult] businesses strung together on that boulevard." (Emphasis added.)

In 1988, **Patrick A. Trueman** was acting director of the NOEU, and took part in the Justice Department's unconstitutional vendetta against several adult mail-order companies, most prominently Adam & Eve, as detailed in Philip D. Harvey's book, *The Government Vs. Erotica*. Now Trueman is director of governmental affairs for the American Family Association (AFA). In that position, Trueman has claimed that the American Library Assn. "will stop at nothing to promote the availability of [online] pornography in libraries, even at the expense of children"; that "Yahoo! continues to make child pornography available to its customers by means of its online 'clubs' [which] feature pictures of young girls, often being bound, gagged, and tortured, all for the sexual gratification of patrons who may purchase the pictures from Yahoo!"; and that the National Endowment for the Arts is "still funding blasphemy and organizations that produce blasphemy" and should therefore be disbanded. Trueman is currently licking his wounds, as is Taylor, at having been passed over by Attorney General John Ashcroft for the top post at CEOS. (Former deputy chief Andrew Oosterbaan, one of the prime movers behind last summer's child porn sting Operation Avalanche, got the "honor.")

Jay A. Sekulow has a friendly greeting for those who visit his organization's Website:

"Hi, this is Jay Sekulow, Chief Counsel of the American Center for Law and Justice,[1] and I wanted to welcome you to our web page for the American Center. You're going to see that our interests at the ACLJ are pretty broad:

* We're concerned about Religious Liberty;

* We're concerned about the Unborn Child;

* And we want to protect Your Family and Your Family's Rights

So enjoy our web page here at the ACLJ, and stand with us, as we stand for Liberty."

Unmentioned is the fact that the group's name was chosen specifically to create confusion with the American Civil Liberties Union (ACLU), not to mention the connections between ACLJ founder M.G. 'Pat' Robertson and the Christian Coalition, the Christian Broadcasting Network (CBN), and *The 700 Club*. Robertson is said to have founded the ACLJ in 1990 simply because he "decided to act to undo the damage done by almost a century of liberal thinking and activism."

For example, as far as mandatory filtering of porn on the Net goes, Sekulow testified before the U.S. Senate Committee on Commerce, Science, and Transportation that, "This is an issue about protecting our children. While the Internet has proved to be a tremendous asset in providing information to our young people, it is also a haven for obscene and pornographic material. The government has the duty and obligation to protect our children. There should be no constitutional crisis when it comes to safeguarding children who use the Internet." And surely there wouldn't be, if that pesky ol' First Amendment weren't in the way.

Alan Sears is a name porn people haven't heard for a while, but he's starting to make his comeback in censorship circles. Those with long memories will recognize Sears as the former director of the Attorney General's Commission on Pornography,[2] more commonly known as the Meese Commission. But while Sears doesn't specifically fight porn anymore, as head of Arizona's Alliance Defense Fund (ADF), he's very concerned about how "tragically, during this time of national grief, many who oppose the gospel remain bent on moving forward to their goal of a secular America." Sears specifically named the American Civil Liberties Union and LAMDA, "a pro-homosexual legal organization," as groups to watch out for, in an article on the AFA Website. "Not a single one of these groups has changed their agenda, not a single one of these groups has withdrawn any of the lawsuits that they filed across America," Sears wrote. ADF is against porn; abortion; right-to-die laws; homosexuals marrying, adopting kids and/or serving in the military; and is in favor of cramming as much religion into public life (and schools) as it can get away with.

Another new name on the scene is **Mathew D. 'Mat' Staver**, president and chief counsel of Liberty Counsel,[3] a "ministry" based in Orlando, Fla., but also self-described as "a nonprofit civil liberties education and legal defense organization dedicated to preserve religious freedom," which claims to have over 400 affiliated attorneys, all of which have allegedly "gone through extensive training in Constitutional and civil rights litigation." Among the primary goals of Liberty Counsel are to sue those who would prevent the posting of "God Bless America" posters and the Ten Commandments in state and federal office buildings and schools, oppose "homosexual union" laws, and support those who'd like to refuse anti-viral vaccination in case of a bio-warfare attack, as would be required under the proposed Model State Emergency Health Powers Act.

The Preachers:

Feel free to append a "Rev." in front of any of these guys, since they've graduated from, or at least been honored by, a bible school or two—but considering their attitudes toward free speech and the sexuality that "God" allegedly gave us, we have to ask, "What Would Jesus Do?"

M.G. 'Pat' Robertson gets to go first, because his brand of Christian fundamentalism is the most media-pervasive. Besides creating the ACLJ, Pat's responsible for inventing the Christian Coalition, the Christian Broadcasting Network (CBN)—It all started on Oct. 1, 1961, "on WYAH-TV [from Yahweh, the Hebrew name for God], a UHF television station with barely enough power to reach across the Portsmouth [Va.] city limits"—and *The 700 Club*. He owns the Ice Capades, a small hotel, several diamond mines, and until recently, International Family Entertainment, parent company of the Family Channel, most of which were started with seed money supplied by CBN, whose main source of income was (and is) donations from listeners.

Of the eight goals spelled out on the Christian Coalition's Website—www.cc.org—the one that will most concern *AVN Online*'s readers is "Protecting young people and our communities from the pollution of pornography." The site also says, "Today, Americans are bombarded with countless political messages from across the ideological spectrum. Because of this, it is becoming increasingly difficult to separate truth from fiction and right from wrong."

See if you can guess which of the following quotes were truly and rightly said by (ex-presidential candidate) Pat:

1. "It is interesting that termites don't build things, and the great builders of our nation almost to a man have been Christians, because Christians have the desire to build something. He is motivated by love of man and God, so he builds. The people who have come into [our] institutions [today] are primarily termites. They are into destroying institutions that have been built by Christians, whether it is universities, governments, our own traditions, that we have.... The termites are in charge now, and that is not the way it ought to be, and the time has arrived for a godly fumigation."

2. "The feminist agenda is not about equal rights for women. It is about a socialist, anti-family political movement that encourages women to leave their husbands, kill their children, practice witchcraft, destroy capitalism, and become lesbians."

3. "Just like what Nazi Germany did to the Jews, so liberal America is now doing to the evangelical Christians. It's no different. It is the same thing. It is happening all over again. It is the Democratic Congress, the liberal-based media, and the homosexuals who want to destroy the Christians. Wholesale abuse and discrimination and the worst bigotry directed toward any group in America today. More terrible than anything suffered by any minority in history."

Yep, you were right; he said 'em all—and if you want to see even more of the same, go to www.geocities.com/CapitolHill/7027/quotes.html.

And speaking of quotes, who said this, and about what:

"The ACLU's got to take a lot of blame for this... throwing God out successfully with the help of the federal court system, throwing God out of the public square, out of the schools. The abortionists have got to bear some burden for this because God will not be mocked. And when we destroy 40 million little innocent babies, we make God mad. I really believe that the pagans, and the abortionists, and the feminists, and the gays and the lesbians who are actively trying to make that an alternative lifestyle, the ACLU, People For the American Way, all of them who have tried to secularize America. I point the finger in their face and say, 'You helped this happen.'"

If you guessed "**Jerry Falwell**," with buddy Pat "totally concur[ring]," about the cause of the Sept. 11 attacks on the World Trade Center and the Pentagon, pick up your kewpie doll at the exit.

Jerry runs Liberty University, which is "[t]raining the next generation of Christian leaders," whose "outstanding graduates are actively serving Christ in government, education, media, medicine, business, law and many other fields."

Jerry's also got a daily radio message airing on "Christian radio"; two weekly hour-long shows airing on (non-Christian) TV, *Listen America* and *The Old Time Gospel Hour* ("also available 24 hours a day on the Internet"); and a monthly newspaper, the *National Liberty Journal*, described as "the conservative answer to the liberal bias of other newspapers in print today... fighting for the strong morals and traditional values upon which our nation was founded." Who could ask for more? Oh; and he invented the Moral Majority... which folded in 1989, having failed to achieve any of its objectives.

Jerry and Pat may be the media frontrunners of this section, but the guy who causes the most mischief is **Donald E. Wildmon**, founder of the American Family Assn. (AFA). Don, as he likes to be called, founded the AFA one evening in 1977 when he was watching TV with his family. "On one channel was adultery, on another cursing, on another a man beating another over the head with a hammer. I asked the children to turn off the

TV. I sat there, got angry, and said, 'They're going to bring this into my home, and I'm going to do all I can to change it.' I brooded for a while and then came up with a plan for our church to turn off the TV for a week. I sent out a press release and the national media picked up on it."

Though he claims a readership/listenership in the millions, a more realistic figure is probably a couple of hundred thousand, with the AFA itself having branches in several states. Typically, Wildmon targets well-known businesses—Disney/ABC, K-Mart, Southland Corp. (7-Eleven), Burger King, S. C. Johnson, etc.—accusing the companies of not toeing the AFA line on "obscenity" and the "homosexual agenda."

Wildmon and crew have created at least two media outreach Websites, AgapePress News Summary, emailed daily to subscribers; and CNSNews ("Cyber News Service," formerly "Christian News Service"), which AgapePress frequently quotes. Several fundamentalist Websites carry front-page links to one or both.

James Dobson isn't much in the news these days, unless you follow the President's Commission on Internet Gambling, on which Dobson serves (guess what? He's against online betting); but the founder of Focus on the Family (FotF) was instrumental in giving porn a big black eye in the '80s.

For a mere seven bucks, visitors to the FotF Website can order a cassette of *Pornography Kills*, the "final interview of serial killer Ted Bundy (given exclusively to Dr. James Dobson) as he warned about the insidious and progressive nature of this lethal but legal killer: pornography."

Trouble is, Bundy had previously blamed his alcohol consumption and his propensity to ogle high school cheerleaders practicing as the motivation for his taking 36 young women's lives—before Dobson came along to fund Bundy's final appeal.

Dobson also served on the Meese Commission, and an anonymous interviewer on the FotF Website asked Dobson to give an industry "update."

"If people understood the debauchery of this business, and what pornography does to the individual addicted to it, they would be far more motivated to work for its control," Dobson responds. "[I]f a man were to go into the sex shops on Times Square or in other large cities in the United States, he would find very few depictions of normal heterosexual activity.

Instead, he would see a heavy emphasis on violent homosexual and lesbian scenes, on excrement, mutilation, enemas, oral and anal sex, instrumentation for the torture of men and women, and depictions of sex between humans and animals.... What has changed since the 1980s is the invasion of obscenity on the Internet. All of the terrible images that we witnessed during the commission, and worse, are now accessible to any 12-year-old with a modem and a high-resolution printer."

Finally, we'd hate to leave out **Phil Burress** and wife **Vickie**, founders of several state branches of the pro-censorship Citizens for Community Values and main sponsors of the National Pro-Family Conference On Pornography referenced above. Though their Website is often way out of date, the Burresses are active: Vickie writes porn-bashing articles for, among others, the AFA, while Phil, a former plumber, campaigns in the Cincinnati area against Larry Flynt and his Hustler Superstores. The Burresses have recently commended Butler County, Ohio and its chief prosecutor Robin Piper for their establishment of a $200,000 commission to fight porn. In the commission's six month-plus existence, near as we can tell, it hasn't done squat.

The Websites:

We've already covered AFA founder Donald Wildmon, the Websites he's founded—AgapePress News Summary, AFA Online, and Cybercast News Service—are each worth a look.

The AgapePress News Summary is ubiquitous across the Religious Right segment of the Web. Several different religious sites carry synopses of its daily stories, and others simply include a link to its homepage, but America's religion- and conservatism-starved masses get the bulk of their news from AgapePress, the *Washington Times* (owned by Rev. Sun Myung Moon), and the WorldNetDaily site.

Interestingly, AgapePress often credits Cybercast News Service (formerly "Christian News Service," and for some reason abbreviated "CNSNews") as a source; yet both are owned by the AFA. So whether a story appears first on AgapePress or CNSNews—or even AFA Online—hardly matters.

AgapePress, however, is a remarkable resource for Religious Right thinking. For instance, type "homosexual agenda" into the site's search engine, and literally hundreds of story links will appear; usually in pairs, since the same story is usually archived at AFA Online as well. A search on "pornography" will produce even more.

"Does The AFA Hate Homosexuals?" one section of the organization's Website asks rhetorically. "Absolutely Not!" is the emphatic answer. "The same Holy Bible that calls us to reject sin, calls us to love our neighbor. It is that love that motivates us to expose the misrepresentation of the radical homosexual agenda and stop it's [sic] spread though our culture."

In their "Pornography" section, one can find, among myriad other articles, "How To Raise Your Son To Be A Porn Addict" by Steve Gallagher, owner of Pure Life Ministries (Rule 3: "Another valuable lesson you can teach him through your own life is to immerse himself in the mentality of this fallen world by watching television, reading secular magazines and spending a lot of time surfing the Internet.") and "Is Pornography Harmless Fun Even If You Are Not Addicted?" by Vickie Burress, wife of Phil Burress, founder of Citizens for Community Values. (Excerpt: "For pornography to be harmless, the people who are depicted in its images would have to be unreal—mere symbols of something philosophical and intangible. However, the women violated in pornography are human beings. Beyond the glossy pages, the naked and used women are real, as real as all other women who work and live side-by-side with men who sustain a regular diet of pornography. Pornography makes women chattel, and all women have reason to fear that the attitudes of the men with whom they live and work are transformed by the images of pornography.")

Each day, the AgapePress writing staff churns out eight to 10 stories about how bad Democrats are, how whatever they're concerned about is all Clinton's fault, how the rights of Christians are being eaten away by non-God-centered legislators, gays, and the Left Wing. The staff includes Rusty Pugh, Bill Fancher, Jody Brown, Fred Jackson, Allie Martin, Chad Groening, and Ed Vitagliano, the AFA's "director of research," though his qualifications to hold that position are nowhere revealed, as well as being the editor of AFA Online. And then there are the columnists: R.

Cort Kirkwood and Jeremy Sisto (not the actor of the same name), plus the occasional guest like Warren Smith, most of whom work for obscure Christian tabloids and magazines scattered across America's heartland.

An offshoot of the AFA is the American Decency Assn. (ADA),[4] also founded by Wildmon but now run by Bill Johnson. The ADA "monitors" Howard Stern's daily radio show in 19 cities throughout the U.S. In addition, it monitors the Stern/CBS TV show in upwards of 10 cities. ADA sends more than 1,000 letters a month to sponsors of the show. The organization claims that, since 1996, it has managed to get more than 12,000 sponsors to withdraw from the Stern show.

After the various AFA sites, porn's second-biggest opponent on the Net is Morality in Media (MIM), headed by attorney Robert M. Peters. Peters joined MIM in 1985 as a staff attorney, and was made president in 1992.

The MIM site provides articles on the alleged effects of porn, on obscenity law, on Internet and other mass media porn issues, as well as links to organizations that "treat" "sex addicts" and other pro-censorship organizations.

Peters hates being called a "censor," which he defines as something only the government can be: "Americans who are fighting against pornography and the declining standards on television are routinely called 'censors' by the porn industry and its allies. It's a buzzword used to discredit, distract, and distort. IT'S A LIE!"

As to Web porn, Peters says: "Clearly, there is a major failure of adult responsibility when almost three out of four teens report they have accidentally come across pornography on the Web. The biggest failure of responsibility lies with federal and state prosecutors who turn a blind eye to obscenity on the Internet. If obscenity laws were being vigorously enforced, the last thing hardcore pornographers would want to do is draw attention to their vile wares by engaging in reckless marketing methods. If vigorously enforced, there would also be much less pornography to accidentally stumble across."

Peters seems oblivious to the fact that one of the main arguments to the Supreme Court last November was that current laws regarding obscenity, which are based on "community standards," cannot apply to the worldwide community of the Web.

One of Peters' main projects has been the National Obscenity Law Center (NOLC), currently headed by attorney **Paul J. McGeady**, with **Robin S. Whitehead** as its senior attorney.

The NOLC acts as a clearinghouse for news of obscenity prosecutions and other legal issues surrounding the adult industry, through their bi-monthly publication the *National Obscenity Law Bulletin*, and also is a reference site for past obscenity prosecutions and anti-porn legislation. Among the publications available (by mail; no Shopping Cart here!) through the site are a three-volume set of the 22 most popular secondary effects reports from municipalities around the country—one suspects that the recent *Flanigan's, Inc. v. Fulton County, Ga.* study, which found no adverse effects from adult businesses, isn't included; but we don't intend to pay the $50 necessary to find out—and the *Handbook on the Prosecution of Obscenity Cases* by George M. Weaver, Esq., which is described as "an authoritative guide that provides the reader an organized understanding of obscenity law by leading the reader through the History, Meaning, Investigation, Trial and Appeal of an obscenity case," all for a measly 10 bucks.

Also heavily involved on the political scene is the Family Research Council (FRC), which has about a dozen "policy analysts," but, oddly enough, no one with a title of "researcher."

For an organization with such a secular-sounding name, the casual surfer might be surprised to find the following in the FRC mission statement: "Believing that God is the author of life, liberty, and the family, we promote the Judeo-Christian worldview as the basis for a just, free, and stable society... God exists and is sovereign over all creation. He created human beings in his image. Human life is, therefore, sacred and the right to life is the most fundamental of political rights."

Founded by failed presidential candidate **Gary Bauer**, the FRC's current head is **Kenneth L. Conner**, a lawyer who has been "deeply involved in state and national political affairs." But the organization's most active spokesperson has been **Jan LaRue**. LaRue, however, has a new assistant, **Miriam Moore**, who's taken over much of the writing for FRC's Website, as well as its two main legal publications, *Legal Facts* and the annual *Supreme Court in Review.* Moore is an attorney who also has a Bachelor's degree in psychology, and is starting to make her mark as a spokesperson for the organization.

Another religious stealth organization is Concerned Women for America (CWA), whose mission is "to protect and promote Biblical values among all citizens—first through prayer, then education, and finally by influencing our society—thereby reversing the decline in moral values in our nation."

Chaired by **Beverly LaHaye**, CWA's main foci, often voiced by spokesperson **Wendy Wright**, have been browbeating the FCC for lax enforcement of its indecency standards, support for other organizations' efforts such as the AFA's "Victims of Pornography Month," and gay-bashing through its own Culture and Family Institute (CFI), whose "senior analyst" and primary spokesperson is **Peter LaBarbera**.

The "homosexual movement" has been attempting to paint conservative Christians, with their biblical view on the issue, as "hate mongers," according to LaBarbera. "Even though we're not haters, we have people writing in and saying that what we believe is hate, calling our site a hate site, and that sort of thing. The homosexual activists... [encourage] people to think that Christians who oppose homosexuality are somehow hateful."

Well, perhaps a look at their site is in order... "We believe it is uncompassionate to promote homosexuality as normal and healthy when well-documented evidence says otherwise," reads the site's overview. "CFI opposes the homosexual movement out of concern for people trapped in that tragic lifestyle and for the destructive effect that the homosexual political agenda is having on America's God-given freedoms... We believe that any society that encourages sinful and unhealthy sexual practices, such as the sanctioning of homosexual 'relationships,' jeopardizes its very survival and the welfare of its citizens... History teaches that civilizations that abandon the objective standards of right and wrong and the marital ideal for human sexuality eventually crumble. We at CFI will work to help America avoid that fate, and pursue the vision of godliness and ordered liberty upon which our great nation was founded."

All told, the Web is rife with religiously based right-wing political organizations and "fellow travelers."

The Politicians:

While adult industry members would be wise to eye most politicians with caution, the following members of Congress in particular seem to have an agenda in tune with the Religious Right.

"Today, this national scourge has begun to find its way across our phone and cable lines into our homes, libraries, and even public schools," wrote Rep. (and former NFL star) **Steve Largent** (R-Okla.), of Internet porn, in a *Washington Times* editorial. "Obscenity will continue to spread like a cancer, creating new addicts, extending its reach to every corner of our culture, provided the Justice Department continues with its current policy and does absolutely nothing."

Largent is a darling of the Religious Right, seeing things their way on nearly every societal issue from abortion to support for tax-paid "faith-based initiatives."

Rep. J.C. Watts, the ex-college football star, shares Largent's philosophy, particularly on abortion issues.

Largent's counterpart in the senate is **Sam Brownback** (R-Kan.). While recently active in congressional moves to ban all forms of cloning, even for medical research, Brownback is best remembered for joining Connecticut **Sen. Joseph I. Lieberman** in attacking the entertainment industry for the "trash and filth that we see and hear in the movies, on television, in music, and in video games." According to an AgapePress article, Brownback was also "upset with vulgar trends in television programming—among them a new Showtime series about homosexuals that features intimate sexual encounters between a man and a teenage boy."

In their letter to the FCC, Brownback, Lieberman, and two other senators blasted broadcasters for the "gross inflation of sex and vulgarity on free, over-the-air television, particularly in the early hours of prime-time," and mentioned several studies that claimed an increase in sexual messages being aired on TV.

Another prime candidate for the Enemies List is Mississippi Congressman **Charles "Chip" Pickering**, whose father was recently under consideration for a seat on the federal appeals bench.

For instance, in May of 2000, at a House Telecommunications Subcommittee hearing, Pickering and Largent attacked Deputy Assistant Attorney General Alan Gershel for the Clinton administration's failure to bring federal obscenity prosecutions. "One of the reasons I believe you have a dramatic increase [in the exploitation of children and child pornography] is because of the lax... effort to address obscenity. They overlap. They are integrated. They contribute to each other. And until you address both, you are going to see a dramatic increase," warned Pickering.

Currently, one of the religionists' primary issues is obtaining the ability of its clergy to endorse political candidates from the pulpit without jeopardizing the church's tax-exempt status. Last summer, Pickering co-sponsored a bill that would prevent the IRS from punishing churches whose ministers speak out about political issues. "We think some conservative Christian groups actually are being targeted by the IRS for their political speech," he said. "This legislation would repeal that, take away any authority the IRS might have to do that."

Most recently, **Rep. Walter B. Jones Jr.** (R-N.C.), has introduced the "Houses of Worship Political Speech Protection Act,"[5] which would "permit churches and other houses of worship to engage in political campaigns." The bill has 112 co-sponsors, all but four of whom are Republicans. Opponents say the bill is little more than a strategy by leaders of the Religious Right to mobilize conservative churches on behalf of conservative candidates, and in fact, the Christian Coalition lost its tax-exempt status several years ago for distributing "voter guides" at churches throughout the country.

While not strictly a politician, U.S. Supreme Court **Justice Antonin Scalia** is an unabashed Religious Right apologist. While addressing a church meeting several years ago, he said, "I'm a fool for Christ. We all are." It was Scalia who told a group in Mississippi in 1996 that Christians should "assert their faith" even if intellectuals dismiss them as "simpleminded."

Aiding Scalia in his quest to spiritualize America is the Attorney General of the United States, **John David Ashcroft**. Ashcroft is the embodiment of "government as defendant" in two of the major free speech cases currently under consideration by the high court: *ACLU v. Ashcroft* (about COPA) and *Ashcroft v. Free Speech Coalition* (about the Child Pornography Prevention Act).

Ashcroft has been biding his time since his confirmation about a year ago, but signals of his views are everywhere. In late January, for instance, he ordered $8,000 spent to cover the historic "Spirit of Justice" statue that's graced the Justice Department halls since the 1930s because he's embarrassed to have his picture taken in front of the statue's exposed breast.

And now that the new head of the Child Exploitation and Obscenity Section, Andrew Oosterbaan, has been installed, reliable sources say that Ashcroft is ready to move with federal indictments against adult video producers and retailers in at least five major cities, possibly based on raids conducted in those cities in August 2000 by the FBI, federal marshals, customs, and IRS agents.

The Rest:
There are some folks out there who aren't politicians, preachers, or attorneys, and who don't operate primarily through their Websites, but who are certainly worth noting.

First among them has to be "Dr." **Laura Schlessinger**, whose doctorate (in physiology) has absolutely nothing to do with psychology, social work, counseling, or anything related to her profession as a radio advice columnist. Schlessinger, who is heard in every major radio market in the U.S., is harmless most of the time. But, for instance, on Jan. 29, Schlessinger went off on a woman who called after finding that her 42-year-old boyfriend had been looking at porn sites on his computer, and was wondering what she should do. "Leave," was Schlessinger's simple answer. "The man is a pervert. He's incapable of having a normal intimate relationship. How can you even think about trying to make a life together with a pervert?"

When the woman vacillated, trying to say that the man had many good qualities, Schlessinger started in on the woman herself. "What do you think it is about yourself that would make you defend a pervert? What is lacking in your life that you would have such a low opinion of yourself?"

"Well, I don't know," the woman answered. "I'm a normal 33-year-old woman who wants someday to have kids..." she began.

"Oh, so you're feeling old and desperate for a relationship, is that it?" Schlessinger countered. "You need to look inside yourself and figure out what it is that attracts you to perverts." Schlessinger launched salvo after "compassionate" salvo for about five minutes—which must have seemed like an eternity for the woman, and in fact was long for a typical call—and eventually brought the woman to tears... but it was just another day in the life of America's most popular conservative religious radio advice columnist. Schlessinger also opposes abortion and unmarrieds living together on religious grounds; claims the American Library Assn. "is boldly, brashly contributing to sexualizing our children" through its anti-filtering stance—"Now the pedophiles know where to go"—and was justifiably raked over the media coals last year for opining that gays were "deviants" and "biological errors." That makes her even more of a "moralist" than porn's other radio arch-enemy, **Rush Limbaugh**.

Also worth mentioning are a pair of "researchers" who've caused their share of trouble for the adult industry. **Victor B. Cline, Ph.D.,** is presently a psychotherapist specializing, he claims, in family/marital counseling and sexual addictions, as well as Professor Emeritus of Psychology at the University of Utah. However, porn veterans may best remember him as one of the star witnesses before the Attorney General's Commission on Pornography, more familiarly known as the Meese Commission.

Cline is considered an "expert" on porn by the Religious Right. Trouble is, according to attorney H. Louis Sirkin, a First Amendment advocate who's often had to challenge Cline's "findings," Cline hasn't done clinical studies on the effects of porn; his conclusions have been drawn from "case histories," "field studies," and "experimental laboratory type studies"—with stress on the word "type"—none of which would be accepted by scientists as empirical.

"In reviewing the literature on the effects of pornography, there is a variety of evidence suggesting risk and the possibility of harm from being immersed in repeated exposure to pornography," a typical Cline "study" might read.

Another Meese witness was the rabidly anti-porn **Dr. Judith Reisman**, a former scriptwriter for the *Captain Kangaroo* television show and now head of her self-styled Institute of Media Education.[6] Reisman has spent much of her career attacking Dr. Alfred Kinsey (yes, the famous one), claiming that he got much of his evidence while molesting the children who gave it to him.

In preparation for her testimony before the Meese Commission, the Justice Department had given Reisman a grant for $734,000 to study the cartoons in *Playboy*, *Penthouse*, and *Hustler*, but according to a paper by David M. Edwards, her grant was "so poorly written and its budget so inflated that it drew criticism from the Senate Juvenile Justice Subcommittee." Further, it emerged that "peer review" of Reisman's findings had been conducted by three vice cops, an FBI agent, and a fellow antiporn activist.

In May 2000, Reisman appeared on a panel on "Porn and the Internet," sponsored by the Pepperdine Law School, where she harangued the audience because none would admit to being "addicted to pornography."

Of course, the problem with any Enemies List, sadly, is that the number of individuals and organizations that can be placed on it is constantly growing. This article has been an overview of some of the main players, but in truth, it barely scratches the surface of what adult retailers and content providers will have to face over the coming months.

What can we say but "Good luck"... and as the much-embattled Boy Scouts of America would probably add, "Be prepared."

I've never met adult nightclub owner Joe Redner, but for a while, he was one of the main voices speaking in favor of adult entertainment in Florida, and at this writing, apparently still going strong even in his 80s.

A STREETCAR (STOP) NAMED DESIRE

March, 2003

TAMPA — When the city of Tampa decided to build a streetcar line between downtown and the historic Ybor City area to the east, it decided to offer the names of each of the 11 station stops to the highest bidders in order to help finance the project.

But since one of the stops is at North Dale Mabry Highway, it was only natural that erstwhile city council candidate Joe Redner,[1] who happens to own the Mons Venus cabaret on that same road, would put in a bid to have that station named after his club.

And that's when the excreta hit the fan.

"The fact that the term 'mons venus' is an anatomical reference that some people find offensive just to say would be essentially the equivalent of naming one of the stations the 'Turgid Erect Member Station,'" said Ed Crawford, a spokesman for HARTline, the historic area rapid transit system charged with building the streetcar project.

So Redner appeared before the Tampa City Council last Sept. 26 to plead his case, and though at least one council member, Rose Ferlita, agreed that Redner should be given an opportunity to buy one of the station names, in the end, on Jan. 6, Redner received a letter from the council rejecting, they were careful to note, the name, though not the individual.

"Since the term 'Mons Venus' can be construed as the name of a female body part, in accordance with the guidelines, it was found to be both controversial, and could be construed as derogatory towards women," the letter, signed by Tampa Historical Streetcar president Michael English, stated.

"Totally expected," Redner sighed. "Very subjective, nothing objective."

Redner said it was unfair to reject the name simply because it included the name of a body part.

"I don't know how they distinguish that from 'eye,' 'foot,' 'nose' or 'ear,'" he said.

Both English and Crawford said that even if Redner had tripled his initial offer of $150,000, the streetcar system wouldn't have gone for it.

"But we'd feel much worse about saying no," Crawford joked.

Sadly, the rejection comes at a time when only five of the stations are sponsored, and at least one of those—the *Tampa Tribune* stop, near the *St. Pete Times Forum*—is being paid for in trade: $125,000 worth of advertising for the streetcar line in the newspaper.

The letter did say that Redner could sponsor a station if he were willing to give it the name of, say, one of his other companies—Joe Redner Enterprises or Xtreme Total Health & Fitness—but Redner wouldn't go for it.

"I have no other intention of using any other name," he said.

Redner had supporters among the city's press, however.

"Just imagine it: Tampa could have a trolley stop named Desire," noted *St. Petersburg Times* columnist Mary Jo Melone.

As for Redner, he plans to run for the city council in District 6, which includes West Tampa; a seat currently held by Mary Alvarez. The seat is up for election in March.

Redner garnered 25 percent of the vote in an unsuccessful bid for Bob Buckhorn's District 3 city council seat in 1999.

You know how all the Very Religious are giving President Biden a ration of shit because though he identifies as a Catholic, he still favors legal abortion? Well, guess what: They've been doing it for more than 20 years, even as far back as John F. Kennedy's presidential campaign. Also noteworthy: blogger P.Z. Myers, though supporting Sam Harris' atheism, accuses him of unworthy racial attitudes.

RELIGIOUS RIGHT GROUPS SUPPORT BUSH – AND YOU PAY!

[Oct 2004]

"A Christian could and should be gay, but the Devil shits on him." – Martin Luther

EL CAJON, Calif. – President Bush might lose yet another presidential election this year—but if he does, it won't be because tax-exempt far right-wing religious groups weren't working their hardest to get out the vote for him.

"This voter's guide helps you cast your vote in an informed manner consistent with Catholic moral teaching," begins the *Voter's Guide for Serious Catholics*[1] from Catholic Answers, a group that's managed to snag the coveted domain catholic.com. "It helps you eliminate from consideration candidates who endorse policies that cannot be reconciled with moral norms that used to be held by all Christians... [S]ome issues are so key, so elemental, that only one position accords with the teaching of the Christian gospel. No one endorsing the wrong side of these subjects can be said to act in accord with the Church's moral norms."

The Guide lists five "non-negotiable" issues, and "Candidates who endorse or promote any of the five non-negotiables should be considered to have disqualified themselves from holding public office, and you should not vote for them."

Those issues are—surprise, surprise!—abortion, euthanasia, fetal stem cell research, human cloning and homosexual marriage—and guess who's the only presidential candidate who *hasn't* "disqualified [himself] from holding public office" under those criteria? And lest anyone be confused by the fact that John Kerry is Catholic, check out point 3 under the section

"How *Not* To Vote": "Do not vote for candidates simply because they declare themselves to be Catholic. Unfortunately, many self-described Catholic candidates reject basic Catholic moral teaching. They are 'Catholic' only when seeking votes from Catholics."

Notably, however, the *Guide* stops short of calling, as some priests around the country have done, for excommunication for those who won't subscribe to the above "non-negotiables." And while the threats of excommunication have made the news, many less-religious people may not understand the depth of that threat: For the 65 million Americans who call themselves Catholic—likely 27% of the voters in 2004—excommunication means, though not "damned for eternity," they are forever barred from participating in the communal life of their church—a real bitch for those for whom church functions are an integral part of their lives—and nobody prays for you when you die.

Sneaky as the Catholic *Voter's Guide* is—not one candidate is mentioned by name—Focus on the Family's (FotF) iVoteValues.org Website takes the prize for being the sneakiest squeakiest clean. One has to go no further than the home page, which quotes Proverbs 29:2: "When the godly are in authority, the people rejoice. But when the wicked are in power, they groan." And whose campaign (and all other) speeches are peppered with "God"?

"As a tax-exempt entity, Focus on the Family is nonpartisan," reads their disclaimer. "The Lord alone is Lord of the conscience and therefore Focus on the Family believes that everyone should vote their own conscience. We do not affiliate with any party or candidate, nor do we seek to influence voting habits. Rather, Focus on the Family seeks to encourage all Americans of faith to exercise their political rights and scriptural responsibilities. Register to vote, be informed, and prayerfully vote your own values."

The key words, of course, are "scriptural responsibilities." If Leviticus 20:13 says, "If a man also lie with mankind, as he lieth with a woman, both of them have committed an abomination: they shall surely be put to death," then "surely" the candidate who proposed the constitutional amendment against same-sex marriage must be the one fulfilling his "scriptural responsibilities."

"God also instructs us to murder people who work on the Sabbath, along with adulterers and children who curse their parents," noted Sam Harris, author of *The End of Faith: Religion, Terror, and the Future of Reason*, in an *L.A. Times* article, "While they're at it, members of Congress might want to reconsider the 13th Amendment, because it turns out that God approves of slavery—unless a master beats his slave so severely that he loses an eye or teeth, in which case Exodus 21 tells us he must be freed."

The FotF site also quotes an AOL/*Time* comparison of Bush, Kerry and Kucinich—Nader and Libertarian Party candidate Michael Badnarik apparently aren't worth considering—on issues like (in order) abortion, gay rights, religion in government, gun control, death penalty and several others. "Iraq" gets the eighth spot; "tax cuts" is 13th, "jobs" only rates 14th, and "environment" is dead last in the priority of issues. And in case that's too subtle, a section of the site titled "Your Values" asks, "What are your core values as we approach Election Day 2004? Would your list include Jobs? The Economy? Health-Care? Education? National Security? As important as those issues are, think about what your core values should be as a follower of Jesus." A recent FotF mailing, complete with voter registration forms, notes, "Rest assured, voter registration is not about Republicans or Democrats, conservatives or liberals. It's about Christians responding to the issues that threaten the future of family, faith and freedom in America."

Hey, according to the conservatively religious Barna Research Group, almost 70 million Americans would favor a constitutional amendment declaring Christianity to be America's official religion—bye-bye Jews, Muslims, Buddhists, etc.—though twice that many oppose it, and Rep. Walter Jones has, for several years running, introduced legislation in Congress that would allow clergy to support particular candidates for office—and word on the street is that Rep. Tom DeLay is planning to attach the bill soon as a rider to some vital appropriations bill.

But as it stands, it's a violation of the IRS Code for a church to engage in partisan politicking, although clergy are allowed to discuss issues of public policy—a vague line that the Religious Right is only too eager to exploit.

Few are more eager than the Rev. Jerry Falwell, who, in a July e-mail and on his Website, exhorted "every political conservative, every evangelical Christian, every pro-life Catholic, every traditional Jew, every Reagan Democrat, and everyone in between to get serious about re-electing President Bush." Americans United for the Separation of Church and State filed a complaint with the IRS over the mailing, but the agency has been notoriously slow to act on such complaints—and certainly none filed in these waning days of the 2004 campaign would be addressed before the election.

Typically, the churches and their supporters try to turn the issue around, claiming their employees are entitled to the same free speech rights as any other citizens—but the average citizen isn't exempt from taxes on whatever donations he or she may receive, which churches are—and they sometimes use those extra funds, overtly or covertly, to support candidates who espouse their conservative ideology.

No one on the Left is trying to take conservative religious folks' beliefs from them—but there are reasons such beliefs shouldn't be enshrined in law.

"In the eyes of most of the civilized world, the United States is now a rogue power—imperialist, inarticulate and retrograde in its religiosity," writes Sam Harris.[2] "Our erstwhile allies are right not to trust our judgment. We elect leaders who squander time and money on issues like gay marriage, Janet Jackson's anatomy, Howard Stern's obscenities, marijuana use and a dozen other trifles lying at the heart of the Christian social agenda, while potentially catastrophic problems like nuclear proliferation and climate change go unresolved...

"It is time we recognize that religious beliefs have consequences... Believe that you are a member of a chosen people, awash in the salacious exports of an evil culture that is turning your children away from God, believe that you will be rewarded with an eternity of unimaginable delights by dealing death to these infidels—and flying a plane into a building is only a matter of being asked to do it. Believe that 'life starts at the moment of conception' and you will happily stand in the way of medical research that could alleviate the suffering of millions of your fellow human beings. Believe that there is a God who sees and knows all things, and yet remains so provincial a creature as to be scandalized by certain sexual acts between consenting adults, and you will think it ethical to punish people for engaging in private behavior that harms no one."

It's that last statement in particular that should be the impetus for adult industry members to get out and vote *their* "faith": The "faith" of sexual freedom and limits on government encroachment on private sexual activity.

As most readers probably know, every year, AVN gives out awards in different categories of sexual expression, including Bondage/Domination/SadoMasochism (BDSM), and the award process consumes several weeks during October and November of each year. But sometimes we slip up...

THE FORGOTTEN NOMINATION

HOLLYWOOD – Although we're accused of it more times than it actually happens, this year *AVN* sorrowfully admits that we actually did forget one important nomination—this time, in the category of Best Specialty Release – BDSM.

Consider this our *mea culpa*.

Perhaps we can be forgiven for missing the film. It was, after all, a foreign language feature and the dialog is hardly what one would call "inspired." And while apparently a big-budget production, the costumes are pretty cheesy—you could probably find some of them at a post-Christmas church rummage sale, and the rest as leftovers from a Steve Reeves "sword and sandal" epic—and the settings are mostly outdoors.

There is a storyline here, but the acting is nothing to write home about, and the characters' motivations, particularly those of the protagonist, seem almost purposefully obscure—and of course, being an S/M movie, there's no sex to speak of, though there is a sort of undercurrent of a love story.

But all that said, the level of violence depicted here is absolutely incredible; far greater and more varied than can be seen in any nominee we've ever had in this category—definitely a new world's record for sustained abuse in any recorded venue anywhere. Once the blood starts flowing, at about the 45 minute point of this two-hour whip-fest, it never stops, relieved only by the occasional brief flashback to pleasanter times.

The protagonist is brutalized without pause by government officials, clergy and even the local townsfolk, and when he isn't being scarred over every inch of his body—and believe us, they don't miss an inch—he's forced to march through the streets carrying a couple of what look like railroad timbers. At the film's climax, his battered, bleeding (and blood-caked, down to his eyelashes) body is suspended by spikes hammered through his hands and feet—and the camera doesn't miss one drop of the blood gushing profusely from each wound. Simply put, this is a sadomasochistic masterpiece; significantly better produced, shot and more stomach-turning than any of this year's nominees, and we apologize to the film's producers for having missed recognizing its gut-wrenching greatness.

The film, of course, is *The Passion of The Christ.*[1] If you're into whips, blood, violence and infliction of pain without let, don't miss it. And even though it's rated R, feel free, as so many churchgoers have before you, to take the kids.

I'm still not sure how I talked my boss Paul Fishbein into springing for all the trips to D.C. I took to cover Supreme Court cases, Senate hearings, National Press Club briefings and the like, but if he hadn't, you wouldn't be reading good stuff like the following. (I particularly love Katharine Harris' Freudian slip.)

VICTIMS OF PORNOGRAPHY SUMMIT REVIVES THE FAITHFUL & FEEDS THE BULL

Speakers Suggest Feds' Next Line Of Attack On The Adult Industry

May 21, 2005

WASHINGTON, D.C. – Although approximately 50 spectators crowded into Room 2322 of the Rayburn House Office Building on May 19 for the "Victims of Pornography Summit," there were surprisingly few "victims" in evidence. No one in the audience identified him- or herself as one, and only three speakers claimed to be, including the summit's moderator, Penny Nance,[1] of the Kids First Coalition.

"I am a victim of pornography," said Nance in her opening remarks. "When I was early in my pregnancy with my first child, I had the unfortunate incident of being attacked by someone who, I later discovered, when talking with the police, was very heavily involved in pornography. It was a very saddening thing to learn."

Nance's statement contained what turned out to be a common theme of speakers throughout the approximately two-hour session: Sexual predators are discovered to have possessed sexually explicit materials; therefore, the use of such materials unquestionably *caused* some subsequent example of abuse or assault or rape or pedophilia. A scientist, however, would simply note, "Correlation is not causation."

The first speaker, Rep. Katharine Harris (R-Fla.), put forth a variation of that theme. Harris, it will be remembered, was Florida's Secretary of State during the 2000 presidential election, and it was she who ordered ballot recounting to stop, thereby assuring Bush's ascension to the Oval Office even though his opponent, Al Gore, was later found to have received the majority of the votes in that state. Her own ascension, less than two years later, to represent what one commentator termed a "safe district" on Florida's southwest coast, with the help of a $3 million war chest and plenty of support from Republicans at the state and federal level, is undoubtedly what the *Miami Herald* referred to as "Harris' lucky streak."

"It's hard to imagine what actually sponsors such unspeakable evil," Harris said, referring to the widely-reported attacks on three Florida children. "There are many contributing factors, but often, we hear about the consumption of pornography and how slowly but surely it's that kind of malignant desensitizer that changes a person's entire perception and becomes often the horrific denominator of crimes against children and women. But many studies have shown that these links between pornography and sexual abuse or violence are—they relate back to pornography, and I think lawmakers can no longer step back and not become more sensitive about that. It obliterates the wall between the individuals' sick fantasies and the compulsion to act upon them, and this is what Ted Kennedy said a day before he went to his execution. Dr. James Dobson interviewed him and it was written about in President Peter—Robert Peters' article for the Morality In Media. It was entitled, 'The Link Between Violent Pornography and Violent Sex Crimes,' and Ted Kennedy said, 'It happened in stages, gradually. My experience with pornography that deals on a violent level with sexuality is one that you become addicted to.' He said, 'I would keep looking for a more and more potent, explicit graphic kinds of material. Like an addiction, you keep craving something that's harder and harder, something which gives you a greater sense of excitement, until you reach the point where pornography only goes so far.'"

For those who don't remember Ted Kennedy—and though there are many Americans with that name, the most famous is the Senator from Massachusetts—being executed in Florida as a serial killer, Harris eventually managed to use the actual name of the person to whom she was referring: Ted *Bundy*. ("Oh, Dr. Freud, your slip is showing...") What she failed to mention was that Bundy's confession to Dobson, after Dobson agreed to fund Bundy's final legal appeal, was actually his third. In his first two, he blamed, in one, his use of alcohol, and in the other, the effect of seeing high school cheerleaders practicing their cheers as the motivators for his multi-state killing spree.

Harris then touched on a theme that first came to prominence during the Senate Judiciary subcommittee hearing chaired by Sen. Sam Brownback (R-Kan.) on March 16: Human trafficking in sex slaves for porn performances.

"If you start doing a Google search on 'human trafficking' or 'sex slaves'," she claimed, "[you can find] literally hundreds of thumbnail images of women of every type of ethnicity and every type of pose. They were bound, they were gagged, they were clearly in distress, they were contorted, and ... these cyberauctions were reaching up to $300,000 in some cases for these women. So this potential marriage of pornography and the Internet and sex slavery is really horrifying, and so we're hoping to really address that."

Harris plans to propose legislation that she refers to as "Carlie's Law," after Carlie Brucia, a 13-year-old girl kidnapped and killed in Florida in 2002. Among other things, Harris' proposed law "would apply the RICO statutes on those sexual predators so that, should they be caught and convicted, there would be the asset forfeiture that we could attack those assets, and that funding would be used for these victims as well as for education in the future," Harris explained, adding, "I think we need to make these links so much more clear in terms of pornography and the extension of the violence and sexual abuse that will follow when it pertains to women and children."

The next "victim of pornography" to speak was Phil Burress, founder of the Cincinnati-based Citizens for Community Values. Burress led off a panel titled "Victimization of Women and Children by Pornography," which also included Marsha Gilmer-Tullis, from the National Center for Missing and Exploited Children; Daniel Weiss of Focus on the Family (FotF); and Dr. Jeffrey Satinover,[2] a former psychiatrist.

"I was raised in a Christian home, and I went to church as much as three times a week, so I certainly knew the difference between right and wrong," Burress began. "But at 14 years old, I was on my way to school one morning and I found a pornographic magazine—and it wasn't pornographic in the sense that's out there today; it was more what they call softcore pornography—and what happened was, I really liked it. I mean, what 14-year-old boy wouldn't like pornography? I didn't even know that this existed. And I pursued it, and I hid the magazine and I kept it, and by the time I was 16 years old and got my driver's license, I was visiting downtown Cincinnati where they had plenty of bookstores on just about every corner; they had bookstores, massage parlors, peep booths and strip bars; it was the home of Larry Flynt—downtown Cincinnati was plagued; it was a red light district. And so I was going to these stores, and they didn't care about my age, and frankly, if I didn't have the money to buy pornography, I was hooked on it so bad, I stole it."

While Burress's story, at least to this point, is probably fairly typical of how some middle-American youth gets exposed to sexual material for the first time, what leaps out is Burress's apparent inability to communicate his new-found obsession to his parents—but since he (and, likely, his parents) went to church three times a week, there's every reason to believe that his parents would not have responded positively even if he had.

Burress went on to claim that his "25-year addiction" to porn led to his divorce from his first wife—no mention what caused the divorce from his second wife—and fantasies about abusing women, but that his "strong upbringing and being in church that built that roadblock that stopped me." Burress's logic seemed to be that since he personally was unable to deal with his obsession about porn, the fault lay not with himself, but with the material, and that's why it should be suppressed.

Imagine if he were obsessed with chocolate; he might now be pushing to drive candy manufacturers out of business and to rename Hershey, Pennsylvania!

"We've done polling in Cincinnati," Burress said, "where now we have no strip bars, we have no massage parlors, we have no—Larry Flynt has a store there, but he agreed in 1998 by court order, by pleading his store guilty of pandering obscenity, he could never again sell X-rated tapes, so Cincinnati is free."

Jimmy Flynt, Larry's son and owner of the Hustler Hollywood store in downtown Cincinnati, took issue with Burress's remark.

"That's bullshit," Flynt countered. "I'm selling a full line of X-rated videos and DVDs in downtown Cincinnati. We've got a very beautiful store. The city of Cincinnati seems to like the fact that we're low-key, we don't create any problems, we're in a good part of town. It's a very attractive store. We get a lot of favorable write-ups in local news. "

But facts have never slowed anti-porn zealots.

"The surveys that we did in the schools, we found that nine years old is the average age of exposure now, and 95 percent of our kids have seen it," Burress claimed. "So the question is, what in the world is happening to our children? What's happening to our young men? And all you have to do is turn on the TV at night and you hear about the sexual crimes; you hear about seven and 11-year-olds raping 4-year-old girls, and the abductions, and I've never met a police officer yet who investigated a pedophile that did not find pornography. Every one of them say that pornography's always on the scene."

Jimmy Flynt, on the other hand, noted that he'd recently read in the newspaper that across the country, rape is down 80 percent and violence against women is down 40 percent, with adult material more available than ever before. A scientist, however, would simply note, "Correlation is not causation."

Marsha Gilmer-Tullis talked about her work combating child exploitation—interesting, but she drew no connections between the availability of sexual materials for adults and, for example, children pressed into prostitution by adults. The audience, however, seemed to be able to fill in that gap all on its own.

Focus on the Family's Daniel Weiss described himself as a "Media and Sexuality Analyst," and his bio on FotF's Website notes that his "knowledge spans pornography and obscenity law to media messages and imagery. In addition to covering legislative and enforcement aspects, Daniel tracks the cultural developments, business trends, and media messages that contribute to the mainstreaming of pornography. Daniel's writings on sexuality, media, and life have appeared in *The Washington Times*, *The Weekly Standard*, *Citizen* magazine, *Boundless* webzine, and *BreakPoint Online*, among others."

In other words, like many of the "experts" trotted out by the pro-censorship forces, Weiss apparently has no academic credentials whatsoever for the work that he does.

Weiss was the first to mention Judge Gary Lancaster's ruling[3] dismissing all charges against Extreme Associates and its owners, which Weiss opined "underscores a growing lack of recognition in the cultural and legal realms of the harm and the threats posed by pornography to individuals, families and society."

"Ultimately, for obscenity law to be effectively and consistently enforced, our culture must understand the facts on pornography," Weiss continued. However, Weiss's "facts" consisted of references to Dr. Victor Cline, a long-time anti-porn advocate, and Dr. Patrick Carnes, who apparently runs SexHelp.com, a "sexual addiction" recovery site, neither of whom, according to a Web search, has done peer-reviewed research; also a claim that "two-thirds of divorce attorneys attending a 2002 meeting of the American Academy of Matrimonial Lawyers said that excessive interest in online pornography contributed to more than half the divorces they dealt with that year," and the results of an online poll conducted by FotF which, since they're well-known as a fundamentalist religious ministry, just might possibly have failed to reach a representative sample of the U.S. population.

Other "facts" mentioned by Weiss were that "a 2001 report found that over half of all sex offenders in Utah were adolescents, and that children as young as *eight years old* were committing felony sexual assaults on their classmates," and that "the porn industry fights laws such as the Child Online Protection Act [COPA], which requires pornographers to use age verification systems, because they know this flood of pornographic imagery is creating a whole new generation of consumers." [Emphasis added] (The adult industry's take on COPA can be found elsewhere in this volume, and the industry has consistently supported parental oversight of children's Internet usage, and the creation of filtering programs that distinguish between sexually explicit material and legitimate sexual education sites that would be beneficial to adolescents. Most importantly, the industry will NOT knowingly use a minor in a sexually explicit production.)

Eventually, Weiss got to the pro-censorship crowd's latest theme: "Although the Supreme Court was clear in *Miller v. California* that hardcore pornography enjoys no First Amendment protection, lax federal and state law enforcement has essentially given obscenity the protection denied to it in the Constitution. *This lack of enforcement has allowed a back-alley enterprise to grow into an unprecedented global trade in human persons.* Pornography turns people into commodities; men and women are seen as sexual objects to be bought, sold, used and then discarded. The last time the United States recognized human beings as consumer goods, it took a civil war to end it." [Emphasis added.]

"We should not be shocked with sky-rocketing STD rates or marital or family breakdown, nor when men rape women and children, or even when children rape one another," he continued. "These developments are entirely consistent with the explosive growth of pornography." What? Nothing about global warming? The tech stock collapse? The Iraq war? The two-headed baby shown on *Oprah!*? Surely they also are "entirely consistent with the explosive growth of pornography." What isn't?

"This is not harmless adult entertainment as some would like us to believe, but a real, measurable and undeniable threat to individuals, families and society." It would probably have been helpful, then, if Weiss had presented some "real, measurable" scientific evidence of his claim. He, and everyone else at the summit, failed to do so.

If there was a star at the summit, though, it was probably Dr. Jeffrey Satinover,[4] an M.D. (1982, U. of Tex.), Board-certified in psychiatry in 1988, who for the past four years has been pursuing a Ph.D. in physics, most recently at the University of Nice, France. Satinover was one of the invited witnesses to Sen. Sam Brownback's November, 2004 hearing on "The Science Behind Pornography Addiction"; however, a Google search of Satinover's website for "pornography" reveals no result. There is no indication that he has ever researched the subject for publication.

Apparently a devout Catholic, Satinover is past president of the C.G. Jung Foundation (suggesting that he follows that psychiatric discipline) and has written several books, most notable of which are *Feathers of the Skylark: Sin, Compulsion and our Need for a Messiah*; *Homosexuality and the Politics of*

Truth (in which he wrote that homosexuality, for which Satinover claims there is no genetic basis, "is but one of the many forms of 'soul sickness' that are innate to our fallen nature."); *Cracking the Bible Code* (Satinover seems to think there actually is one); and *The Quantum Brain*, which one critic described as "a fusion of neuroscience and quantum physics for the audience of soap-operas and talk shows."

Satinover also displays a couple of interesting fetishes on his site. For instance, he refers to his Bachelor of Science degree from M.I.T. as a "S.B." rather than the more common "B.S."—and clicking on a menu button on the site labeled "Dan Rather" takes one to a blurry "reproduction" of a (typewritten) letter from George Washington predicting that a "Dan Rather" who will one day work for CBS News is a "forgery."

Hence, Satinover's preconceived biases and his qualifications to make statements like, "in fact, international trafficking in human beings, and in particular sexual slavery, has become now the third largest international organized crime source of money after drug trafficking and arms trafficking, and experts in the field, including Ambassador Miller of the State Department here, recognize, along with ... radical feminists, that the driving source for the rise in international sex slavery is pornography" and that "the driving source for sexual slavery around the world is the intense, basically addictive nature of pornography" both (all!) open to question.

"Unfortunately," Satinover charged, "what has happened is that you will hear ... critics of pornography addressed in a kind of sneering tone by people who think they're enlightened, that this is just some innocent entertainment, and that anybody who criticizes it is either some kind of ignoramus, an evangelical ignoramus, or a hyper-intellectual on the left, and without a brain in their heads. I happen to have degrees from MIT, Harvard, Yale, I teach at Princeton—as I said, I do research in theoretical physics. I think I have a fair enough background in the intellectual arts to claim that I know what I'm talking about."

Well, no. It would be stupid to consult a theoretical physicist such as Dr. Albert Einstein (even if he weren't dead) on the best way to remove an appendix, and an equally bad idea to rely on baseball legend Tommy

Lasorda to solve America's balance-of-trade deficit. Expertise in one field doesn't necessarily translate into expertise in another.

So when Satinover makes statements about porn such as, "Its purpose is not in any way whatsoever to entertain. Its purpose is to generate very intense states of arousal and stimulate the viewer to masturbate and to achieve orgasm as rapidly as possible," one is led to the conclusions A) that Satinover is deficient in his understanding of the functions, historically, of art and free speech, and B) that he doesn't find masturbation or orgasms entertaining.

Satinover also mentioned a magnetic resonance imaging (MRI) study done in Europe that indicated physiological responses within the brain to viewing sexually explicit images, but since he gave no details of the study nor the researchers who performed it, it's impossible at this point to know if the study has been peer-reviewed or subjected to proper controls. For instance, it is well-known that the human brain responds with a release of endorphins to any number of pleasurable stimuli, including religious ecstasy and eating a favorite food. In fact, Satinover almost concedes this later in his statement.

"I have here in my testimony before the Senate hearing on pornography that was sponsored by Sam Brownback, a whole set of research studies, essentially pointing toward the fact that the craving state—this is not just the arousal state, but even the craving state in somebody who has experienced a lengthy process of pornographic viewing, arousal and orgasm—in other words, an addictive cycle—the changes in the brain are essentially identical to that which you find in any other behavioral or even chemical addiction," Satinover said. But he'd better be careful; if brain changes due to "behavioral ... addiction" are grounds for criminalization, he may go to his church some morning and find a padlock on the door because it's been found that too many parishioners are getting off on the Sunday sermon.

Very troubling, also, was Satinover's statement that, "I'm presently involved in helping the city of Los Angeles develop what I hope will turn out to be a model for a very aggressive anti-sexual-slavery trade project for the city of L.A.... I hope it will become a pilot project for other projects across the country, which specifically attempt to suppress the sexual slavery trade, and at the same time, go after the pornography industry primarily because of the role that it plays in creating sex slaves as has been described by other people here on this panel. I'm pleased to hear that that intersection was described, how pornographic tapes of women being raped and tortured are in fact an integral part of the international pornography industry, not to mention children as well."

AVN.com approached one well-known manager in the adult industry who frequently represents women from Europe, to ask if he is aware of any talent in the industry whom he would describe as a "sex slave."

"I've never heard of it," he responded. "When you say 'sex trafficking,' that's like what they have in Europe, where they basically kidnap girls from eastern Europe and bring them into western Europe and have them work as hookers. Nothing like that happens here. Any girl that comes in, does so voluntarily. I never recruit girls, so it's all by word of mouth; they call me, and I turn most of them down. I turn down two or three girls a day."

"I've had people approach me before, like in Hollywood," he continued. "I guess there's a lot of Russian hookers or eastern Europeans that they bring over and have them hooking. I've had people say to me, 'Yeah, we could hook you up with these [girls],' but besides the fact I don't want them doing it for moral reasons if they don't want to be doing it, also, you know, they wouldn't be doing a good job if they don't want to be doing it. I don't want to deal with somebody who's scared all the time that somebody's gonna kill them."

During the question-and-answer period that followed the panel, Burress made one good point about the content of adult video: "In Cincinnati, if you want to deal with X-rated tapes, come to Cincinnati and open up a store like Larry Flynt did and start pandering, guess what? You're gonna end up in court and the jury's gonna be looking at the material and determining whether they want this material in their community."

What is true in America 2005 is that video producers each decide what they want to communicate through their products, and then must decide what communities will accept that "message"—or be prepared for a court battle.

But as Burress later noted, "We have lost as many cases as we have won in Cincinnati, but the way the system is set up, what most people do not understand is that this is the only law that I know of on the books where we go to trial to see if a crime has been committed"—a rare admission from a member of a subculture that assumes that *all* sexually explicit material is outside constitutional protections.

The next speaker was John C. Richter, acting head of the Justice Department's Criminal Division, who assured the attendees that Attorney General Gonzales is serious about prosecuting obscenity—and that there's too much hardcore material around, particularly on the Internet.

"The pornography industry have made great use of the Internet for their own insidious purposes," he claimed. "As a result, for the first time in human history, hardcore pornography was made available to everyone, at home and away. Adults and children could find it when they looked for it and pornography found them even when they weren't looking for it. Today, you don't have to drive down the dark back alleys of a big city to find hardcore pornography. Instead, the Internet brings pornography right into our homes. That means our kids see it, our spouses see it—frankly, too many people see it."

"That also means that a lot of people are enticed by it," Richter continued. "It also creates an even greater danger, however, that because obscene material is so accessible, many may fail to realize that availability does not equate to legality."

That statement seemed potentially at odds with the *Miller* requirement that in order to be found obscene, a work would have to offend contemporary adult community standards—and if sexually-explicit material is sold in many places in the community, that would militate for its tacit acceptance by the community.

Richter also mentioned the recent indictments[5] of retailers John Kenneth Coil and Edward Wedelstedt, noting that Coil "recently pled guilty to racketeering offenses, to tax offense, to obscenity offense, and as part of his plea, he had to give up his essential criminal enterprise, 40 pieces of real estate and more than 20 stores. We've taken it down. The judge, of course, has sentenced him to more than five years in federal prison."

What Richter didn't mention—and possibly doesn't know—is that Coil's sentence exceeds the plea agreement he made with federal prosecutors, and even the no-longer-mandatory federal sentencing guidelines, and Coil is therefore contemplating an appeal.

"I hope that you realize that we aren't backing down on the purveyors of obscenity," Richter summarized. "Our response to their increased sophistication is to increase our technical expertise. Our response to their increased brazenness is to redouble the efforts of our best prosecutors, our professionals in the law enforcement realm, to fight them. We are fortunate, I hope, that we have allies such as persons here in this room and elsewhere who are supportive of us, and I would ask those of you here in attendance today for your support of the Department as we continue to move forward on this front."

Sen. Sam Brownback also put in an appearance at the summit, and quickly placed the whole "freedom of speech" issue into perspective—religious perspective, that is.

"I hope you recognize the greatness of the moral cause you're involved in," he began. "It's kind of easy to quickly get drug into the reeds on this and think, 'Okay, this is just something I've gotta fight for,' but lift yourself up and look at the cause. This is about allowing people to be souls and to be honored rather than to be treated as material objects just for somebody else's pleasure."

Brownback also let the summit attendees in on some of his plans.

"We're going to try to host a hearing just with the Attorney General to talk about, 'Here's what we're doing on pornography prosecution'," he said. "I chair the Constitution subcommittee. We've held one hearing on this already; we hope to have a couple of others, one with just the Attorney General; a second one with people that have been trafficked into the United States for purposes of pornography, and tying the two topics of trafficking, human trafficking in with pornography, because we're now finding—we just had Dr. Jeffrey Satinover in to testify. He has been building this linkage in the primary areas in southern California where the pornography industry is located, of people, women primarily, actually trafficked in there for pornography purposes, and we're trying to put together that hearing of the two being tied in together."

AVN would also be interested in meeting "women ... actually trafficked in[to the Los Angeles area] for pornography purposes." Hopefully, Brownback will announce the date of that proposed hearing well in advance, unlike all the other hearings that he's held regarding the adult industry.

During a break following Brownback's talk, moderator Penny Nance expressed her appreciation for *AVN's* attendance at the conference, but when it was pointed out that a more comprehensive sex education curriculum in the public schools might reduce the need for another such gathering, she expressed confusion as to the connection.

Moreover, Ricci Levy of the Victoria Woodhull Foundation reports that when she (Levy) suggested that for a more rounded picture of the issue, future conferences might want to include attorneys or spokespersons from the adult industry, Nance told her that no industry guests would be invited to participate. In fact, attorney Paul Cambria, founder of the Adult Freedom Foundation, offered to Rep. Joe Pitts (R-Penna.), one of the summit's sponsors, to provide "a pool of attorneys, researchers and industry executives who are experts on the adult entertainment industry" who would be willing to address the summit, but the offer was rejected.

Pitts himself did address the attendees, interrupting the event's second panel, "Experts on Pornography and the Law," but not before the first panelist, attorney Jan LaRue, chief counsel for Concerned Women for America (CWfA), got to tell of her own victimhood.

"The reason I do this," she said, "is several reasons, one of which is, I too was victimized by pornography as a young child and also as an older minor. I was involved in looking at pornography with several businessmen, some of whom I worked for, and once a month, it became part of my job description to go out and buy the latest issue of *Playboy* magazine, go back, lock up the office, turn off the phones, mix the martinis—I was a minor—and look at the magazine with my bosses, and some of their business friends that they would invite over at the time. These were all executives; these were lawyers, CPAs, executives in the insurance industry, and one was a Superior Court judge. They all knew my age. I had no idea the impact it was having on my life by both looking at pornography and consuming alcoholic beverages at the same time. But one day, these men, after I had too many martinis, convinced me that I was prettier than the women in the magazine, and wouldn't I like to pose for them, and one of them just happened to have a camera with him."

LaRue went no further with the tale, leaving it unclear whether she actually posed for the pictures—does simply being asked to pose for photos, presumably in some state of undress, qualify as victimization?—but the experience apparently formed the basis for LaRue's current view that, "I'm not saying that everybody that looks at pornography becomes a child molester or a rapist or an addict, but a significant number of them do, and the crimes are so horrific that one victim is one too many."

LaRue then delved into a short history of obscenity law, quoting Justice William Brennan's statement in *Roth v. United States* that, "Implicit in the history of the First Amendment is the rejection of obscenity as utterly without redeeming social importance. This rejection for that reason is mirrored in the universal judgment that obscenity should be restrained, reflected in the international agreement of over 50 nations, in the obscenity laws of all the 48 states, and in the 20 obscenity laws enacted by the Congress from 1842 to 1956. We hold that obscenity is not within the area of constitutionally protected speech or press," but failing to note Brennan's repudiation of that position in his dissent[6] in *Miller v. California*, the foundation of modern obscenity law.

LaRue quoted several paragraphs from Chief Justice Warren Burger's majority opinion in *Miller*, including the three-prong test as well as some examples that Burger termed "plain examples" of material that could be suppressed. She noted that, "The court went on to say, 'Sex and nudity may not be exploited without limit by films or pictures exhibited or sold in places of public accommodation any more than live sex and nudity can be exhibited or sold without limit in such public places. At a minimum, prurient, patently offensive depiction or description of sexual conduct must have serious literary, artistic, political, or scientific value to merit First Amendment protection.'"—again failing to note that to Judge Gary Lancaster, that meant that Extreme Associates' *mailing* of its videos to an undercover postal inspector in Pittsburgh did not fall under *Miller's* prohibitions. She did however claim that Judge Lancaster's similar ruling as to Extreme's Websites "has no support under *Stanley* [*v. Georgia*] or any Supreme Court ruling, including *Lawrence v. Texas*, which the judge chose to rely on." CWfA has filed an amicus brief with the Third Circuit opposing the dismissal of the indictments against Extreme.

LaRue talked briefly about adult material on the Internet, noting the "exponential increase of pornographic Web sites" since 1998 to approximately 2.1 million sites with 420 million pages.

"It's commonly believed that most of these Web sites are owned by fewer than 50 companies," she said. "I have personally looked at hundreds of them; more than I want to think about, and I can tell you that virtually all of them display hardcore prosecutable material, and it's easily accessible to children, and children are doing so."

Fortunately, LaRue herself is apparently immune from the claimed ill effects of viewing so much "hardcore prosecutable material."

Rep. Pitts, whose district includes most of Pennsylvania's ultra-conservative Amish community, then gave his presentation, a slide show that also dealt with minors' access to explicit material on the Web.

"May is Victims of Pornography Month," he began, "and while every month could be called this, May is our opportunity to shed light on the violence, on the rape, on the child abduction, on the murder, the other heinous crimes against women and children by Internet predators. As these cases unfold before our eyes, all too often, we identify a common thread: The perpetrator is addicted to pornography, often child pornography, and to effectively reduce crime against women and children, we have to deal with the root of the problem: pornography—its content, its sources, its distribution. We often hear about the danger of drugs in our society. Pornography, while not a chemical, is just as addictive and corrupting, and just like drugs, it's too easy to gain access to pornography."

Pitts also unwittingly made the case for community acceptance of the material: "The pornographic industry is also a huge money-making industry. *There is unfortunately an alarming demand for it*, and our laws have not kept up with the demand and the modes of distribution." [Emphasis added.]

Pitts specifically targeted peer-to-peer (P2P) networks, claiming that many filtering programs fail to stop access to hardcore P2P file-sharing.

"Look at what happens when little Susie types in the name of her teen idols, the Olson twins," he said. "Look at all the results advertising nudity and pornographic on this site. These sites pop up even with the so-called 'offensive content' filter activated."

But Pitts has a solution.

"In the coming weeks, I will be introducing legislation to confront peer-to-peer pornography to strengthen criminal controls, to promote truth in file labeling to protect our children, not just from pornography itself but from the individuals who use pornography to prey on the innocent."

Adult Webmasters may want to start pruning their meta-tags now.

Rep. Mike Pence (R-Ind.)[7] also spoke, a talk peppered with religious allusions. He said that it was after he'd Googled the phrase "Declaration of Independence" and got a multitude of adult links that he authored the Truth In Domain Labeling law, but that much more needed to be done.

The Supreme Court "seems more enamored these days of protecting sexual speech than it does political speech," he claimed, leading to a "tidal wave of obscenity" that's taken over the Internet. He also said that he was considering support for a top-level domain devoted to "the 'dot-filth' world."

The final speakers were George LeMieux, the Deputy Attorney General of Florida, who had flown up specifically to attend the summit. He told the audience about a new cybercrimes unit that had been formed in his office, and of "escape schools" that teach children how to avoid child predators, and how to escape from them if caught.

Finally, Bruce A. Taylor, Senior Counsel to the Assistant Attorney General for the Justice Department's Criminal Division, was on hand to answer questions—but when no one seemed to have any, this reporter asked when the new 2257 regulations would be available. Taylor said that they were undergoing final proofreading at the Government Printing Office, and would include not only the regulations themselves, but commentary on which suggested changes proposed by, among others, Free Speech Coalition and other free speech advocates had been accepted and why others were rejected.

The conference ended a bit late, but remarks overheard from the departing crowd indicate that most felt it was a great success. The adult industry probably won't have to wait long to see how correct that assessment was.

Brownback, it should be remembered, was later elected Governor of Kansas, and thanks to tax cuts which he pushed through the state legislature in 2012, almost bankrupted the state[1]*. Way to go, Sammy! It is perhaps noteworthy that "virtual reality" was still in its infancy in 2005, so way to go, Bobby! I've also written quite a bit about Extreme Associates, which even in the relatively freewheeling porn industry had a piss-poor reputation, but those articles will be saved for a future volume. And yes, porn performers* are *sex workers. And no, there is no sex trafficking in the Los Angeles-based porn industry. And I'm not sure why I was reticent to admit that porn performers are sex workers.*

SENATE SUBCOMMITTEE HEARING ON PORN PROSECUTION DELIVERS FEW SURPRISES

March 22, 2005

WASHINGTON, D.C. – With the federal court decision dismissing the obscenity indictments against Extreme Associates still fresh in conservatives' minds, Sen. Sam Brownback (R-Kan.) presided over a March 16 hearing of the Senate Judiciary Committee's Subcommittee on the Constitution, Civil Rights and Property Rights titled "Obscenity Prosecution and the Constitution"—with Brownback himself the only senator in attendance, though Sen. Russell Feingold (D-Ca.) did put in a momentary appearance between floor votes on his legislation.

But the hearing, which was originally scheduled for February 16, meaning it had to have been conceived just days after the January 20 *Extreme* decision, held few surprises, though it did provide clues to the direction conservatives may take in attempting to suppress sexual speech.

Sen. Brownback, in his opening remarks, claimed that Judge Gary Lancaster had "cobbled together hand-picked strands of 14th Amendment substantive due process, decisions from *Roe*, *Lawrence* and others and ruled that the statutes at issue [in the *Extreme Associates* case] violated an unwritten constitutional right to sexual privacy" and that "just recently, we have in Southern California examples of human trafficking, of individuals trafficked into the porn industry for use by the porn industry." Neither statement was factual, but accuracy was hardly the point of this hearing.

Sen. Brownback then introduced Prof. Robert Destro,[2] of the American Catholic University, who had some ideas on ways to head off First Amendment defenses of adult material.

"[Y]ou can start by looking at this as a question of market regulation, and focus on the pornography industry," opined Prof. Destro. "That has certain advantages to it, in that, you know, what you're really talking about is business transactions and lots of money and lots of—lots of illegal behavior. And if you focus on it from that perspective, you never really even get to the First Amendment unless you are of the view, as Justice Douglas was, that sex acts between consenting adults were a form of free speech, and he talked about that in *Griswold v. Connecticut*. But setting that aside, nobody else really takes that view.

"Or you could look at it as a perspective of, we're going to be regulating content. That then gets you into the content and the perspective of speech, and in really almost an endless morass of First Amendment analysis where you get into the question of how much redeeming social value is there in this particular movie or videotape or Website or virtual reality, and you get into kind of almost unanswerable questions about just how—you know, how much, you know, under the Court's decisions, does this really appeal to someone's prurient interest? I suppose the easy answer to the question is that if they're willing to pay for it, it must appeal to them."

Prof. Destro went on to claim that Judge Lancaster's opinion opens the door to the legalization of prostitution, which is what he apparently believes goes on any time someone shoots an adult feature.

"He [Judge Lancaster] creates a right to privacy that, if taken to its logical conclusion, would legalize outcall prostitution," Destro said, "because if indeed you have a right to sexually explicit material that's made by others out in Hollywood or wherever they make it, I suppose you could make the same argument that under *Griswold* [*v. Connecticut*] and *Lawrence* [*v. Texas*], you would have a right to have it made right in your living room. At least, under the judge's reading of the—of those 14th Amendment cases, the

Congress's power to regulate the economy and the industry just drops out of the equation altogether."

Prof. Destro bolstered his view by quoting a law review interview with Larry Flynt.[3]

"[A]s many of you know, Larry Flynt has always been held up as the paragon of the defenders of First Amendment values," Prof. Destro recounted. "Larry Flynt's interview was actually quite fascinating, because, you know, they asked him about the First Amendment; he says, 'Well, no, that wasn't really the point.' He said that his goal really was to open up—and I'm putting words in his mouth, but it's the rough equivalent—he wanted to have a chain of sex stores, you know, that in the end, he thought that there should be a freedom to buy and sell sex just like you did any other commodity. I thought, well, finally, you know, he's actually—you know, when you get the Larry Flynt unvarnished, he's a salesman, and that's what I would suggest that we're looking at here, is that we're looking at the sale of sex as a commodity; we're looking at sex slavery and trafficking, which is a serious problem not only here in the United States but around the world."

Interestingly, the professor didn't attempt to make the same argument against the First Amendment status of, for example, the nightly news on television, which, after all, is presented with commercials selling products, which ads pay for the news program. Similarly, newspapers with advertisements are sold on most city street corners, but the professor didn't argue that the news between the ads is not constitutionally protected.

In his written testimony, Prof. Destro was even more forceful – and even less accurate.

"ENFORCING OBSCENITY LAWS: DOES THE CONSTITUTION PROTECT THE 'SEX TRADE'?" the professor's heading screams. "The answer to this question is an emphatic 'no.' I will leave to others the task of describing the individual and community devastation (including slavery, brutality, and murder) caused by those engaged in the sex trade, but I do want to take this opportunity to describe why this Committee needs to view the 'pornography issue' in a more global context.

"The production and distribution of pornography is part and parcel of a global sex trade that employs 'sex workers', film and video producers, distributors like Extreme Associates, IT experts, and the financiers who provide the capital to bring these 'productions' to market. Broadband and cable providers provide the final link in a worldwide distribution chain that allows willing consumers to watch as 'sex workers' around the globe ply their trade."

"Sex workers" are what porn performers may well be—one could just as easily call them "actors" or "performers"—but they are willing, well-paid adults who enter the profession freely and with knowledge of what their work will entail, not as slaves, not to be brutalized and not to be murdered.

In his prepared testimony, Prof. Destro goes on to trash Judge Lancaster's decision, in the process casting aspersions on Lancaster as an "activist judge." At the hearing, the professor also had thoughts on how sexually explicit material on video could be prosecuted irrespective of the First Amendment.

"In the case of Extreme Associates, you're looking at exploitation, at battery and at all kinds of other behaviors that certainly can be regulated under the criminal law," Prof. Destro opined, apparently forgetting his written references to slavery, brutality and murder. "So my suggestion to the committee is that ... you too can avoid the First Amendment. You can do it if you're clear and if you focus on the commercial aspects of what's going on."

In some ways, the March 16 hearing dovetailed nicely with a November 18, 2004 hearing, over which Sen. Brownback also presided, of the Senate Committee on Commerce, Science, and Transportation's Subcommittee on Science, Technology, and Space, titled "The Science Behind Pornography Addiction." At that hearing, Dr. Mary Ann Layden testified that pornography is "toxic mis-education about sex and relationships," while "Dr." Judith Reisman[4]—her doctorate is in communications, not biochemistry—claimed that porn images "imprint and alter the brain, triggering an instant, involuntary, but lasting, biochemical memory trail, arguably, subverting the First Amendment by overriding the cognitive speech process." She called those biochemical memory trails "erototoxins."

So if a viewer doesn't have to think about sexually explicit material in order for it negatively to affect him/her, and if the message conveyed by the material can be given secondary status somewhere below the acts performed that convey the message which, without the message component, may already be illegal acts, then pornography—not just obscenity, but porn in general—has effectively been stripped of its constitutional protections without a First Amendment fight. That clearly seems to be where Sen. Brownback is headed with his hearings.

The chairman also heard from Patrick Trueman, an attorney currently working for the ultra-conservative Family Research Council, but who, in the late 1980s and early '90s, headed up the Justice Department's Child Exploitation and Obscenity Section.

"To those who argue that the prosecution of obscenity crimes is a waste of time or an unwise use of resources," Trueman said, "I'd like to point out that during the time that I was chief of CEOS, we received more than $24 million in fines and forfeitures as a result of our aggressive prosecution efforts. That is more than the budget of CEOS during those years."

Could that possibly be a not-so-subtle message to Congress that if harsher anti-porn laws are enacted, they won't impact the already-out-of-control federal deficit? You be the judge!

After boasting of the number of convictions his department obtained under Project PostPorn,[5] which targeted adult mail-order companies, and Project Wormwood, which targeted Los Angeles producers and distributors of adult materials, Trueman espoused his philosophy of which materials should be brought to trial.

"We didn't just select the hardest of the hardcore material," Trueman said of the Wormwood busts. "We wanted juries to decide what they found to be obscene in their district, and that's the nature of what *Miller v. California*, the seminal obscenity case by the Supreme Court, allows. We believed it was important to let juries decide what was obscene, and we found that juries, looking at a variety of materials, from the hardest to the most mild of what we considered to be obscene, regularly said that the material was obscene and were willing to convict. I've done several grand juries myself, where we asked the people in the jury to decide whether the material is obscene, and my own experience has been that people who regularly watch movies that are obscene, will ask questions in the grand jury about—saying that they didn't know it was obscene; are they doing something illegal? But yet those people, when told that yes, in fact it may be obscene, will also vote for an indictment on obscenity against a pornographer."

Leaving aside the questionable assertion that grand jurors who regularly watched porn would nonetheless vote to indict material they themselves had seen and found to be harmless, Trueman in his statement further blurred the already indistinct boundary between putatively illegal "obscenity" and perfectly legal "pornography." He also failed to note that most of the material convicted in the '80s would be laughed out of court by juries today.

Trueman also made the claim that it was because of Justice Department prosecutions that porn producers, in the late '80s and early '90s, stopped using the themes of "rape, incest, bestiality [and] pseudo-child pornography" in their features, when in fact those themes had always been marginal to the industry, and had all but disappeared on their own 10 years earlier.

The tiny voice of semi-sanity at the hearing was the next witness, Prof. Frederick Schauer,[6] a Frank Stanton Professor of the First Amendment at the John F. Kennedy School of Government, Harvard University.

After assuring the subcommittee that he was not among the "many people who believe that obscenity law as it now exists is unconstitutional and violates the First Amendment," Prof. Schauer opined that, "The inquiry then moves to the question of, under what circumstances would the constitutionally-permissible-under-the First-Amendment prosecution of obscenity be desirable?"

The professor listed three cautions that he urged the government and federal prosecutors to consider in deciding what to prosecute.

"[I]gnoring the law in favor of their own agenda is not only a judicial vice," said Prof. Schauer of federal judges such as Judge Lancaster, "but is also potentially a prosecutorial vice. I raise this issue because I believe the same applies to prosecutors."

Prof. Schauer also advised both the legislature and the courts to adhere closely to the obscenity standards set forth in *Miller v. California*.

"I would ask you, Mr. Chairman, in investigating this issue, to seek assurance on behalf of the committee [that] the prosecution will be in accordance with the *Miller* standards strictly defined rather than be used as a way of modifying, expanding, changing, redefining, resuscitating or in some other way changing the existing, and as I said, in my view constitutionally-permissible-under-the-First-Amendment law of obscenity," he said.

Prof. Schauer, who authored the conclusions set forth in the *Report of the Attorney General's Commission on Pornography* (better known as the Meese Commission Report), also suggested that benign material should be left alone by federal prosecutors.

"One of [the Meese Commission Report's] central teachings was that it divided the category of *Miller*-defined legal obscenity into the categories of material that endorsed and promoted explicitly violence against women, material that endorsed and promoted explicitly the degradation of women, and material that was neither endorsing of violence against women nor that was endorsing the degrading of women," Prof. Schauer assessed. "In light of those three categories, the Attorney General's Commission recommended prosecution of legal obscenity in the first category and in the second category, but as to the third category, the commission made no recommendation.

"I am troubled here in part by the attempt to use the Report of the Commission as endorsement for the prosecution of legally obscene materials that neither promote nor endorse explicitly the violence against women," he concluded.

In a question-and-answer session between Sen. Brownback and the witnesses which followed the witnesses' remarks, the senator returned to his contention that at least some porn performers in Southern California are trafficked-in sex slaves.

"[S]ex trafficking ... [is] one of the lead slavery issues in the world today, and what we're finding in this, apparently, we're seeing people trafficked into the pornography industry for porn," Sen. Brownback claimed, referring to a *Los Angeles Times* article of March 5. "This is just a quote here from the article: 'A lot of people are promised jobs once they come here, but when they get here, they're forced into labor or the sex trade.' That's a lawyer with the Department of Health and Human Services, and apparently this is a lucrative business to move people into."

None of the witnesses were willing to go on record in the hearing in support of the idea that any Southern California performers are sex slaves, so Sen. Brownback widened his claim.

"I've been working on this for some period of time," Brownback said, "and this is really an awful trade, and I've met with girls who've been trafficked in Nepal and Israel and Thailand and America, and that's where this is taking place, and we're even finding reports—we haven't verified this, but people [are] doing the pornography filming in a foreign country, developing country, and then shooting it in here—because then you don't have to traffic somebody in; you just traffic the film in."

This concerned Sen. Brownback, because Prof. Schauer had previously testified that even if a video's content had been produced with sexual slave labor, and that if caught during the taping, the slave masters could be prosecuted, the content itself could not be prosecuted simply because it featured unwilling participants.

"All I'm suggesting is that in order to get at the product, existing law would have to be changed dramatically," Prof. Schauer responded. "I don't deny the economics of the fact that when one dries up the product, one makes it harder to engage in the underlying conduct ... I would agree with you entirely, the underlying conduct is something we should deal with. I would like to deal with it within the boundaries of existing law, because attempts to change the existing law are always fraught with danger."

"My suggestion is that, you know, what you do is that you focus on the underlying behavior that's going on here," added Prof. Destro. "I mean, these people are accessories to prostitution, and the—you're going to have to, just like you do in trying to interdict the drug trade, to figure out where the important pressure points are going to be, and so if you can—you can easily prosecute someone for the—not so much under a 'pornography' theory but under an 'accessory to prostitution' theory."

Sen. Brownback then turned his attention to the ex-Justice Department prosecutor.

"Mr. Trueman, if [the decision in] the *Extreme Associates* case is allowed to stand, upheld, will we be able to prosecute any obscenity cases in the future?" the senator asked.

"No, I can't imagine that you would," came the reply. "I think that *Extreme Associates*—the ruling itself is so extreme that obscenity prosecution would go by the wayside."

"[T]his industry is a very large industry now," Sen. Brownback continued. "Is it because of the lack of prosecution that we see the pervasiveness of pornographic material in America today?"

"Yes, I certainly think it is," said Trueman, who went on to opine that owing to the "nine or 10 attorneys" of the "pornography defense bar" who can easily overwhelm local prosecutors with motions to dismiss and other pre-trial matters, that most obscenity prosecutions, he felt, should be handled at the federal level by Justice Department prosecutors "because they can match, shot for shot, the defense bar in these cases. The Justice Department won't be overwhelmed, they won't stop to take a case just because it's been drawn out and expensive to do, so I think it's vital that the Justice Department gets back to a point of vigorously prosecuting."

Interestingly, there was no mention at this hearing of the indictments[7] against Goalie Entertainment and its principals and employees that had been filed just five days before, even though the indictments represented the largest federal move against an adult retailer in more than a dozen years.

What actions Sen. Brownback will next take are anybody's guess. He announced at the beginning of this hearing that it was the first of several that he planned to conduct on several different topics, but with the testimony adduced so far, the senator or one of his colleagues could easily introduce an anti-porn bill soon, using the "porn addiction" hearing and this one as the "scientific basis" to prevent First Amendment defenses in obscenity trials. Only time will tell.

18 U.S.C. §2257, better known in the adult industry simply as "2257," has been the subject of lawsuits since the early 2000s, and thanks to the very hard work of attorneys J. Michael Murray and Lorraine M. Baumgardner, most of its more onerous provisions have been struck down—not that the law served any real purpose anyway... but that's a story for another day.

MISINFORMATION ABOUNDS AS REACTIONARIES RAMP UP ANTI-ADULT CAMPAIGN

May 31, 2005

WASHINGTON, D.C. – Fast on the heels of the May 18 "Victims of Pornography Summit," and the earlier Senate subcommittee hearings on "Obscenity Prosecution and the Constitution" and last year's "Science Behind Pornography Addiction," religious reactionaries are pushing ahead with their anti-adult agenda—and unsurprisingly, they have no problem using lies to do it.

At the beginning of the Memorial Day weekend, two prominent procensorship activists, former Justice Department prosecutor Patrick A. Trueman and Meese Commission witness "Dr." Judith Reisman, reached out to their constituencies with misleading claims and outright lies regarding the adult industry, in an attempt to further blacken the industry's reputation in the public's mind.

On Friday, subscribers to Focus on the Family's e-zine CitizenLink were informed that "U.S. Attorney General Alberto Gonzales recently signed rules that force producers of pornographic material to keep a record of the names and ages of their performers."

"The effort comes in response to charges that a lot of pornography includes minors—and the belief by many porn producers that ignorance will keep them out of trouble."

Perhaps CitizenLink's writer, Kim Trobee, can be forgiven for being ignorant of the fact that the legislation underlying the record-keeping requirements, 18 U.S.C. 2257,[1] was introduced way back in 1988, and that the regs have been in effect since 1995—and that if the Justice Department actually thought that they served any purpose other than harassment of the adult industry, it might have conducted even *one single investigation* in the *10 years* before the regs' official update last week—but it didn't.

Moreover, the only ones making "charges that a lot of pornography includes minors" are the anti-adult zealots, some few of whom are on the Justice Department's payroll, but most of whom staff pro-censorship groups like Concerned Women for America, Family Research Council (FRC) and American Family Association (AFA).

One such zealot is Trueman, who was one of the three witnesses at Sen. Sam Brownback's "Obscenity Prosecution and the Constitution" hearing on March 16. Since Trueman's leaving the Department of Justice in the early 1990s, he has worked for several pro-censorship organizations, including the FRC and AFA.

"The problem is, for the pornographers, most of those films have no records whatsoever," Trobee quoted Trueman as saying. "That allows the FBI to charge with a crime the seller of that material as well as the producer."

Admittedly, Trueman has been out of the Justice Department loop for so long that he would not have had any official contact with either the original 2257 regulations or their update, but if he knew anything about the adult video industry, he would know how assiduously such records are kept. There's a very good reason for that: Adult producers know that violators of even the original regulations stood to spend five years in federal prison for each improper or missing record.

So for Trueman to claim that "most of those films have no records whatsoever" betrays either an incredible ignorance on the part of a person who has been intimately involved in the anti-adult fight for more than 15 years, or a deliberate lie (unless he has been misquoted by Trobee).

Similarly, "Dr." Judith Reisman—her doctorate is in communications, not any branch of science, psychology or sociology—vented her own anti-adult spleen in a May 27 article for WorldNetDaily, which Alexa.com described as the "No. 1 most-visited conservative Internet site," and whose founder, Joseph Farah, an ex-employee of arch-conservative Richard Mellon Scaife, has called for the destruction of the ACLU, and has prescribed,

"The very first step in my program to take America back is to get down on our knees and ask God for revival and renewal in our lives."

Upset that adult actress Mary Carey and producer Mark Kulkis will be attending a fundraiser for President Bush,[2] Reisman opined that, absent a White House revocation of Kulkis' and Carey's invitation, "The public might conclude we are compromised, financially and legislatively. The public might think someone gets paid off to keep the Erototoxin flood flowing. The public might conclude we talk tough, but are soft on sexual crime, exposing ever more millions of women and children to sexual violence, disease, despair and death." ("Erototoxins," of course, are Reisman's paranoid version of endorphins, the natural substances released by human brains experiencing pleasure.)

"Maybe Laura Bush's speech writers can use some Mary Carey jokes," Reisman wrote. "Like the one where Carey says 'a little girl-on-girl action' might appeal to 'sexy' Karl Rove. However, pornography is no joke. Thousands of children are kidnapped each year and forced into sex slavery—commonly preserved as pornography."

Reisman, of course, must know that the adult industry doesn't use or record children having sex, whether forced or not, and a more honest statement would have inserted the word "child" before "pornography"—but Reisman's apparent purpose is to blur the lines between adult industry product and recorded child sexual abuse. Moreover, her language supports the latest right-wing smear that adult performers are "sex slaves" when in fact all perform voluntarily and are well-paid for their efforts.

Just a few lines later, Reisman claims that a "typical news item" relates that "WTOL News in Toledo, Ohio, reported the way pornographers commonly secure 'girl-on-girl action.' Two teenage girls were abducted in East Toledo. The kidnappers took 'the girls to several truck stops and forced them into prostitution.'"

Exactly how "kidnappers" in Ohio who "forced" teenage girls into prostitution have anything to do with adult video producers, mostly based in California, who pay established, willing performers to act in sexually explicit videos, is never explained. Perhaps it wouldn't be such a bad idea, as

Reisman claims at the beginning of her article, if "the administration would screen *us* [Reisman and her fellow anti-adult zealots] for mental illness."

Still later, Reisman charges that, "Despite present denials, pornographers would like to see us legalize prostitution and child pornography, as well as all mind-altering drugs like marijuana, LSD, cocaine." While various adult industry professionals have spoken out against America's insane drug policies, and in favor of the right of consenting adults to engage in and pay for prostitution services, none advocate employing minors in sexually explicit productions.

"The pornography business lobbies for its interests and against the public interest," Reisman concludes. "These callous racketeers appear to spend their money on Republicans they support, and against those they want to remove. Don't look for a crackdown on pornography very soon. It has been my experience that the Sex Industrial Complex has friends in high places."

To which we can only respond: "WHO? WHERE?"

Sadly, Pamela Paul is currently the editor of the New York Times Book Review, and considering her rabid anti-porn views, I'm guessing this volume may not get a Times review, or if it does, it won't be complimentary. However, it's been a while since she mentioned porn, so perhaps her views have changed?

BROWNBACK HEARING AGAIN EXPLORES PATHS AROUND FIRST AMENDMENT PROTECTIONS

January, 2006

WASHINGTON, D.C. –Sen. Sam Brownback (R-Kan.) continued his attempts to find a way around First Amendment protections for sexual speech, this time in a hearing titled "Why the Government Should Care About Pornography: The State Interest in Protecting Children and Families," held on Nov. 10.

The hearing was conducted by the Constitution, Civil Rights and Property Rights Subcommittee of the U.S. Senate Committee of the Judiciary, which Brownback chairs, and on which Sen. Russell Feingold (D-Wisc.) is the ranking Democratic member. That division of authority allowed Brownback to choose three of the witnesses to testify before the subcommittee—Pamela Paul, author of *Pornified: How Pornography Is Transforming Our Lives, Our Relationships and Our Families*; Jill Manning, a sociologist at Brigham Young University as well as a Fellow of the ultraconservative Heritage Foundation; and Richard Whidden, executive director of the National Law Center for Children and Families—and Feingold to proffer two: Leslie Harris, senior consultant and incoming executive director of the liberal Center for Democracy and Technology, and Rodney Smolla, Dean of the University of Richmond (Va.) School of Law.

Both the Free Speech Coalition (FSC) and the Adult Freedom Foundation (AFF)[1] had contacted Brownback's office to offer expert testimony to the subcommittee on the topic at hand, but both organizations were rebuffed.

"Your past two hearings have featured former prosecutors and critics of the Adult Entertainment Industry, while discounting our requests to provide attorneys, researchers, and Industry experts to present both sides of the story," wrote attorney Paul Cambria, general counsel for the AFF.[2] "For example, researchers have shown the educational value of pornography and its role in enhancing communications between couples. AFF also has experts who will testify that claims of 'porn addiction' are 'bogus,' and based on flawed research."

Several free speech supporters attended the hearing, however, including representatives of The Raben Group, FSC's congressional lobbying group, and Ricci Levy, director of the Woodhull Freedom Foundation.[3]

The slant of the hearing was never in question, and was summarized by Brownback in a statement to Pete Winn, an associate editor of Citizen-Link, the daily e-newsletter of the religio-reactionary Focus on the Family.

"I think most Americans agree and know that pornography is bad," Brownback told Winn. "They know that it involves exploitive images of men and women and that it is morally repugnant and offensive. But what most Americans don't know is how harmful pornography is to users and to their families. Few Americans know or appreciate the serious and imminent risk it poses to families—especially to children."

That view was echoed by Judiciary Committee member Sen. Orrin Hatch (R-Ut.).

"Pornography and obscenity present a problem of harm, not an issue of taste," Hatch wrote in remarks submitted for the subcommittee's record. "The days are long gone when concerns about the impact of pornography consumption can be dismissed with clichés or jokes about fundamentalist prudes imposing Victorian values... Surveys, government commissions, clinical research, and anecdotal evidence have long confirmed that pornography consumption correlates with a range of negative outcomes. Its effects are protracted, progressive, and profound."

That last was certainly the view of Pamela Paul, who claimed to have "interviewed more than 100 people" and to have "commissioned the first nationally representative poll" (which asked loaded questions such as "Is using pornography cheating?" and "How does pornography affect the children who view it?") from Harris Interactive before drawing her conclusions about porn.[4]

"Despite the claim that porn is harmless entertainment, the use of pornography has serious, negative effects," Paul said in her prepared remarks. "Countless men described how, while using porn, they have lost the ability to relate or be close to women." (Since Paul claims to have interviewed approximately 80 men in the course of her research, it's unclear how "80" translates to "countless.")

Moreover, while Paul does not disclose the date of the poll to which she refers, Harris Poll #76, conducted Sept. 20-26, 2004 (approximately one year before the publication of Paul's book), found that less than half (48%) of the 2,555 adults surveyed agreed that porn "changes men's expectations of how women should behave"; only 40% agreed that it "harms relationships between men and women"; and just over one-quarter (27%) felt that porn is "demeaning towards women."

Sadly, this poorly-constructed poll (which suggests that it *is* the one Paul created) asks the participants to choose which of several statements "best describes your opinion about the impact of pornography on children who see a lot of it." While a full 21% were either unsure or refused to answer, only 30% thought that its primary impact was to "[distort] boys' expectations and understanding of women and sex," while 25% answered that it "makes kids more likely to have sex earlier than they might otherwise." Given the loaded nature of the possible responses (see the full list at harrisinteractive.com), it's understandable that just 9% thought it didn't have any of the effects listed.

The poll's final section, which asked, "Which one of the following statements best reflects your opinion about what the government should do about pornography," was at least as loaded as its prior one. Choices included "The government needs to regulate Internet pornography specifically so that children cannot access X-rated material" (42%); "*Whether one likes it or not*, people should have full access to pornography under the Constitution's First Amendment" (23%); "The government should regulate pornography in a similar way to how cigarettes are regulated—with warning labels and restrictions *so that harm is minimized*" (13%); "The government has no role with regard to pornography" (10%); and "The government should fully legalize *all* forms of pornography" (1%). [Emphasis added.] It seems likely that the lay people who participated in this poll were unclear as to the constitutional distinctions between regulating cigarettes and regulating speech. In any case, it's no wonder that a full 12% of them were unsure which of the statements "best reflect[ed]" their opinion, or simply refused to answer.

As one might guess, Paul concluded from her "research" that porn hurts everyone, from the men who "found themselves wasting countless hours looking at pornography"; whose "relationships soured"; whose "work days became interrupted, their hobbies tossed aside, their family lives disrupted," to the point that, "Some men even lost their jobs, their wives and their children."

Nor have women escaped porn's appeal.

"While many women continue to have mixed or negative feelings towards pornography, they are told to be realistic, to be 'open-minded,'" Paul reported. "Porn, they are told, is sexy, and if you want to be a sexually attractive and forward-thinking woman, you've got to catch on. Today, the pornography industry has convinced women that wearing a thong is a form of emancipation, learning to pole dance means embracing your sexuality and taking your boyfriend for a lap dance is what every sexy and supportive girlfriend should do."

And then, of course, there's the kids. Paul quotes Judith Coché of the Coché Center[5] in Philadelphia (which advertises retreats where couples can learn "how to 'keep the erotic pot bubbling' year after year with the one you love") that when it comes to children and porn, "We have an epidemic on our hands."

"Coché describes one case in which an 11-year-old girl was found creating her own pornographic Web site," Paul reported. "When her parents confronted her, she said that pornography was considered 'cool' among her friends. Perhaps it wasn't a very good idea, the girl admitted, but all her friends were doing it." (Undoubtedly Brownback and his supporters would find this credible, but few others would or should.)

"Pornography is wildly popular with teenage boys in a way that makes yesteryear's sneaked glimpses at *Penthouse* seem monastic," Paul continued. "Like all good marketers, pornographers know it's important to reel consumers in while they're young. MTV recently announced the launch of a

Stan Lee/Hugh Hefner collaboration, *Hef's Superbunnies*, an 'edgy, sexy animated series' from the creator of the Spider-Man comic book series featuring a buxom team of specially trained *Playboy* bunnies."

Paul also has a problem with Jenna Jameson's and Brianna Banks' images appearing on one brand of snowboards and with a "Playboy: The Mansion" videogame.

"Kids also absorb pornography very differently from the way adults do," Paul claims. "Not only are kids like sponges, they are also quite literal. Even young teenagers are generally not sophisticated enough consumers to differentiate between fantasy and reality... Watching pornography, kids learn that women always want sex and that sex is divorced from relationships. They learn that men can have whomever they want and that women will respond the way men want them to. They learn that anal sex is the norm and instant female orgasm is to be expected." (That is, of course, unless their parents talk openly and realistically with them about sex—though such parents apparently don't exist in Paul's universe.)

After that opening salvo, it might seem that any following testimony might be anti-climactic, but sociologist Jill Manning,[6] a former Mormon missionary who "became interested in the impact of pornography on families while she was working as a therapist with LDS [Latter-Day Saints] Family Services in Edmonton, Alberta" and "has studied the many destructive consequences caused by exposure to pornography," was ready with the news that, "Since the advent of the Internet, the pornography industry has profited from an unprecedented proximity to the home, work and school environments. Consequently, couples, families, and individuals of all ages are being impacted by pornography in new and often devastating ways."

According to Manning's findings from "studies published in peer-reviewed research journals," she concluded that, "When a child or adolescent is directly exposed the following effects have been documented: Lasting negative or traumatic emotional responses; earlier onset of first sexual intercourse, thereby increasing the risk of STD's over the lifespan; the belief that superior sexual satisfaction is attainable without having affection for one's partner, thereby reinforcing the commoditization of sex and the objectification of humans; the belief that being married or having a family are unattractive prospects; increased risk for developing sexual compulsions and addictive behavior; increased risk of exposure to incorrect information about human sexuality long before a minor is able to contextualize this information in ways an adult brain could; and, overestimating the prevalence of less common practices (e.g., group sex, bestiality, or sadomasochistic activity)." (Almost needless to say, Manning never identified which "studies published in peer-reviewed research journals" she relied upon.)

The final Brownback witness, attorney Richard R. Whidden, Jr., traced some of the history of Supreme Court decisions suppressing public access to sexually explicit materials, particularly *Paris Adult Theater I v. Slayton* (whose rationale for prohibition is currently being challenged in the *Extreme Associates* case) and *Ginsberg v. New York*, where the high court established a simple rational-basis test for whether the material was harmful to minors, and suggested that technological advances were overtaking law enforcement's ability to prevent minors' access to the material.

"It has also been established that the law may address the methods of distribution of pornography," Whidden wrote in his prepared remarks. "Justice Sandra Day O'Connor wrote about the regulation of Internet pornography in a way that is analogous to the zoning laws, allowing a segregation of harmful material. Specifically, the government may address the secondary effects of pornography on children and families in the time, place, and manner of the distribution." (In other words, government should try to "segregate... harmful material" on the *World Wide Web*! Yeah, that'll work!)

Whidden concluded by urging legislators to consider "research concerning the effects of pornography on children and families" as well as "the effects of this material on the human brain and its addictive nature," and "legislation that allows parents to hold illegal pornography distributors responsible for the harm done to their children." (We'd definitely like to be present in court for the evidence and arguments in those lawsuits.)

When Leslie Harris'[7] turn came, she told the senators exactly what they didn't want to hear. She summarized the findings of the COPA Commission, which was established by the Child Online Protection Act to "identify technological or other methods, if any, to help reduce access by minors to material that is harmful to minors on the Internet," and the Thornburgh

Committee, named after the attorney general who chaired a similar study undertaken on behalf of the National Academy of Sciences.

"The most critical two conclusions are (A) in light of the global nature of the Internet, criminal laws and other direct regulations of content inappropriate for minors will be ineffective, and (B) education and parental empowerment with filtering and other tools are far more effective than any criminal law," Harris wrote in her prepared remarks.

"The Thornburgh Committee determined that approximately three-quarters of the commercial sites offering sexually explicit material are located outside the United States," Harris continued. "According to the report, there are hundreds of thousands of non-U.S. sexual web sites. This substantial number of sexually explicit sites outside of the United States means that U.S. criminal statutes or censorship will be ineffectual in protecting minors from sexual content on the Internet. Simply put, even if it were possible (and constitutional) to somehow make all U.S.-based sites completely inaccessible to minors, minors would still have hundreds of thousands of overseas sexual sites available to them."

Harris noted that both studies endorsed the use of filters and other end-user technologies by which parents and other caregivers could control their children's access to the Web.

The final witness, Dean Smolla,[8] spoke generally about historic Supreme Court decisions affecting the content of speech, with emphasis on an analysis of the two high court hearings dealing with the Child Online Protection Act. However, his prepared remarks only provided an outline for his live testimony, which apparently dealt with the difficulties faced by legislators and law enforcement in attempting to prevent access to sexual speech while still adhering to the constitutional prohibition on abridging free speech rights.

"One sort of common-sense thing to keep in mind is: This may not be a matter of needing new legislation," he said during the hearing. "It may simply be a matter of making the decision at the local level, the state level or the federal level to put more resources into prosecution."

This latest Brownback hearing was well-received by conservative religious groups, which continue to call on the federal government to suppress sexual speech. Patrick Trueman, former head of the Justice Department's Child Exploitation and Obscenity Section, predicted that, "Because of the pressure of Sam Brownback and the support of the American public, and the good will of the Attorney General, we are going to see the Justice Department have a strong effort against obscenity very soon."

Meanwhile, several more hearings on this and similar topics are planned. Sen. Ted Stevens (R-Aka.), who has stated that he believes that cable and satellite programming should be held to the same FCC-mandated decency standards as broadcast media, held a day-long "forum on decency" on Nov. 29, which was open to the public but to which Stevens had invited various cable and broadcast industry and other telecommunications representatives to attend, and has scheduled a pair of hearings for Jan. 19 on the topics of "decency" and "Internet pornography."

Sen. Ted Stevens got quite a bit of press in 2005 for adding $398 million into a federal budget bill earmarked to construct a bridge from Ketchikan, Alaska to Gravina Island, which had just 50 residents and the Ketchikan International Airport—an island that was already served by a ferry. Trouble was, pretty much all the legislators who weren't Alaskans opposed the project, calling it a "bridge to nowhere," and eventually the project was dropped. Sen. Ted was later indicted for receiving cheap home remodeling and other gifts from the VECO Corporation and was convicted on seven counts of making false statements. However, the convictions were voided after it was revealed that the feds had concealed evidence, but within about a year later, Stevens was dead. Not sure why it took me a week to cover the afternoon session of Stevens' hearing, so I've kept the stories separate rather than trying to combine them into one.

NEWS ANALYSIS: THAT INDECENT INDECENCY HEARING

November 29, 2005

WASHINGTON, D.C. – In a country whose Constitution prohibits its legislature from making any law abridging freedom of speech, it might seem strange that one of those legislators would hold a public forum on "Indecency in the Media"—but this is America 2005, and Sen. Ted Stevens (R-Aka.), fresh from losing funding for his pork-barrel "bridge to nowhere," was ready to tackle this allegedly pressing issue today in the Dirksen Office Building.

The hearing began at about 9:30 a.m. Eastern time, and was scheduled to last the entire day, but in fact concluded just before 4 p.m., with the afternoon session devoted to confrontations between the morning's speakers and members of the general public.

The morning, however, brought a docket of some 20 speakers that included several senators, plenty of religio-reactionaries, several broadcast and cable/satellite industry executives—but no one from a recognized free speech group, unless one counts actor Joe Pantoliano of the Creative Coalition or the representative from AFTRA, the television performers' guild, neither of whom called the hearing for what it was: An attempt to censor broadcast and cable/satellite speech even more than it already is, as well as an attempt to browbeat cable companies into allowing consumers to pick and choose just which cable channels they will pay for, rather than requiring them to buy packages of channels, some of which several of the speakers seemed to find offensive.

"We're not involved in this to bring about censorship," Stevens claimed in his opening remarks. "We're here to give an opportunity for those who represent the families of America to listen to those of you run the media, that they currently believe does not fulfill their wishes to have the kind of moral compass that our country should have for our young people."

One might have thought that providing a "moral compass" was something more properly the province of a family's church, synagogue, mosque, ashram, etc., or perhaps the children's parents ... but this is America 2005, and reinforcing Judeo-Christian morality is everyone's business, especially that of the people in charge of parents' favorite electronic babysitter, the television.

"I still have the same feeling that parents have the right to try to protect their children from some of the things they can run into in the media," Stevens said cautiously, "and with the tumbling technology we've got in this country now, it's hard for those of us in government to know what to do."

Stevens' lack of clarity was not shared by the next speaker, Sen. Jay Rockefeller (D-W.Va.).

"The entertainment broadcasting industry has proven itself unable, essentially, in my judgment, or unwilling, or both, to police yourselves," Rockefeller declared. "As a result, I have introduced, along with Sen. Hutchinson, the Indecent & Gratuitous & Excessively Violent Programming Control Act.[1] The name I don't like, but the bill I do. It gives parents sets of tools and lays out some ground rules which are not available today."

One might have thought the "ground rules" might have been deduced from the Constitution's clear prohibition against the abridgement of free speech by Congress ... but as the man said, this is America 2005.

"My bill is not intended to limit artistic expression nor is it my purpose to impose the will of Congress on decisions that properly belong to parents or to the FCC," Rockefeller claimed. "My legislation does require the FCC commissioner to begin a comprehensive review of existing technologies ...

of the V-chips and other things that are out there, to see how they're doing with the technology, to make a study of them, get back to the Congress committee, and then the FCC can begin a proceeding to find additional benefits should they feel it necessary to protect children from this content. That sounds rather mild; I don't intend it to be that way."

Actually, it sounds pretty severe, especially since both houses of Congress are already considering bills that would raise the maximum fine the FCC can impose for each instance of "indecent" programming from $27,500 to as much as half a million dollars. For instance, S. 193, introduced by Sen. Sam Brownback (R-Kan.), would raise the fine to $325,000 for every instance where a broadcaster has been "determined by the [Federal Communications] Commission ... to have broadcast obscene, indecent, or profane language."[2]

"Profane," of course, means "showing disrespect for God, any deity or religion," and one might have thought that in a country whose Constitution prohibits its legislature from "establishing" any religion, showing disrespect for one would be something Congress would not be able to take notice of, much less fine someone for so doing ... but this is America 2005.

By the way, that $325,000 may be for a single violation, but the bill also authorizes that amount of fine for "each day of a continuing violation, except that the amount assessed for any continuing violation shall not exceed a total of $3,000,000 for any single act or failure to act.'"

But it took the third speaker, Sen. Mark Pryor (D-Ark.)[3] to mention, finally, the "p" word.

"I don't only want to mention violence; I also want to mention pornography and sexually explicit things that people all across this great land can see on television, especially children, and that concerns me greatly," Pryor said. "I do think when it comes to pornography and sexually explicit material, the people around this table, they have a responsibility and I think it is a must that you own up to your responsibility, that you take responsibility for what is being shown not just on the airwaves but on cable. And of course, the Internet is another factor that's come on board in the last few years, but if I could just focus on cable just for a moment, my impression is that the cable industry is complicit in promoting pornography and sexually explicit material in our homes."

"Complicit in promoting pornography and sexually explicit material in our homes"? So now, making something available (for a price) for consumers to choose to watch in the privacy of their own living rooms, and maybe running commercials for same in the same medium, is "complicity in promoting"? This is through-the-looking-glass logic, where words mean whatever Humpty Dumpty wants them to mean.

"And I think if you look back at the track record of the pay-per-view world, the premium channels, late night cable—I mean, you can go through a long list of ways that it's happened," Pryor continued, "but I think the bottom line is for the cable industry and for satellite TV and to a lesser extent broadcast, but I think the bottom line is that this is a profitable business; that pornography and sexually explicit material is profitable. I think we need to acknowledge that; we need to be open about that, and I think we in Congress want to do something, not about the profitability of it, but about making sure that our children and people who should not be exposed to this are not exposed to it. Like Sen. Rockefeller, I'm not talking about censorship, but I'm talking about sitting down in this room in a forum here in the United States Senate and the Congress as a government working to clean up our act. We all bear responsibility, including members of congress, with this."

In a forum where everyone acknowledges that the V-chip exists, that almost all TV sets have one, as well as on/off switches and channel changers, and that no one is forced to subscribe to cable or satellite providers at all, it's not easy to understand exactly what "act" Pryor wants the program providers to "clean up" that *doesn't* involve "censorship" and *doesn't* affect "the profitability of it" ... but this is America 2005.

"I hear from some in the industry," Pryor continued, "whether it be the so-called Hollywood industry or cable or broadcast or whatever it may be—I hear people say that this is legal, and it is; it is legal. But I also have in mind what the tobacco industry said years ago. They came to this body, came to the U.S. Senate, came to the Congress and said, 'What we're doing is legal.' Well, what you do as 'legal' is not always the best thing for the country, is not always right, and I think that all your industries, everyone seated at the table here, I hope will sit down in good faith and talk about these issues with members of the Senate, members of the House, members of the administration, and try to clean up your act."

It's interesting that Sen. Pryor doesn't seem to understand that providing television programming is a First Amendment-protected activity and selling cigarettes isn't ... but this is America 2005.

But whatever problems may exist with television programming, it fell to FCC chairman Kevin Martin[4] to first enunciate what the Bush/Rove administration sees as a solution.

"Most consumers today can choose among hundreds of television channels, including some of the best programming ever produced, but television today also contains some of the coarsest programming ever aired," Martin claimed. "Indeed, the networks appear to be increasing the amount of program designed to push the envelope and too often the bounds of decency. ... As the broadcast networks have become edgier to compete with cable, prime time on broadcast television has become less family-friendly; cable and satellite television offer some great family-oriented choices, but parents cannot subscribe to these channels alone. Rather, they are forced to buy the channels they do not want their families to view in order to obtain the family-friendly channels they desire."

Ah, the answer to everyone's concerns: Don't sell cable programming packages; sell individual channels "à la carte," so each household can watch only the channels it thinks it can be comfortable with. No longer, as depicted in a recent commercial touting the V-chip, where mom had blocked a particular channel so the kids wouldn't look at it, will dad have to ask, "Honey, can I please have the unlock code?" In the commercial, mom gives a flat "No"—but now she won't have to; the government will arrange it so that she won't even have to subscribe to that channel—undoubtedly, much to dad's chagrin.

And such a system isn't just a good idea; it's absolutely necessary, claimed L. Brent Bozell,[5] president of the ultraconservative Parents Television Council.

"We hear a lot about freedom of speech, and that's a sacred thing," Bozell said, "except we know what the Supreme Court has said about this, and we know what we're talking about here. We're talking about the hours from 6 in the morning till 10 o'clock at night. We're talking about a safe haven for families. We're talking about providing a freedom that parents have, that families have as well, and the Supreme Court has upheld it."

And besides, who's it going to affect?

"Look at the number 1 show on television last year; it was watched by less than 10% of America, so where's the grand market demand for this type of programming?" Bozell asked. "Every single market study shows overwhelmingly, the market wants less raunch, less violence, less filth, so why not give the market what it wants?"

He might ask 19th century philosopher/economist John Stuart Mill that question. In the treatise "On Liberty," Mill noted that, "If all of mankind minus one were of one opinion, mankind would be no more justified in silencing that one person than he, if he had the power, would be justified in silencing mankind."

But in fact, Kyle McSlarrow,[6] President of the National Cable and Telecommunications Assn., had a more practical answer.

"If you're talking about mandatory à la carte [cable channel sales], I think this is a very dangerous idea," McSlarrow opined. "It would be very strange and I would think unthinkable if somebody went to the newspapers and said, 'You know what? I like the sports section; I don't really read the business section that much, so I'm going to tell you that you need to sell sports sections and business sections separately.' That is no different than what we're talking about with à la carte if it's mandatory in terms of the cable industry... The reason we have all these cartoon networks, the reason we have the family networks, is because the cable industry invented diversity of programming, and the reason those networks survive is because they are bundled together, allowing them an opportunity to be offered, to gain new subscribers and new viewerships so they can survive and thrive, and if you take that away with an à la carte system, you end up in our view not only violating the First Amendment but hurting the very customers you want to help."

Sadly, there's no easy way—in fact, there may be no way whatsoever—for consumers to determine which particular cable channels are profitable and which channels are not but are being supported, essentially, because they're sold in packages with more profitable ones. We already know that the major cable suppliers are adamantly silent about what portions of their profits are derived from sexually-oriented programming; it's not too much of a stretch to understand that they might be equally silent about how profitable other channels are, if for no other reason than that a diligent researcher who knew how much profit the non-sexual channels make could deduce what profit percentage the sexual channels account for.

Beyond the question of packaging versus individual channel sales, some witnesses actually dealt with the subject of the hearing: Indecency. And for several of the witnesses, it wasn't enough that the FCC decency standards apply only to broadcast TV and radio; they wanted it to apply universally to all content providers, whether over-the-air or subscription—and it quickly became clear that the motivation of "free TV" providers to have cable offerings regulated for decency was a very old one: Profits.

"Indecency is not just a radio or TV, or cable or satellite problem," claimed Jessica Marventano,[7] Senior Vice-President of Clear Channel Communications. "It is an industry-wide challenge and we all must take responsibility to see that it is addressed in a fair and consistent basis. Otherwise, two bad things happen. One is, children are insufficiently protected. To a 9-year-old, whether indecent programming is on broadcast cable or satellite is really a distinction without a difference. Second is that edgier, more popular programming migrates to cable and satellite and our free over-the-air broadcasting system becomes less accessed by the audience and more endangered. Neither outcome is good public policy."

Hmmm—fewer people looking at over-the-air channels because cable programming is sexier means lower ratings for the broadcasters, which means lower advertising rates, which means ... lower profits!

And indeed, the excessive fines for indecency proposed by Sen. Brownback and others aren't bad because they trample of citizens' free speech rights; they're bad because ...

"The worst thing Congress could do would be to impose draconian station-shutting penalties on over-the-air broadcasters while at the same time placing a flashing neon sign above their cable and satellite competitors proclaiming that indecency on these platforms is permissible," Marventano argued. "Not only would such a course put at risk the only media outlets that are truly focused on and responsive to local communities; ultimately, it would put children at greater risk of exposure to indecent content."

That same point was hammered home by Preston Padden,[8] representing the Walt Disney Company and ABC Television.

"There is no longer in our view a constitutionally sustainable basis to distinguish between broadcast and expanded basic cable and satellite TV with regard to indecency," Padden announced. "If you go to the *Playboy* case, I'd like to read a single sentence from that Supreme Court decision. The Court said, 'The key difference between cable television and the broadcasting media, which is the point on which this case turns, is that cable systems have the capacity to block unwanted channels on a household-by-household basis.'

"Well, as you've heard over and over this morning, today, V-chip technology and set-top boxes provide parents with the opportunity to block unwanted programs whether they originated on broadcast, cable, satellite, or ... the new telephone systems," Padden continued. "So the same reason that the court invalidated the regulation of cable in the *Playboy* case is now equally applicable to broadcast; namely, technology now provides a less restrictive means for parents to protect children. None of the other alleged distinctions between broadcast and basic cable and satellite justify continuing to regulate indecency on only broadcast TV. A kid with a remote control and 50 channels to click through has absolutely no idea where any of those channels originate. Regulation of only a handful of those channels, only the broadcast channels, is not only constitutionally suspect but also plainly ineffective."

Of course, Padden's comments could be read as a *condemnation* of the attempt to regulate indecency in either broadcast or cable TV, but it seems more likely that the Disney position is that indecency *should* be regulated in *both* types of media.

John Casoria,[9] of the religious Trinity Broadcasting Network, made the basis of the argument about indecency on cable even more clear.

"Applying indecency regulations to cable would also serve to eliminate the competitive imbalance between cable and broadcasting," Casoria warned. "It would do this by granting parents effective control over the content of the cable industry which liberally exposes their children to some of this questionable programming."

One of the few executives to voice a real understanding of the problem with indecency laws was NBC's Alan Wurtzel.[10]

"I'd like to offer just one point about the broadcast indecency bill that was recently passed by the House," he said at the close of his remarks. "That bill contains several provisions that would put station licenses at risk for a few seconds of indecent programming. Indeed, one indecency violation may be used by the FCC to preclude an application for a license, a license transfer or a renewal. Three violations trigger a license revocation proceeding. We believe that these penalties are completely out of proportion to the offense, especially where the First Amendment is so clearly and directly implicated. Enactment of any such provision would not only have an enormous chilling effect on broadcast programming, but would also have a depressing effect on the entire broadcast industry."

Unless, of course, the fines could be levied against subscription cable offerings as well!

The penultimate witness, Jim Dyke,[11] of the newly formed liberal group TV Watch, summed up the anti-censorship position fairly well.

"Mr. Chairman, look at almost any survey of public opinion and you will find at least 80% of Americans who see something on television that they don't like," Dyke noted. "It is the statistic most often cited in a call to government action. Mr. Chairman, I am here to tell you that I am one of those Americans, but I am not calling for government action because I am also one of the 92% of Americans who want to make their own content decisions rather than the government making those decisions."

Today's "forum" was simply a prelude to more formal hearings on television indecency scheduled for Jan. 19 before Sen. Stevens' committee. In the meantime, however, both houses of Congress will be considering several different pieces of legislation proposing media censorship of one level or another, and with conservatives in control of both the legislative and executive branches of the federal government, and a majority of the FCC commissioners now apparently amenable to foisting "decency" standards on subscription cable and satellite channels, the outlook for free speech in 2006 and beyond doesn't look good.

News Analysis: Advocates Show Their Colors at Decency Hearing

December 6, 2005

Jack Valenti,[12] the creator of the Motion Picture Association of America, the group that supplies all the Gs, PGs, Rs and NC-17s for Hollywood movies, rarely had a good word to say about constitutional free speech while he headed the MPAA. But in the years since his retirement, Valenti seems to have reconsidered where his expression values lie, and in the afternoon session of Sen. Ted Stevens' (R-Aka.) "Decency in the Media" forum on Nov. 29, he gave the attendees an earful of it.

Valenti's remarks were apparently inspired by the censorious tone and wild exaggerations of another speaker, L. Brent Bozell, III, head of the Parents Television Council (PTC), which group, by most accounts, has been responsible for 98 percent of the indecency complaints received by the Federal Communications Commission (FCC) over the past few years.

"I think we're discussing the wrong issue here," Bozell stated, referring to proposals from various broadcast and cable media moguls to strengthen public awareness and use of the V-chip, the device installed in all modern TVs which can block programming based on the show's assigned rating for sex, language, dialog and/or violence. "We're having a grandiose debate about—and the analogy that I've drawn before is the analogy of a pothole on 14th Street. We're all discussing ways of putting warning signs to alert motorists to a pothole on 14th Street: What size V-chip, what size warning label, content descriptors and everything else. But no one's addressing the potholes. They're still on 14th Street.

"If we are to say that we shouldn't address that pothole, then what we're saying is that we—there is a need, a demand, a call, a protection, a something for indecency on television," Bozell claimed. "And we're not talking about little indecencies here. We're talking about big, big indecencies. And I would ask the people around this room, and my friends in the networks, to tell me where there is a market demand for the kind of things that we're now talking about protecting, because we're saying V-chips and everything else is to protect the right to watch what? To watch pedophilia; to watch bestiality—it's on television now—to watch incest, to watch necrophilia—that's on in prime time now. Are we really so impassioned about defending some sort of a market right to watch this, or would we just be doing ourselves a big favor if we were to simply say that it doesn't matter what the law says; it's a simple function of decent civilized behavior? One does not put this on television when youngsters should be watching. And not to mention, by the way, adults, too—I don't know why adults would be wanting to watch this, but children, for goodness sakes. Do we have to have V-chips, or can we just not say—can we just say, we're not going to do that? And then we wouldn't be having these hearings."

Bozell's claim that depictions of adults having sex with children, with animals and with dead bodies was outrageous enough—that doesn't even happen on cable, much less broadcast TV, the only venue where the FCC currently has control—and Bozell neglected to name even one program that depicted any of those acts.

He did, however, attempt to bolster his claim by citing a Pew Research poll which indicated that even the most popular show on TV (which he likewise did not name, but *Desperate Housewives*[13] is a likely candidate) was watched by less than 10% of the population—yet if sterile, non-sexual fare were more popular than titillation, wouldn't shows like *Seventh Heaven* regularly outscore *CSI* in all its incarnations and *Law & Order: Special Victims Unit*?

For Bozell, the V-chip was just the tip of a slippery slope that began with TV-MA ("mature audience") ratings and presumably would end with hardcore sex.

"As we predicted would happen when the V-chip debate began," Bozell warned, "beware of the law of unintended consequences. As soon as we got the V-chip, what we also got was almost immediately some of the lowest offensive programming and indecent programming ever on television. Why? Because now you could do it, because we had a V-chip and we had a rating system, and we could just put TV-MA and drop that bomb, because we had TV-MA... All I'm saying is that the V-chip has allowed some who have wanted to push the envelope ... to push it with the protection of the V-chip. And then we come back here two years later, all the more upset."

Bozell's comments seemed to inspire Valenti to remember his constitutional roots, though his initial argument was more a challenge to the degree of television's indecency than any defense of it.

"There's 2400 hours of television on the air today; 2400 hours a day," Valenti began. "How much of that is indecent? This is an imperfect world we live in."

But soon, Valenti hit his stride.

"What has made America great is, it's a free country, and when you are a First Amendment person, you must allow into the marketplace that which you find to be meretricious, untidy, unwholesome and sometimes just plain stupid, but that's the price you pay for democracy," Valenti rightly argued. "A democracy is quite messy. If you want to have a pristine television show, you go to Burma or you go to North Korea, and you'll find yourself in a pristine world where nothing that the government doesn't want on the air is on the air. That's the price you pay, Brent, for a democracy."

Picking up on Bozell's failure to mention which shows had depicted sexual acts, Valenti then gave some advice to Sen. Stevens.

"Mr. Chairman, I think you'll find that it's very fine to say you could have standards, but now when you begin to fine people, when you begin to force people, then you must be precise," he cautioned. "You cannot indict a man for a crime without defining what the crime is ... What is the standard? What is 'too much' violence? Where do you draw this line? The idea that the whole country, all of us get upset about a three-second version of an artificial breast to me is the most absurd thing in the world, this Janet Jackson thing.[14] It made no sense. And yet you can go in any museum, you can go anyplace and see nude women. Venus de Milo is known around the world. The point is, this thing got out of hand, it seems to me, that to have three, four seconds of a silicone breast and the country became ecstatic about it—I mean, it just doesn't make any sense."

If Valenti knew that Jackson's nipple was in fact exposed for less than half a second, he might have been even more outraged.

Earlier in the hearing, ABC's Preston Padden had mentioned that about one-third of his network's affiliates had decided not to air a repeat broadcast of Steven Spielberg's *Saving Private Ryan* due to worries that the FCC might level fines for the violence and vulgarities contained in the movie. But Valenti argued that lawmakers must look past the objections of modern puritans and deal with the core message of the film: War is hell.

"When you look at, say, *Saving Private Ryan*, is the classic example; is that too much violence?" Valenti asked. "Most would say not, because men are being killed. You saw the brutal realisms of a war, and yet I think every young boy in this country, particularly young boys and young women under the age of 12 ought to see that movie because it has to do with war, and every now and then, we go to war. What is it like? So this is very delicate ground we're on. I'm saying to you, there's no way that we can do what Brent wants, and that is to scour the airwaves of everything that offends his sense of decency, which might be different than somebody else's, but I say to you again, if you're going to indict somebody, you must be precise, what it is they're violating."

That latter point was exactly what no one on the pro-censorship side could address, though Bozell took a stab at doing so by attempting to distinguish between "artistic" and "gratuitous" violence. But first, he had to admit that, like obscenity, no one had yet defined "indecency."

"There's been this discussion about how does one define indecency," Bozell said. "I don't know how to do it. It's not that one says that it can't be done; I just don't know how to do it, and I don't know of anyone who's come up with a definition of indecency."

Bozell's lack of ability to define the term hasn't stopped his organization from urging members and the general public to flood the FCC with complaints about "indecent" programming, but rather than own up to this basic contradiction at the heart of PTC's entire program, Bozell changed the subject.

"Note that we're not talking about obscenity, and so much of what is on television today is obscene in the Webster definition of the word 'obscenity,'" Bozell claimed. "And yet it isn't legally obscene because the word 'obscenity' has been defined in such a way that I believe it must include visual insertion, so nothing can be obscene on the radio. So this is the slippery slope you get into when you get into a full definition."

"Full definition?" How about *any* definition that doesn't run smack up against the First Amendment's prohibition against Congress making *any* law that abridges freedom of speech? But no definition, full or otherwise, was to be forthcoming at this hearing.

"But there's another point, senators, that needs to be hammered home here," Bozell pressed on. "Contrary to what we heard across the table, which is flat-out wrong, it is not a function that the public doesn't care and doesn't want government to do something. The Pew Center shows that 75 percent of the public wants tighter enforcement from the government on these rules. Now, why is that? These airwaves are owned by the public. They're not owned by any company represented here, and they're not owned by the Parents Television Council either. They're owned by the public. The law states that you have to abide by community standards of decency. Now, there's going to be some gray area here, but there's a black-and-white area here as well. There are things that are on broadcast television that are simply indecent, and I really don't care about how many Band-Aids we talk about it. Senators, the law says you can't be indecent. And people who violate that, willfully violate that, gratuitously violate that—*Saving Private Ryan* wasn't gratuitously violating anything, and that's a smokescreen. I'm talking about programming that gratuitously violates community standards of decency should be fined."

Bozell was just digging his hole deeper. Despite his inability to define "indecency," now he assured the audience, including Sens. Stevens and Daniel Inouye (R-Hi.), that there were both gray areas of non-definition and black-and-white areas of same—a contradiction that Valenti would later seize upon. But Bozell, like Supreme Court Justice Potter Stewart, apparently knows indecency when he sees it; he just can't tell anyone else exactly what it is—except, of course, that it's "gratuitous," as evidenced by some imagined poll of "community standards of decency." Sadly for Bozell and his compatriots, the Constitution requires much more than a "show of hands."

Sen. Stevens, however, apparently recognized Bozell's problem and attempted to save him.

"I believe that it would be correct to say that the FCC has interpreted the criminal law and has said, according to a note that I have here, that 'indecent' is language that—or material that depicts or describes sexual or excretory activities or organs in terms of patently offensive as measured by contemporary community standards for the broadcast media," Stevens declared. "Now, that's pretty vague, but it is defined by past FCC decisions. That's what you're talking about, and greater enforcement of that standard, is that right, Brent?"

Bozell probably would have agreed with that, and perhaps would even have been happy that Stevens had described the FCC's standard as "pretty vague," but before Bozell could respond, Valenti chimed in.

"Mr. Chairman, again, that standard is not an indictment, it's not a description of a crime," Valenti properly pointed out." As a matter of fact, in the motion picture business, we have obscenity laws in about 40 states pertaining to motion pictures. The last time that an obscenity case was filed against a motion picture was in Albany, Georgia, and the picture was ... *Carnal Knowledge*, and it went all the way to the Supreme Court in a 9-0 decision; they threw it out.[15] The reason why is, we go by the *Miller* standard, which is prevailing community standards. That is a loophole big enough for 10 Hummers to get through, and as a result, no district attorney, no attorney general has filed any obscenity charges against a motion picture because it'll get thrown out in the higher court because of a lack of precision."

Sadly, Valenti had apparently bought the claim that the Supreme Court's decision in *Miller v. California* had defined and legitimized "community standards" for "obscenity" in some manner that, it was clear, had not been done for "indecency," but thankfully, Valenti then returned to his point about the need for specificity of definition when bringing criminal charges, or even FCC fines.

"Now, when Brent talks about all of this terrible stuff is on television, I'd like him to make a catalog of it," Valenti requested, "because what you find is, nobody can make this judgment. When I first started the motion picture rating system, I retained two social scientists, one child behavioral expert and a psychiatrist, and I said, 'What I need from you is, I'm doing this rating system; put down on a piece of paper exactly where the demarcation lines are in these various categories that we have, but it's got to be specific, because otherwise we go back to subjective standards again.' Guess what? They couldn't do it... I say again, standards are different from a specific definition that is lacking, and that's what you have in the Supreme Court today, and that's the reason why, to repeat, in the last 25 years, there have been no cases filed because the district attorneys understand there's no case there."

However, with four bills dealing with "indecency" in the media currently pending before Congress, and with Stevens himself having scheduled another hearing on the subject for Jan. 19, it is unlikely that Stevens had the "ears to hear" what Valenti was saying. Therefore, even fans of the soft adult material available on both broadcast and cable/satellite TV and radio should gear up for court fights on this issue, perhaps as early as the spring of 2006.

George Lakoff is one hell of a sociologist, and all adult industry members and fans should read his book Whose Freedom?: The Battle over America's Most Important Idea, *not to mention,* Moral Politics: How Liberals and Conservatives Think.

CHRISTIANITY, CHOICE AND CONTENT

May, 2006

Adult content, that is. You know: Where women 18 years or older, who theoretically are mature enough to choose whether to smoke cigarettes, drink alcohol and/or have an abortion, also are theoretically mature enough to choose whether they want to have part of their sex lives recorded for all to see.

What? Women have choice? When did that happen? Well, *you* may not be asking that question, but plenty of folks out in Middle America are.

According to George Lakoff,[1] professor of linguistics at UC-Berkeley, conservatives view women's free choice about pretty much *anything* to be a crime against culture and a subversion of the woman's proper place in society: A step or two below that of daddy, the "strict father."

"What is the notion of a moral authority?" asked Lakoff in a lecture to the Commonwealth Club of California in January. "A moral authority is the father who knows right from wrong, who has the power to punish and the power to tell you what to do, and that's good because he is moral. Morality and power *should* go together and there's a hierarchy of that. The way to tell who is moral is to look at traditional forms of power. So you have God above man; man above nature; adults above children; western culture above non-western culture; America above other nations, and that's part of general conservative thought. And then you get a bigoted extension: That is, an extension to men above women; whites above non-whites; Christians above non-Christians; straights above gays. And that is what I'll call the 'moral order,' and that's a very important part of conservative thought—at least, the first part of it is general conservative thought, and then you get the not-so-nice extensions of it."

And if there's one thing the adult industry is familiar with, it's those "not-so-nice extensions of it."

Enter Supreme Court Justice Antonin Scalia.

"The *core* of [St. Paul's] message is that government ... derives its moral authority from God," Scalia wrote[2] in the May, 2002 issue of *First Things*, a conservative religious magazine. "The reaction of people of faith to this tendency of democracy to obscure the divine authority behind government should not be resignation to it, but the resolution to combat it as effectively as possible... All this, as I say, is most un-European, and helps explain why our people are more inclined to understand, as St. Paul did, that government carries the sword as 'the minister of God,' to 'execute wrath' upon the evildoer."

Among the more familiar "evildoers" that the government, as "the minister of God," has "execute[d] wrath" upon are Reuben Sturman, Ferris Alexander,[3] Russ Hampshire,[4] Susan Colvin[5] and Chris Mann,[6] with wrath scheduled for Eddie Wedelstedt and, no doubt, Sherri Williams[7] and Rob Black. [UPDATE: All except Colvin, Mann and Williams spent time behind bars.]

Because, as Sam Harris[8] pointed out in his monumentally important work, *The End of Faith*, "In the United States and in much of the rest of the world, it is currently illegal to seek certain experiences of pleasure."

"Behaviors like drug use, prostitution, sodomy, and the viewing of obscene materials have been categorized as 'victimless crimes'," Harris continued. "[W]hat is startling about the notion of a victimless crime is that even when the behavior in question is genuinely victimless, its criminality is still affirmed by those who are eager to punish it. It is in such cases that the true genius lurking behind many of our laws stands revealed. The idea of a victimless crime is nothing more than a judicial reprise of the Christian notion of *sin*."

Between them, Lakoff and Harris have got religio-conservative philosophy exactly right: Under their "strict-father" morality, God orders, man obeys—that's it!—and if *you* have any doubt about what God (as interpreted by Falwell,[9] Robertson,[10] Wildmon[11] and the rest) wants, it's the rack for you, with Scalia, Alito, Thomas and Roberts as our modern Torquemadas.[12]

"[Conservatives] want to go back and undo each of those things [social safety nets, child labor laws, environmental legislation] that has to do with freedom," Lakoff explained. "Voting rights is freedom from tyranny. Public education is freedom from ignorance and access to knowledge where knowledge is power. Civil rights is freedom to participate in society... Media extension [is] freedom of speech. These are freedoms and they have been extended over time, and that is what we stand to lose right now."

To that list, of course, the adult industry adds: Freedom to fuck, and to have others see us fuck. Trying to legislate against that, as Robert Heinlein[13] analogized in another context, "is like trying to teach a pig to sing: It wastes your time and annoys the pig."

But perhaps more importantly, this industry understands, as perhaps no other group does, that sex is life: Sex creates life; sex is one of life's great enjoyments, and in the largest sense, sex is freedom.

"We cannot let them have life," Lakoff demanded. "Life is a progressive value. It's *our* value."

Damn fucking straight!

Every once in a while, I've examined how intellectually inferior a lot of these Religious Right types are, and below is one such examination. Sadly, I don't remember much about the CNN debate Peters and I took part in, but I'm sure what I related below is accurate.

IS IT JUST ROBERT PETERS WHO'S SCIENCE-DEFICIENT? OR IS IT THE WHOLE RELIGIOUS RIGHT?

July 7, 2006

NEW YORK CITY – In light of the plummeting rape statistics nationwide, and the temerity of one *Chicago Tribune* columnist to question whether that drop could be attributable to more people watching more porn, Morality In Media president Robert Peters[1] has decided to weigh in on the question of whether that cause-and-effect exists. In the process, Peters reveals how little he knows about science.

"Even if it were true that the viewing pornography is cathartic for some," Peters states, "that alone does not disprove a causal link between viewing pornography and sex crimes, including rape."

Um ... Bob? In *science*, you don't prove negatives. You formulate a theory—f'r'instance, "an increase in viewing sexually explicit material in society decreases the incidence of rape in that society"—and then examine statistics and conduct experiments to find support for the theory. Even if you fail to find such evidence, it certainly doesn't mean that the *opposite* is true; it just means that you've failed to find experimental support for your proposition.

"One possible explanation for the high 'rape' rates in the 1970s, when the statistics Mr. Chapman relies on begin," Peters continues, neglecting to explain why he puts the word "rape" in quotes, "is that the 1970s were a time of social transition when some males and females may have viewed the 'boundaries' between consenting and non-consenting sex differently. It is also noteworthy and relevant that by the early 1970s the proverbial pornography 'horse' was out of the 'barn' and on the run, changing the way people view and presumably have sex." (Gosh, Peters certainly does love his meaningless internal quotes!)

Just a couple of problems there. The fact that the sexual revolution was in full swing by the early '70s brought with it the idea that women had the right to be in control of their own bodies—a concept the anti-abortion Peters opposes—and with that recognition came the power to say "no" to unwanted intercourse; a power that quickly began to show up in codes of conduct on college campuses, which outlawed "date rape" by mental coercion. If anything, those policies would have led to a decrease in date rapes. Moreover, porn was hardly prolific in the early '70s. Although *Deep Throat* and a few other XXX movies were playing in theaters, the earliest home VCRs didn't come along until 1975, and the earliest porn tapes not until a couple of years after that—in fact, just in time to (perhaps) account for a decrease in rapes.

That's the only *evidence* (such as it is) that Peters brings to the question of porn's effect on rape. He mentions high school sex ed courses as discouraging intercourse, but admits that they didn't accomplish that goal very well. He also implies that law enforcement has taken "many sex offenders out of circulation," but serial rape was rare even back then. He notes that "schools, women's groups and others have also worked hard in recent times to teach girls and women how to avoid being raped and to make boys and young men more aware of the legal line between consenting and nonconsensual sex," but he's already admitted that plenty of them are having *consensual* sex.

Of course, it was inevitable that Peters would drag out the theocrats' resident "sex expert," Dr. Victor Cline[2]—and in the process, shoots himself in the foot.

"As observed by Dr. Victor B. Cline in his monograph, 'The Effects of Pornography on Adults and Children,[3]'" Peters claims, "the fourth stage of pornography addiction is the increasing tendency to act out sexual behaviors viewed in the pornography. 'Willing' partners include spouses who 'consent' to sexual behaviors they find abhorrent, until there is a separation or divorce. Unwilling partners include prostitutes who are sexually assaulted. Criminal violence against prostitutes, however, is rarely reported."

Peters brought up the concept of "porn addiction" in a debate he and I had on CNN's *Showbiz Tonight* in April, where I explained that porn addiction is not a recognized psychological disorder. On the other hand, obsessive-compulsive disorder (OCD) *is* recognized, but that condition may lead a person to obsess about *anything*: Hand-washing, avoiding crowds, even praying.

But what Peters seems to be saying is, the fact that partners of OCD sufferers and the prostitutes hired by OCD sufferers haven't reported being raped is somehow evidence that they *were* raped, and that pornography, rather than this recognized psychological disorder, was the cause of it.

Peters also quotes a retired NYPD lieutenant commander on the "proliferation" of "serial murder events as well as sex related homicides," many of which, Peters claims, involve prostitutes—but he's on even shakier grounds there. At least one of the more recent serial killers, Gary Leon Ridgeway,[4] the "Green River killer," targeted prostitutes *because* they sold sex, while Dennis Rader,[5] the "BTK killer," was sexually aroused by watching people die—scenarios *not* depicted in any adult industry fare.

"I picked prostitutes as my victims because I hate most prostitutes and I did not want to pay them for sex," said Ridgway, who thought of prostitutes as an "infestation," in his confessional statement. "I also picked prostitutes as victims because they were easy to pick up without being noticed. I knew they would not be reported missing right away and might never be reported missing. I picked prostitutes because I thought I could kill as many of them as I wanted without getting caught."

Finally, Peters gets to the meat of it:

"The effect that pornography has in the commission of sexual crimes is difficult to measure scientifically," Peters concludes. "*Conclusive scientific data, however, is not necessary. Common sense should inform us* that when persons feed their minds on pornography that depicts the exploitation and degradation of women, their sexual 'appetites' can become warped. Social science research also indicates there is a causal relationship between pornography and sexual violence. There is also a mountain of anecdotal evidence showing that pornography is linked to sexual crimes." [Emphasis added; useless quote marks in original]

Need we really list the myriad fallacies that "common sense" has "informed" us of? We could start with the earth being flat and also the center of the universe—and for all we know, since "conclusive scientific data ... is not necessary," Peters may believe both of those propositions, and many similar ones. However, "social science research" has only shown a link between violent sexually explicit material and violence in general—and it's still unclear whether the first causes the second, or simply that people with a propensity toward violence are drawn to violent material. And as for the "mountain of anecdotal evidence" ... well, anyone can check out what Wikipedia has to say about that in terms of its scientific validity (oops; forgot; "conclusive scientific data ... is not necessary") ... or you can just keep walking in a straight line, and when you come to the edge, you'll know the earth is flat.

But if you don't, will you then know it isn't? That's the question Peters can't answer.

Most people don't seem to know this today, but historically, far-left Democrats were referred to as "radical," while far-right Republicans were termed "reactionary"—a term which seems to have fallen out of use today. But guess what? They still are.

THEOCRATS CALL ON JUSTICE DEPARTMENT TO BUST HOTEL PAY-PER-VIEW

August 8, 2006

CINCINNATI – Spearheaded by Phil Burress' Citizens for Community Values (CCV), 13 religio-reactionary groups have placed an ad in today's *USA Today* calling on the U.S. Department of Justice to investigate and prosecute companies which supply adult videos for hotel pay-per-view systems. The ad, which can be found on the CCV and the Family Research Council's websites, apparently appears only in the D.C. and New York City editions of the newspaper.

The specific targets of the ad, which is titled "If what begins with a click can end as a *registered sex offense*, it's time we rethink hardcore porn," are OnCommand and LodgeNet,[1] which are termed "two companies ... largely responsible for flooding U.S. hotels with the majority of highly alarming and pornographic video content." Not explained in the ad are why such videos are "highly alarming," nor which particular sex offenses are "registered."

However, the ad does quote "the usual suspects": Dr. Mary Anne Layden,[2] who's testified several times before U.S. Senate subcommittees whose objectives have been to attempt to find ways to prevent Americans from viewing sexually explicit material, and former FBI agent Roger Young,[3] another oft-quoted anti-adult activist.

"It is a known fact that registered sex offenders use adult hardcore pornography as a high-octane fuel to direct dangerous sexual behavior toward others including children," the ad's text begins. "The often-addictive nature of pornography—which many view as a private act—continues to have drastic public consequences."

In fact, all legitimate studies have shown that pedophiles are completely uninterested in "adult hardcore pornography"; it doesn't turn them on. Moreover, it's unclear what the organizations mean by "dangerous sexual behavior toward others": Not using condoms? Getting blowjobs while driving? Most responsible adult producers oppose those practices as well—but it's doubtful that that's what the ad is directed toward.

But these organizations are already well on record as opposing premarital/extramarital sex and consensual sodomy—the kind that sometimes takes place in hotel rooms—and the U.S. Supreme Court as well is already on record, in *Lawrence v. Texas*,[4] as declaring that such activities are outside the purview of the government.

The ad also disingenuously quotes from a 1983 study conducted by Dr. William Marshall of Ottawa, Canada, who, the ad says, has "found that 86% of serial rapists studied admitted to consumption of hardcore porn, with 57% admitting imitation of actual scenes from the material in the commission of their crimes." It is likely that, if questioned, more than 86% of serial rapists would admit to having consumed beef and milk at some point before committing their crimes, suggesting that the scientific motto, "Correlation is not causation," once again applies.

But science has never found much favor nor carried much weight among the theocrats.

"We are calling on the Department of Justice and Federal Bureau of Investigation to immediately investigate the companies that distribute it to determine whether 'adult' videos being sold in hotels by *OnCommand* and *LodgeNet* violate long-established Federal and State laws regarding distribution of obscene material," said Burress, who over the past few years has attempted to convince various Ohio and northern Kentucky prosecutors to strong-arm hotels into banning adult pay-per-view.

Indeed, the ad notes that, "Even Sweden, an otherwise liberal bastion of sexual tolerance, has banned government officials from staying in hotels that offer pornography. Their decision this April followed the lead of the Netherlands in 2003."

What the ad doesn't say is that it's not the *governments* of those countries that's banning officials from hotels with adult, it's the military leaders who are responsible, since it is the military's job to "negotiate[] deals with hotels which then apply to all other public sector officials traveling on business," according to *The Local*, a Swedish online newspaper.[5] *The Local* also notes that the move came in response to pressure from ROKS,[6] a Swedish women's pro-censorship organization, which convinced the military leaders that preventing military officers and enlisted personnel from being able to access adult movies in hotel rooms would aid in recruiting women into the armed forces. Moreover, Sweden is hardly a "liberal bastion of sexual tolerance," having outlawed prostitution some years ago while it remains legal in several other Scandinavian and European countries, including the Netherlands.

"Pornography also contributes to addictive sexual behaviors which, in turn, help fuel the increasing proliferation of sex crimes against women and children by sexual predators who live in our neighborhoods," the ad claims. However, as behavioral psychologists and researchers know, there is no such thing as "porn addiction"; the disorder that may involve adult materials is "obsessive-compulsive disorder," which can manifest itself in an unhealthy fixation on anything from porn to gambling to prayer.

And finally, the ad opines that, "It's high time America began thinking less of profiting from debasing women and more about prosecuting—under current laws—those who produce, sell and distribute hardcore porn." But sexually-explicit material is constitutionally protected unless a jury finds that it violates the standards set forth in the U.S. Supreme Court's *Miller v. California* decision—and "debasing women" ("lowering in quality or value," which adult does in no greater measure than any other entertainment medium) isn't one of those criteria.

In addition, the CCV website lists more than 50 PPV offerings that it claims "account[] for the tragic human and cultural expense from which [adult producers, distributors and hotels] profit," and the list includes features from every adult company that supplies the PPV systems.

"The lists speak for themselves," claimed thrice-married CCV President Phil Burress. "This is not mere nudity. We're talking about every conceivable form of degrading, distorted sex. We're talking about the types of material, which are addictive in nature, which men are lured into viewing in the privacy of their hotel rooms, and which have been responsible for sexual crimes and for the breakdown of countless marriages, families and careers. And we're talking about a company and its leader who care more about the dollar than about those men, women, children and families."

Several of the theocrat organizations sponsoring the ad are also signatories to a letter from the Interfaith Stewardship Alliance,[7] which urges religious people to ignore scientific findings proving the existence of global warming, and all oppose comprehensive sex education in schools, as well as condom distribution for HIV prevention in Third World countries.

Yeah, *they* care about "men, women, children and families"!

I've been a fan of the writings of Dr. Marty Klein for a very long time, and am proud to call him a friend. However, that has nothing to do with my positive review of his ground-breaking book, which I consider to be a "must read" for anyone interested in how American government and most major religions deal with sex.

REVIEW: 'AMERICA'S WAR ON SEX'

By Marty Klein, Ph.D.; Praeger Publishers, 88 Post Road West, Westport, CT 06881; 212 pp; $29.50
November, 2006

Almost since its founding 23 years ago, *Adult Video News* has reported on the government's attempts to suppress sexually explicit video, and in recent years has expanded its coverage to include many more aspects of the interaction between American culture and a wide variety of sex-related topics—and if we do say so ourselves, we've done a damned good job of covering that subject.

It is against that background that we can state that Dr. Marty Klein's[1] recently published volume, *America's War On Sex*, is quite simply the best book yet written dealing with the collision between the adult industry, sex-positive activism and the Religious Right. Every single page contains valuable information and analysis for anyone involved in the adult industry, and should be considered required reading for anyone who wants to understand why so many people in the United States, particularly the so-called "cultural leaders," are so screwed up when it comes to all subjects sexual.

"[T]hose who are trying to 'clean up' America say they're fighting for a number of critical reasons: the family, marriage, morals, education, community safety," Klein perceptively notes at the outset. "But this isn't really true. *It's a war against sex*: sexual expression, sexual exploration, sexual arrangements, sexual privacy, sexual choice, sexual entertainment, sexual health, sexual imagination, sexual pleasure."

The war, he says, is between "those who fear and hate sexuality ('erotophobes')" and "those who appreciate or tolerate sexuality ('erotophiles')"—and as things stand now, the erotophobes are winning.

"Today's domestic conservative/fundamentalist political and social movements present a clear (though horrifically distorted) picture of sexuality" in almost every form, Klein assesses. "The goal of this war is to control sexual expression, colonize sexual imagination, and restrict sexual choices."

Sound familiar? Sound like something you yourself have thought?

Klein's thesis is broken into several chapters dealing with such subjects as sex education, reproductive rights and the media, both broadcast and Internet, but as becomes quickly evident, those are really just different aspects of the same war, fought with the same weapons, using the same (mis)information and targeting the same objective: To control and restrict everyone's sexuality, even their own.

And what better place to start than with the kids?

"The battle over sex ed is the battle over childhood and adolescent sexuality," Klein notes. "The Right and government at all levels ... [are] asking kids to join them in an unholy alliance to deny sexuality: teaching kids to fear sexual feelings, while adults fear sexual information."

The "anti-sex educators" received $200 million in 2006 alone to teach "abstinence education," but as Klein explains at length, it's a doomed enterprise.

"Kids using abstinence *this weekend* will have sex," Klein states. "They've promised they won't, but they will. How do we want to prepare them for this? We tell kids to wear seatbelts, even though we don't want them to crash. We tell kids to call if they'll be late, even though we want them home on time. What do we offer kids who don't refuse sex the way we want them to? Nothing—no backup plan, no mnemonic devices, no support, no information to protect themselves. Ask an abstinence proponent what a kid should do if he or she has sex, and they reply, 'Don't have sex.'"

And this year's $200 million is hardly the entire price tag of this program, Klein notes. Among the other, perhaps more important costs are "unfamiliarity with, and mistrust of, contraception"; "reinforcement of belief that sex is bad and dangerous"; "ignorance of appropriate personal sexual decision-making"; and "shame, guilt and isolation when chastity vows are broken." In fact, it all makes a pretty good case for the concept that kids are, as Klein puts it, "a minority targeted for discrimination."

Another discriminated-against class is women in general, whose rights to abortion, birth control and "morning-after" pills are routinely subverted if not outright denied—and as Klein correctly states, the Religious Right is working ever harder to restrict those rights even further.

"It starts with a belief that the only legitimate purposes of sex are reproduction and marital intimacy," he explains. "Contraception symbolizes sex for other purposes—that is, pleasure. Thus, an attack on contraception is an attack on sex-for-pleasure... For [the Religious Right], sex is either authorized or unauthorized. And sex is authorized only between legally married heterosexual couples, generally limited to penis-vagina intercourse... This means that most Americans are having unauthorized sex."

And how do the religious conservatives combat unauthorized sex? One of the main methods is by increasing the unwanted consequences of such acts.

"Those who war on sex," Klein warns, "depend on a simplistic hypothesis proven wrong repeatedly throughout history: That if you increase the possible dangers of sexual expression, people will stop having sex."

This strategy has already been employed in nearly every conceivable way: By teaching people, especially youngsters, to fear sex; by withholding contraception from them, both before and after the fact; and by claiming bogus health consequences of the use of contraception, of the new HPV vaccine, and of "porn addiction," among many others. Moreover, religiously-motivated government actions have contributed to the problem by ignoring scientific evidence in making decisions about sex-related subjects, by subtly encouraging the takeover of hospitals that have performed abortions by religious institutions that oppose access to the procedure, and by enacting laws that give "rights" to fetuses and "rights" to physicians and pharmacists to withhold treatment and drugs.

"Legal recognition of fetuses' rights is *not* the same thing as criminalizing abortion—it's *worse*," Klein charges. "Nor is it the same as declaring when life begins. It's more pervasive, with a cascade of awful effects. This is not an incremental change; it is an earth-shaking event counter to every founding document and principle in American history... Law has taken moral and metaphysical beliefs and made them facts."

Many of these assaults on sexual culture are perpetrated by what Klein calls the "Sexual Disaster Industry" (SDI), which he says "involves federal and local government, conservative religion, 'morality' organizations, right-wing think tanks, victim parade daytime talk shows like Montell and Maury, and news programs looking for a bump ('Isn't it awful the way people go to strip clubs? Film at 11!')"

"The Industry is continually inventing and warning us about new sex-related disasters-in-the-making," Klein continues. "And although government, religion and civic groups are working overtime creating more and more solutions, everyone agrees that our safety and peace of mind is further away than ever. It would seem that our sex-related problems are just too big, that American sexuality (actually, human sexuality) is just too degenerate. That's why programs need more money, citizens need to be more vigilant, people need to give up more rights, and government has to pass ever-stricter laws."

If that sounds as if it means that suppression of sex will go a long way to creating a theocratic dictatorship in America, the evidence for that future is incontrovertible.

Consider also the provably false sexual mythology that, according to Klein, the SDI promotes:

"1) Kids are damaged by exposure to sexual words, pictures and concepts;

"2) America is full of sexual predators—and the situation is getting worse;

"3) Ultimately, people can't explore sexuality safely;

"4) People interested in sexual stimulation, exploration or unusual stuff are 'them,' not 'us';

"5) Eliminating venues for sexual experiences will eliminate sexual behavior;

"6) Feeling scared about sexuality is responsible citizenship and common sense."

"Together, these six assumptions create a landscape of danger and powerlessness, in which suspicion of one's own and others' sexuality is sensible,"

Klein concludes. "Surrounded by this much danger and potentially explosive eroticism, fear (and resentment) isn't just plausible, it seems responsible."

Objects of that fear/resentment include everything from porn to strippers to swingers to gays (and same-sex marriage) to prostitution, and true believers would even throw in such innocuous fare as *Buffy The Vampire Slayer* and Janet Jackson's millisecond breast exposure ... but as Klein notes, "The Sexual Disaster Industry's goal isn't to address the real problems of real people. It's to 1) inspire us to fear sex; and 2) to provide society with excuses to restrict sexual expression."

Ding! Ding! Ding! Anybody out there worried about his/her store getting busted? Website getting shut down? Production company indicted for failing to index records properly even though no kids are involved? Thank the Sexual Disaster Industry! And as Klein properly assesses, "sexual conservatives are devoted to finally, completely winning this conflict by any means necessary short of nuclear weapons."

"So it's not the busted neighborhoods, ruined virginal strippers, kids playing Nintendo with hookers, or bored, philandering husbands that are the real issue," he continues. "It's sex as entertainment. It's people arranging for sex to serve them, rather than people being enslaved by sexual repression. It's the acknowledgement that erotic novelty is not only desirable, it's possible. And it's the assertion that men and women who choose to use sex in this way can make responsible choices in the rest of their lives. For those who fear sex, tolerating adult entertainment means collapsing the crucial distinction between good people who repress their sexuality and bad people who don't (and who suffer as a result)."

For *AVN*, those "bad people" would certainly include its readers as well as adult entertainment customers, producers, performers and anyone else employed in any manner by any adult business... but as Klein understands, it's far more than that.

"Somehow, they [religious conservatives] neglect to mention that it's the consumer choices and other preferences of *their own constituents* that are 'the problem.' It is average, working-class and middle-class Republican voters in Charleston, Abilene and Spokane that are watching porn, having affairs, buying vibrators, going to strip clubs, and keeping *Sex & The City* on the air. People may tell pollsters and even politicians that they want more 'decent' programs and products. But that's not what people are discussing, buying and watching. Religious people, conservative people, 'decent' people demand—and get—the *Gilmore Girls*, a Hitachi magic wand, Jenna Jameson, a lap dance."

But the hypocrisy of XXX's critics, as important as that is to understand, is hardly the point of this book. It's about human rights, and for U.S. citizens, constitutional rights as well.

"Americans have had so many rights of expression, economic choice and privacy for so long that most have trouble envisioning their world without them," Klein rightly notes. "For people who enjoy a little porn once a week, it's hard to imagine our constitutional structure turning on such a seemingly trivial thing. The righteous anger of the Right, enthroned in federal and state government, clearly sees what the average porn consumer still doesn't: The profound connection between the personal and the political."

As the adult industry trade publication, *AVN* has long tried to make this exact point—but never has it done so as eloquently as has Dr. Marty Klein in this vitally important book.

I've taken the several articles I wrote about the 2006 Values Voter Summit and combined them into one for continuity and easier reading. One thing which may not be clear is the creepy feeling I had every minute I was in attendance at this event, seeing all the apparently normal attendees supporting ideas and actions that should make any real American blush—and grow angry. Also of interest: in 2006, the Supreme Court hadn't yet ruled that religious adoption agencies could legally discriminate against gay parents. For those who don't remember Hurricane Katrina, it did $125 billion in damage to New Orleans and its surroundings—and guess who paid most of that? If you guessed "government," you're smarter than most of these fools. Of course, this group's defamation of the alleged current crop of "activist judges" is a laugh, considering how many right-wing activists are on the courts now. Also, remember the days when Kellyanne Conway was just a "right-wing pollster"? Ah, memories! And don't forget to Google "spreading Santorum"!

THE "VALUES" ARE CLEAR AT THE 2006 VALUES VOTER SUMMIT

Report begins September 22, 2006

WASHINGTON, D.C. – Think of it as a sort of "Night of the Stars"[1] for the Religious Right—and this was just the first day of the 2006 Values Voter Summit, part of a series of meetings of religious conservatives that co-sponsor Family Research Council (FRC),[2] through its openly-political arm FRC Action, calls "The Washington Briefing."

The event was held at the Omni Shoreham Hotel, a stately older establishment that also hosted the Conservative Political Action Conference in February. The venue may have been selected because the Omni chain does not offer its guests any adult pay-per-view choices on the hotel cable system—no doubt a plus for summit supporter Citizens for Community Values, which co-sponsored an anti-adult-pay-per-view ad in *USA Today* in August, and which runs the CleanHotels.com website, devoted to—guess what!

All the big names were here: FRC head Tony Perkins; Rev. Jerry Falwell, who spoke at an exclusive "FRC Action Breakfast for Pastors"; Dr.

James Dobson,[3] founder of Focus on the Family (*and* FRC *and* the Alliance Defense Fund, whose current head Alan Sears, formerly of the Meese Commission, also spoke); Sen. George Allen (R.-Va.); Sen. Sam Brownback (R.-Kan.); Rep. Mike Pence (R.-Ind.); Rep. Marilyn Musgrave (R.-Colo.); Gov. Mitt Romney (Mass.); Gov. Mike Huckabee (Ark.); L. Brent Bozell III, founder of the Media Research Group and Parents Television Council (you know, the group that filed more than 98% of the FCC's indecency complaints over the past few years); Dr. Ted Baehr,[4] who runs the theocrat film rating magazine and website MovieGuide.com; plus several more "personalities" whose names would only be familiar to those who read a lot of religious right websites.

Also scheduled for later Friday evening were former FRC president Gary Bauer,[5] now head of Americans United to Preserve Marriage & American Values—an obvious attempt, like Pat Robertson's American Center for Law & Justice (ACLJ), to create a name similar enough to an existing *non*-theocrat organization (ACLU)—in this case, Americans United for Separation of Church & State—that some will be confused when doing a web search—and the lovely (some would say "anorexic") Ann Coulter,[6] who undoubtedly would be talking about the public reception of her latest book, *Godless*, which trashes just about anybody who's ever had a good thing to say about The Left, including a group of New Jersey widows who lost their husbands in the 9/11 attack. (This author couldn't bring himself to stay for *that* virtual bloodbath.)

Oh; and they were also bringing in Steve Bridges, the George Bush look-alike whose humor was well eclipsed at last spring's National Press Club dinner by Comedy Central's Stephen Colbert's "homage" to Bush. (Remember "Reality has a well-known liberal bias"?)

In truth, there was little talk here about pornography or the adult industry—but they did talk at length about the next best thing: Bringing religion back (some would say "farther") into government, which for the adult industry portends to be at least as bad.

The event got off to an early start; Falwell's breakfast was scheduled for 7:15, and attendees got to choose between that ticketed event and another pay-for-pray feast sponsored by Bauer's organization. Then, as the doors to the Shoreham's ballroom opened, the crowds were greeted by an invocation by Father Frank Pavone, national director of Priests For Life, which, surprisingly (or maybe not), is not an anti-Iraq War organization; a "presentation of colors" by the Armed Forces Color Guard; a recital of the Pledge of Allegiance (this version, of course, containing the "under God" reference which was added to the pledge in the early 1950s) and a rendition of the Star Spangled Banner.

Pence was the first speaker; introduced by Perkins as "a man, a conservative and a Republican, in that order." Pence made one of the day's few mentions of illegal immigration, which was being floated just a few months ago as the issue that would get conservatives out to the polls in November ... until somebody realized that it was those conservatives—the well-heeled ones, anyway—who were *employing* plenty of the "illegal aliens." Pence's plan, which grew out of his "commitment to justice," was to "do border security first," after which he and his 110 fellow House conservatives would "reject amnesty" but be in favor of a "guest worker program" that wouldn't lead to citizenship but would require the "guests" to learn English ... and would require a "partnership between business and government" that would include fines and penalties for hiring illegals.

Gov. Romney spoke next, and can you guess what his "Topic A" was?

Yep; "American society is built on the foundation of family life," he claimed, but the Massachusetts Supreme Court "struck a blow ... against that value." How? They ruled that the state can't discriminate against gays when it comes to marriage.

But the gay marriage issue isn't about adults getting married, according to Romney: "Marriage is primarily about the development and nurturing of children." And how can children be properly developed and nurtured when gays are insisting that birth certificates no longer read "mother" and "father" but "Parent A" and "Parent B"? And when parents aren't allowed to take their kids out of classrooms when the teacher reads books about, f'r'instance, two princes who decide to get married? And when religious adoption agencies can't place kids because the law won't allow them to discriminate against would-be gay parents?

"Liberals love democracy only so far as the outcome is guaranteed to be in their favor," he declared, claiming that the main plank in the Democrats' party platform was—you guessed it again!—same-sex marriage.

But who knew that gay marriage being legal in just one state actually affects child development and nurturing in *all* states? Call it the "virus theory" of same-sex marriage, and Romney's against it; he wants a federal law banning the practice ... and he's sure it will happen: "Great people come forward when there's great need," he assured.

Same-sex marriage was also the main focus of the panel that followed Romney's talk. That panel consisted of Dobson, Perkins and Sears, and several times broke down into a mutual admiration society—and what the hell was Perkins doing bringing up some story about Dobson going bear hunting?

Among the things the audience "learned" from these three were:

• When states put the same-sex marriage question on the ballot, an average of 71% of the people vote against the practice.

• In Alabama, an anti-same-sex ballot initiative got 79% of the vote—but according to them, nobody in the mainstream media reported that fact.

• According to Perkins, whose group has worked with pastors to create anti-same-sex marriage initiatives, "The other side is working aggressively to stop these initiatives," but in order to do so, they "must stop the churches."

• The ACLU relies on "fear and intimidation" to silence churches, and "uses every type of national disaster to advance their agenda" (something these folks, of course, would *never* do) (Ahem, 9/11, ahem, ahem...); however, Perkins promised, "No longer in America when a pastor stands up [to same-sex marriage] will that pastor stand alone."

• Realizing there might be some in the audience who didn't share their views—for instance, Barry Lynn,[7] head of (according to Perkins) "Americans United for the Division of the Country," had bought a membership to the summit—Perkins was careful to note, "This is not about endorsing candidates; this is about talking about concerns." (Ri-i-i-ight!) However, he recommended using the letter Lynn was sending to clergy, advising them of IRS restrictions on church politicking, to line bird cages.

• "Everything we say [here] is approved by lawyers," Dobson added, also noting that, "Barry Lynn makes his living off me."

It was definitely shaping up that the theocrat leadership would be attempting to use the same-sex marriage issue to bring "the flock" to the polls in '06 just as they had in '04—but in '04, the Iraq War was still fairly new and (to some) arguably winnable, the Republicans still had some credibility left, and Bush was still scoring over 40% in the polls.

The next panel was dedicated to—you guessed it (dang, you're good!)—same-sex marriage, this one featuring Prof. Robert George[8] of Princeton University; Rep. Musgrave,[9] and syndicated columnist Maggie Gallagher[10]—and the soundbites flowed like wine.

"We must avoid complacency," George declared, or else New Jersey, which has yet to pass a law to prevent official recognition of same-sex marriages performed in other states, "could become a Las Vegas" of gay marriage, because even with the confirmations of John Roberts and Samuel Alito, "The [U.S.] Supreme Court continues to be a threat to marriage."

"This issue that's in front of us today is very important," assured Musgrave. "If we have gay marriage, our religious liberties are gone... The future is grim unless we do what we need to: Elect people to positions of authority in the state and United States Congress to fight the good fight for our children and ourselves."

"The procreative dimension of human love" is threatened by gay marriage, intoned Gallagher, who also claimed that gay marriage was responsible for pretty much everything that's wrong with children in society today, from juvenile delinquency to promiscuity to poor grades in school.

Gallagher also attempted to distinguish the gay marriage rights movement from the black civil rights movement of the '60s, but noted that those who oppose gay marriage would likely suffer the same legal and societal penalties as had those who had discriminated against blacks. (Obviously, that analogy didn't work very well for her cause, but the audience hardly noticed.)

The morning's penultimate speaker was anti-porn crusader Sen. Sam Brownback, but he never got around to mentioning the subject he's held at least three Senate hearings on. Instead, he spent most of his time talking about "the dignity of personhood," which, for him, means "honor[ing] God in the public square and not throw[ing] him out"; opposing assisted suicide and embryonic stem cell research, which he claimed had produced no results(!!!) even though a quarter of a billion dollars had been spent on it already; and pushing a bill that would require that a fetus be anesthetized if it were over 20 weeks old and to be aborted, because fetuses at that age "have more pain receptors than adults."

Brownback was also not without his aphorisms: "*Roe v. Wade* is going to be overturned in the future," he assured, and "The best way to raise a child is with a man and a woman bound together for life."

Brownback, who said he was raised to be an auctioneer, was outdone, however, by the morning's final speaker, Gov. Mike Huckabee,[11] a former pastor—and it showed.

"The people's priorities haven't necessarily been Washington's priorities," Huckabee said, sounding the familiar conservative refrain that the common folk can handle most problems better than government—like, for instance, the aftermath of Hurricane Katrina: "When the government failed, the American people did not."

Huckabee is in favor of having more "people of faith" in politics, but they should be "people of compassion"—perhaps not the best choice of words, since Americans might still remember what became of one famous "compassionate conservative."

Huckabee sounded the familiar anti-same-sex marriage refrain, but with a bit more humor: "Until Moses comes down with two stone tablets from Brokeback Mountain, let's keep marriage what it is," he advised.

Noting that he is "pro-life," Huckabee snuck a bit of environmentalism past his audience, by suggesting that being pro-life not only means opposing abortion, but also being in favor of clean air and pure water.

However, Huckabee was the only speaker so far to mention porn—though in a sort of backdoor fashion. He had no truck with feminists, he said, but "if we could work with feminists to oppose pornography and child abuse and battery of women, we should do it."

☆☆☆

"Greetings from the President of the United States!"
That's how Bush press flack (formerly Fox News talking head) Tony Snow[12] began his segment Friday afternoon.

Gee; d'ya s'pose Tony would bring similar greetings if *AVN* asked him to speak at its Expo in January? Maybe not ...

But Snow wasn't the first speaker on the summit's afternoon agenda; that honor went to the three members of a panel, "Hollywood In The Heartland," which included Don Feder[13] (author of *A Jewish Conservative Looks At Pagan America*); Dr. Ted Baehr, publisher of the (Catholic) *Movie Guide*; and Rev. Tommy Tenney, whose movie *One Night With The King*—no, it's not porn; it's the biblical story of Esther who, according to the movie's publicist, "saves the Jewish nation from annihilation at the hands of its arch enemy while winning the heart of the fiercely handsome King Xerxes," which is scheduled to be released in mid-October.

Feder, who got to speak first because he had to be home before the start of Rosh Hashonah that evening, said he could sum up his talk in just a few words: "If you're a Christian, Hollywood hates you."

"When I say 'hate,' ladies and gentlemen," he continued, "I'm not talking about vague contempt or mild disdain. I mean Hollywood hates you, the way Hamas hates Jews, the way George Clooney hates George W. Bush."

Of course, some might see a difference between Hamas, the Palestinian terrorist organization that was elected to run Israel's West Bank and Gaza Strip, and George Clooney, the star of *Syriana* and *Good Night And Good Luck*—but not this crowd.

Feder went on to cite a couple of recent instances of alleged anti-Christian bias—Rosie O'Donnell comparing "radical Islamists" to "radical Christians"; the fact that the dictatorship in *V For Vendetta* is composed of "not Muslims... not Marxists, but Christians"—and claimed that "Christians are regularly portrayed as fanatical, hypocritical, stupid, cowardly, avaricious, lustful, sadistic and/or buffoonish in a long line of feature films." Of course, so are Jews, Muslims, rednecks, cops, anti-war protesters and at least a dozen other identifiable subgroups ... but Feder was on a roll.

"What's more interesting than *how* Hollywood hates Christians is *why* Hollywood hates Christians," he continued. "It hates you, views you as the enemy, because you stand in the way of the Hollywood Left achieving all of its cherished agenda."

So ... all Christians are right-wingers? Good to know! (Of course, some in *AVN*'s audience and elsewhere might dispute that ... but certainly no one at *this* convention!)

Yup; "Hollywood's religion—and it *is* a religion—is diametrically opposed to the Judeo-Christian ethic," Feder stated. "Hollywood's worldview contains the following doctrines: Sexual liberation; the glorification of premarital sex including adolescent experimentation; adultery; promiscuity; homosexuality; the sexualization of children—in other words, Hollywood wants all of us to live the way they live... Don't worry about tomorrow; your goal should be to maximize pleasure now."

See! There's not so much difference between Hollywood and the adult industry after all! Hell, any day now, they'll all be lining up to join the Free Speech Coalition!

Yup; any day now ...

Any ... day ... now ...

"The next tenet of Hollywood's religion: Radical secularism," Feder continued. "The belief that religious expression is dangerous and should be purged from our public lives; that the so-called mixing of politics and religion leads to a theocracy like Iran."

That'll be by 2012, some figure, though optimists who aren't as familiar with people like yourself, Don, have put it at 2016.

But every preacher needs a big finish, and Don had one:

"And finally, the normalization of homosexuality—the dogma that people are born homosexual or heterosexual and are absolutely unable to change; that all voluntary sexual activity is equally good, and that homosexual liaisons should be afforded the same recognition and respect as heterosexual marriage—and that to question this dogma is to condone violence against gays."

See? And you thought he'd never get around to the purpose of the summit: Fanning the fear of same-sex marriage to drive fundamentalists to the polls in November to elect Republicans.

Tenney then spoke briefly about his movie, which features Peter O'Toole, Omar Sharif and John Rhys-Davies in minor roles, showed a clip, and warned of Hollywood that, "Any battlefield we abandon, we lose by default."

No worries there; 20th Century Fox has inaugurated its FoxFaith division, which should do for feature films what Fox News has done for news programming. (Insert frowny face here.)

"Every week, more people go to church in the United States than go to movies," noted Dr. Ted Baehr. Trouble is, according to Baehr's own statistics, kids are spending more time with movies than with church, and as anyone here could tell you, that's a Bad Thing.

But there's hope:

"Hollywood loves money," Baehr revealed, "and they know where the money is, is in moral and Christian films, and moral films and Christian films do better throughout the world, not just in the United States. As a result of our statistical analysis, since 1991, there are many more moral films being made and there are many more Christian films... Hollywood is looking to survive, and is going through a freefall right now... Hollywood is just like the Soviet Union on the eve of collapse... Don't let them bamboozle you. Don't become a sheeple. Stand for the truth. You can make a difference and take every thought captive in Hollywood for Jesus Christ."

This, of course, was greeted with thunderous applause... but not quite as thunderous as when Tony Snow took the stage shortly afterwards.

"September 11, 2001, people in the United States who may not always have thought in terms of matters of faith or family, were reminded in one swift and horrible morning that evil exists in this world," Snow claimed. "One of the other things we learned about September 11, 2001 is that some of the evil people around the world have decided that Public Enemy #1 is the United States of America, in part because we are a nation bound by faith."

Hmmm... wasn't it Sam Harris who noted, in his book, *The End of Faith*, that most wars over the past several centuries have been caused by clashes of religious faith? Good to know that Snow's president is keeping up with tradition!

Snow also revealed that his president isn't someone who thinks much about the future.

"George W. Bush is not a man who's going to sit around thinking about his legacy," Snow assured. "He thinks about the job he has to do right now... He doesn't give a rip about polls."

Indeed!

Sen. George Allen also stopped by, repeating the homilies he's used for several weeks on his reelection campaign trail—he's for less taxation, for more healthcare and energy independence—and he assured the audience that, "Preserving our foundational values, ladies and gentlemen, is very important." He reserved the last part of his talk, however, for another bugaboo of religious conservatives: "Activist" judges.

"Where our values are under attack so often are from these unelected, appointed-for-life federal judges who ignore the values and the will of the people," he intoned.

Um, George? That's *why* they're unelected: So they won't be influenced by the whims of the electorate (aka Boobus Americanus) and can concentrate instead on upholding the law as given by the Constitution. It's called "checks and balances"; you may have heard of it.

But no; George has a problem with the Ninth Circuit upholding the lawsuit about taking "under God" out of the Pledge of Allegiance; with courts requiring the Boy Scouts not to discriminate against gays if they want to meet in public buildings; with judges striking down laws criminalizing late-term abortions; and with the Supreme Court's abridgement of the Fifth Amendment's "taking" clause.

"My friends, this is why we need more men and women on the Supreme Court of the United States like John Roberts and Sam Alito," he announced. "They're to apply the law, not invent the law, and we must have judges who stop legislating from the bench... I firmly believe that marriage should be between one man and one woman."

Cue the thunderous applause.

A "political pundits" panel followed, featuring Kellyanne Conway, a fairly well-known right-wing pollster, and Charlie Cook, editor and publisher of *The Cook Political Report*, and moderated by Terry Jeffrey, the editor-in-chief of *Human Events*, the country's best-known reactionary magazine.

Cook, the least ideological panelist, spent his minutes essentially explaining why the Democrats are likely to gain several congressional seats in the upcoming election—"It's a challenging environment for Republicans," as he put it, noting that the war in Iraq is "70% of the problem"—leaving it to Conway to attempt to soften the blow.

"For 2006, Charlie's absolute right: The numbers are unbelievably poor for the party in power; nobody should be able to spin that for you," Conway said. "Does that end up being fatal to the prospects of the Republicans holding onto majorities in both houses? Not necessarily... But the people do know that 'conservative' is a more palatable word than 'Republican,' but 'liberal' is a less palatable word than 'Democrat,' so you often see it [in the media] being 'Republican and Democrat' instead of 'conservative and liberal.'"

Next up were two attorney generals, one former, Mark Earley of Virginia, and one current, Phill Kline of Kansas. Earley was apparently chosen because his organization, Prison Fellowship, was sued by Americans United for Separation of Church and State for having used tax money for evangelism in prisons in Iowa (they're appealing their loss), but it was Kline who really delivered what the crowd wanted.

"America ... stands for the recognition of the value of human dignity," Kline preached. "It is found in our nation's founding document that we hold these truths—not cultural preferences; not the tides of the times or whatever the proclivities of a people are—these truths to be self-evident, that all men are created equal, endowed by their creator with certain inalienable [sic] rights. The divine promise of America is that our government, with all its power, will not just be there for the powerful, but it will answer the call of the most vulnerable and the most innocent, especially when their fundamental rights are at risk."

Of course, that doesn't include gays, but it apparently also doesn't include minors who have sex, since Kline is currently in court[14] trying to open kids' medical records on the basis that any minor female who can be shown to have had sex must have been raped.

"The ACLU is arguing that it violates the constitutional right of the privacy of a child for us to be able to obtain the medical evidence to take the child's rapist to court and prosecute them for child rape," he said. "As we stand here today, the ACLU is making the argument that a child has the inherent constitutional right to choose an adult sexual partner, and that state statutory rape laws are an unconstitutional violation of that child's privacy."

Um, Phill? You're from Kansas. Kids can legally marry at *15* in Kansas—and that only because the state found it couldn't prosecute a 14-year-old from Nebraska who'd skipped out of the family home to marry her 22-year-old boyfriend in Kansas, so the legislature decided it was time to set an actual "age of consent."

Of course, what he's actually after are the records of minors' abortions, as a pretext for shutting down women's clinics. Federal law, y'see, prohibits federal funds—in this case, $227 million—from being granted to institutions that fail to report child rape, and what better evidence is there of a minor's rape than a pregnancy?

In case anyone had any doubts that the Values Voter Summit was a religious event, the next speaker was Bishop Wellington Boone,[15] an Atlanta-based preacher with a major online presence. He's semi-famous for, among other things, having written an article titled, "The Rape of the Civil Rights Movement," subtitled, "How Sodomites Are Using Civil Rights Rhetoric To Advance Their Preference For Sexual Perversion."

"Gays have no right to redefine marriage or to pressure *politicians* to redefine it according to a definition that is contrary to God and His Word and the opposite of centuries of American jurisprudence," the article reads in part.

And Boone was in fine form here.

"I'm offended about the so-called gays, which you know is a misnomer, trying to get on the bandwagon of civil rights," he said. "You know that that should be an offense to every black person everywhere as though that that whole issue of gay so-called rights is the same issue as the civil rights that relates to black Americans... I'd hate to be in slavery for several hundred years and then having a war to be fought for the sake of the freedom, and then by 1877, going to an 1877 compromise, be thrown back into segregation, Jim Crow laws and a Voting Rights Act as late as 1965—now you tell me that a gay has a right to get in on some of that?! Get outta here!"

Boone also claimed to be quoting from several "founding documents," each of which had some religious test for holding office—and all of which would have been voided by the U.S. Constitution's prohibition of such tests once it was ratified.

The day's penultimate event was a panel titled, "What Feminist Majority? American Women And The Values Agenda"—a panel which, of course, would not have existed but for women protesting and asserting themselves in all walks of life over the past 30 or so years, just so the three females on this panel could tell them how worthless their struggle had been.

"People are always telling women what they should want, especially the media," claimed panelist Myrna Blyth, former editor-in-chief of *Ladies Home Journal*. "And what happened over the years? Instead of seeing choices for women as opportunity, we began to hear in the '80s and '90s and still today that instead of opportunity, women are victimized by their choices... The notion that women are victims, seeing the world victim-first, is a very liberal point of view, and the women in charge of media, the 'spin sisters'... know each other, they agree with each other, and they have the terrible presumption to assume that they reflect the ideas and values of the women of America. Media tends to act, like Diane Feinstein, that they speak for the women of America, and if you're a woman in this country, you have to be a Democrat or liberal."

Of course, the people who are actually telling women that they're victims are the Dr. Lauras of the world, who want women to quit their jobs, stay home, raise babies and shut up.

Following that same line of thought, Citizens for Community Values honcho Jennifer Jarrow, who's pumped out nine (9) children so far, wanted to "take a little snapshot of where we're at after this 30-plus years of empty advocacy from the feminist movement."

"First, let me talk about a story that my niece told me just this year," she began. "She goes to Miami University, and she was talking about a friend of hers, and of course, all of us know that a lot of kids nowadays, they sleep together; they have multiple partners, and this girl had broken up with her boyfriend, and because she was bored, she had a fraternity president hitting on her and calling her up late at night, 'Oh, come on over, you know.' She went over; she had a relationship with him every couple of nights for two weeks, late at night, and then got back with her boyfriend. And then he called one night when the boyfriend was there, and she said, 'You know, I forgot to tell you, I got back with my boyfriend.' He started to scream in the phone to her: 'Did you tell him we did this and we did that and we did this?' And as she's retelling the story to my niece, she stops and she says, 'And at the end, he said, "You're nothing but a cheap whore!"' And then she stopped and she said, 'Oh my gosh, I *am* a whore!' And the reality hit her, that all she has been doing is sleeping around with boys at college in-between having a boyfriend. *That* is what we can thank the feminist movement for: Telling our daughters that sex is a plaything outside of marriage."

Hate to break it to you, Jen, but one of the hard-earned lessons of feminism is that women can make many of the same choices about their sexuality that men can—and oddly, you don't brand either of the *guys* who fucked this woman as a "whore," even though they were just as promiscuous as she was; why is that?

Jarrow also doesn't like women in the military, co-ed dorms or sperm banks—and guess what: They're also "products of the feminist movement"! And don't get her started on gay adoption!

"We have news for Rosie O'Donnell: The ultimate child abuse is placing a child in a gay home, where they have not two parents but two selfish individuals who are in it for their own parenting experience," Jarrow claimed.

Yeah; "selfish" gays are just *lining up* to adopt unwanted kids or patronize sperm banks just so they can spend hundreds of thousands of dollars clothing, feeding and educating the little monsters because it's *so* much fun and/or to have a trophy to show off to their friends! Right!

"I'm representing the single female professional working woman who is also pro-marriage, pro-man and pro-family," began Jennifer Marshall, late of the Family Research Council. "The messages about casual sex have hurt women above all. Sixty-seven percent of young people who have engaged in sexual activity at a young age tell us they regret it, but the number is even higher among young women; it's 77% for young girls who engage in sexual activity early. The rate of depression is three times higher among young women who engage in early sexual activity. So this idea of safe sex really damages women emotionally and also physically, with all the STDs to which young women are prey."

Two-thirds of young people—male and female!—regret fucking??? Get serious! Is there anybody outside of this summit and its supporters who'd believe such horseshit?

Friday's final speaker was L. Brent Bozell III, head of Media Research Center, one of the main "news" sources for right-wing fundamentalists. They played the music from the NBC Nightly News as he walked in, and he had a few choice things to say about that network—none of them complimentary.

"Let's talk about Madonna," he began. "Some of you may know she's on tour again. She has what she calls her Confessions tour. In her Confessions tour, as some of you know, she begins the concert by appearing on the stage mounted on a cross with a crown of thorns, mimicking, mocking the crucifixion of Jesus Christ. It's a worldwide hit, what she's doing. Unfortunately, she's had $400 million worth of ticket sales worldwide. She began her concert, by the way, one half mile from the Vatican, on purpose. NBC—remembering the soundtrack—NBC thinks this is a wonderful idea, and so they've now announced that they're going to do a two-hour special next month with this concert on national television, on your public broadcast airwaves. Now, some people thought, well, maybe this is wrong, and we ought not to be doing something that insults 85% of the American public. Well, NBC executive Kevin Reilly responded; he said, 'Madonna felt that this part of the concert was the cornerstone of the show. We viewed it and we didn't see it as being inappropriate.' Now, in the wake of outpourings of outrage, led by the likes of the American Family Association, the Catholic League and others, NBC now suddenly is rethinking their position. Now they're saying, and this is just as of yesterday, that it is awaiting the delivery of the special, and 'Once we see it in its entirety, we can make a final decision.' Which begs the question, how long does it take to make a decision as to whether or not it is or isn't appropriate to mock Jesus Christ? But anyway, they've got to look at it. I do too."

A couple of points: The phrase "public broadcast airwaves" puts one in mind of the public broadcasting system, PBS. In fact, NBC is *advertiser* supported, and rest assured, if NBC's advertisers find the programming offensive, they won't buy ads during it and NBC will lose money. That's the *marketplace* in action; something these conservatives are usually in favor of. Secondly, I'll go out on a limb here and say that almost all TVs have a little gadget called an "on/off switch" and another little gadget called a "channel selector," and anybody who doesn't want to watch Madonna on her cross with her crown of thorns can employ either of those gadgets to avoid so watching.

Bozell—commentator Keith Olbermann aptly calls him "Bozo the Clown"—was also upset about NBC's purchase of the religiously-oriented *Veggie Tales* cartoon series for Saturday morning broadcast. What irks Bozell is that NBC, in some misguided attempt at ecumenism, ordered the Bible verses that begin and end each episode snipped, as well as all references to "God" and "the Bible," allegedly for time constraints, but in fact because it didn't want to offend viewers who weren't Christians.

Bozell had a few more gripes—the *New York Times*' reporting on the Pope's recent slur against Islam; the premier episode of NBC's *Studio 60 On The Sunset Strip*, which referred to an anti-Christian comedy skit—but to Bozell, those are only symptoms of the real problem.

"It's easy to say that this is secular moral relativism run amok," Bozell said, referring to the controversy about the Pope, "that this is a media that doesn't believe in transcendent truth; that for them, there are no absolutes; for them, there is no right, there is no wrong, there is no true good and there is no true evil. But I don't think that's altogether true, and it's simply—and I don't mean to suggest that it applies to everyone in the press. They do have a moral code, but it's a rather interesting moral code. They do believe that George Bush is evil. They do despise conservatives. They do have a disdain for Christianity. On the NBC series *Studio 60 On The Sunset Strip*, Christianity a couple of weeks ago was defined as 'a psycho-religious cult,' and they have a special disdain for conservative

Christians. And then there are, in my case, there are Catholics, and boy are we in their gunsights. But what do we Christians believe? We believe there are truths. We believe there are absolutes. We believe there's right. We believe there's wrong. We believe there's good and we believe there's evil, and therefore, if we do that, we must understand that if we ever want to regain the popular culture, if we want to restore a sense of moral clarity in this troubled world that is in front of us, we have to confront the press. We have to document, we have to expose, we have to confront and we have to control it... I don't understand why some of my conservative brethren have such a hard time understanding this and have such a hard time standing up for simple beliefs and simple truths, because if we can't stand for those beliefs, if we can't take a stand and say to a network, and say to a reporter, 'You will not insult my religion any longer; you will not insult my God any longer,' why do we bother with anything else? What else is important? Tax cuts aren't important; spending isn't important if we can't defend God."

As expected, that got a big round of applause from the audience—you know, from the same people that you'll find picketing your video store or dance club next weekend.

And to a large extent, that's what this "summit" was all about: "Defending God" by controlling *you*—and they intend to use the government to do it.

Pretty good first day, eh?

And then Saturday rolled around, and before entering the Omni Shoreham's ballroom for the beginning of the second day of the summit, I decided to check out what was actually in the "goodies bag" I'd been given at registration, as well as a few items I'd picked up in the course of Day 1.

Besides the convention booklet itself, one of the most useful inserts would undoubtedly be the "Contact Information for Senate and House Congressional Members" booklet, beautifully done up in red, white, blue and gold, with Republicans in plain type, Democrats in italics, and "Members who have died or resigned" in bold brackets.

Young Americas Foundation (formerly Young Americans for Freedom, the seminal Republican college campus crusade) was giving out copies of its magazine *Libertas*, this issue featuring on the cover an article titled "Teachers' Pets"—and can you believe it? Of the eight people pictured, every single one is a Democrat!

Particularly interesting was the "Memorandum" from Grover Norquist's Americans For Tax Reform, which, oddly enough, had little to do with what most people think of as "tax reform." Instead, it was all about the "IRS 'crack-down' on religious speech," including a "Letter in Support of the House of Worship Free Speech Restoration Act"; "HR 235, House of Worship Free Speech Restoration Act of 2005"[16]; "Articles on the IRS attacks on houses of worship"; "Memo from our lawyer detailing lobbying and political activity houses of worship can legally engage in"; and "A report from the Congressional Research Service for Congress on acceptable political activity for tax-exempt organizations." In other words, the "reform" these folks were interested in was rewriting the tax laws to allow churches to support political candidates and issues, and by maintaining the churches' tax-exempt status, still have the taxpayers pay for it!

And then there were the brochures: "The Truth About Same-Sex 'Marriage'"; "Unique New Textbook For Academic Study Of The Bible In Public High Schools"; "Why You Should Be Involved," from Family Research Council (FRC), subtitled, "A Biblical Case for Social and Political Involvement": a strange one titled, "The Future of Tax Exemption and Homosexual Behavior"; and one on why James Dobson's "Focus on the Family" quasi-political organization was tax-exempt, but James Dobson's "Focus on the Family Action" spin-off fully-political organization wasn't.

Finally, there were a couple of large postcards: One advertising a book, "God's Grace and the Homosexual Next Door" ("*Where? Where?*" as John Cleese might say); and one that rather boldly asked, "How Would Jesus Vote?", advertising an Oct. 5 debate featuring, from the left, Sen. Barack Obama and Rev. Jim Wallis, and from the right, radio talker Janet Parshall and Rev. Richard Cizik.

Saturday's lead-off speaker was, according to Dobson, "one of the most effective and articulate people in the country, a man I respect very highly—I mean, this guy is getting it done... This is a great American,"

Almost needless to say, that was Fox News talk show host for the past 11 years, Sean Hannity.

"Actually, Alan [Colmes, Hannity's pseudo-liberal on-air partner] wanted to be here tonight," Hannity joked, "but he had to race off to Massachusetts ... where he belongs ... hanging out with Ted (hic) Kennedy. Don't worry; Alan is driving."

Hannity was referring, of course, to Kennedy's 1969 car accident in which his companion, Mary Jo Kopechne, was killed, and as they say, an elephant never forgets ... unless it's whether or not he's taken a bribe from a lobbyist.

Hannity's 45-minute speech mixed humor, often in the form of Clinton jokes, with right-wing rhetoric, including a "phenomenon" he described as "Bush derangement syndrome."

"It doesn't matter, whatever you talk about, there is this instinctive, reflexive—it's almost like conditioning, that if you talk about George W. Bush, this vitriol, this hatred starts coming out from liberals," he explained. "And they have this compulsion, if you mention George W. Bush, you can take a stopwatch and you can start counting and find out how long it's going to be before they say, 'Liar!'"

Must be a genetic variant on the vastly more common "Clinton derangement syndrome," where if there's anything wrong with the U.S. today—the economy, the "war on terror," 9/11, whatever—reactionaries will find some way to blame it on Clinton.

At one point, after reading a series of anti-war statements from Democrats, Hannity reflected, "Now, you decide; put it in the context of where we are. We're in the middle of World War III. We've had the worst attack in American history. I don't care what Hugo Chavez says. I don't care what Ahmadinejad said. We know they're our enemy. When Nancy Pelosi, who also said that our president is mentally unstable, and Harry Reid calls our president a loser in front of school children, the depth and the magnitude and the depravity of this type of rhetoric, at a time when America ought to be united, ought to be unacceptable to the American people."

In other words, you Democrats and other would-be free speakers, just shut up and follow orders!

Needless to say, Hannity got rousing applause for that one!

"These are people that use religion to justify their madness, their brain-dead hypnosis, their lobotomized mindset," Hannity said, describing Islamists. "In their sickness, they actually believe and think in their hearts that they are doing the right thing. Their numbers are far more numerous that we ever thought in the beginning, and we have got to confront this evil, and it ought to be the one thing that unites good people all around the world."

To an outsider, however, it could just as easily seem as if Hannity were talking about the fundamentalists in this very audience!

But Hannity did let slip some good news: "In the meantime, while all of this is going on, 40 House members have joined with John Conyers to sponsor Resolution 635, to create a select committee to investigate the grounds for impeaching George W. Bush. It reads, 'Creating a select committee to investigate the administration's intent to go to war before congressional authorization, manipulation of pre-war intelligence, encouraging torture, retaliating against critics, and to make recommendations regarding possible grounds for impeachment.'"

Hannity then offered this bit of hypocritical thinking: "I want you to think deeply about this, because this is where the insanity began, and where the Democratic Party lost its soul. Bill Clinton said under oath the following; think deeply about this, and you must: 'We were alone, but I never really thought we were alone.' You'd tune into Hannity & Colmes that night, and we'd be debating that idiotic statement. There'd be some liberal there—doesn't matter which one; they're all the same at this point; they'll defend anything. They would start explaining to us the concept that nobody is ever really alone, and they would take Bill's cue, because Bill would explain it to them and give them the talking points."

And of course, this crowd ate that up. Never mind that shortly after Bush ordered the invasion of Iraq, the alleged "weapons of mass destruction" that were the impetus for the invasion and were supposed to be all over the place there suddenly became "weapons of mass destruction *programs*." Never mind that Bush claimed there was "overwhelming evidence" of a connection between Saddam Hussein and Al Qaeda when just the opposite was true. Never mind that Bush claimed that Iraq had an ongoing nuclear weapons program and was seeking to buy enriched uranium, when it had no such program and no such intention. Hypocrisy only counts if you're a Democrat.

Hannity ended his talk with his "six principles," which came out sounding more like a dozen. They included such right-wing talking points as supporting the PATRIOT Act, "spreading liberty," Reaganomics, securing the borders, more tax cuts, energy independence, opposition to "activist judges" and the "liberal court system"—he wants judges who are "originalists"—and supporting "traditional values."

"The stakes can't be higher," said Hannity. "The differences can't be more clear."

No shit!

But if Hannity came off as a sort of more charismatic, better-spoken George Bush, the next speaker, former drug czar William Bennett, seemed to be channeling a slightly less testy Dick Cheney.

"I want to talk about the culture, the talk underneath the politics; the way we think, the way we respond," Bennett began. "Melanie Phillips, in her book *Londonistan*, talks about 'preemptive cultural surrender,' the feeble state, discourse about the current world war in which we are involved. I think she is right... It has not been a great couple of weeks. We issued a travel visa to the former president of Iran so he could spread his deceptions throughout churches and colleges in our nation, including the National Cathedral. At the United Nations, we were treated to a speech by the current president of Iran where he called us occupiers, aggressors and violators of international law on primetime television. He called us all of those things: Occupiers, aggressors and violators of international law. The next day, we were treated to Hugo Chavez calling our president the Devil as he crossed himself, saying we were exploiters, pillagers. He called us real fascists and genocidal; this, in our own country. Our official response was not to respond. That was a mistake. This is a far different day than the day I served with Jeane Kirkpatrick in the Ronald Reagan administration. I remember her standing up and saying it was a new day at the U.N.; 'We will not stand for it. We will not take it anymore. Every calumny will be addressed and responded to.'"

Apparently, Bennett is unfamiliar with the wisdom every child knows: "Sticks and stones may break my bones but names will never hurt me." And in case anyone missed it, we *were* "occupiers, aggressors and violators of international law."

"There is too much tentativeness among us now. We are too tentative about things that matter the most," he continued. "Right now, when an administrative official or member of Congress is asked when we will leave Iraq, they shunt the question to the generals: 'When the generals say we can.' Wrong answer, wrong posture, wrong response. 'We will leave when the job is done.'... We will teach the enemy a lesson, that American life is not cheap and that barbarism will be extremely expensive."

In other words, we will never leave. Thanks for the tip, Bill!

And for those who have always bought Bush's lie about the "connection" between Iraq and the September 11 attack, Bennett had this to offer:

"When a reporter asks what Iraq had to do with 9/11, stop saying, 'Nothing'," Bennett advised. "9/11 was the beginning of our war against terrorism, and Saddam Hussein's Iraq was a terrorist-sponsoring state. Saddam Hussein was a terrorist; don't apologize for saying it. Abu Abbas, Abu Zarqawi, Abu Nidal were in Iraq; they were in Iraq long before 9/11. They were not in Iraq preaching Quakerism. Invitations to Bin Ladin were not for high tea, and there were many such invitations."

Guess it was just Bill's bad luck that the day after the summit ended, the news broke that last April's National Intelligence Estimate expressed the opinion of America's intelligence community that there was little to no "terrorist-sponsoring" going on in Iraq before the U.S. invaded, but that there's plenty of it now. And another recent item noted that in fact Hussein and Bin Ladin hated each other; high tea together would have been the last thing on their minds.

Here are a few more Bennett soundbites that garnered massive applause from this crowd:

• "When the former president of Iran, the current president of Iran, or the president of Venezuela seek a visa to come to the U.S. to speak, to spread propaganda and poison at the U.N. or in our churches or universities, *you deny them the visa.*"

• "I understand we have 100 members of the press here. Glad to see them. When reporters here at home print leaked classified wartime intelligence, *they should be prosecuted.*"

• Regarding the CIA interrogations: "I will say that if the choice is between water-boarding and picking up the bodies of 3,000 people, I will be for water-boarding."

• "Put real strictures on the U.N., and act like we own it, which is what we do in terms of the amount of money that we put forward. Ronald Reagan [said], 'I paid for this microphone,' and you're not going to soil it by calling the president of the United States a devil."

Next on the agenda was Georgette Forney, who, the announcer said, "had an abortion at age 16, and 19 years later, she experienced healing, forgiveness and reconciliation [but] through her healing and restoration experience, she developed a greater understanding of the negative impact that abortion has on women and on society" ... so of course, now she organizes women who regret their own abortions into the "Silent No More Awareness Campaign," which is "a national effort to raise awareness about the physical, the spiritual and the emotional harm that abortion does to women." However, about the only thing worthwhile in Forney's talk was the (predictive) statistic that "43% of women under the age of 45 will have had an abortion" ... and possibly the fact that Jennifer O'Neill, whom a certain number of readers will remember was the sexy female lead in the classic film *The Summer of '42*, is this group's celebrity spokeswoman.

Embattled Sen. Rick Santorum (R.-Pa.) was supposed to be the next speaker, but "family matters" kept him away from the conference, so he sent in a videotape which was long on rhetoric but notably short on content.

That, however, didn't stop the next speaker, Paul Weyrich, co-founder of the neo-con Heritage Foundation and more recently CEO of the Free Congress Foundation, as well as publisher of the *Conservative Digest*, from jumping [sic] on the Santorum bandwagon. (Weyrich is legless and confined to a wheelchair.)

"Rick Santorum is the most important United States Senator we have in this country at this time," Weyrich said, later describing him as "extraordinary," "fearless" and "one of the most decent people we've ever had in the United States Senate." Now *that's* "spreading Santorum"!

Weyrich has great hopes that the current makeup of the U.S. Supreme Court will lead to an overturn of women's abortion rights. To that end, he sees a win on the November referendum on South Dakota's complete abortion ban as "the beginning of the end for *Roe v. Wade*." (UPDATE: It wasn't.)

And as for the anti-same-sex marriage amendments that are on the ballot in eight states in November, "I predict that every single one of these is going to pass, and pass by a large margin."

"We are on the move, and we're on the move in the right direction," Weyrich stated. "The other side, of course, makes it sound as if they have all the troops and they have the media, they have this and they have that—well, we have something that we didn't have when we began these battles back in the early 1970s, and that is talk radio. Let me tell you, if the Democrats win control of Congress, they intend to reinstate the Fairness Doctrine, which would do away with talk radio... A Rush Limbaugh or a Sean Hannity or a Dr. Laura or any of the people that have an enormous following in this country will be shut down if that is the case."

Yeah; what a shame it would be if citizens had the power to force an accounting of the lies and slanders delivered on a minute-by-minute basis by the 1100-plus right-wing talk show hosts on the public airwaves around the country!

Even worse, Weyrich claimed, "[O]ur enemies want to regulate the Internet and want to block organizations such as ours."

"The Internet is a God-send," he said. "I know there are a lot of terrible things on the Internet, but it still can be used for God's purposes... So we've got to fight to keep the Internet from being regulated the way that these people want to regulate it. I have no objection to regulating the pornography and the filth that's on the Internet, but that's not what they want to do. They want to leave that alone. They want to regulate our kind of material that goes out instantly to people, telling them what's going on and what to do."

Next up was the morning's only panel, "The Role Of Churches In Political Issues," and its star was Dr. Richard Land,[17] a major player in the ultra-conservative Southern Baptist Convention. Also on the panel were Rev. Dr. John Guest, a pastor in Sewickley, Pa., and Rev. Herb Lusk, described as "an advisor to President George W. Bush," but *AVN* readers may remember him as the host of FRC's last judge-bashing "Justice Sunday III."

Land got to speak first, since he had to leave early for his regular radio show ... but he let the audience know that he has a hotline to God.

"It is our job as pastors and as church workers to take the truth of God's word and apply it to the moral and social issues of our society, and to call our society to adhere to the biblical standards," Land declared. "Let me be clear here: God is not a Republican. God is not a Democrat. God is pro-life. God has a side when it comes to pro-life: He's on it. He's pro-life; he's pro-heterosexual marriage; he's anti-pornography. I have no doubt about that whatsoever. All I have to do is look at the clear teachings of God's word."

And that, of course, is the problem: Land "knows" what God wants, and anybody who thinks different will feel God's wrath ... and if God itself doesn't see fit to visit that wrath on "sinners" (like adult industry members), well golly gee, Land and his minions will be only too happy to visit that wrath on them for God and in its name.

And that's perhaps the biggest problem with the coming theocracy that all the participants at this summit, whether they're conscious of it or not, are promoting.

The panel's moderator, Dr. Kenyn Cureton, asked Land why, according to the IRS, "churches are not completely free to do as they please when it comes to political issues."

Needless to say, it was a Democrat's fault.

"Lyndon Johnson was very upset at the preachers who were criticizing him in his 1954 election campaign for the senate in Texas," Land explained, "so in the dead of night, he passed [sic] some extra language into an authorization bill that put particular restrictions on churches, and according to those regulations, churches cannot endorse candidates."

"Now, let me be very clear here," he continued. "I do not believe that churches should be endorsing candidates; I believe we should be looking for candidates who endorse us, endorse our values and endorse our beliefs. I don't think we should align ourselves with any particular party. We should be looking for party platforms that align themselves with us. But I also think that this should be a decision that is made by churches and made by ministers, not made by the government, and so I think the IRS regulations need to be changed. I believe they're an unwarranted intrusion of the government into the free exercise of our faiths."

Well, tell ya what, Dick; there's a real easy way to keep the government, and in particular the IRS, from "intruding into the free exercise of [your] faith": GIVE UP YOUR CHURCH'S TAX EXEMPT STATUS! Then you can talk all you want about candidates, legislation, whatever your little heart desires—you just can't do it on the taxpayers' dime!

Because what we've seen happening around the country is that some clergy—not *you*, of course, Dick—are doing their level best to figure out ways to endorse Republican candidates and all manner of unconstitutional legislation, while still milking the public tit to pay for it—and the clear indication is that if the IRS backs down from enforcing the provisions of Sec. 501(c)(3), the clergy will do even more of it.

But prompted by Cureton, Land seemed to be offering a way around the IRS's restrictions on clergy.

"A pastor has the freedom, and I believe the obligation, to speak prophetically to his congregation on the issues of the day. As the abolitionists preached prophetically about the sin of slavery, as preachers preached and often sometimes lost their pulpits for preaching biblical truth about the sin of racial segregation, we have just as much of an obligation to preach about what the Bible says about unborn life. There's a reason why the Jewish civilization was the only civilization in the Mediterranean basin that didn't practice infanticide and abortion. The reason was because their God, who is the one true God, had made it very clear that life begins at conception, that God's involved when conception takes place, and that abortion is the taking of a human life and it is not to be done except to save the mother's life."

Just a couple of problems with that: 1) The Southern Baptist Convention, of which Land is a high-profile member, was preaching the sanctity of slavery well into the 20th century; 2) Jews in biblical times *were* practicing abortion, using certain well-known herbs to induce miscarriages; and 3) although various religious leaders have taken various positions on abortion through the centuries, it was generally agreed until recently that an abortion up to the 18th week of a pregnancy was just fine with the church.

Land also had advice for pastors who receive a letter from Rev. Barry Lynn of Americans United (the good one) regarding the limitations of politicking by clergy: "I would ignore it, and if you have questions, I would go to a more objective intrinsic source such as Family Research Council or Focus on the Family or the Ethics and Liberty Commission if you want real advice on what you can and can't do, and not from someone who's doing their best to make sure you don't do anything."

After Land took off for his radio gig, Rev. Guest—a Brit by birth—launched into a comparison between anti-war protesters and Bush critics in America and his own country's appeasers of Hitler before WWII.

"I am scared for a country that will not—speaking of an America which I have become one of, and one of you—I have actually said from my pulpit that it is treacherous and traitorous to be condemning, destroying, belittling and bringing down our president in time of war," Guest said. "All you're doing is setting stage for the kind of misery we saw in England and in Europe at that time [WWII]."

Right; the U.S., with its massive atomic arsenal, should be worried about a disorganized bunch of Muslims 6,000 miles away in Iraq who can't even decide which sect should be in power in their own country—or Iran, a few miles farther away, that's at least a decade away from its own atomic bomb.

But with Land gone, Rev. Lusk, whom the religious would undoubtedly consider a fairly charismatic guy, became the star of this panel—and once he got on a roll, there was no stopping him.

Here's a taste of Lusk's "sermon," which was punctuated by applause at just about every turn of phrase:

"Nehemiah asked a civics question," Lusk began. "He was in the palace—and boy, I've been to some of our churches, and some of us pastors, we're in the palace—and said, 'How are things back home?' They told him that the walls were down, the cities were in disarray, and that the remnant was there and struggling in depression and all kinds of upheaval. And Nehemiah began to weep. He visualized the fact that the walls were down, that-that-that-that-that the city was in disarray. But I'm going to ask you a question: How are things back home? And your answer's going to be the same as brother Nehemiah: The walls are down; the cities are in disarray—and you can't hide it, you can't put your head in the sand; you got to see and visualize exactly what took place. Visualize it. And I think he visualized what took place; he agonized; he began to pray. And he began to cry, he began to weep, and one of the problems that we have today is that we have a dry-eye church; churches don't weep ... And after he visualized, after he agonized, then he organized, and that's what Tony [Perkins, FRC head] is doing right now! That's what Dr. Dobson is doing right now! That's what Dr. Land is doing right now! That's what my friends in the Modesto Bishopric are doing right now! We're organizing! But now, before you do anything else you organize, you've got to get permission. You've got to go to the Team of Teams! You see, the worst thing you could do is to know the right thing to do and get ahead of Him who *is* the right! Him who *is* the protection! And we have to ask for protection! And my friends, we need protection, because the enemy is out there, and we've been calling the guy's name, but I don't want to call his name: Barry—I won't call his last name, because the more you call your enemy's name, the larger he becomes, and for our preaching in this particular place, that we do not call his name no more today!"

That "enemy," of course, was Rev. Barry Lynn of Americans United for the Separation of Church and State; supposedly a "man of God" in his own right—but in this place, at this time, it was not enough to be a man of God; you also had to be a man of Bush.

Lusk went on for several more minutes, much of it barely intelligible over the applause, "Amens" and "Hallelujahs," which Cureton summed up by saying, "Folks, just imagine—just imagine what Bible-believing Christians could do, what kind of impact we could have on the moral health of our country, on the direction of our nation and the character of our leadership, if we would simply live our values and vote our values."

And if people in the adult industry, and others who believe in the U.S. Constitution, don't watch out, they may very well find out what happens when fundamentalists like these "vote [their] values"—and rest assured, we won't like it.

Colin Hanna, described as "a County Commissioner" and "the lead defendant in a lawsuit against the county by the ACLU, demanding that the county remove a bronze plaque containing the full text of Ten Commandments which had stood on the outside walls of this historic Chester County courthouse for more than 80 years," spoke next, mostly on the topic of the "Christian perspective on immigration."

Turns out his "Christian perspective" is mostly summed up in the name of his website, WeNeedAFence.com, "which gives you an idea where we come from," Hanna admitted.

Liberals, you see, "falsely equate amnesty with forgiveness," Hanna explained. "Now, a biblically literate Christian knows that forgiveness is preceded by confession. 1 John 1:9 lays it out quite simply: If we confess our sins, He is faithful and just and will forgive us our sins. Now, that's *Christian* forgiveness, and it's quite different from amnesty. Amnesty is forgiveness without confession, or to put it another way, amnesty is sin without consequence. Therefore I would argue, amnesty is not Christian."

Indeed; because we all know that every sin has a consequence—and if God itself doesn't see fit to deliver one, God's followers will do their level best to pinch-hit for The Almighty ... and screw illegal immigrants (and us) to the wall.

Hanna cut his talk a bit short since Hannity had run so long, and because nobody wanted to miss another of the morning's highlights: Rev. Donald Wildmon, founder of the American Family Association (AFA), a major pro-censorship group.

But Don wasn't here to speak about porn; bashing porn won't get out the vote this November.

No, the Rev. was here to recount his longstanding fight against ... the Ford Motor Company.

"About two years ago, a TV program called *Will & Grace* had two lesbians kissing each other," Wildmon recalled. "And I asked our special projects director, I said, 'Randy, find out who sponsors that program.' And he came back, and he said, 'Ford.' 'Ford?' 'Ford.' I said, 'All right; I'll tell you what to do: Look and see what you find about Ford.'"

To make a *very* long story short, he found that Ford was gay-friendly.

"I couldn't believe it. I really couldn't," exclaimed the astonished bigot. "They were into everything, nearly everything that the homosexuals were doing. They were helping fund, they were giving them automobiles[!], they were giving them preferred positions—I mean, the whole bit!"

Needless to say, Wildmon couldn't let *that* go on!

"So we put all the materials together ... and we asked for a boycott," Wildmon said. "And the mailing went out and Ford began to get some e-mails and some calls, and I began to get some e-mails and calls, and I got a fax from a dealer in the Dallas, Texas area, and the fax said in essence—it wasn't a hateful fax, it wasn't a mean fax, it wasn't cursing me out; it was a fax that said, 'Please don't do this. I'm a dealer. I have 750 people who work with me, and your boycott will put me out of business. Please don't do this.'"

Well, Wildmon ruminated over that fax, and then suggested that he and the dealers get together and talk—a conversation that led to several meetings with Ford executives.

"They were two gentlemen who understood us, who are part of us, who believe like we believe, who work for Ford, have very high positions in Ford," Wildmon recounted. "And we worked out an agreement ... In essence, what we asked Ford to do was to remain neutral in the homosexual cultural, homosexual marriage wars."

Ah; but Wildmon didn't get it in writing!

"Well, they went back," Wildmon continued. "Within a week, the homosexuals had a meeting with Ford, and Ford threw out the window every agreement that we had reached because of pressure from the homosexual groups... When they did that, they left us with two choices. We could forget having a boycott and have not one ounce of integrity left in our organization, or we could go forward and boycott."

Guess which one they chose?

"I hesitated for three weeks about boycotting Ford. It's the toughest decision I've had to make regarding boycotts in 30 years. Here's the situation: If we boycott, we're gonna hurt some people, and that's not funny. But if we don't boycott—I mean, 40 Christian leaders, every one of them you would know, wrote Ford a letter, said, 'Please, would you just remain neutral in the cultural wars?' And in essence, Ford wrote back and said, 'Sorry, take a flying leap.'"

If only!

"If we had the boycott, we're gonna hurt some people, and that's no fun," Wildmon repeated. "But if we *don't* boycott, we have no integrity left, *and* we're going to hurt more people in the long run."

Wildmon never specified just what integrity his group had in the first place, or which "more people" those were, but the audience seemed to know already.

"You would be utterly surprised how strong the homosexuals are in corporate America," Wildmon charged. "They run, as far as culture; they run a number of these companies. They have free play. They get their way."

That may come as a surprise to some of *GayVN*'s readers; bet they didn't know how much power they really have—which, with an additional $2.95, will get them a latte at Starbucks...

Anyway, to make a long story short, sure enough, AFA launched its boycott ... and there's a good chance that Ford has lost upwards of a dozen sales because of it. Undoubtedly, the summit attendees went to lunch with the warm feeling of having done The Lord's work.

That happy feeling engendered by knowing that no true conservative, thanks to Rev. Don Wildmon's boycott, would ever again buy a car from Ford didn't last for those who went outside the hotel to eat. Just at the edge of the Shoreham's parking lot was a group of about 10 anti-bigotry protesters carrying placards bearing slogans like, "Gays Are People Too." Too bad the summit's attendees didn't have the eyes to see them.

Worse, when the attendees returned from lunch, there was another protest group to greet them—this one apparently from Americans United—bearing signs that read, "America: It's Not Just For Fundamentalists Anymore" and "Focus On Your OWN Family!"

<*sigh*> It's getting tougher to be a bigot in America these days ... (UPDATE: No, it isn't.)

The summit moved into high gear after lunch, leading off with a talk from Sen. James Inhofe,[18] a third-term senator who's also served a couple of terms in the House—and in both places, he's been in charge of the weekly prayer breakfasts—and in-between those duties, he's been using his government office to proselytize the "political philosophy of Jesus Christ" in Africa. Must be why they love us so much over there...

In a sense, Inhofe was one of the most honest politicians to speak at the summit. He said he supports "core conservative values," which, when you look at them, he explained, "you'll find these things are all scriptural.'

"I could name about 10 of them—you can talk about flag burning, you can talk about 'one nation under God,' you can talk about homosexuals, you can talk about abortion—but I will only use two just as an example, and they are the abortion and homosexuality," Inhofe stated. "When we talk about 'litmus test,' to me a litmus test is something that's scriptural. If it's scriptural, it's a litmus test, and it should be. So I'm going to give you the scriptures ... so when you go out among other people that *don't* believe, you'll be able to carry something with you."

Well, aside from Inhofe's little mistake about what a "litmus test" is—it's a *scientific* (not scriptural) test of the acidity or alkalinity of a substance—what he made unquestionably clear is that he bases all of his legislative decisions on the Bible—and as an American living under the Constitution, if that doesn't scare the bejesus (hee-hee) out of you, I don't know what will.

And religion has been very good to Inhofe. Take, for instance, the little yellow cards they used to give out in church, that gave the legislative and philosophical views of candidates for office—selected views, that is, on issues that were important to the church, like abortion and homosexuality.

"Quite frankly, when I left the House to come to the Senate in 1994, I probably would not have been elected if it hadn't been for them [yellow cards]," Inhofe said. "Right now, that [church voter guides] is under attack, as you probably know."

But, warned Inhofe, the liberals have been searching for years for an issue that they could bring before the public that would distract people from important things like abortion and homosexuality—and they've found one!

"They chose an issue—and this is ingenious ... and a lot of you are going to be real mad at me," he prefaced, "because 70% of you out there believe that global warming is a reality."

"We were just about to sign the Kyoto Treaty when I became chairman of the committee, Environment and Public Works," Inhofe continued. "Now, in this committee, we have jurisdiction over all these areas, so I thought, 'We need to find out what the truth is about global warming.'"

Of course, that "truth" turned out to be that global warming doesn't really exist—and if it does, it'd cost too much to fix.

Curse those liberals! Don't they realize that the possible extinction of all life on earth pales in comparison to such weighty issues as whether gays can marry or women can maintain control over their own bodies?!?

And in case you couldn't guess, Inhofe doesn't think too highly of animal rights activists—see Romans 1:23-25—or the U.N., either.

Next up was former Judge Charles Pickering,[19] the Mississippi-based U.S. District Court judge who'd been nominated by President Bush for an appeals court position in 2002, and after failing confirmation for two years, Bush eventually placed him on the Fifth Circuit through a recess appointment in January of '04. However, since recess appointments must be confirmed by the Senate before the end of the next congressional term, and Pickering's wasn't, he resigned his position in December of that year.

In a sense, Pickering picked up where Inhofe left off.

"Today in America, we're engaged in another of those great debates; it's called the culture war," Pickering said. "The issue that drives that debate is abortion in its most extreme forms—partial-birth abortion, abortion without parental or spousal consent or even notification—in other words, abortion on demand. But that's not the only issue. Another issue—in fact, a separate issue—is whether reference to God will be banned from the public square, the public arena, the public buildings, institutions and ceremonies, and even in the Pledge of Allegiance; pornography in its most extreme forms—hardcore pornography, even child pornography—and the definition of marriage; these are the issues that are involved, and I compare them in this debate to these other great debates, because as Bill Bennett said this morning, the result of this debate will determine the character of our nation. It will determine the kind of America in which your children and grandchildren and my children and grandchildren will live."

Actually, Pickering thinks it's *judges* that will determine the result of the debate—and sure enough, he thinks not enough of them hew to what he considers to be the original meaning of the Constitution.

"The judiciary was never intended to be a political branch of government," Pickering stated. "It is ill-equipped to make political decisions. It has no process to receive public influence. It has no way of forging a consensus while making compromises. It is extremely bad policy for the judiciary to be become a political branch of government."

Um ... maybe you don't know it, Chuck, but making the judiciary political is exactly what the people at this conference want to do, by having the Senate confirm judges (like yourself) that reflect the rampant prejudices of religious reactionaries in defiance of several of the rights granted by the very Constitution they'll swear to uphold and then ignore when it suits them.

On second thought, maybe he does know it:

"In the 1970s, in the midst of the state Senate, I supported a proposed constitutional amendment to reverse *Roe v. Wade*," Pickering admitted in discussing the course of his appeals court non-confirmation. "And in 1983, as president of Mississippi Baptists, I made that statement that they found so disturbing, 'The Bible is the absolute authority by which we should judge all of life's activities.'"

That, of course, got a big round of applause from an audience which probably will never understand the concept that in America, all of life's *legal* activities are supposed to be judged by the *Constitution*.

Nonetheless, Pickering declared, "We're fortunate that our Founders gave us a carefully crafted system of checks and balances, so no branch of government can become too strong, but that carefully crafted system of check and balances and separation of powers has been violated in recent years. To correct the process, we need to pass a constitutional amendment that says, in the future, the only way to change, alter or modify or to add to the Constitution is through the amendment process; that judges of the future will not change, modify or alter the Constitution because they will interpret it according to the common understanding of the relevant provisions at the time it was adopted."

Great idea! And since the First Amendment guarantees freedom of speech and of the press, and since in all the states, there was only one obscenity law on the books between 1789 and 1821, that must mean that all sexually oriented speech is protected, right? (Somehow, I don't think Pickering would agree...)

The afternoon's last scheduled speaker was Ron Luce,[20] founder of Teen Mania Ministries—and in some ways, the most interesting speaker (at least as regards the adult industry) of the whole bunch.

"I would like to inform you of something you may not know about, and that is that you have terrorists living in your living room," Luce began.

Al Qaeda? Nope. Tim McVeigh? Uh-uh. Democrats? Close!

"You have them in your computer; you have them in your iPods—you all know what iPods are?—terrorists lurking of a different nature, of a different kind."

Luce then related a story from "the R-rated part of the Bible," about how a guy whose concubine is raped and killed by "the wicked men of the town"—so the guy cuts her body into 12 pieces and distributes a piece to each of Israel's 12 tribes as an object lesson of what can happen in Israel—*Israel*, of all places!—and Luce just happened to have on stage a mannequin that he'd cut into 12 pieces to signify that "in America ... we have a very similar situation happening to an entire younger generation. They're being carved up, destroyed, pillaged, right in front of our face; right before our eyes. In fact, we're here this afternoon to mourn the departure of a younger generation. It's really being carved up in a number of different pieces. Let me just describe the acts of violence that have been portrayed and bestowed upon them."

You can probably guess what some of those "acts of violence" are—well, maybe not ...

"We've got all kinds of things that are destroying our kids," he said. "We've got depression. You know, one out of eight teenagers are clinically depressed right now; one out of eight, all over the country, and there's data that shows that there's a direct relationship between the more time you spend on the Internet, the more likely you are to be depressed."

So, kids, you'd better stop surfing over to CNN.com!

"We've got video games," he continued. "You know, eighth graders are the ones that play the most. $20, $25 a week, they're playing—but you know, we're not talking about Pong and Pacman; we're talking about video games that teach them how to solicit prostitutes, how to plan murders—this is entertainment?"

He was talking about Grand Theft Auto, and read to the crowd a news story from Michigan about a couple of kids who played the game, hopped into their car, ran down a stranger, went to breakfast, came back and "stomped the guy into a coma, and then went home and played the game some more."

Sure; happens all the time—NOT!

"You know, we can talk about music," he continued, "the references to violence, the references to sexuality. You know, there's all kinds of documentation, the more that you hear this stuff, see this stuff on music videos and so forth, the more likely you are both to be violent and to be sexual... Here we've got M-TV, probably one of the largest culprits. These people, one documentation shows that 3,000 times a week, there's a soft-core porn image that comes across M-TV—3,000 times a week! And the data shows that Christian young people actually watch M-TV more than secular young people!"

Yeah, right! Hmmm... wonder why...

Luce ticked off a few other "acts of violence" including self-cutting, suicide, STDs and "identity theft"—"And I'm not talking about credit cards and that kind of thing; I'm talking about young people that are aimed at by advertisers to brand them with some sort of identity so they can get their money from them the rest of their lives!" (Of course, the *church* would never do that!)

The final "acts of violence" include the Internet, where kids have "pseudo-friendship relationships; they don't know how to interact with real people because they've got all these pseudo-people online"; drugs ("There was a clear drop in drug use once President Bush came in and began to spend more money on prevention."); and "point-and-click pornography."

"Probably one of the worst culprits we have that this generation is facing, that no generation has ever had to face before, and that's point-and-click pornography," Luce explained. "Now, we all know that's bad, but do we really know how bad it is? How many of you have ever been online before and you were trying to get to—and something popped onto your computer of a sexual nature and you clicked to try to click it off and another one came up? You know, that happens to 90% of teenagers online doing their homework. Ninety percent! Eighty percent of kids have had multiple exposure to hardcore pornography. Think of the implications! Eighty percent of this generation, multiple exposure. Now, there's no barrier to enter. It used to be you had to convince a guy behind the counter to give it to you and then hope your parents or neighbors didn't see you bring it home, and now it's click, free, click, free—oh, now, a slave. And if we think a 50% divorce rate now is bad, what's it gonna be when *these* kids start getting married? You know, there's data that shows that people who have had multiple exposures to all this pornography, they get married and then they can't have a normal sexual relationship with their spouse because of what they've exposed their mind to? So now they need Viagra just to have a normal sexual relationship? What is going on here? How many of you have daughters? How are you going to find a decent husband for them, if 80% of their peers have had multiple exposures to pornography, hardcore pornography? And you know what the data shows? It's 12- to 17-year-olds; it's not the dirty old men, that are the longest viewers of pornography online."

Luce thought it was "time we sent a message," and the audience heartily agreed.

"Do we understand what's going on here?" Luce asked. "The train is about to go off the tracks to post-Christian America, and I know we're not here to talk about evangelism today as much as we are how to shape our culture and laws and so forth, but can we just say this real quickly? If we end up with 4% Bible-believing Christians, do you know what kind of laws they're going to make? What kind of judges they're going to put into office? What kind of people they're going to vote into office? What kind of campaigns they're going to support? Do we understand what's going on here? ... If we don't start looking to kids, what's going on with these young people, everything we're doing now is going to be moot, because they're going to come and make all kinds of new laws, and our whole culture is going to wash down the drain."

Actually, Ron, some of us *do* understand what's going on here. When you say "our whole culture is going to wash down the drain," you mean the U.S. Constitution guarantees Americans so much freedom which has so permeated the American culture that you and your kind can't put enough propaganda out over the airwaves, in the newspapers, in the schools and in the pews to convince enough of them to toe the line of your anti-sex, anti-pleasure, anti-freedom agenda.

So I guess you're just going to have to steal it.

And that was the topic of the Summit's final free event. (Well, aside from Sunday morning's worship service, which I didn't attend...) Following Luce's talk, attendees were given a choice of six "break-out sessions," each on a different topic, such as "The Future of Health Care"; "Impacting the Culture Through the Church"; "Training the Next Generation of Pro-Family Leaders"; "Using the Media to Communicate Our Message"; and "In Defense of Mixing Church and State from Acts 16."

As tempting as that last one was—hell, they were *all* tempting!—I chose "Getting Church Voters to the Polls," run by Connie Marshner,[21] director of international programs for the Leadership Institute, which calls itself "the premier training ground for tomorrow's conservative leaders."

The "course materials" for the session was a booklet, originally prepared for Sen. Rick Santorum's 2000 reelection campaign in Pennsylvania, titled, "Voter Identification And Turnout: A Church Plan," by Marshner herself. What she hoped to do over the course of the hour-long session was to teach the attendees how to target their fellow parishioners who might be theocrat-friendly and get all of them to the polls.

"Many people come into politics with the idea that, 'Oh, truth is on our side. We have the right ideas. We have proper philosophy. All we need to do is get our message out and people will naturally agree with us, and we will win.' I call this 'the Sir Galahad Theory of Politics'; 'I will win because my heart is pure'," Marshner explained. "That's good for King Arthur's legends. It's not reality.

"The reality is that in any given political climate, whichever side is best able to motivate and activate the greater number of volunteers has the greater chance of winning," she continued. "That's the real nature of politics."

But while the session did explain how to find volunteers to work on a candidate's campaign, at least half of it was devoted to how to secure like-minded voters and get them to the polls—and Step One was to get a hold of a "church or parish directory"—preferably one's own, but these folks weren't that particular; any directory would do, because studies have shown that people who attend church regularly are more likely to vote for conservative candidates. The prime targets, however, were churches that are "relatively independent, relatively small, and where most people are likely to agree."

Once those directories were secured, the next step was to get some number of volunteers to go through each directory and call each member to try to feel out how he or she felt politically—but Marshner stressed that it was important that this be done as an "anonymous survey" by someone whose voice was completely unknown to the person being called.

According to a script in the booklet, the caller should say, "Hello, I'm with ABC Polls. We're calling in your area to find out the level of interest in the upcoming [U.S. Senate/House of Representatives/state assembly/town council/school board/etc.] election."

The idea of this "poll" was "to identify 'our' voters," Marshner said. "You don't want to get the other side's voters to the polls."

Marshner cautioned callers, "I wouldn't tell them you have a copy of the church directory." When one of the attendees—her collar suggested that she was a clergywoman—asked what to say if the caller were asked directly if he or she was using a church list, Marshner replied, "I haven't heard a perfect answer to that question. It's a delicate answer." Callers were also to avoid admitting they supported a particular candidate: "Just say 'I'm collecting information about the candidates'," was Marshner's advice.

"Religious Right groups love to lord their moral superiority over the rest of us," noted Rev. Barry Lynn of Americans United for Separation of Church and State, who attended the summit, "yet the devious approach they endorse shows that these groups suffer a deficit of values."

If the person being called admitted that they were against the conservative candidate, they would never be contacted again. But if the "callee" said he or she was in favor of the conservative, leaning in that candidate's direction or just didn't know much or anything about the candidate, then the caller would deliver that name up the line to a "church coordinator" for follow-up "eyeball-to-eyeball" contact with that person as a potential volunteer to work on the candidate's campaign.

The booklet spends a couple of pages detailing who is—and more importantly, who is *not*—a good potential recruit. Good recruits for volunteer work are "busy people" who "know how to keep a commitment." They should also be "attractive" and "non-controversial"; people who are "organized" and "know how to manage [their] time."

Some people, however, are "not right."

"It is best to avoid individuals who have been involved in church controversies, or too strongly identified with any movement outside of the mainstream of the church family," Marshner wrote. She also warned the group to be wary of people who showed too much enthusiasm; what they really needed was people who understand the concept of commitment—the ability and willingness to follow through on the tasks required.

Once all the volunteers were lined up and the church members who would be voting for the conservative were identified, all that remained was to make sure that every one of them went to the polls on election day and voted—even if it meant calling them several times that day, and even arranging for transportation to the polling place if necessary.

"The goal is to reach every single person in your shoebox [list of voters] as soon as possible—and to keep calling them until the polls close," Marshner said. "You simply have to keep calling until you know that every voter in every one of the 50 families for which you are responsible has actually cast his or her ballot. That's where we win or lose the election."

"If 30 of your 50 identified voters actually vote, you have won the election in your parish," she concluded.

Remarked Lynn, an ordained minister in the United Church of Christ, "It looks like the 'value voters' have embraced a 'win-at-any-cost' strategy that is far removed from the ethical principles taught by the religion they claim to cherish."

No shit—but Marshner's session was the best education imaginable for anyone who wants to know how the theocrats have amassed so much political power in America today. Now, all progressives have to do is figure out how to overcome the tremendous advantage these ready-made conservative voter lists give them.

It won't be easy.

By their own words shall ye know them! Also, I've always wanted to get a copy of the "homosexual agenda," but sadly, none of these folks have seen fit to reprint it.

ANALYSIS: THE RELIGIOUS RIGHT AND THEOCRACY: A MATTER OF PERSPECTIVE?

May 9, 2007

WASHINGTON, D.C. – James L. Lambert,[1] a self-described "former pornography addict" who now sells mortgages, posted a column Tuesday on OneNewsNow, the American Family Association's successor to its AgapeP-ress News Summary daily emailer, which covers the news (and occasionally makes it up) from a conservative religious perspective.

Lambert's column, titled, "Perspectives: Left's hysteria growing in closing months of the Bush administration"—("closing months"?!?!? Try *21 of them*!) (Are italics too "hysterical"?)—charges that, "Editors of *Adult Video News*, the porn industry's advocacy magazine, claim the 'religious right' and President Bush are drawing America into a theocracy."

That's a pretty strange way to phrase it, since what "Editors of *Adult Video News*" have actually claimed is that the Religious Right and President Bush have declared full-scale war on secular America. They're attempting to turn the executive and judicial branches of the government into arms of the Southern Baptist Convention through everything from federal judge and Supreme Court nominees to the establishment of the Office of Faith-Based and Community Initiatives which reports directly to the president.

But since Lambert impliedly denies that this is going on, we thought we'd take a short stroll through the religio-conservative emails we received that same day to see what evidence they might contain that might bolster *AVN*'s contention.

First, there's a special email from Family Research Council (FRC), exhorting its readers to "Thank President Bush Now for Defending the Unborn!" Bush, you see, has "courageously" sent a letter to the majority leaders of both houses of Congress "vowing to veto any legislation that would force U.S. taxpayers to fund the destruction of human life." Now, you might think—well, hope, anyway—that the Prez was referring to some promise to veto any bills that would continue funding the war in Iraq, where over 3,200 American human lives have been snuffed and tens of thousands wounded ... but no; FRC wants readers to thank him for promising to veto federal funding for "research that requires the killing of human embryos" a.k.a. embryonic stem-cell research.

"Unfortunately," notes FRC, "due to the change in who controls Congress, we can expect leftwing efforts to undermine pro-life provisions in several spending bills." Since FRC's definition of "pro-life" stops at a woman's labia, we think it's safe to classify its advocacy for "pro-life provisions in several spending bills" as yet another attempt to bring conservative (if not fundamentalist) religious views to bear on the supposedly secular federal budget process.

OneNewsNow itself is another reliable advocate for more religion in government, and for the past several weeks, various articles have railed against federal "hate crimes" legislation, which would make it a crime for anyone to "willfully cause[] bodily injury to any person or, through the use of fire, a firearm, or an explosive or incendiary device, attempt[] to cause bodily injury to any person, because of the actual or perceived religion, national origin, gender, *sexual orientation, gender identity* or disability of any person," but would exempt "any expressive conduct protected from legal prohibition by, or any activities protected by the free speech or free exercise clauses of, the First Amendment to the Constitution." [Emphasis added]

In other words, clergypersons can rail all they want from the pulpit about how Leviticus 20:13 prescribes that, "If a man also lie with mankind, as he lieth with a woman, both of them have committed an abomination: they shall surely be put to death"—that's protected speech. What the Act *doesn't* protect is those parishioners then going to their local bar and beating the shit out of one of its patrons because those good Christians (or Jews) think that person is a "fuckin' queer."

But, notes a story on OneNewsNow, "Representatives from groups like the Southern Baptist Convention, Concerned Women for America, Vision America, and Jews Against Anti-Christian Defamation held a press conference in Washington, DC, to voice their displeasure with what they view as an attack on Christian expression."

Hey, "press conference ... to voice their displeasure"—no problem! It's the American way! But then, as so often happens with these articles, the lunatic fringe takes over:

"Janet Folger[2] of the ministry Faith 2 Action says the hate crimes bill passed by the House is aimed at pastors or anyone else who has the 'audacity' to disagree with the homosexual agenda," the article recounts. "'Mike is standing at a football bar, or he's standing at a restaurant, watching a game,' she posits; 'Bruce comes out of the restroom, and he's touching up his makeup. He's a cross-dresser with red-nail polish and a five o'clock shadow. He comes out and hits on Mike. Maybe he puts his arm around him or maybe he brushes or puts his hand through his hair.' The average man would 'maybe want to push off such unwelcome advances,' Folger observes. However, she warns, 'That, if you touch him, is a hate crime.'"

Um ... no, Janet, it isn't. The law requires that the person "willfully cause bodily injury to" the person, and just pushing them away—in the 10 or 12 times this century that that scenario has actually played out in real life—would not cause the required injury. The bill in no way "attack[s] ... Christian expression"; in fact, it protects it.

What Folger and her ilk want is the *carte blanche* to beat up gays *because their religion encourages them to do so*, and not suffer any additional penalty for that; in other words, a religious exemption for bigotry that results in violence.

And when religious bigotry gets special protection from government, that's a problem.

Another OneNewsNow story that caught our attention is headlined, "*Coral Ridge Hour* launches campaign to improve nation's public schools."

Well ... we here at *AVN* are all for improving our nation's public schools ... but we're also a little suspicious when the guy who bankrolled the placement of a two-and-a-half ton rock engraved with the Ten Commandments in the Montgomery, Alabama federal courthouse—it was, of course, later ordered removed at *taxpayer* expense by a federal judge—claims he knows how to do that.

"Throughout May," the article announces, "three television programs will be aired during *The Coral Ridge Hour*, the weekly show produced by the Florida-based ministry of Dr. D. James Kennedy.[3] The programs will investigate problems with the U.S. public school system, including the role and influence of the National Education Association, the nation's largest teachers' union."

Religio-conservatives have had a hard-on for the NEA for several years, since the teachers' union has generally supported Democratic politicians and has had the temerity to suggest that school kids could use *less* proselytization of religion in the classrooms rather than more.

And sure enough, "Senior producer Jerry Newcombe says ... Dr. Kennedy, for years, has been 'banging the drum that we should apply the mind of Christ and the Bible to all of life, not just our spiritual life—and that would include education.'"

It has, of course, escaped Dr. Kennedy's attention that not all public school children believe in Christ, and that facilities already exist where kids can get all the Christian upbringing they can stand.

They're called "churches."

The attempt by religionists to "apply the mind of Christ and the Bible" to public school instruction is an attempt to meld religion with a primary governmental function: Public school education. If one needed an example of the dangers of that "unholy alliance," one need only look at the recent hubbub surrounding Monica Goodling, graduate of Pat Robertson's Regent University Law School, who's about to be offered immunity to testify before Congress as to the Justice Department's attempts to pad its ranks with religio-conservative Republicans.

But speaking of churches, "A Florida Christian has filed suit to block the construction of a Muslim mosque in an area of Pompano Beach where very few Muslims live," write OneNewsNow "reporters" Chad Groening and Jody Brown, further noting that, "He is concerned that the imam has ties to terrorism and that the facility will pose a threat to his neighborhood."

"Attorney Larry Klayman says his client"—Rodney Wright, a member of the Antioch Missionary Baptist Church—"believes the relocation of the Islamic Center of South Florida 'presents a substantial harm to the well-being, safety, and health of the community' ... Klayman, founder and former chairman of the watchdog group Judicial Watch, says the lawsuit demonstrates that the mosque 'has ties to radical Islam and [that the imam] invites terrorists and people who support terrorism to the mosque.'"

Perhaps it's just poor reporting on the part of Groening and Brown, but nowhere in the article do they state just what evidence Klayman or Wright have that the mosque either has ties to "radical Islam" or that its leader "invites terrorists" and their supporters to the mosque. That evidence would be kinda important in a "news" story like this, wouldn't you think? Otherwise, someone might suggest that this was simply another turf war between Christians and Muslims, with the Christians trying to bring the power of government to give their faith a legal edge over the equally valid beliefs of the Muslims.

And if they succeed, that might be viewed as another instance of the government establishing Christianity over Islam, which the Constitution says is a *big* no-no.

Another favorite daily email is the Alliance Alert, from the Alliance Defense Fund (ADF),[4] one of the small group of law firms or associations that represents Christian organizations (no Muslims need apply, and Jews are scarce to non-existent as well) in lawsuits against government entities. The organization was founded by Alan Sears, formerly best known as the executive director of the Meese Commission.

On Tuesday, the Alliance Alert alerted us to Dick Otterstad and his son Luke, leaders of the 20-member Church of the Divide, which has "staged dozens of demonstrations in recent years to expose what they view as Christian persecution," according to a linked article in the *Sacramento Bee*.

Most recently, the Otterstads have organized rallies against Dave Terwilliger, the principal of the San Juan High School in Sacramento, for having suspended 35 students for wearing t-shirts bearing anti-gay slogans and Bible verses on the April 18 "Day of Silence," an annual student protest in support of gay rights—and in an amazing coincidence, the Otterstads own a store, No Gay Gear Inc., that sells the shirts!

"Trent Allen, a spokesman for the San Juan Unified School District, said the problem with the shirts worn by San Juan students isn't that they espouse religious beliefs, it's that they target a particular group or refer to a sexual act," wrote Tod Milbourn for the *Bee*.

But that wasn't good enough for the Otterstads, who decided to follow Terwilliger home and pass out flyers to his neighbors reading, "Your neighbor is persecuting Christians. You need to confront him over his tyrannical behavior at a public high school." They also picketed outside Terwilliger's church, carrying signs calling him a hypocrite and calling for his excommunication.

Another ADF link brought an article titled, "NC Supreme Court Upholds Crimes Against Nature Statute." Seems a 14-year-old kid and his 12-year-old partner were discovered engaging in oral sex and intercourse in the back of the girl's mother's SUV, and eventually, the county district court ruled that he was a "delinquent" for committing a "crime against nature." One might think that all such "crime against nature" laws were thrown out after the Supreme Court's ruling in *Lawrence v. Texas*, but the boy's lawyer never argued that point, and the North Carolina Supreme Court ruled that, "Besides the goal of promoting proper notions of morality among our State's youth, the government's desire for a healthy young citizenry underscores the legitimacy of the government's interest in prohibiting the commission of crimes against nature by minors."

Frankly, we suspect that ADF just gets off on the court referring to consensual sodomy as a "crime against nature."

"ACLU Asks Government to Investigate Evidence of Taxpayer Dollars Funding Religion in Oregon Abstinence-Only-Until-Marriage Program" was another ADF link. The article refers to the ACLU calling on the federal Department of Health and Human Services to investigate grants given to an abstinence-only "sex ed" program called "Stop and Think." According to its own contracts, the Stop and Think program required its presenters and supervisors to "possess an authentic relationship with Jesus Christ; possess knowledge of the Word of God, and the ability to communicate it's [sic] truth; exhibit a loving and merciful spirit; [and] attend a Bible believing local church or fellowship"—which the ACLU took as evidence that the program was religiously based, and objected to taxpayer funds going to the program. This is exactly the sort of program that ADF defends.

All in all, we found about a dozen articles *just on Tuesday* depicting religious organizations and their supporters attempting to influence government or government-funded entities in favor of religion—in fact, in favor of Christianity, and often in favor of the fundamentalist variety of that religion. There were swipes at presidential candidate Rudy Giuliani's having made personal donations to various chapters of Planned Parenthood, a particular boogeyman of the religious right; applause for John McCain's assertion that although it's not impossible for a Republican candidate who favors abortion rights to win the nomination, such a candidate would "face long odds"; claims that government-mandated TV ratings are a "sham" when it comes to notifying parents of sexual content in those shows; and outright lies about a Zogby poll that supposedly showed that parents of public school students overwhelmingly support programs that preach sexual abstinence over programs that promote safe sex with condoms.

Yes, Mr. Lambert, America is fast falling toward theocracy—a state where religious beliefs dictate government policy—and the articles on the website that publishes you, as well as similar sites, prove it rather dramatically. The only question is, why don't you see that?

Or is it possible that you just don't want to?

AIM, of course, was the Adult Industry Medical Healthcare Foundation, which was driven out of business by people who wanted to take over all STD testing for adult performers.

EDITORIAL: HOW THE RELIGIOUS RIGHT CREATES PORN STARS

April, 2008

The former Christian News Service (CNS), now renamed Cybercast News Service, got bent out of shape because Planned Parenthood's teenwire.com website told teens that it was okay to look at porn.

Teenwire's stated purpose is "to provide medically accurate sexual health information for teens on the Internet," and to that end, it offers facts and advice like:

• "Masturbation is not physically harmful in any way. In fact, masturbation has a number of physical and mental health benefits, such as relieving stress and physical tension. Many people masturbate to relax and to feel good, and it can help some people fall asleep."

• "People who oppose comprehensive sex ed incorrectly say that teaching teens about preventing pregnancy and infections encourages them to have sex, but this has been scientifically disproven. In fact, a recent study by Columbia University researchers found that while teens who took virginity-until-marriage pledges were abstinent longer, they were less likely to use condoms when they stopped abstaining—which most are likely to do before marriage."

• "There's no such thing as a 'normal' age for becoming sexually active."

• "Despite overwhelming scientific evidence to the contrary, anti-choice organizations continue to spread the false idea that it is common for abortion to have severe, emotionally negative effects. They want people to believe that most women who choose abortion suffer severe and long-lasting emotional trauma. This is not true."

• "Steven, 19, says that the abstinence-only program at his high school just seemed like a way for teachers and staff to avoid talking about sex. Since most states don't allow same-sex marriages, telling lesbian and gay students to abstain until they are married is hurtful and doesn't really make sense."

Despite the fact that much of the advice given is moderate to the point that it could form part of the sermon at some liberal churches, Cris Clapp, lobbyist for the anti-porn group Enough Is Enough,[1] has a problem with the idea that, according to her interpretation, "overall, teenwire.com has painted a picture that pornography is harmless fun."

And, of course, nothing could be further from the truth; just ask serial killer Ted Bundy (well, of course, he's dead now, but still...) like Focus on the Family founder James Dobson did, and you'll find out that Bundy, who got Dobson to fund his final death-row appeal, and who had previously blamed his killing spree on alcohol and having been excited by watching high school cheerleaders practice, had settled on the *real* main "contributing factor" to his homicides: Violent porn.

"I'm no social scientist," Bundy told Dobson, "but I've lived in prison for a long time now, and I've met a lot of men who were motivated to commit violence. Without exception, every one of them was deeply involved in pornography, deeply consumed by the addiction."

Thanks (probably) to the CNS article, and a later one reporting that several House Repugnicans (including the ever-popular Steve King of Iowa and Joe Pitts of Pennsylvania) were calling for the termination of Planned Parenthood's federal funding, the organization has removed the porn references from Teenwire. But a cut-off of funding would remove *all* of PP's sexual advice from the Web, not to mention diminish its ability to provide birth control and abortion services ... which is just what the sex-negative activists want.

How many single mothers are there in the porn performer community? How many adult actresses have had abortions? How many performers of either gender are "lapsed Catholics" or refugees from the orthodoxy of some other religion? How many women didn't realize, before they got into porn, that they were more attracted to their own sex than the opposite one, or that they were innately bisexual? (Of course, lifesitenews.com has found an "expert" who says that, "I believe that the genetic evidence for homosexuality is just not there. It's the values and politics of homosexuals and their supporters that is driving the gay gene agenda, not good science.")

No one's yet done a survey to find the answers to those questions—we hope AIM will consider doing one, just for statistical purposes—but we suspect we can count on the fingers of both hands, plus maybe a toe or two, the number of actresses who had the benefit of a thorough-going sexual education ... and one hell of a lot more who got that "education" in the back seat of a car or its equivalent.

In January, for instance, some kids at Parkland High School in central Pennsylvania were under police investigation for recording themselves having sex and sending the images to fellow students' cell phones,[2] while in December in Ogden, Utah, a 13-year-old girl was convicted of "sexual abuse of a child" for having had consensual sex with her 12-year-old boyfriend—as was he, for having had sex with her!

But there are a number of extremely powerful groups in this country who are dedicated to preventing minors from having any idea how to perform safe sex—hell; how to perform sex of any kind!—and if they figure it out for themselves, to keeping them ignorant of how to avoid pregnancy, life-threatening diseases and, almost as importantly, of how to do it in a way that will give them maximum enjoyment.

In October, for example, the Righteous were all up in arms about the plan by King Middle School in Portland, Me., to allow the school's health care provider—an independently-operated clinic—to prescribe contraceptives for the girl students and give condoms to the boys.

Meanwhile, Pastor Bryan Longworth is sure there will be "even higher rates of Chlamydia, Gonorrhea, HIV, and other STI infections if the Graphic, Explicit, Risky Condom Ed Curriculum 'Get Real about AIDS' is Implemented in St. Lucie County, Florida!" (Hey, they're not *our* caps!) And Pastor Ken Hutcherson is "upset" over a poster for his local school's Gay/Straight Alliance which displays "silhouettes of three teenage couples—one male-female, one female-female, and one male-male—all embracing in front of a rainbow, as if they are about to kiss." (He also didn't want his daughter being taught by "two pro-homosexual teachers.")

Robert Knight[3] of "Bozo" Bozell's Culture and Media Institute has a hard-on for a "kiddie sex book" titled *It's Perfectly Normal*, which is "full of colorful drawings of nude people, sexual activities including masturbation by both sexes, and even a girl leaning over and holding a mirror between her legs, so she and the reader can examine her nether regions."

"If you felt violated just reading this description," warns Knight, "imagine how kids feel when looking at the pictures." (Amused? Curious? Less ignorant?)

And while all the Usual Suspects are promoting "abstinence (non-) education" to the tune of another $191 million this year, no matter how ineffective a review[4] in the *British Medical Journal* may have found such programs to be, and despite the fact that the U.S.'s teen birth rate rose last year for the first time in 15 years, Parents Television Council (PTC) can always be counted upon to bemoan the "death" of the "Family Hour" on TV, and to file millions of protests with the FCC over Janet Jackson's half-second Super Bowl nipple exposure, Charlotte Ross's two-second ass exposure on *NYPD Blue*, 10.5 seconds of pixilated tits 'n' ass on *Married by America*, Jane Fonda saying "cunt" on *Today* and Diane Keaton saying "fuck" on *Good Morning America*—all to support the pretense that nobody in America actually has sex or talks about it.

But indeed they are, as evidenced by the findings in sociologist Mark Regnerus' new book, *Forbidden Fruit*,[5] which reports that "evangelical teens tend to have sex first at a younger age, 16.3, compared to liberal Protestants, who tend to lose their virginity at 16.7," and that "young evangelicals are far more likely to have had three or more sexual partners (13.7 percent) than non-evangelicals (8.9 percent)"—and by the fact that Kevin Giedd's "40 Days for Life" protest group has been videotaping women entering the Lynchburg, Va. Planned Parenthood clinic—and specifically focusing on the ones sporting Liberty University parking stickers—you know; Jerry Falwell's law school—with intentions of turning their tapes over to school officials for fining those students, forcing them to engage in community service and possible expelling them altogether.

Well, that's okay; if the gals can't be uptight fundamentalist lawyers, there'll always be room for them in front of Porn Valley's cameras.

KERNES ADDRESSES SOCIETY FOR THE SCIENTIFIC STUDY OF SEXUALITY

AVN editor notes 'Legal and Social Obstacles to Sexual Communication'

April 13, 2008

Following is the complete text of Mark Kernes' April 12 speech to the Society for the Scientific Study of Sexuality:

Our topic is "Legal and Social Obstacles to Sexual Communication," and in my work as Senior Editor of Adult Video News, that's pretty much all I deal with on a daily basis. In a sense, it's difficult for me to talk about this topic, because as an ardent follower of what political and religious conservatives are saying, it's obvious—to me, at least—that the entire right-wing side of the political spectrum, and a good portion of the left, are fueled by a fundamentalist religious reaction to all things sexual. In other words, scratch the surface of many political positions taken by Republicans and Joe Lieberman Democrats and you'll find an underlying sexual component.

I probably don't need to convince anyone here of that. Everyone remembers the fact that a president of the United States was impeached essentially because he accepted (and possibly solicited) blowjobs from a member of his staff and, good ol' Southern boy that he was, dissembled and lied about it to the American people. Even his lying didn't rise to the constitutional requirement that impeachment be for "high crimes and misdemeanors," but religious conservatives smelled the semen-salty air and moved in for the kill. A similar fate was visited only last month on New York Governor Eliot Spitzer, who arguably violated the Mann Act, another sexual "crime" whose high-profile victims—actors Charlie Chaplin and Rex Ingram, architect Frank Lloyd Wright, musician Chuck Berry—have all generally been political targets as well.

As a writer, what concerns me most in the struggle between sexual repression and sexual sanity is the words themselves. Most of you hopefully have received my handout, "Needed: A Factness Doctrine," which deals with one level of this issue: the provably false statements about political issues and figures that have become commonplace on radio and television, not to mention the plethora of religio-political websites scattered across the Internet—but the problem dealt with in the handout is even more critical when applied to sexual speech and all sexually-related topics ... which, as I plan to demonstrate, include almost all issues which we as a society hold to be important to our health, mental and physical, and even to our survival as a species.

As most of you probably know, beyond actual knowledge of the subject, linguistics is the most important factor in any public discussion of sexual issues. In a news story, whether a person or group is described as "pro-life" or "anti-abortion," "pro-choice" or "pro-abortion" often says as much about the writer as it does about the subject. I highly recommend that everyone here read linguistics professor George Lakoff's *Whose Freedom?*, which applies the concept of framing to non-sexual political and social issues, but it doesn't take much reading between the lines to see those same memes at work in discussions of sexuality as well.

Aside from *The New York Times* and various articles linked from Google-News, most of my daily reading consists of emailed articles and website postings from the major religio-conservative pro-censorship groups. These include the Media Research Center, Family Research Council, Focus on the Family, Morality In Media, the American Family Association, Concerned Women for America, Parents Television Council, the Alliance Defense Fund, Community Defense Counsel and Citizens for Community Values. (Incidentally, I've found that a good rule of thumb is, if a media-related organization has either "family" or "research" in its name, it's probably a religious pro-censorship group.)

Moreover, *Talkers Magazine* lists Rush Limbaugh, Sean Hannity and Michael Savage as the three "most important" talk radio hosts in the country, followed by Laura Schlessinger, Glenn Beck and Laura Ingraham. All of them can be counted upon to promote sexually repressive religious viewpoints, even if they don't follow those precepts themselves.

The writings from the above-named groups cover the entire spectrum of sex-related topics—even ones that the average person may not consider to be sex-related. For example, most of the religious right sites have been posting reviews of the premiere of talk-show host Ben Stein's so-called "documentary," *Expelled: No Intelligence Allowed*,[1] which claims that "intelligent design" is a legitimate topic for debate in high school biology classes. I might note that reviews of the movie have *only* appeared on religious right sites, because audiences at the movie's showings, which have largely been in church venues, have been carefully screened to try to keep out critics of intelligent design. Of course, the import of the idea that an other-worldly "intelligence" created humans, rather than their having evolved from simpler forms, has vast implications for human sexuality.

Then there was the article on christianpost.com which purported to identify "America's most sinful cities." In the "Most Lustful" category, Denver was ranked first, followed by Charlotte, San Antonio, Seattle and Providence. How did they determine the lustfulness of these cities' inhabitants? The AC Nielson research firm used sales figures for contraceptives, adult DVDs and sex toys in ranking the list. "Sin," of course, has powerful negative connotations for the religious.

Just last week, Albert Mohler,[2] president of Lexington, Kentucky's Southern Baptist Theological Seminary, came out against sexual surrogacy, claiming that "introduc[ing] a third party as an agent in the biological equation" creates "complex moral issues for Christians" because "Surrogates carry babies ... for married couples, *unmarried couples*, *gay and lesbian couples*, and *single adults* of all walks of life." [Emphasis added.] And as any conservative Christian or Jew or Muslim knows, sex is only for procreation and babies are only for married heterosexual couples.

Incidentally, I'm not the only one who thinks that religion is a sexual issue, although Rev. Mike Young of the First Unitarian Church of Honolulu put it exactly the opposite way. "Sexuality is a religious issue," he said. "It is the most powerful human motivator after air and water for the human species. The dynamics of sexuality touch every aspect of the life we share together. For that reason, priests have been trying to forbid it, control it or co-opt it from as early as there were priests."

I propose today to discuss some of the most important social issues where religious dogma clashes with sexual sanity, the most prominent of which is abortion. As the 2008 presidential election approaches, one of the primary talking points for Republican supporters will be the concept that only a Republican president will appoint Supreme Court justices who will overturn *Roe v. Wade*. It's an issue that all of the religio-conservative groups have been harping on since before the 2004 election, and which, allegations of voting fraud aside, along with the fear of legalization of same-sex marriage, was what drove conservative voters to the polls to reelect President Bush.

But while the "judicial activism" meme will be used more and more as the election approaches, Family Research Council is currently floating another method to attack abortion choice: It's launched a campaign to deny all federal funding to Planned Parenthood, based on previous claims that the organization provides contraception to anyone—even minors—who asks for it, that it helps cover up child abuse by providing abortions to underage girls and that it's engaging in a eugenics program.

The "evidence" for that last charge is that abortion opponents have been calling up various Planned Parenthood clinics and offering to donate money as long as they can be assured that the funds will be used to abort only "black babies." Of course, Planned Parenthood doesn't have programs aimed at aborting fetuses of any ethnicity, but its staff, happy to get any donations offered, probably figured it couldn't hurt to agree to accept the funds on whatever basis the donor wanted to give them—not realizing that the calls were being recorded and would be used by the anti-abortion groups for propaganda purposes.

"For decades, Planned Parenthood has made its livelihood aborting tens of thousands of black babies," FRC said in its Thursday email. "Over 80 percent of its clinics are located in minority neighborhoods where America's largest abortion provider has cashed in on the vulnerability of young women."

If FRC can actually manage to cut off Planned Parenthood's federal funds, that will go a very long way toward effectively denying legal abortions to any women who seek them. Jane Jiminez, a regular columnist for the American Family Association's OneNewsNow website, recently wrote, "In one of the greatest public relations scams of modern times, America is being duped by the King of Lies—doing business as Planned Parenthood." The "King of Lies," of course, is another term for Satan.

And speaking of lies: Google UK has just announced that it would be refusing to accept anti-abortion ads from the Christian Institute, declaring, "We only allow ads that have factual information about abortion."

Also on the horizon is the "Prenatally and Postnatally Diagnosed Conditions Awareness Act",[3] Senate Bill 1810, introduced by fundamentalist Sen. Sam Brownback, which will force physicians and women's clinics to pressure pregnant women not to abort simply because the fetus will be born with Down's syndrome, cerebral palsy and other adverse genetic conditions. Banning abortions on the basis of such genetic defects is the next logical step after banning late-term abortions. Just last month, legislators in Minnesota, at the behest of Minnesota Citizens Concerned for Life, introduced a bill to ban all saline abortions, calling them "one of the most brutal and inhumane medical procedures performed today."

Finally, let me note that protesters outside the Planned Parenthood clinic in Lynchburg, Virginia, have been videotaping women entering the clinic, and have been paying particular attention to those driving cars with parking stickers from nearby Liberty University School of Law, founded by Rev. Jerry Falwell. The protesters have announced plans to report those students to Liberty's administrators, with the aim of having the women expelled from the school for possibly having had abortions.

Another frequent topic on the religio-conservative websites is sex education: Both support for so-called "abstinence education," plus vehement opposition to anything that even hints at the idea that post-pubescent teens might be having sex, and that adults should help the kids avoid both pregnancies and sexually-transmitted infections. In fact, on February 26, Family Research Council teamed up with the National Abstinence Education Association to host a "training session" for federal legislators and their staffs on the "positive impact such programs have had on the attitudes and behavior of young people." This was apparently to counter the conclusions of a study prepared for Rep. Henry A. Waxman which concluded that 11 of 13 abstinence-only "sex ed" programs contained distortions and outright lies, particularly as to the effectiveness of contraceptives, the risks of abortion and of contracting STIs, the comparative horniness of boys and girls, and whether God cares when and if they have sex.

Incredibly, religious and conservative groups have used the recent finding, reported in *The New York Times*, that one in four girls ages 14-19 has at least one sexually-transmitted infection—most of them, HPV—as evidence that true sex education doesn't work, and that more abstinence propaganda is necessary. Of course, those same groups have been campaigning around the country to stop legislatures from making HPV vaccination mandatory for young girls.

"The current contraceptive-based education approach offered in 75 percent of U.S. schools not only relies on an overly narrow focus on physical health that is spurring an epidemic, but it also completely ignores the emotional consequences of premarital sex," declared Family Research Council.

"Abortion providers like Planned Parenthood should not be supplying our students with information about sexual health," said Missouri Gov. Matt Blunt, who signed a law last year banning Planned Parenthood from conducting sex ed classes in public schools. (No; obviously, Missourians should get their sex ed from church groups!)

Moreover, Mathematica Policy Research Inc., in a study[4] of four abstinence programs begun in 1999 and concluded in 2006, found that roughly the same number of abstinence-indoctrinated students had had sex as in the control group—that is, about half—and that the average age of first sexual experience was 14 years, nine months—which of course would be illegal in most states. And many more abstinence-indoctrinated youth have substituted oral and anal sex for vaginal in order to remain "abstinent"! Even so, the teen birth rate rose in 2007 for the first time in 15 years.

In all, as of late 2007, 14 states have rejected federal funding of abstinence-only programs, and in an op-ed piece for the *Washington Post*, First Lady Laura Bush advised Americans to "practice safe sex," use condoms "every time" and get tested for HIV. Imagine that: An intelligent Bush!

But even when something approaching real sex education is the approved curriculum, as it was for Brevard County, Florida schools for the first time this year, that doesn't mean that's what the kids will actually be getting. For instance, teachers there are forbidden to discuss "three district-defined 'moral issues': Abortion, masturbation and homosexuality," and they're supposed to stress abstinence.

"I really think that when we teach health, that we should talk about healthy behaviors ... and the healthy behavior for unmarried teenage students should be *no sex*," said Florida high school health teacher Brandi Morford, who has taught abstinence education for four years. "Just because they're all doing it doesn't mean it's a healthy behavior."

Indeed, kids *are* having sex—and getting busted for it! In December, 2006, the Utah Supreme Court found a 13-year-old girl guilty of sexual abuse of a child for having had consensual sex with her "victim," her 12-year-old boyfriend—and found him guilty of the same thing for having had sex with her!

Just this past January, Pennsylvania State Police began checking the cellphones of Parkland High School students to see if their classmates had sent them nude pictures of their fellow students. Apparently, 40 Parkland students had them on their phones. Last month, four 12-year-old Daphne Middle School students in Daphne, Alabama were arrested and charged with possession of material harmful to minors for using their cellphone cameras to snap nude photos of themselves and exchanging the images with each other.

And who can forget the furor over the Sundance Film Festival's 2006 showing of *Hounddog*, in which 12-year-old actress Dakota Fanning was shown being raped. Interviewed later, Fanning thought the scene had been a good experience for her development as an actress.

Family Research Council has also had some success in retargeting the funds in the President's Emergency Plan for AIDS Relief (PEPFAR). The bill now recommends using the $50 billion allotment in a "balanced approach" between contraception and abstinence promotion—while allowing funded religious groups to avoid discussing contraception and abortion altogether, and maintaining the ban on all fund recipients from providing services to prostitutes in the targeted countries.

On the home front, Morality In Media has taken the NYC Department of Health to task for its media campaign to promote condom use, advising New Yorkers in ads to "Get Some." Condoms, that is, which the Department is handing out free.

"I think it will be perceived by many people—young people, in particular—not just to get condoms but to get promiscuous sex," predicted MIM president Robert Peters. "The NYC Department of Health now targets all 'New Yorkers,' including children and adults whose religion teaches them that use of condoms is sinful. To the extent that the campaign is aimed at married couples, it is not only pro-promiscuity but also anti-children."

That's funny; I thought it was okay for *married* couples to be "promiscuous"—that is, have a lot of sex with each other—and is Peters seriously saying that when married people *do* have sex, they should expect that the woman will get pregnant and do nothing to try to prevent that?

The fundamentalists were up in arms just last month when Barack Obama had the temerity to suggest that in addition to abstinence education, sex ed should include "information about contraception, because look, I've got two daughters, 9 years old and 6 years old. I'm going to teach them first of all about values and morals, but if they make a mistake, I don't want them punished with a baby. I don't want them punished with an STD at the age of 16. You know, so, it doesn't make sense to not give them information."

The Religious immediately went into high dudgeon. Rather than focusing on the point of Obama's statement—that sex education should be more than just telling kids not to "do it"—Wendy Wright,[5] president of Concerned Women for America, focused on the "baby as punishment" concept, telling LifeNews.com, "Stigmatizing the babies conceived by teenagers is not the way to reduce teen pregnancies. Instead, it provides an excuse for aborting them." Concerned Women for America also opposes comprehensive sex ed.

Sex education is one of the driving forces behind the home-schooling movement, which in recent months has become much more prominent among the religious. Websites like OneNewsNow and Focus on the Family's Citizenlink have run dozens of scare stories about Gay-Straight Alliance clubs in schools; about children sent home for wearing t-shirts with slogans like, "Be *Really* Gay—Go Straight"; about how more and more districts are shunning "Intelligent Design" in favor of actual science in biology classes; and about how many schools are turning down abstinence funds and teaching comprehensive sex ed. The sum of these has been to convince many parents that the public schools will morally corrupt their children and drive them away from the church—and they're fighting back by attempting to home-school the kids so when they go out in the world, they'll *know* that the Earth is only 6,000 years old, that God made fossils and carbon-dating just to fool scientists, that gay people are sick if not actual agents of Satan, and that godly children have perfect control over their sexual urges.

Oh, yeah; and they're also opposing California bill AB 2943, which would "criminalize the non-injurious swat of a child with virtually any object, such as a ruler, newspaper, or paddle"—apparently before the kids get a chance to decide if they're into spanking sex-play.

I've already referred a couple of times to the fundamentalists' opposition to gay rights, and not a day goes by that there aren't multiple stories about Christians being discriminated against by having to accept gay employees, by a municipality allowing public facilities to be used by gay groups, by reported proposals for unisex bathrooms at schools, and by publicly-traded companies like UPS and McDonald's providing benefits for same-sex partners—all the while continuing to claim that "*Gays Can Be Cured!*" This, despite the fact that Pastor Ted Haggard,[6] who resigned from his parish in 2006 after his homosexual relationship with a prostitute was revealed, has asked the team of ministers overseeing his "spiritual restoration" recovery program to "end their oversight." However, "officials with New Life Church say the termination of the relationship is premature." Translation: He's still gay or bi.

Of course, I've saved my favorite topic for last: Pornography.

First, we might ask, "Just what *is* pornography?" You might think you know, but consider that the American Family Association wants *Redbook* magazine taken off supermarket shelves for printing articles like "Handbook: Your Sex Life," which contains 56 suggestions for how to "feel sexy in a flash!" Among the article's suggestions: "Got ten minutes? Swap your coffee break for a visit with your vibrator!" The American Decency Association wants Wal-Mart to move *Maxim* magazine and *Sports Illustrated*'s swimsuit calendars away from checkout areas, both of which ADA president Bill Johnson contends "feature pornographic photographs of women." On Thursday, Parents Television Council called on supporters to complain to the FCC about the CW Television Network's having broadcast an episode of *America's Next Top Model* that featured a momentary glimpse of a computer-blurred woman who apparently had no clothes on under the blur—and in primetime, no less!

And in case you're still not sure what porn is, Dr. Gail Dines[7] will teach you this summer at Wheelock College near Boston. She's sponsoring a symposium titled, "Media Madness: The Impact of Sex, Violence and Commercial Culture on Adults, Children and Society," which will feature such topics as "How media images perpetuate and legitimize sexism, racism, consumerism and economic inequality" and "How media affects children's ideas about sexual behavior and relationships with others." Dines has written *Pornography: The Production and Consumption of Inequality*, and my invitation to the 3-day, $475 event—$2,025 if I want three graduate credits for having taken it—came from an organization called StopPornCulture.com.

But despite yet another study showing that porn, however you define it, is harmless—this one from Denmark, done by Martin Hald and Neil Malamuth, which found that the Danes generally believe hardcore porn to have had a positive influence on their lives—we still have groups like Concerned Women for America sending 16,000 signed petitions to the Justice Department "respectfully demanding" that the nation's obscenity laws be "properly enforced"; "experts" like Dr. Mary Anne Layden claiming that porn is an "equal opportunity toxin"; and the heads of most of the censorship groups I named earlier sending a letter to Attorney General Michael Mukasey last November requesting a meeting with him "to discuss this rapidly growing pornography epidemic." No word on Mukasey's reply.

And then there are the so-called feminists like Robert Jensen,[8] who claim that pornographers' presence in mainstream culture "shouldn't be surprising, because they represent mainstream values: The logic of domination and subordination that is central to patriarchy, hyperpatriotic nationalism, white supremacy and a predatory corporate capitalism." Who knew?

You also may be familiar with the case concerning celebrities saying "fuck" and "cowshit" on national TV during award show telecasts that's working its way toward the Supreme Court. The broadcasters—Fox Television, of all people—won at the Appeals Court level, with the Second

Circuit finding that the FCC had provided no reasonable basis to fine the networks millions of dollars over the so-called "fleeting expletives."

It's looney-tunes like these who inspire people like Knoxville, Tennessee resident Kent Blackwelder to file a lawsuit against Delaware-based Specialty Publications, a gay porn company, for having sent him a DVD of *Titan Men's Farm Fresh* in an envelope marked "Free DVD"—which Blackwelder's 12-year-old daughter opened, thinking for some reason that it was a Disney movie, and was "horribly shocked to see numerous sexually explicit photographs of completely nude males." That "great pain of body and mind and emotional distress", he claims, is worth $4 million.

That also may be why everyone seems to want to tax adult entertainment to the hilt these days. California Assemblyman (formerly Senator) Charles Calderon, who's been introducing porn tax bills for most of the last decade, now wants to tax porn downloads from the Internet. A couple of states want to tax porn sales or strip club door fees to support everything from battered women's shelters to health care for the poor, and municipalities all over the country are passing ordinances designed to keep adult material out of their towns—often when nobody's even tried to bring it into their towns! These attempts often fail because porn has a legal right to be sold, though the Supreme Court claims that obscenity doesn't—although the 1969 opinion in *Stanley v. Georgia* recognized people's right to own "obscene" materials in their own homes. This legal schizophrenia has led to the current crop of obscenity prosecutions, the latest being the Evil Angel bust for two movies—one featuring milk enemas, the other depicting squirting—and a trailer.

By my count, there are currently five other ongoing federal obscenity cases: Extreme Associates, Max Hardcore, Movies By Mail, Karen Fletcher's RedRoseStories.com and Ira Isaacs, a couple of which will be coming to trial this summer.

Yeah, it's that *Robert Mueller. Sorry.*

THE REV BLOWS IT AGAIN ON CHILD PORN

April 30, 2008

NEW YORK CITY – Robert "The Rev" Peters, President of Morality in Media (MIM), has a little problem with child pornography: He can't seem to distinguish it from adult pornography. Here are a couple of clues, Bob: 1) Child porn is illegal; adult porn isn't. 2) Child porn has kids in it; adult porn doesn't. And according to the latest data, we might add 3) Adult porn—the better stuff, anyway—is mostly Made in America™ these days. Kiddie porn is mostly made in Russia, and the vast majority of it that's available on the World Wide Web is on Russian servers.

The Rev would know that if he'd bothered to ask the people who have to deal with child porn on a regular basis, like Joan Irvine of the Association of Sites Advocating Child Protection (ASACP)[1] or Ernie Allen, president of the National Center for Missing and Exploited Children's CyberTipline, both of whom (and their organizations) check out reports of child porn on the Web and forward verified sightings to the FBI.

But facts have never stood in the way of a good press release (or fund-raiser) for The Rev, so of course he had to weigh in on FBI Director Robert Mueller's statement to the House Judiciary Committee last week, when asked by Rep. Trent Franks (R-Ariz.) about child porn on the Web, that, "We're losing."

"It is growing on the Internet, exponentially is probably too strong a term, but just about every crime there is has gravitated to the Internet, and in certain cases, the Internet has provided the vehicle for expansion that otherwise would not be there, and that's certainly true with child pornography," Mueller told[2] Franks and the rest of the committee.

"It doesn't surprise me that we are losing the war against child pornography," The Rev wrote to Mueller. "I still recall the shock I felt upon hearing that the U.S. Justice Department's focus under Janet Reno was on apprehending suspected child molesters, not on curbing child pornography as such." [Translation: It's still all Clinton's fault.]

"Thankfully, former Attorney General Ashcroft began to change that policy," Peters continued, "but from what I read it would appear that law enforcement energies are still focused primarily on apprehending suspected child molesters. Meanwhile, child pornography proliferates."

Well, y'see, Rev, that's because the FBI isn't Interpol or Russia's Federal Security Service (the replacement for the KGB); it can only arrest those involved with child porn here in the U.S., and for the most part, that would be *viewers* of child porn, because for the most part, the *makers* of the child porn and the ones putting most of it on the Internet are in *Russia*, where the FBI can't touch them.

But never mind all that; The Rev was on a roll!

"The FBI also makes it difficult to successfully wage war against child pornography by refusing to devote more than token resources to combating obscenity and by refusing to investigate obscenity crimes that do not depict the most extreme hardcore pornography," he wrote to Mueller. "The explosion of obscenity contributes to sexual exploitation of children in a number of ways. First, child molesters use 'adult' obscenity (i.e., no minors depicted) to entice, arouse, desensitize and instruct their child victims... Second, there is growing evidence that many men arrested on sexual exploitation of children charges began their downward spiral by viewing not child pornography but 'adult' obscenity."

But according to the article Peters cites for his first point—FBI Agent Kenneth Lanning's report, "Child Molesters: A Behavioral Analysis"[3]—pedophiles use multiple methods to "entice, arouse, desensitize and instruct their child victims" including simply paying attention to them, showing affection toward them, giving them gifts (especially toys, dolls and model planes or boats), behaving like clowns or magicians; decorating their homes in ways that would attract kids, such as hanging posters of rock stars or anime characters, or including items like toys, games and popular music CDs; and even using "seduction techniques, competition, peer pressure, child and group psychology, motivation techniques, threats, and blackmail." Showing them sexually explicit material may be one facet of a seduction technique—but Peters doesn't suggest outlawing Barbie dolls or Monopoly games or Pokemon cartoons because they also may be used.

The report also suggests that parents watch out for "high-status authority figures" who could turn out to be child molesters; you know, people like "teachers, camp counselors, coaches, *religious leaders*, law-enforcement officers, doctors, judges" who could "present even greater problems in the investigation of these cases. Such offenders are in a better position to seduce and manipulate victims and escape responsibility." [Emphasis added]

Boy, ya can't trust anybody these days—*except adult video producers, who have to keep records of who they hire to perform sex!*

As for the second item, it's pure crap. A pedophile—someone attracted to pre-pubescent minors—would no more get aroused by looking at "adult obscenity" (he probably means "adult pornography," but then, he has trouble making distinctions about *anything* sexual) than an adult heterosexual would "turn on" by looking at gay male porn. And Peters' source for this amazing revelation? The Oct. 17, 2007 issue of the *Buffalo News*; specifically, an article titled "An Addiction He Couldn't Break Away From."

The article refers to former greenhouse worker (and now-convicted child molester) Clarence A. Johnson, who "once enjoyed the adult pornography sites he viewed on the Web. But after a while, the thrill was gone. So Johnson started clicking on some of the advertisements that popped up on his computer screen above the naked men and women he was staring at. He was seeing something new—young teenagers, and even young children, posing in the nude, having sex with each other or being molested by adults. At first, the 49-year-old Batavia man was appalled. But once the shock wore off, Johnson couldn't get enough."

While the article doesn't give the time frame in which Johnson allegedly looked at adult sites, clicked on their ads and was taken to child porn sites—newspaper reports have, after all, been known to contain fabricated anecdotes used to bolster a point—that scenario is exactly the type of thing that Joan Irvine's group and the CyberTipline people have been combating for several years now, and Irvine reports that it's been a long time since she's found any adult porn site where the click-through leads to actual child porn. Moreover, no scientific study is referenced in the article; merely the statement of David G. Heffler, a local "psychotherapist who is appointed by the courts to counsel child pornography offenders" who claimed, "Many men told me they started out looking at adult porn and never intended to look at children. But after looking at adult porn for a long time, they get bored. They want to try something different. They start looking at children. Then, they can't get enough of it."

Part of the difficulty lies in the phrase "looking at children"—who, according to the legal definition, would include anyone aged 17 years 364 days and younger. Peters faults the Supreme Court for its decision in *Ashcroft v. Free Speech Coalition*, which struck references to "young-looking adults" from the Child Pornography Prevention Act, but there's a huge difference between being turned on by post-pubescent girls with breasts and pubic hair and pre-pubescent girls without them. Many adults would find the former attractive; few would find the latter exciting, and it's impossible to tell which group Heffler and/or his patients are referring to.

But for Peters, that "17 years, 364 day" dividing line doesn't really exist, since he rails against "obscenity featur[ing] teens who may be at least 18 but who are promoted for their youth." Get it straight, Bob: Seventeen years, 364 days=illegal; 18 years or older=legal. And adult industry producers *do* check IDs!

The Rev has similar myopia regarding who's hooking these days:

"[T]here is growing evidence that many men who are addicted to obscenity use prostitutes to act out their porn-fueled fantasies... To the extent that addiction to pornography helps maintain or increase the demand for prostitutes, it also helps maintain or increase the demand for women and children who are trafficked into prostitution."

So: First Amendment-protected expression should be criminalized because some men who view it may hire prostitutes, whose profession should be decriminalized and allowed to be practiced openly ... which would make it much harder for traffickers to force women (and certainly children) into the business in the first place? Good thinking, Rev!

And, of course, inevitably, Peters gets around to, "addiction to obscene materials is also destroying countless marriages, which puts children at greater risk for sexual abuse."

Do we really need to go into the fact that there is no such thing as porn addiction—"Dr." Laura Schlessinger actually admitted that fact on her radio show on Tuesday—but only "obsessive/compulsive disorder," which can focus on anything from porn to gambling to praying to hand washing? Do we really need to remind everyone that marriages don't fail because of porn, but may fail in part because the partners are unable or poorly able to communicate with each other about their sexual fears and desires? Or that porn viewing has nothing to do with child sexual abuse?

"In addition to protecting children from sexual exploitation," The Rev continues, "the Justice Department and FBI should also be doing all they can to protect children from exposure to Internet obscenity."

Great news, Rev: Computer programmers have developed this thing called "Web filtering," which can be set to screen out anything hinting of sexual material: breast-cancer exams, Betty Boop cartoons and lots more. In fact, your pals at the American Family Association will let you subscribe to their own ISP which will do all that filtering for you! And besides, aren't you the guys who keep ranting about how parents should be in charge of their children's sexual education? Wouldn't part of that consist of monitoring what their kids look at on the Web? I mean, isn't that their ***job***???

But of course, once again, it's the Supreme Court's fault for not having upheld unconstitutional laws like the Communications Decency Act and COPA.

"It wouldn't require a tremendous allocation of investigative and prosecutorial resources to substantially reduce traffic in obscene materials," Peters claims, "because much if not most hardcore pornography is controlled by a relatively small number of companies based in the U.S. But it would require a commitment."

Um ... no. In case you hadn't heard, the Internet is often referred to as the "World Wide Web," and there's a clue in that phrase as to why "commitment" by a U.S.-based law enforcement agency just won't cut it: Servers can be located anywhere in the world, and a click on a URL can bring in images from Denmark or Antarctica just as easily as it can from right next door—maybe easier.

In his Morality in Media Newsletter, Peters boasts that his ObscenityCrimes.org website recently scored its 70,000th citizen complaint, and although he says he forwards all such complaints to the Justice Department and local U.S. attorneys, he doesn't mention how many of those complaints have resulted in prosecutions. We're guessing zero, zip, nada, since the people who subscribe to his newsletter, and complain on his website, even get offended by the covers of *Redbook* and *Cosmo* at the supermarket checkout line.

But ... "In 2002, MIM also retained the services of two retired law enforcement agents to follow up on select complaints and prepare investigative reports which provide information about various pornographic websites. MIM also forwards these reports to the Justice Department and local U.S. Attorneys." And we're guessing that it's because that stuff has been so valuable that two years ago, Congress cut off the funds it was donating to keep the website running.

So remember: Keep those donations coming!

OBSCENITY DAY AT THE NATIONAL PRESS CLUB HOLDS NO SURPRISES

May 19, 2008

WASHINGTON, D.C. – It was billed as "Speeches/Press Conference Against Illegal Obscenity," with the title itself belying its creators' understanding that, at least according to the Supreme Court, obscenity already is "illegal."

But never mind: At least 16 representatives of conservative religious groups gathered at the National Press Club this morning to make known their opinion that the U.S. Department of Justice (DOJ), despite nearly a dozen federal obscenity indictments during the current presidency, still isn't doing its job when it comes to suppressing "smut" a/k/a constitutionally-protected sexual speech.

While a recording of the morning's press conference was (reportedly) on its way to *AVN* (**Update**: It never arrived), Family Research Council has released its encyclical on the subject, most of it either provably false or all-too-revealing.

"The porn industry and their friends at the ACLU seek an America where there are no legal limits on pornography—no limit to how graphic it may be, no limit to the people it can exploit for profit, including children," said Cathy Ruse,[1] senior fellow for Legal Studies at FRC, and wife of Austin Ruse, president of the Catholic Family & Human Rights Institute, which targets United Nations family planning initiatives. "And they're winning. Not because what they're doing is legal, but because they're getting away with it."

Actually, no. Adult XXX companies don't use minors in their productions, and in fact, several have called for an agreement to raise the minimum age of performers from 18 to 21. As for porn being legal, the Supreme Court has unequivocally said that it is, so there's no need for the adult industry to "get away with" anything.

"There is no First Amendment right to make or sell hard-core pornography that's 'obscene'," FRC's press release's quoting of Ruse continues. "That's a legal battle the other side lost a long time ago. And without the law on their side they've turned to ridicule, obfuscation, and intimidation to get their way. They mock the word 'obscenity' and make fun of Potter Stewart saying it's hard to define but 'I know it when I see it.' They aim their hired guns at townships threatening to bankrupt them. And they personally and viciously attack anyone who upholds the law."

Of course, Ruse leaves out the fact that it's completely legal to *own* obscene material, which begs the question of where that material is supposed to come from. Most people don't make it themselves, and for the Supreme Court to rule that sexually-explicit material can be prosecuted at any point *until* it crosses the threshold of a person's home or apartment is schizophrenic, to say the least.

As for the adult community resorting to "ridicule, obfuscation, and intimidation to get their way," Ruse needs to hold up a mirror to herself and the organizations she represents. The industry does indeed "mock the word 'obscenity'" because any constitutional scholar can see that the First Amendment provides no exception allowing its prosecution. The United States is a government of laws, not of men, with the Constitution the highest law of the land, and the sensibility of the late Justice Potter Stewart that he "knows [obscenity] when he sees it" doesn't pass *that* smell test.

Ruse can throw around the term "hired gun" all she likes, but the adult industry thankfully has a good body of attorneys willing to defend its right to exist and market its product, and to the extent that municipalities try to thwart that right, those attorneys will go to court to defend it. And as for who's trying to bankrupt whom, Ruse might want to look at the case of *PHE, Inc. v. U.S. Department of Justice*,[2] where the DOJ, following the advice of the man who now heads its Obscenity Prosecution Task Force, devised a strategy to indict adult companies in multiple jurisdictions around the country in an avowed effort to bankrupt those companies with legal fees, knowing that it couldn't win its obscenity cases on the merits!

"But the law says obscene material is that which a jury finds: appeals to the prurient interest, is patently offensive, and lacks serious value," Ruse continued. "So it doesn't matter what the porn industry or what the ACLU thinks. All that matters is what a jury thinks, and that means ultimately it's up to the American people to decide what's illegal or not. The people become disenfranchised when obscenity laws are not vigorously enforced."

Actually, the American people become disenfranchised when obscenity laws *are* vigorously enforced, because it takes from them the decision whether to buy the material or not, and leaves that decision in the hands of government prosecutors, and in some cases, juries composed of up to 12 citizens who often don't understand the concept of "prurient interest" no matter how a judge explains it to them, and most of whom have never talked about their sexual preferences with their families or next-door neighbors, let along strangers elsewhere in their cities in order to know what the "community standards" of their community *are*! And as for the "American people [deciding] what's illegal or not," one of the reasons the Constitution exists is to protect minorities—like the adult industry—from persecution by the majority—or in this case, by a highly vocal minority: Fundamentalist Christians and Jews.

"Our voice is the jury verdict," Ruse boasts. "Without obscenity prosecutions there are no juries, and no juries mean no verdicts, and no verdicts mean the people have no voice. And that leaves the porn industry to set the standards for the culture."

Over 921 million adult tapes and DVDs were rented and sold in 2006, the last year for which such figures are available. The population of the United States is only just over 300 million, including children, but that strongly suggests that adult entertainment enjoys widespread acceptance across the United States. Therefore, for Ruse to claim that her fundamentalist followers' views are "the jury verdict" is both laughable and provably false. Conservatives are so fond of claiming that the free market should be the determiner of commercial laws, let her and her cronies apply the same principle to adult entertainment so they can finally realize that it isn't the porn industry that "set[s] the standards for the culture," it's the average American consumer. Feeling a little jealous, are you, Cathy?

"We call on the Bush Administration and on the next President of the United States to give us back our voice, and vigorously enforce this nation's obscenity laws," Ruse concludes. But what she's really calling for is for the government to embrace her religious doctrines at the expense of everyone else's free speech rights.

The place to peddle that hooey is in Communist China or Vatican City, not the United States of America.

Porn fans will be glad to know that Brandi Love is still around and as entertaining as ever.

PENN & TELLER TACKLE "THE WAR ON PORN"

June 20, 2008

LOS ANGELES – Comedians/magicians Penn Gillette and partner Teller kicked off their fourth season of *Penn & Teller: Bullshit!* on Showtime last night with a topic vital to free expression: America's war on porn.

"You're watching this to defend America's Constitution," Penn says in voice-over while on-screen, Jay Huntington and some unidentifiable actresses engage in close personal contact. "Porn is part of what makes us great; it's as American as B-movie actors [photo of Ronald and Nancy Reagan] and pilgrims... With the Internet, pornography has become more accessible and more accepted than ever."

The show includes plenty of footage from adult tradeshows—notably Adultcon[1]—and XXX movies (though nothing hardcore is shown) and features mini-interviews with psychologist Dr. Marty Klein and sociologist Dr. Daniel Linz[2]—as well as with what Penn terms "The Three Stooges Reincarnated": Wheelock College professor and anti-porn activist Dr. Gail Dines, anti-porn author Dr. Diana Russell[3] and XXXChurch[4] pastor Craig Gross.

Penn notes that an early government non-prosecutorial attempt to censor sexual speech began with the Lockhart Commission,[5] empanelled by President Lyndon Johnson to study the effects of adult material on society, which found no problem with the genre, followed only a few years later by the Meese Commission, empanelled by President Reagan, which "pissed away a lot more of our money," Penn states.

Also featured are housewife Brandi Love and husband, who "are the proud owners and stars of a high-tech website, brandilove.com."

"I think many people love the idea, whether they'll admit it or not," Brandi opines, "that they could get paid and make a very comfortable living having sex on camera... For us, it's the American dream."

Of course, plenty of shots of naked Brandi are shown.

About 10 minutes into the show, however, the pro-censorship trio are given their chance to speak.

"This is a national emergency!" cries Dines. "As far as I'm concerned, access to pornography, to the hardcore violent pornography that exists, is the #1 public health issue of our time... Is it okay to become aroused to images of sexual torture, which is what pornography is?" (LIAR!)

Penn and Teller, though, point out that in areas which have the most access to the Internet, and hence to online porn, rapes are down, while in areas with the least access, rapes are up—possibly a coincidence, Penn admits, but a lot more likely than the idea that porn causes rape (and child abuse), for which no peer-reviewed scientific studies exist."

"Men can become predisposed to rape from viewing pornography," claims Russell. "That is my theory."

And she has a diagram to "prove" it.

"I think this theory, I have to say myself, is really very powerful," Russell continues. "I don't know anybody who has been able to refute it."

"Really?" says Penn.

"There's no proof, there's no peer-reviewed scientific data that people who look at pornography are more likely to commit violent or sexually-deviant acts than anybody else," Klein, author of *America's War On Sex*, responds.

"Not only is there no evidence that looking at pornography makes people more violent than people who do not look at pornography, there's actually evidence to the reverse," he continues. "The good news is that most pornography shows happy people doing things that happy people do when they're in bed with somebody they want to have sex with."

But then the show cuts to a lecture by Dines, where she claims that pornography "has to keep ratcheting it [violence] up to keep it interesting," and links adult porn with child abuse—an idea that Klein completely rejects.

The show also features one of Gross's "Porn & Pancakes" anti-porn events, which he holds at churches around the country, and even briefly interviews a reformed "porn addict."

Perhaps most important, however, is Dines' final point, when asked about "the studies that are out now":

"You keep pushing me on this," she retorts. "I've said enough. There's nothing else to say. I mean, there are no good studies."

And indeed, there aren't—except the ones done back in the '80s and '90s that show that most porn is completely benign.

Of course, there's much more stuffed into the show's half-hour than can be related here, but one thing's for sure: It's an experience that no member of the adult entertainment community should miss.

HOW CAN I BULLSHIT THEE? LET ME COUNT THE WAYS

Morality in Media releases another bogus 'porn report.'
October 9, 2009

NEW YORK CITY—Robert Peters, president of the religious pro-censorship group Morality in Media, has issued a report, "How Adult Pornography Contributes To Sexual Exploitation of Children,"[1] which a press release accompanying the announcement says was compiled from "information from hundreds of news articles and from court cases, social science studies, books, Congressional testimony, and other sources" by Peters himself.

Of course, one doesn't have to look further than the introduction to find the manure that forms the backbone of this "report."

"The explosion of hardcore adult pornography on the Internet and elsewhere is contributing to sexual exploitation of children in a variety of ways," the report claims. First on the list is, "Perpetrators use adult pornography to groom their victims." The word "groom" in this context apparently means showing the kids pictures of adults either naked or having sex, and convincing the child that he/she can do that also. The concept is hardly new, and certainly wouldn't fall into disuse if all adult XXX material were to disappear tomorrow. Pedophiles have been using *any* sexual and pseudo-sexual material for such purposes at least as far back as the Sears catalog[2] has printed pictures of people in underwear, and there are a whole host of highly-respected Hollywood movies used for the same purpose: *The Last Picture Show*, *Midnight Cowboy* and *Blue Lagoon*, just to name three prominent ones.

"Also at this time, there was much debate about whether adult pornography was harmful," Peters writes of his early days as a staff attorney at MIM. "Much of the debate focused on the question of whether adult pornography 'causes' sex crimes. In my opinion this is a dishonest question because when it comes to human behavior, 'causation' is difficult to determine conclusively. The unresolved question of 'causation' notwithstanding, it seemed to me then, and now, that the use of adult pornography by predators to arouse, instruct and desensitize their child victims is an example of how adult pornography contributes to harm."

In other words, Peters wants to have the best of both worlds: He's willing to leave open the (actually already settled) question of whether porn causes sex crimes—it doesn't, and there are numerous scientific studies showing that to be the case—but he's willing to assume it does when adults use it to "lure" kids into sexual acts.

But the right (and especially the religious ones) might want to think twice before blaming (legal) media for the (illegal) actions of its users. For example, the U.S. Department of Justice has recently opened investigations into whether certain CIA interrogators "exceeded the limits" placed on their torture of Guantanamo prisoners by the legal opinions authored by White House counsel staffers John Yoo and Jay Bybee—so if legal porn can be blamed for the illegal acts by pedophiles, that same logic would suggest that Yoo and Bybee are ripe for prosecution for conspiring, through their writings, to torture detainees.

And of course, the vast majority of articles Peters uses to prop up his charges were authored either by law enforcement personnel, anti-porn laypeople or journalists with no expertise in sexuality at all. Missing is any scientific evidence, and for good reason: There isn't any.

"For many perpetrators there is a progression from viewing adult pornography to viewing child pornography," is Peters' second claim, and the key word there is "many." The vast—in fact, overwhelming—majority of adults interested in adult pornography have no interest in kiddie porn; they're just not attracted, for both moral and esthetic reasons, to minors. Are there some adults who will progress from adult to child porn? Of course—but that has nothing to do with the adult material itself. Rather, there are some adults with a predilection for children's sexuality, and for them, adult porn is unattractive since it doesn't fulfill their fantasies. Again, it's the *people* who need treatment, not the material that needs banning.

Here, Peters props up his charge by quoting Dr. Victor Cline, an anti-porn "researcher" who claims that "porn addicts" go through four stages of their "illness": Addiction, escalation, desensitization and acting out sexually. But Cline plays fast and loose with the "scientific research" he claims to use. For instance, while it's correct that Drs. Neil Malamuth and Edward Donnerstein—both legitimate researchers—found that violent porn tends to increase males' acceptance of the fantasy that women like to be raped, the other side of that coin is never mentioned: That non-violent porn has little to no effect (other than temporary arousal) on its viewers. Cline is more at home quoting Drs. Dolf Zillmann[3] and Jennings Bryant[4]—both anti-porn crusaders—who allege that porn "increase[s] callousness toward women," "devalue[s] the importance of monogamy," "distort[s] perceptions about sexuality," causes "an appetite for more deviant, bizarre or violent types of porn," and causes those exposed to "view non-monogamous relationships as normal and natural behavior." (Oooh, unmarried people having sex—real scary, boys and girls!)

And finally, in Cline's section titled "Research methodology," he admits that there is no causal link between porn and any of the sexual deviancies he chronicles: "Correlation alone never demonstrates or proves a causal relationship, though it can be suggestive or raise that possibility."

"Johns act out what they view in adult pornography with child prostitutes and pimps use adult pornography to instruct child prostitutes," is Peters' third charge, and again, the scientific evidence is absent. Peters quotes Cline's fourth step, "Acting out sexually," wherein Cline, citing no scientific evidence whatsoever, claims that "porn addicts" engage in "compulsive promiscuity, exhibitionism, group sex, voyeurism, *frequenting massage parlors*, having sex with minor children, rape, and inflicting pain on themselves or a partner during sex." [Emphasis by Peters]

The reader can perhaps be forgiven for failing to understand how porn viewers becoming patrons of prostitutes translates into those viewers patronizing *child* prostitutes and acting out porn fantasies with them, and of course, Peters' only evidence for that is his claim that, "To the extent that viewing adult pornography on the Internet is linked to prostitution in general, it is also linked to sexual exploitation of children trafficked into prostitution, if for no other reason than that so many prostitutes are children."

Peters' statement is difficult to assess since no one knows how many prostitutes are currently working in the world, much less in the U.S.... and of course, Peters himself provides no reliable statistics. Beyond that, his only evidence that prostitution patrons are seeking children are unsubstantiated claims that they're looking for hookers who are "young."

Similarly, there is no scientific evidence provided for the claim that "Children imitate behavior they view in adult pornography with other children." Oh, there are several press accounts of kids molesting or sodomizing other kids, usually with some adult opining that the molesters learned their sexual deviancy by watching either their parents' porn collection or going online to adult sites, but no one even attempts to factor in kids' normal post-pubescent sexual curiosity and inventiveness nor the incidence of sociopathic behavior in minors. And indeed, most of the reports of adolescent sexual behavior can just as easily be traced to their natural sexual curiosity without the need to bring in dark conspiracies by porn sites to allegedly attract youngsters. Rather, it is the unwarranted (though in religious circles extremely common) assumption that kids have no sexual thoughts until some adult instructs them, or they view porn, that informs Peters' claim, rather than any assessment of reality.

So it's almost a breath of fresh air when Peters claims that, "Perpetrators use adult pornography to sexually arouse themselves." Can you say, "Duh"? Porn's purpose is arousal; the conveyance of an erotic message that says, in effect, "Sex is a normal part of human existence, and people who see other people having sex can revel in their enjoyment of it... as well as perhaps get some ideas to improve their own sex lives." Even the U.S. Supreme Court understands that!

But again, Peters has difficulty separating the fact that porn arouses people from the fact that some people, when aroused, will commit antisocial acts. That has nothing to do with the porn itself, but rather the psychology (and possibly physiology) of the perpetrator of the crime. Even in the absence of porn, bad people commit bad acts—even bad sexual acts.

Finally, Peters claims that "Addiction to adult pornography destroys marriages and children raised in one-parent households are more likely to be sexually exploited." We've noted several times that so-called "porn addiction" is simply another manifestation of obsessive-compulsive disorder (OCD), and that those who suffer from OCD may express their disease in any number of ways, from excessive hand-washing to excessive orderliness (indifferently expressed by the main character in the TV show *Monk*) to excessive religiosity... to excessive porn viewing. The disorder is treatable, but the disorder itself has nothing to do with porn.

And as for the claim that kids in one-parent households are more likely to be sexually exploited, Peters devotes exactly one paragraph to the concept, citing a British study, "Children under 12 years with Sexual Behaviour Problems in London and Middlesex County: Trends and Professionals' Perceptions."[5] However, what that study actually found, after surveying "social service professionals," was that roughly one-third of all kids who came in contact with those social service personnel had sexual behavior problems, which the study attributed to the kids having been exposed to "domestic violence, alcohol and substance abuse problems, unstable living arrangements, different and often temporary caregiving figures, poor parenting skills, poverty"... and, yes, "adult sexual activity and pornography."

In answer to the question, "What predicts sexual problem behaviors in children," the British study states, "Research in this field suggests that many boys and girls who act out sexually have witnessed adult sexuality paired with violence, been sexually, physically and emotionally abused, and experienced significant neglect of their physical and emotional needs by their primary caretaker... Child maltreatment is very strongly correlated with sexual behaviour problems." [Citation omitted] Single-parent families are barely mentioned.

So if readers hadn't already guessed, Robert Peters' "study" of "How Adult Pornography Contributes to Sexual Exploitation of Children" is just another sorry attempt to justify the censorship of adult material by claiming a scientific basis for harm. And indeed, one might suspect that the entire purpose of the "study" was the press release announcing it—and, once one clicks through to the website, soliciting donations—since the majority of people who go to the trouble of downloading the "study" won't even read the whole thing, won't think about it analytically, and won't investigate Peters' alleged sources for his "information."

But then again, that's probably exactly what Peters is hoping for.

Too bad, Bob!

The Barry Goldman case got little media attention. The actor/director created several BDSM movies which were mail-ordered by an FBI agent—and he wound up being indicted in New Jersey, which had almost no connection to the movies or their mailing. Also, what's most fascinating about sexts sent by minors is that when those kids are prosecuted, both the sender and the recipient are charged with creating and/or receiving child pornography—which they created themselves! BTW, Alliance Defense Fund later changed its name to Alliance Defending Freedom—and they got to keep the same monogram!

RIGHT RAMPS UP ANTI-PORN EFFORTS

Posted November 2, 2009

JESUSLAND—Accusing adult producers of being "those who would destroy [the next] generation's future for personal gain," former Meese Commission general counsel Alan Sears, who founded the ultra-conservative/ultra-religious Alliance Defense Fund (ADF), charged in an editorial on Sunday that the U.S. Department of Justice has dropped the ball on prosecuting porn.

In a sense, Sears' op-ed piece for the Washington Times, founded by the fundamentalist preacher Rev. Sun Myung Moon, was a follow-up to a letter which several major pro-censorship groups like Family Research Counsel, American Family Assn., Morality in Media and Focus on the Family, as well as several hundred followers, had sent to Attorney General Eric Holder, taking him to task for allegedly not living up to certain anti-porn sentiments expressed in a memo he wrote while a deputy attorney general under Janet Reno, to all of the U.S. Attorneys around the country.

In the July 15, 2009, letter as well as the Times op-ed, Sears specifically reminds Holder of his 1998 admonition to the U.S. Attorneys: "Priority should be given to cases involving large-scale distributors who realize substantial income from multistate operations and cases in which there is evidence of organized crime involvement," but that "prosecution of cases involving relatively small distributors can have a deterrent effect and would dispel any notion that obscenity distributors are insulated from prosecution if their operations fail to exceed a predetermined size or if they fragment their business into small-scale operations." Holder also suggested targeting the adult internet, the investigation and prosecution of which "is particularly suitable for federal resources."

Several knowledgeable First Amendment attorneys have suggested that Holder's memo, from the waning days of the Clinton administration, was written in an attempt to pacify the growing religio-conservative political forces which had played a significant role in encouraging Congress to impeach President Clinton for his dalliances with intern Monica Lewinsky, and to deflect their wrath from Reno, who had not brought a single federal obscenity case (though she had brought several child porn cases) during her tenure as attorney general.

In his editorial, Sears expresses his dismay that the only response to the July 15 letter was a "one short form-letter paragraph two months later from a department official assuring us our input was valued and our concerns were being considered 'carefully' [and] Since then ... nothing but crickets."

But according to Sears, in the 10 years or so since Holder's memo, "the evil has proliferated"—meaning simply that the number of adult DVD producers and webmasters has increased, but that the Justice Department, which targeted just four (arguably) high-profile adult producers during the Ashcroft/Gonzales/Mukasey years—Extreme Associates, Max Hardcore, JM Productions and Evil Angel Productions—has, under Holder, "tak[en] a profoundly laissez-faire attitude toward a criminal enterprise making pervasive use of the Internet to facilitate the efforts of child molesters to infect children with their profoundly warped and perverse ideas about sexual activity and deviancy."

Of course, as a Meese alumnus, Sears likely sees any company that deals with sexually explicit expression as a "criminal enterprise," but he fails to provide any details for his claim that the mainstream adult industry in any way "facilitate[s] the efforts of child molesters to infect children" beyond simply existing. He gives passing notice to the fact that the Child Online Protection Act (COPA) was struck down by the Third Circuit Court of Appeals, but that suit was brought by mainstream artists and publishers, not adult producers—and COPA's demise had nothing to do with Holder's Justice Department.

Sears claims that between the Justice Department's non-interest in prosecuting adult material—he is apparently unaware of this past summer's indictment of Barry Goldman in New Jersey—and the overturning of COPA, "the gates of the mental playgrounds [are] wide open for those who believe, in the favorite phrase of the North American Man Boy Love Association (a major beneficiary of the government's passivity), that 'sex after 8 is too late,' and that every child is 'fair game.'"

Of course, there's nothing in the law (or certainly in the policies of the Washington Times) that requires Sears to be sane in order to publish an opinion article, but the concept that the adult industry is interested in portraying sex with minors (let alone pre-pubescents) or in fact targeting children in any way is in no way borne out by the evidence. And the implicit linking of the (completely legal) adult industry with an organization that encourages pedophilia—NAMBLA[1]—is apparently no longer beyond the pale for religious zealots like Sears.

However, as an attorney, much less one who oversees a large, well-funded legal hit squad like ADF, Sears can't seriously believe that in order to support the constitutional protections for free speech, including sexual speech, "You have to believe that the men who wrote our Constitution despised Christian faith and morals and were indifferent to the concerns of parents for their children's mental and emotional well-being—but were always deeply committed to the protection of deviants and pornographers."

Of course, most of the "men who wrote our Constitution" were Deists, not Christians, and exactly what constituted children's "mental and emotional well-being" was poorly understood at the time, about 100 years before Freud developed the first theory of psychoanalysis, though certainly a topic of discussion—but there's little unclear about the First Amendment, which says, in pertinent part, that "Congress shall make no law ... abridging freedom of speech, or of the press." If the Founding Fathers had intended the phrase "no law" to somehow exempt "deviants and pornographers" from First Amendment protections, the evidence of that is nowhere to be found in the literature of the day. In fact, as Eugene Volokh notes—writing in The Heritage Guide to the Constitution,[2] published by the far-right Heritage Foundation (of which Sears is a member)—"There was only one state law banning pornography, and that appears to have been unenforced until 1821." Much more common were anti-blasphemy laws, all of which have now been declared unconstitutional under both the First and Fourteenth Amendments.

"You have to believe that immersing oneself day after day in deviant sexual imagery has no discernible impact on one's mind, morals, habits, attitudes or relationships with children and people of the opposite sex," Sears continues. "You have to believe that—if the government would just leave them alone—young people living in a culture awash with hypersexualized imagery, language, programming, fashion and entertainment and given instant and unlimited access to technology, will deliberately discipline themselves not to send 'sext' messages or lewd pictures of themselves and others over their cell phones, laptops and home computers. In other words, you have to believe the unbelievable to justify defending the indefensible."

Of course, the underlying implication of Sears' statements is that there's something wrong—or, indeed, unexpected—about the idea that once children reach puberty, there's some reason that they shouldn't take some steps to explore their new-found sexuality—hopefully guided by knowledgeable, non-neurotic adults. It's hardly surprising that kids are sexting each other in order to be playful or to attract members of the opposite sex. What's saddening, however, is that Sears would want to thwart kids' natural sexual expression and figuratively, if not literally, dress them in burqas and apply medieval (or in today's terms, Shari'a) moral law to them, possibly stoning adulterers to death and righteously murdering rape victims and "loose women."

Several books have touched on modern religious anti-sex attitudes, from the discussions of religio-conservative authoritarianism in John Dean's Conservatives Without Conscience[3] to Christian paternalism in George Lakoff's Whose Freedom?—and of course, the "bible" of religious anti-sex activism, Dr. Marty Klein's America's War on Sex.

"Of course, the pornographers have the best lawyers and public relations teams billions can buy—and besides, they'll get their money back and then some," Sears concludes. "But their profits, and this Justice Department's passivity, are already costing the rest of us two things a great nation can ill afford to lose: the high moral ground and the souls of our children."

Leaving aside the nostrum that adult industry moguls have "billions" to spend on attorneys and P.R. flacks, apparently, Sears' "rest of us" doesn't include the millions of Americans (some of whom, we're guessing, are church-going Republicans) who rent the roughly three-quarters of a billion DVDs from video stores and on the internet each year, nor the "high moral ground" staked out by prostitute-patronizing Republican Sen. David Vitter,[4] Rev. Ted Haggard and Rev. Jimmy Swaggart; adulterous Republican Sens. John Ensign and John McCain, former Republican Reps. Charles "Chip" Pickering and Newt Gingrich and evangelist Jim Bakker; not to mention attempted-child-seducing former Republican Rep. Mark Foley.

Fortunately, despite Sears' alleged concern for President Obama, "a man who so beautifully and publicly demonstrates his love for his daughters," it's likely that Sasha and Malia will grow up sexually sane under the influence of their two sexually normal parents ... who, if the majority of American citizens are lucky, will give Sears' editorial all the consideration it deserves—as bird-cage liner.

NEW WEBSITE MAKES OLD CLAIMS ABOUT PORN

Why is Utah so porn-obsessed?

Posted January 21, 2010

SALT LAKE CITY—The heart of Mormon country has spawned more than its share of anti-porn crusaders, but a new site appears to be aimed at giving Morality In Media a run for its money... literally.

FightTheNewDrug.com, a new website that claims that viewing adult content is tantamount to using addictive chemicals, got its hard launch on Tuesday, at a "special kickoff breakfast" at the Little America Hotel here, attended by, among others, Utah Gov. Gary Herbert and Attorney General Mark Shurtleff.[1]

The site is the brainchild of four activists, Ryan Werner, Cameron Lee, Clay Olsen and Beau Lewis, about whom little is known beyond what they themselves have written on the site: Werner runs triathlons; Olsen "loves teaching" and has a "background in marketing"; Lewis, who's listed as the founder of the 501(c)(3) organization, is an accountant; and Lee is a "networking genius"... not to mention, president of the Latter-Day Saints Student Association, a credit not listed on the site. It's unclear whether the other founders are also Mormons.

As is typical of anti-porn sites, there's a section called "Stories," where so-called "porn addicts" get to tell their tales of woe, but for a site that claims that its mission is based on science, and urges visitors to "Hear the facts directly from the fighters," there's precious little actual science available there. The "Fighter Facts" button leads to a screen with no content whatsoever (but they're supposedly "Coming Soon"), while the "Science" button leads to three areas: "The Physical Effects of Pornography," "The Un-Sexiness of Pornography" and "The Pornography Pandemic."

"We have always known that children's brains change constantly as they develop, and the assumption was that adult brains became 'set' and fixed in a particular way that was stable for the rest of one's life," reads the introduction to the "physical effects" section. "Recently, however, neuroscientists have been surprised to discover the degree to which adult brains change over time, a phenomenon known as 'neuroplasticity' (with 'plastic' expressing the idea 'malleability'). For instance, recent studies have shown that when individuals learn a language, their neural networks expand[;] when they start a meditation routine, their brain pathways adjust[;] and when individuals are abused, neural pathways are similarly altered. If learning new languages or peaceful moments of meditation change the brain, what about even more intense or stimulating activities? In what way might watching something on a television or computer screen shape the brain?"

Yes, that's right: All these folks have is speculation; there really is no science that has produced experiments that link the dopamine produced by the brain's pleasure center—production that can be stimulated by addictive drugs—specifically to viewing sexually explicit material... rather than, say. taking part in any other pleasurable activity, like eating or sex... or running a triathlon.

"With all addictive behaviors, however, it is more than a dopamine spike itself that occurs," the site continues. "Repeated exposure to pornography, or any drug of abuse, over time, will inevitably affect the dopamine system—most commonly leading the VTA-NAc pathway to develop a tolerance to the chemical. That is, in order for an individual to get the same sensation that he or she used to get, more dopamine is needed to produce a similar feeling or 'high.' As happens with any drug, this growing tolerance requires increases in both frequency and intensity of the drug to compensate for the decreased pleasure."

Trouble is, every single reference to this alleged increased tolerance leading to decreased dopamine production (others have claimed that endorphin production is the culprit), which in turn leads to increased use of the stimulant, is to studies of *drug abuse*; not a single one references even video-game playing, much less porn.

So much for any attempt to use actual science.

The other two sections make typical claims about porn use: That it subverts actual interpersonal relationships, and that its prevalence in society, even though the site admits that "Pornography is naturally appealing," is "exerting more cultural influence than ever before," and has "become a public health issue."

But aside from the site's claim that it's the nexus of a "global campaign against pornography," it's really just another tired attempt to roil the proles—something with which Utah is well familiar.

Despite the fact that Utah has more subscribers to adult websites per capita than any other state in the union, Attorney General Shurtleff seems to have devoted his life to suppressing sexual expression in the state. Recall, for instance, his creation in March of 2000 of the administrative post of "porn czar,"[2] one of whose duties was supposed to be to draft a new state definition of obscenity, to help local municipalities restrict, suppress or eliminate porn and to offer "information" about the "dangers of obscenity." The job lasted about three years, sucked up about half a million tax dollars, and produced no results... except to inspire an "adult entertainment tax" of 10 percent on all nude dancing and escort services in the state. The tax was supposed to bring in $1 million annually to state coffers, and though it's been in existence for about six years, having withstood a lawsuit by strip clubs, just how much revenue the tax has brought in is not available through public records.

So watch out, Morality In Media: Looks like the Mormons intend to give you fundamentalist Protestants a run for your (supporters') money!

Truth is, I was going to do a review of The Social Costs of Pornography *but never got around to it, and at this point, I'm not sure why I didn't. Also, the late Shelly Lubben was a former adult performer—she appeared in all of 14 movies under the stage name Roxy—who turned anti-porn activist, spoke at a lot of anti-porn events, and even formed a foundation that did little but support her lifestyle; great scam she had going. BTW, check out "Jesusland" on Wikipedia; it's a hoot.*

THE WEIGHT OF BULLSHIT

Send in the clowns, er, 'scholars'
Posted May 27, 2010

JESUSLAND—Mary Eberstadt, a "research fellow" at the conservative Hoover Institution, has just the right credentials to write about the harms of porn. No science, psychology or sociology training, of course, just a good list of publications in conservative/right-wing whackadoodle journals like the *Weekly Standard*, the *American Spectator*, *Policy Review* and the *Wall Street Journal*. Moreover, she used to be a speech writer for Reagan's Secretary of State George Schultz and a "special assistant" to Reagan's U.N. Ambassador Jeane Kirkpatrick. How much more "qualified" can you get?

So perhaps it's not too surprising that she doesn't know shit about the effects of porn on either individuals or society—but that didn't stop her from writing "The Weight of Smut"[1] for *First Things*, a fundamentalist Catholic magazine.

Of course, lots of people are concerned about their weight these days, and Eberstadt uses an *Atlantic* article "America the Obese" as her jumping off point to claim that there's an "emerging social phenomenon" called "sexual obesity," which anti-porn zealot Dr. Mary Anne Layden—she's a favorite witness for anti-porn Sen. Sam Brownback—defines as "the widespread gorging on pornographic imagery that is also deleterious and unhealthy." Not surprisingly, though, that "gorging" won't show up on the bathroom scale.

"She [Layden] also knows what most do not," Eberstadt intones. "Quietly, patiently, and irrefutably, an empirical record of the harms of sexual obesity is being assembled piecemeal via the combined efforts of psychologists, sociologists, addiction specialists, psychiatrists, and other authorities." (Well, that might be true if one puts "conservative" in front of each of those specialists ... and while "empirical" means "based on observation or experiment," you can bet it's exclusively the former; one thing anti-porn zealots *don't* do is "experiment," 'cause if they did, they'd have to publish ... and watch *real* scientists tear apart their methodology and results.)

"Young people who have been exposed to pornography are more likely to have multiple lifetime sexual partners, more likely to have had more than one sexual partner in the last three months, more likely to have used alcohol or other substances at their last sexual encounter, and—no surprise here—more likely to have scored higher on a 'sexual permissiveness' test," Eberstadt claims, as if those are Bad Things.

"They are also more likely to have tried risky forms of sex," she continues. "They are also more likely to engage in forced sex and more likely to be sexual offenders."

"Risky forms of sex"? Does she mean without condoms? Nah, couldn't be; she and her ilk oppose comprehensive sex education in schools. Does she mean anal sex? Gay sex? Who knows—and Eberstadt ain't sayin'; it'd ruin the soundbite-iness. And when she claims that porn viewers are "more likely to engage in forced sex," does she mean more likely to *be* raped or to *commit* rape? Probably the latter, but there's no scientific evidence for that, and Eberstadt doesn't provide any links or footnotes—but that's okay; the bulk of this article is a set-up to plug *The Social Costs of Pornography*, which Eberstadt "prepared" with Layden, based on a symposium conducted by the ultraconservative/ultrareligious Witherspoon Institute. But more on that later ...

"As for the all-purpose cop-out that 'all this shows is correlation'...[n]o one reasonable would doubt that there is a connection between watching sex acts and trying out what one sees," Eberstadt claims, "especially for adolescents, who rather famously and instantly ape the other influences on their lives, from fashion to drug use and more, as has also been copiously studied."

No, actually, it hasn't... unless by "studied," she means the "empirical record" claimed above which conservatives have no problem pulling out of their asses. To be fair, sure, people—mostly adults—who watch porn sometimes try to emulate what they've seen on the screen, usually to add "spice" to their relationships ... which is why many porn movies begin with a disclaimer that "the sex acts depicted in this movie are performed by professionals, and should not be attempted at home." But the idea that a 12- or 14-year-old boy can watch porn and go out and pick up a babe off the street (or at the local mall) and fuck her like a porn star fucks is simply adolescent (conservative) fantasy.

"[E]vidence also shows that sexual obesity does share with its counterpart this critical common denominator: It afflicts the subset of human beings who form the first generation immersed in this consumption, many of whom have never known a world without it—the young," Eberstadt later claims.

Let's see: Sex is pleasurable. When boys and girls reach puberty, they become interested in sex—and quickly find that just about every adult in their lives, including just about every school and church official, is scared shitless to talk to them about it except in vague, uninformative terms, with the first words out of their mouths usually something like, "You don't want to try it; you're too young." And with that attitude, we expect kids *not* to seek out porn?

Yes, of course, it's more available now, and from a wider variety of sources than ever before, but kids have *always* sought out porn, whether it's "French postcards," 8mm loops, "little dirty comics," erotic novels, *Playboy/Penthouse/Hustler* or what-have-you. In fact, ACLU attorney Marjorie Heins[2] actually wrote a book which discusses the history of kids and porn, aptly titled, *Not In Front of the Children*.

But when you start with the assumption that looking at pictures or videos of other people having sex is a Bad Thing, almost any statistic evokes horror.

So when Eberstadt moans that, "One 2008 study focused on undergraduate and graduate students ages 18 to 26 across the country found that more than two-thirds of men—and one out of every ten women in the sample—viewed pornography more than once a month," the first question that should pop to mind is, "So?"

Likewise, when she claims that, "Another study showed that first-year college students using sexually explicit material exhibited these troubling features: increased tolerance, resulting in a turn toward more bizarre and esoteric material; increased risk of body-image problems, especially among girls; and erroneous and exaggerated conceptions of how prevalent certain sexual behaviors, including risky and even dangerous behaviors, actually are," it's reasonable to point out that while she uses the *language* of addiction—"increased tolerance"—nowhere has she demonstrated that viewing sexual material is in any way comparable to *actual* addiction like, say, heroin or methamphetamine use; that when she talks about "body-image problems," surely porn has to take a back seat to the plethora of TV, magazine and billboard ads hawking everything from makeup to fashion to jewelry to diet foods to exercise equipment; and that she actually has no conception of what much of America is doing in the privacy of its own bedrooms when it comes to "certain sexual behaviors," some of which she calls "risky and even dangerous." (Again, *what* behaviors? Condomless? Anal? Pedophilia? Surely not erotic asphyxia, which over-the-counter porn movies don't show? Of course she never deigns to define what a "risky" or "dangerous" sexual behavior is.)

"Finally, to connect the dots between 'monkey see' and 'monkey do,'" Eberstadt claims, "a 2004 study in *Pediatrics* reported, in the words of its title, that 'Watching sex on television predicts adolescent initiation of sexual behavior'—an ominous connection, given that Internet sex is vastly more realistic than anything available on television ... A Kaiser Family Foundation study from 2005, for example, revealed that the number of sex scenes on television doubled between 1998 and 2005. The Foundation had previously noted that some 70 percent of youths aged 15 to 17 accidently [sic] came across pornography online."

Yeah; kids—whaddya gonna do with 'em? They reach puberty, their hormones start flowing, and next thing you know, they're thinking about the sex those hormones are stimulating them to have! Sure, their parents and grandparents used to get off (literally) on the underwear ads in the

Sears Catalog, and turn-of-the-(20th)-century newspaper editorials (and religious revivalists) used to warn about "dandies" always looking for the turn-on of catching a glimpse of a young girl's "smartly-turned ankle" under floor-length dresses—but all of that pales before the "sex scenes" kids can now see on TV!

Of course, there *are no* "sex scenes" on TV. Hell, you can't even show a half-second glimpse of Janet Jackson's nipple without the FCC trying to fine you millions of dollars. No, you can see about as much "sex" (by which the censorship types usually mean the "bare skin" of "certain anatomical parts") on TV as you can in the average Calvin Klein or Victoria's Secret ad in a magazine—or on a five-story high billboard in Times Square.[3] And if parents are dead set against their kids seeing bare tits 'n' ass on cable, there are parental controls on every TV set nowadays, and for the internet, just about every fundamentalist religious group has a "porn-free" ISP you can subscribe to, and beyond that, several companies sell filtering software that will block similar fare ... until your kids get computer-savvy enough to work around it. (Hormones, remember?)

But of course, Eberstadt and her ilk aren't really worried about whether the kids are seeing bare skin or (God forbid) people actually having sex; to them, the *mere existence* of sexually explicit content is the *real* problem:

"But even this impressive array of data cannot answer a question almost as ubiquitous as pornography itself: So what?" Eberstadt writes. "Why should people who are not part of that consumption even care about it? The varieties of the libertarian shrug extend even to those averse to it. Pornography indeed may be morally wrong, many of those people would also say (and of course major religions would agree); but, apart from the possible damage to the user's soul, if you believe in such a thing, what really is the social harm of smut?"

And as if you couldn't guess, that question is simply a set-up to plug her "book" (at 57 pages, little more than a pamphlet, really), *The Social Costs of Pornography*, supposedly "A Statement of Findings and Recommendations" that "is not the work of one or two but rather scores of people[,] most of them academics and medical professionals."

AVN will soon be taking a more in-depth look at "The Social Costs of Pornography"—or rather, the so-called "academic studies" underlying the claims in that pamphlet, since the pamphlet itself contains almost no scientific data—much as it frequently references "voluminous amounts of data," "abundant empirical evidence" and "professional and expert agreement." And of course it's written in "academically neutral language"—to disguise its (all too obvious) agenda.

And speaking of "agenda," get ready to try to find the actual science behind "the very human stories that went into it all: the marriages lost or in tatters; the sexual problems among the addicted; the constant slide, on account of higher tolerance, into ever edgier circles of this hell; the children and teenagers lured into participating in various ways in this awful world in the effort to please romantic partners or exploitive adults."

It's not there, of course—well, at least not here—but Eberstadt's article tries to whet the reader's appetite with a couple of anti-porn claims, beginning with the concept that "Pornography use is a private matter."

"Perhaps the queen bee of lies about pornography, this is also the easiest to take down," Eberstadt boasts. "For while consumption of the substance may be private (or not, as airline travelers[4] and library patrons and others in the public square have lately been learning), the fallout from some of that consumption is anything but."

And what evidence does she have? Well, "[a]dolescent users of pornography are more likely to intend to have sex and to engage in more frequent sexual activity." "Intend"? Most people *intend* to be rich someday, but it'd be a mistake to bet the house on that. Beyond a claim that these same adolescents are "more likely to test positive for chlamydia"—somehow, the fact that the disease is often passed to babies during childbirth has escaped Eberstadt's attention—"Three separate studies have found among adolescents a strong correlation between pornography consumption and engaging in various sexual activities." Didn't anybody ever mention to these "academics and medical professionals" the well-known statistical axiom that "correlation is not causation"? (That's probably Day 1 of any course in statistical analysis.)

Eberstadt's other "evidence" for porn use not being private? Sixty-two percent of the 350 attendees at a matrimonial lawyers' conference reportedly said "the Internet had played a role in divorces during the last year"—not "porn"; "the Internet." She also quotes "research not yet published"—or peer-reviewed, one might add—from a "General Social Survey" on divorce of which a couple of economists are "examining data ... to assess the negative impact of pornography on other aspects of marriage." Of course, one might ask what expertise *economists* have in assessing the effects of porn on divorce, but perhaps it would just be better to wait until their "research" is completed and see what actual social scientists and statisticians have to say about it.

But in fact, science isn't held in high regard by Eberstadt and her ilk. Just a couple of paragraphs later, she assures her readers that "not everyone needs it [science] to know that pornography is more than just a private thing." *Common sense*—that's all they *really* need! Or maybe just a feeling in their gut ...

"Imagine your teenage daughter walking down the beach," she continues. "Half the men on it have been watching sex on the Internet within the last few days, and half have not. Which ones do you want watching her? How can their 'private' behavior possibly be said to be confined to home, when their same eyes with which they view it travel along with them everywhere else?" What's that a proscription against? The "hairy eyeball"? Cooties? Forget daughters; how is *any* woman harmed by a guy looking at her—no matter what he's looked at before? (Of course, the implication is that porn viewers are more likely to try to seduce—or rape—the girl, but since there are no statistics to back that up—in fact, the stats say exactly the opposite—Eberstadt has to leave it at an implication.)

Another "untruth" Eberstadt wants to debunk is, "Pornography use is a guy thing. It only bothers women." The temptation is to give her that one: Most porn is watched by men, and men can be just as crazy (in a bad way) about sexual speech as women can—and if Eberstadt had stopped there, there'd be little argument.

But no; she's got to quote Pamela Paul, who "interviewed in depth more than 100 heterosexual users of pornography" for her 2005 anti-porn screed, *Pornified*.

"Countless men," Eberstadt quotes Paul summarizing her interviews, "have described to me how, while using pornography, they have lost the ability to relate to or be close to women." How disingenuous can she be? One hundred porn users is hardly enough of a sample to base any conclusions upon—and it's one hell of a lot less than "countless"!

"At least some of the shame and disgust that users sometimes report to therapists may be due to another phenomenon well documented about chronic pornography use: habituation and tolerance," Eberstadt writes, referencing the work of "medical authorities" including Dr. Norman Doidge.[5] "Just as heavy drinkers and drug users over time require higher doses of substances to achieve the same effect, so apparently do some chronic users of pornography come to require harder-core and edgier material ... This same descent into the particular pit of knowing that one is doing something wrong, and still being unable to stop oneself, echoes through other accounts by clinicians of what they hear from some patients."

Gosh, what do we call people who are troubled by "intrusive thoughts that produce anxiety, by repetitive behaviors aimed at reducing anxiety, or by a combination of such thoughts (obsessions) and behaviors (compulsions)"? That's right: *Obsessive-compulsives*! But that's got nothing to do with porn; obsessive-compulsives can obsess over anything from hand-washing to hoarding to overeating ... to praying. And sure enough, Eberstadt trots out quotes from a couple of people who've had firsthand experience with an obsessive-compulsive person—because after all, science doesn't really matter when it comes to porn bashing.

The final "untruth" Eberstadt wants to debunk here is "It's only pictures of consenting adults," because "pornography is never only about pictures. Every single person on the screen is somebody's sister, cousin, son, niece, or mother." Apparently, the fact that those folks voluntarily want to show the world, through photos, videos or the internet, that they're less sexually screwed up than the general population is of no consequence. Porn is bad and anyone who would do it is bad as well.

One might expect some mention of anti-porn activist Shelly Lubben at this point, but Eberstadt simply makes the unsubstantiated claim that the porn community is "a world rife with everything one would want any genuinely loved one to avoid like the plague: drugs, exploitation, physical harm, AIDS." It's all bullshit, of course, and if Eberstadt ever wants to check that out for herself, visits to porn sets and offices for her and her fellow ignoramuses can easily be arranged.

Another "finding" of Eberstadt's "research" is that porn and trafficking of women and children for sex are "associated" because "cameras and film equipment [are] found when trafficking circles are broken up." Hey, swingers (and parents): Better hide that Nikon!

But, "Once again, who even needs all that social science?" Eberstadt asks, sadly likely *not* rhetorically. "Perhaps the most telling response to the 'pictures' defense is rhetorical. Ask even the most committed user whether he wants his own daughter or son in that line of work—and then ask why it's all right to have other people's daughters and sons making it instead."

Um ... because this is America? You remember: "Land of the free, home of the brave"? You probably read about it in school ...

But beware: "Several experts have also noted one more interesting phenomenon that most people who have ever written on this thankless subject will verify: Telling the truth about pornography is practically guaranteed to elicit malice and venom unique in their potency from its defenders."

Gosh, thanks! We try!

But seriously, these people wouldn't know "the truth about pornography" if every producer, director and actor in the business camped out on their front doorsteps. And that most certainly includes *National Review Online*'s Kathryn Jean "K-Lo" Lopez[6] and Family Research Council "Senior Fellow" Cathy Ruse, who "served for several years as the chief spokesperson on human life issues for the U.S. Catholic Bishops," both of whom got "terrifying," "horrible" emails[7] when they wrote their own bogus anti-porn screeds.

"Such unique vituperation," Eberstadt writes, "which has so far gone unremarked in any public discussion of pornography despite the fact that it is commonplace, demands inspection in its own right. In fact, it may be the surest proof altogether of just how addictive Internet pornography can be. Although academic experts may continue to battle over exactly what is meant by 'addiction,' surely the tremendously defensive response in the public square by itself settles the question to any reasonable person's satisfaction."

First of all, pretty much all the anti-porn crowd *does* when it isn't spreading lies about the industry is to whine about how badly they're portrayed in the adult-friendly press. (Concerned Women for America's chief counsel Jan LaRue once called us "domestic terrorists.") Beyond that, it's a no-win situation for defenders of adult content if their only choices are either to ignore the falsehoods of Eberstadt, Layden, Lopez, Ruse and their ilk or to give those bozos' apocalyptic rhetoric the derision it deserves. So if "some reliable subset of defenders can be counted on to respond more like animals than like people," it's only because we (occasionally) sink to your level, Mary.

So ... what do Eberstadt and her cronies want to do about "this other obesity epidemic"?

"For starters," she advises, "we could use a campaign that might promise to do to pornography what was ultimately done to tobacco—a restigmatization based on the evolving record of fact. What's needed is nothing less than the kind of leadership that turned smoking, in the course of a single generation, from cool to uncool—one eventually summoning support high and low, ranging from celebrities, high-school teachers and principals, counselors, former users, and anyone else who knows they belong in the coalition of the willing on this wretched issue. Perhaps when the First Lady concludes her campaign against 'regular' obesity, she or someone else of similar public stature can spare time for this other epidemic, too."

There's just one problem with that: There's verifiable, falsifiable, peer-reviewed scientific proof that tobacco use causes lung cancer, among other ailments, while on the porn side, there's ... absolutely nothing with scientific validity that indicates harm.

And once again, it is (or soon will be) Obama's (or his wife's) fault.

But believe it or not, there's *hope*!

"After all, just look at the tremendous effort that goes into attempts to break the habit," Eberstadt writes. "Look at the energy fueling all those attempts to repair the damage done—the turns to counseling, the therapists, priests, pastors, and others working in these awful trenches to help the addicted get their real lives back. Look at the technological ingenuity too—the new software, the filters, the countercultural and uphill efforts here and there to thwart pornography's public crawl. To survey that multifaceted record of struggle, fledgling but growing by the day, against the also rapidly growing empirical record of the beast's harms, is to grasp a truth about this new obesity beyond the ridicule of the jaded or the vituperative recriminations of those still in the pit."

First of all, "beasts"? Seriously? And then the "fledgling but growing" struggle? Who does she think she's kidding? These assholes have been trying to get porn banned since even before Gutenberg invented the printing press. They're well-funded by a combination of well-meaning but clueless religious types and the conservative political machine that sees suppression of sexual speech as a means to regain political power in government in order to "protect" everyone's kids from the possibility that they might get an inkling of what those below-the-waist body parts might do someday besides tinkle—not to mention, "protect" parents from having to answer the questions their kids are bound to ask the first time (and there *will* be a first time) the kid sees a bare tit, an erect penis or a hairy (or even shaved) pussy: "Mommy, what's that for?"

Because that's what Eberstadt and her "coalition of the willing" are all about: Controlling the population by controlling sex. It's an epic battle that won't end anytime soon—but it's one that needs to be fought for the survival of the American (if not humanity's) way of life.

Consider this a cautionary tale about taking anything about the sociology of porn use at face value.

BOGUS PORN 'STUDY' CLAIMS KIDS SEE HARDCORE BY AGE 11

Hey, if you can't trust a magazine whose masthead says 'Put Porn in its Place,' who can you trust?

Posted June 10, 2010

JESUSLAND—Monday's edition of the e-newsletter for the religio-conservative law group Alliance Defense Fund (ADF) linked to a story headlined, "Study: 1/3 of kids have viewed porn by the time they're 10," which touted a "pornography study" allegedly conducted for the Portman Clinic,[1] part of Britain's National Health Service. The clinic, according to one UK city's website, "offers a psychotherapy service to children and adolescents who have problems with delinquency, criminality, violence, sexually inappropriate behaviour and sexual behaviour which causes harm to others or to the person themselves."

Trouble is, the study doesn't really exist.

Of course, it takes following a couple of links to find that out. ADF linked to a *New York Daily News* article which claimed, " One third of children age 10 and younger have access to online porn, and more than 8 in 10 teens regularly view hardcore pictures on their home computers, according to a British survey reported in the *Daily Mail*."

The *Daily Mail*, it will be remembered, was the sensationalistic paper that "broke the story" that climate scientists at the University of East Anglia had allegedly sent each other emails "revealing" that human-caused global climate change was a hoax—a claim that was later widely debunked by the scientific community.

In any case, the *Daily Mail* reported on the "shocking study" (or was it a "disturbing survey"?) allegedly conducted by "leading sociologist Michael Flood" which was reported in *Psychologies* magazine, which allegedly found that "[a] third of children have accessed online pornography by the time they are ten years old" and that "more than eight in ten children aged 14 to 16 say they regularly access hardcore photographs and footage on their home computers, while two-thirds watch it on their mobile phones."

Apparently oblivious to the difference between a "study" and a "survey," the *Daily Mail*'s writer claimed that Flood had "interviewed hundreds of secondary school pupils for the survey" and found that, "There is compelling evidence that pornography has negative effects on individuals and communities."

Of course, before delving into the meat of what Flood allegedly told *Psychologies*,[2] it might be helpful to know that the magazine's masthead exhorts its readers to, "Put Porn in its Place—Join Our Porn Campaign." Moreover, its editor, Louise Chunn, put the lie to the claim that any actual "study" had taken place:

"Back in the *Psychologies* office we started to talk about what the wide-scale consumption of porn was doing to people, and we focused not on the ironic adults but on teenagers and younger children," Chunn wrote. "*Without a watertight study proving harm*, we invited half a dozen psychologists and counsellors who specialised in sexual relationships to come to a lunch to tell us what they thought. It was their unanimous condemnation of internet porn, and *belief* that it posed a special danger to teenagers' ability to form loving relationships, that formed the basis of our story (written by well-known journalist Decca Aitkenhead) asking if porn is destroying the next generation." [Emphasis added]

That noted, we turned to Aitkenhead's article, and lo and behold, not a single mention of "leading sociologist Michael Flood"!

Rather, Aitkenhead frets that whereas previous generations might have gotten their sexual jollies from "the underwear pages of a Kays catalogue" or "softcore porn magazines such as *Playboy*," "today's children are just a click away from a world of 'scat babes' (women covered in excrement), 'bukkake' (women weeping in distress while several men ejaculate over their faces), or websites offering an entire menu of rape scenes, from incest to raped virgins."

"The average child sees their first porn by the age of just 11," she continues. "Between 60 and 90 per cent of under-16s have viewed hardcore online pornography, and the single largest group of internet porn consumers is reported to be children aged 12 to 17[!]. There is nothing new, of course, about pornography. But this is the first generation to grow up seeing rape and sexual violence before even losing their virginity."

What would be nice would be *any* reference to a peer-reviewed scientific study that contained the above statistics, but almost needless to say, none is mentioned in Aitkenhead's story.

Rather, the reader finds, "The impact of porn on boys, according to sex therapist Dr Thaddeus Birchard, is particularly profound. 'Boys tend to create their sexual template by images—either in their mind, or on the page,' he says. 'These pictures become watermarked on to the fabric of each individual's sexual repertory. That's how male sexual function gets set up.'"

There is reference to a "recent Australian study" which found "'compelling evidence' of a link between boys watching pornography and regarding sexual harassment as acceptable," but surely she isn't referring to *The Porn Report*[3] by Prof. Alan McKee, Dr. Katherine Albury and Prof. Catharine Lumby of the University of Melbourne, who found that just 2 percent of porn consumers felt that porn "causes them to objectify people."

Similarly unidentified are the "researchers in Sweden [who] have found that only limited exposure to porn changed boys' attitudes towards their girlfriends—they found 'normal' sex boring, and wanted to experiment more."

Vague claims rather than even the semblance of scientific evidence continues to be the rule in Aitkenhead's article:

"Couples therapist Val Sampson *suspects* the new popularity of anal sex is entirely due to its prevalence in pornography," while "[t]he Portman Clinic in London, which treats sexual disorders, *has noticed* a dramatic increase in referrals of young girls using the internet to become amateur porn stars." [Emphasis added]

"Once you start to expose impressionable young people to porn, they become desensitised," claimed "sex and relationship therapist" Mo Kurimbokus.[4] "They start looking for something more in terms of excitement, and they can become sexually deviant," while, "Porn is even more addictive than alcohol or drugs," agreed John Woods, a psychotherapist at the

Portman Clinic." (Ah, *there's* that Portman Clinic! Guess it doesn't matter whether it's Michael Flood or John Woods who's quoted ...)

"And like any addiction, the user's tolerance threshold quickly rises," Aitkenhead adds. "*It is still too early for us to have solid empirical data* on how exposure to online pornography will affect the adult relationships of today's teenagers. Even if most of them won't grow up to become addicts, experts' *predictions* for their adult sex lives are troubling." [Emphasis added]

In other words, "We have nothing but our own prejudices that there's something wrong with viewing porn, so we'll have to make do with *predictions* about what will happen to users in the future."

And sure enough, "Dr. Patrick Carnes,[5] who runs a sexual disorder treatment programme in Arizona, says there is no way of knowing who will have a problem with cybersex."

Supposedly, there are "case studies" of teenage porn users in the July issue of *Psychologies* where Aitkenhead's article is to be found, where the kids "feel they are perfectly capable of distinguishing between reality and fantasy, and that only those already damaged by life can be damaged by porn. It is an appealingly reassuring argument—and could they be right?"

Anyone care to hazard a guess?

"[Couples therapist Val] Sampson[6] isn't persuaded," the next paragraph begins. "I think we are all influenced, no matter how stable we are, by what we see," she says. "Every experience to some degree scars us, for good or for bad. I would suggest that choosing to watch violent pornography will be scarring you, whether you like it or not. And it will have an impact on your behaviour. We're being naïve if we think it's the same as watching gangster movies." (Did we forget to mention? Apparently, "impressionable young people" who are "exposed to porn" become "desensitised" and "start looking for something more in terms of excitement, and they can become sexually deviant." Hence the reference to "violent pornography.")

"The only solution, every expert we've spoken to agrees, is regulation," Aitkenhead concludes ... but it's a far cry from any "study" showing that "'There is compelling evidence that pornography has negative effects on individuals and communities,' sociologist Michael Flood, who spoke with hundreds of young people for the survey, told *Psychologies* magazine," as stated in the ADF's *Daily News* link.[7]

Oh, well, if one bogus "scientific" claim doesn't work, try, try again ...

I have no idea what percentage of the content of this volume came from Flynt himself and how much from his co-author Dr. Eisenbach—but whatever it was, both authors deserve the praise of a grateful nation!

'ONE NATION UNDER SEX'–A REVIEW

Hustler owner Larry Flynt has once again produced the definitive American political potboiler

September 22, 2011

LOS ANGELES—Viewers of last week's ABC News Special, *Jacqueline Kennedy: In Her Own Words*, may have noticed something missing from the network's distillation of eight-and-a-half hours of taped interviews with the former First Lady, recorded just four months after her husband's assassination: Sex. Fortunately, Larry Flynt's new book, *One Nation Under Sex: How the Private Lives of Presidents, First Ladies and Their Lovers Changed the Course of American History*, written with the assistance of historian Dr. David Eisenbach,[1] more than remedies that oversight.

Yes, there are two whole chapters devoted to JFK's and Jackie's and Bobby Kennedy's affairs, but they're hardly the most interesting subjects this top-notch historical work covers. Rather, the book (which screams, "Make me into a two-hour special on The History Channel!") begins with America's earliest days, and traces the sexual activities and proclivities of presidents, politicians and other prominent historical figures beginning with the third president—Does Sally Hemings ring any bells? How about James Madison's wife Dolley?—and concluding with the overblown (no pun intended) Clinton/Lewinsky affair, revealing information and trivia that generally didn't make the morning papers (even colonial ones) or the evening newscasts.

If we wanted to sum it up, we'd probably simply say that roughly half of the presidents, if they weren't gay, had mistresses and other lovers, but what fun would that be? For instance, it'd leave out the fact that there was a whorehouse on the construction site of the first White House, and that

Benjamin Franklin, while serving as an unofficial American ambassador in France, conducted plenty of policy negotiations in the bedroom.

It would also gloss over the history that then-34-year-old Treasury Secretary Alexander Hamilton, whom John Adams described as "a man who's [sic] excessive production of secretions no number of whores could draw off," paid to fuck 23-year-old Maria Reynolds for more than a year, with full knowledge of her pimp husband—and that the pair later blackmailed Hamilton for $1,000 (in 2011 bucks: $28,000) and then had the gall to hit him up for a series of "loans" while Hamilton continued to pay-for-play with Maria. (To be fair, Flynt estimates that one in every 25 urban colonial women was a full-time prostitute.)

But let's not forget that the subtitle of this book talks of how all this sex "changed the course of history," so we probably should mention our first gay President, James Buchanan, who carried on a 32-year love affair with Alabama Sen. William Rufus King, a slave owner for whom Buchanan was also a protege—thus making Buchanan pro-slavery enough that he failed to head off southern secession, which led directly to the Civil War.

And then there's the sentence, "Contemporaries of young Abe [Lincoln] were puzzled by his utter lack of interest in girls," which might bear on the fact that shortly after being admitted to the Bar, Lincoln spent four years as the roommate—and bedmate—of one Joshua Speed, and later, after becoming president, Lincoln gave full White House access to one Capt. David Derickson—and slept with him whenever Mrs. Lincoln wasn't home.

Other presidents who were known to frequent bordellos were Woodrow Wilson and Warren G. Harding, but as Flynt notes, "Fortunately for these presidential lotharios, American journalists in the early twentieth century had adopted a code of professional ethics that prohibited reporting on the sex lives of politicians." How far we've come since then! Of course, Wilson was savvy (and bold) enough to marry one of his mistresses, and Edith Wilson actually ran the country during Wilson's final days, thanks to his having been laid low by a stroke.

But perhaps the most interesting presidential couple was Franklin and Eleanor Roosevelt. Seems Eleanor, an unattractive child put down by her parents for her lack of beauty, had little interest in sex, so FDR had to make do with a couple of mistresses, most notably secretaries Lucy Mercer (with whom he continued his affair after she married) and Marguerite "Missy" LeHand, who hardly ever left his side during his entire presidency. But Eleanor eventually found joy in sex—sex with two lesbian couples, and later with journalist Lorena Hickok, who actually moved herself into the White House in a room adjoining Eleanor's.

Flynt also devotes an entire chapter to "America's Sex Czar," FBI director J. Edgar Hoover, who detailed his agents to dig up sexual and other scandals on every politician and celebrity he could think of, and who used the information gathered to retain his job for nearly 50 years—all the while sharing the bed with one of his top agents, Clyde Tolson. (However, Flynt thinks the various stories of Hoover being caught prancing around in a dress or lingerie and high heels is probably a myth.)

The first chapter on the Kennedy era begins, "When John Kennedy was elected president in 1960 his speech-writer Ted Sorenson predicted, 'This administration is going to do for sex what the previous one did for golf.'" Sadly, however, it didn't, even though Kennedy was the consummate tomcat, having fucked Hollywood sex idols Angie Dickinson, Kim Novak, Janet Leigh, Jean Simmons, Jayne Mansfield, Marlene Dietrich and Marilyn Monroe. Indeed, Kennedy once told British prime minister Harold Macmillan that if he didn't "get a strange piece of ass every day," he got migraines.

As it turns out, however, Jackie was no sexual slouch either, having had affairs with actor William Holden, Fiat chairman Gianni Agnelli, sister Lee Radziwell's billionaire boy-toy Aristotle Onassis... and her brother-in-law Bobby.

Well, we could go on and on—certainly the book does, for 264 pages plus footnotes and index—but what would be the fun in that? The point is, *One Nation Under Sex* may be one of the most important books of the past 200 years, if for no other reason than the studied lack of attention that's being paid to it by the mainstream media because, after all, everyone knows that presidents, politicians and the rich 'n' famous are pure as the driven snow—just ask the mainstream media during non-sweeps weeks!

One Nation Under Sex: How the Private Lives of Presidents, First Ladies and Their Lovers Changed the Course of American History by Larry Flynt and David Eisenbach, Ph.D., is published by Palgrave/Macmillan, a division of St. Martin's Press, LLC, 175 Fifth Avenue, New York, NY 10010; 264 pp; $25

You'll be happy to know that at this writing, Dawn has been named Chief Executive Officer at Morality In Media's official reincarnation, the National Center on Sexual Exploitation (NCOSE). Can you say, "Failing upward"? Also, this is one of my favorite articles.

DAWN HAWKINS' TERRIFYING PORN FLIGHT

Hey, Dawn: It's why 'God' gave you eyelids!

February 24, 2012

JESUSLAND—Over the weekend, we received word from Morality in Media PR flack Dawn Hawkins—in the form of a solicitation for donations, natch!—about a terrifying flight she took from Baltimore to Detroit where <gasp!> some old guy who was in the seat "directly in front" of her was looking at "violent child-themed pornography," the sight of which rendered her "speechless for a moment."

Of course, we should pause for a moment to ponder just what Dawn considers to be "violent child-themed pornography." We already know that Morality in Media (and likely Hawkins herself) considers anything that depicts nudity to be "pornography," and if those in the photo or video are young-looking, to them that's "child-themed" no matter what age the performers actually are. And of course, people engaging in consensual BDSM activity, whether clothed or unclothed, are bad, bad, BAD no matter how you look at it.

So when Dawn writes that, during the moment that she was speechless, the guy had "enough time to... flip through at least 8 images of very young Asian girls, one of them was of a girl whipping another girl," it's probably worth taking that description with a grain of salt—as is the concept of how she could see this guy's iPad screen if he was sitting directly in front of her. Who knows; maybe she has x-ray vision?

But as a good Right-thinking American, Dawn leapt into action, because she "couldn't help but say something."

"I asked, somewhat loudly, 'Are you really looking at pornography right now? On an airplane at 6 am [sic]? Are you really looking at porn right here?'"

It will probably come as a surprise to Dawn, but normal folks think about naked people a lot of the time—even as early as 6 a.m. and sometimes even after midnight... or as late as 4 or 5 or—oh, what the hell?—6 a.m.!

So when the guy told Dawn she didn't know what she was talking about—and it's certainly possible she didn't, since her idea of "pornography" would probably encompass half the billboards in Los Angeles—she doubled down and said loudly, "You are! You're looking at porn! I can see it on your screen."

For some reason, we're reminded of the (probably apocryphal) story of the woman who called the police to report that her neighbors were "having sex right out in the open!" When an officer arrived and asked to see what the woman was talking about, she led him to her upstairs bathroom and pointed to the small window above the toilet, saying, "There they are! That couple next door has no sense of decency, having sex in the middle of the day with the window open and the shades up where anybody can see it!" So the officer walked over, took a glance out the window and said, "Lady, you're crazy—I can't see anybody doing anything out there." "Stand on the toilet!" the woman exclaimed. "Stand on the toilet!"

Anyway, by this time, everyone in the cabin was looking at her, so Dawn told a nearby flight attendant, "Sir, this man is looking at pornography right now. Will you please do something?" Supposedly, the guy refused, saying there was nothing he could do, but if this were a true story rather than an apocryphal one to solicit cash for MiM's shrinking coffers, the attendant's more likely response would have been to ask the guy either to better shade his screen or switch to some different material—or if the images had been *actual* child porn, the attendant probably would have reported the guy at least to the other attendants and possibly the pilots and/or airline staff at the landing gate. However, according to Dawn, the guy did put his iPad away while she was ranting.

But of course, that wasn't enough for a True Defender of the Faith™!

"A few seconds later, in a quieter voice directed at the man in front of me, I said, 'I am on my way right now to speak at a conference about pornography and sex trafficking. You are contributing to the problem. You are victimizing and exploiting thousands of women. I cannot believe you would do that right here on an airplane.'"

Yeah; actually, what we *can't* believe is that this guy was "victimizing and exploiting thousands of women... right here on an airplane"... and apparently at least one other passenger felt the same:

"THEN, an older woman in her 50s stood up, turned around and said to me, 'Be quiet. No one cares.'" [Emphasis in original]

"Words cannot explain how I feel right now," Dawn writes. "It is bad enough that a man was looking at violent child-themed pornography in public, right in front of me. It is bad that the airline would do nothing about it. But, I cannot believe that a middle-aged woman would be so ingrained with this pornified culture, that she would say 'No one cares.'"

Yeah, Dawn, it's just amazing that some people (dare I say "most"?) find depictions of nudity and sex unremarkable—though I can understand how someone who makes her living trying to censor other people's access to such depictions would be shocked that someone would actually tell you the truth to your face. And again, we only have your word that the material was "violent child-themed pornography"; it could just as easily have been adult women going topless and practicing a bit of domination play—and which scenario seems more likely to have been displayed on a commercial airline flight?

"During the flight, I went through a million emotions," Dawn continued. "I felt hopeless and as though there's just nothing we can do to stop this."

Gosh, that's a lot! We're guessing that even in the most stressing of circumstances, most of us would go through about 999,990 fewer emotions than you did. And you definitely should feel hopeless: Sex and porn are here to stay.

And then comes the pitch:

"But, then, I remembered, that even though I felt alone, I know that millions of Americans are on my side," Dawn imagines. "I am not alone in feeling like this is extremely exploitative of women. I am not alone in feeling like this is wrong. I realized that we just have to fight harder. We have to be louder. We have to make sure people understand that pornography harms. This woman has no idea that pornography is wreaking havoc in the lives of millions, tearing apart countless families, destroying our kids' chance of having a normal relationship, contributing to the demand for sex trafficking and so much more. She is WRONG! Millions care. You care."

Yeah, but what we care about is know-nothing religious busybodies trying to be the "porn police" for all of society, so FUCK YOU for claiming that sexually explicit material made by, for and with consenting adults hurts ANYBODY who doesn't already suffer from obsessive-compulsive disorder—one symptom of which might be standing in the middle of an airplane aisle ranting loudly about what some other passenger is looking at on his iPad.

UPDATE:

Uh-oh! Looks like the anti-porn crowd is reading our stuff again:

"Soon after the video was up, the porn industry, through their trade magazine, Adult Video News, attacked Dawn in an editorial, not the man looking at porn on the plane, for being uncomfortable at being forced to look at porn in a public place," wrote Dawn's boss, former Obscenity Unit prosecutor Patrick Trueman, in an email sent to supporters today.

The "video" Trueman's referring to is this one,[1] which we *didn't* see before writing the article—but check out how emotional Dawn gets about this incident, even a full day after her flight. We mean, she appears in the video to be in her mid-20s, yet she's still crying about this! Talk about lack of emotional maturity!

Here are some of the more interesting details from the video, which mostly shore up the concepts that A) this is a tempest in a teapot, and B) Dawn is even more shameless than her email in shading the truth... if not outright lying:

"I sat back for enough time for him to flip through about eight images," Dawn reported. "They were all of very young girls. I couldn't tell if they were 14 or 18; they were definitely young. They were all Asian, and a couple of the photographs were very violent in nature. One even had one girl whipping the other girl with a whip."

Isn't it important, when you're accusing someone of looking at "child-themed" sexual imagery, that you ascertain whether the images are of actual minors (the "14" rather than the "18")? Because if they're not, it's just regular porn, which has received Supreme Court protection at least since their 2003 decision in *Ashcroft v. Free Speech Coalition*, which said that for something to be child pornography, it has to involve actual children.

"The flight attendant, he just stood there, did nothing," Dawn stated. "He said there was nothing he could do. He could have just asked the man to put it away, not look at it. I was astounded. I couldn't believe that he refused to do anything, especially because it was making me and other passengers so uncomfortable, and I'm sure it was making the other passengers uncomfortable as well."

We can only wonder why Dawn is so sure "it was making the other passengers uncomfortable as well." After all, no one said anything in support of Dawn's position, at least as far as Dawn reported in her video, so how does she know? Or could it just possibly be a little projection on Dawn's part? After all, she's anti-porn, so she apparently assumed that most other adults shared her view.

"A few minutes later," she continued, "I leaned forward and in a much quieter voice directed just at the man, I said to him, 'Sir, I'm heading right now to speak at a conference about pornography and sex trafficking. You're contributing to the problem. You're exploiting millions of women and children. You're creating the demand. You're the one contributing to all this harm."

Yeah, a guy looking at "dirty pictures" of what are most likely adults engaged in some domination play is "exploiting millions of women and children" apparently by "creating the demand" for images of adults engaged in sex play with other adults, with no evidence that the women in the photos were coerced in any way—so how in hell is the guy "contributing to all this harm"?!?!? What harm? People—adults!—getting paid to have sexual fun, or just amusing themselves for free? That ain't harm, lady!

Also, it turns out that the lady who told Dawn to "Be quiet. No one cares," was "probably in her 50s"—certainly old enough to have a better sense of what's accepted in modern adult society than the hyper-emotional 20-something Dawn.

"I could not believe that a woman of all people would stand up and tell me to be quiet," Dawn sobbed. "She didn't tell the man to stop looking at pornography; she didn't say anything about that; she just said no one cared that he was looking at pornography, what was likely child pornography, on the airplane, right in front of all of us. She said to just let it go."

Of course, since Dawn was the only one to make a big deal out of the guy's in-flight entertainment, there's a good possibility that the 50-ish woman was right: No one cared. And again, Dawn accused the guy of looking at child porn with no evidence whatsoever beyond her own jaundiced opinion of what the images depicted.

After going through her "million emotions, most of which were disbelief and extreme sadness and hopelessness in the fight against pornography," Dawn continued, "I couldn't believe that a woman of all people, an older woman, wasn't on our side, didn't see anything wrong with the exploitation and degradation of women and likely children right then and there."

Well, Dawn, perhaps the woman was old enough to have heard that we have this thing in our country called the "First Amendment," which even the Supreme Court agrees guarantees each person's right to look at sexual imagery, and even to possess obscene materials in the privacy of his/her own home! And again, Dawn couldn't seem to make her point without another claim, still without proof, that the photos were of children. In fact, as the response video[2] by "JordanOwen42" (whom Trueman refers to as a "foul-mouthed man") notes, many Asian women look younger than they actually are, so one should be extra careful in assuming that they're kids.

After that, the assumptions come quickly and furiously:

"We know that pornography is *so* addictive, and that man was likely very addicted to where—that's why he was looking at porn right then, that early; he couldn't help it. I feel really bad for him, part of me does, just because I understand that he must be struggling with these urges and I'm sure that he doesn't [understand]. He's not happy and he doesn't want that, but it hurt even more that a woman would tell me that people don't care about this. It's a danger to children, pornography, especially if children were going to be exposed to it on an airplane. It is no place for pornography, on an airplane. I feel like even most porn users would agree that there's no place for pornography on an airplane. A wealth of research today demonstrates that pornography consumption is the leading cause for sexual violence and sexual assault. This is a safety hazard also. [chuckles] In a public place as tight and small as an airplane, we can't have that."

Where to start? Where to start?

OF COURSE porn is not a "danger to children," whether on an airplane or anywhere else, and if children were being brought up by parents who are sexually sane and who would explain what sex (and porn) is about from the earliest age the kids are developed enough to understand it, they'd barely notice it when they see it—and "a wealth of research today" shows that until children begin puberty, they have little or no interest in porn (or sex) at all—unless, we suppose, some assholes like Trueman and Hawkins and their ilk make a big deal about it.

And of course, it's a lie that ANY peer-reviewed scientific research has "demonstrate[d] that pornography consumption is the leading cause for sexual violence and sexual assault." Alcohol and an upbringing that teaches kids (as most religions do) that women are second-class humans are the main causes of *that*!

But contrary to our previous assumption, apparently Dawn *did* do something about the "problem" when she got off the plane.

"I got off the airplane and I reported it to a police officer, who promised to investigate. He went to the man's next gate, especially because the likelihood it was child pornography was pretty high[!], but he said that if it was adult pornography, there was nothing he could do because Delta and many other airlines have no policy about this kind of content on their flights."

And since, according to our internet search for child porn arrests, none was reported as occurring at Detroit Metro Airport over the weekend, we guess we can assume that either the porn on the guy's iPad was not child porn, or (more likely) the officer Dawn spoke to simply shined her on and told her what she wanted to hear, and didn't see any point in bothering the other passenger over that kind of horseshit.

"Needless to say, airlines need to have a policy; it needs to be spelled out that obscenity and pornography is not allowed on airplanes; this is a danger to all passengers, to flight attendants. It would be a very unhealthy working place, workplace; that would be sexual harassment anywhere else."

Well, it *might* have been sexual harassment if the porn-viewing passenger had been a fellow airline employee, but one suspects that flight attendants have generally been trained to ignore pretty much anything a *passenger* does that doesn't directly harm others or cause actual problems for the flight or the crew.

But no; the only "danger" porn causes—or, at least, caused in this instance—was to make poor little fundamentalist-minded Dawn Hawkins shed a few tears, which sadly *weren't* about lamenting her lack of understanding of the proper place(s) of sex and porn in the modern *real* world.

It continues to amaze that the Ninth Amendment isn't cited more often in civil rights cases—like the Mississippi anti-abortion case that was decided last summer by the Supreme Court!

THE RIGHTS YOU DON'T KNOW YOU HAVE

August 17, 2012

If there's one thing that probably confuses every member of the adult entertainment community from company owners to performers to secretaries to warehouse personnel, it's the question of, since adult content is produced in the adult industry only by willing adults for sale to and viewing by other willing adults, why are there laws that make certain types of sexually explicit content illegal?

After all, we've all read the First Amendment, which states, in pertinent part, that "Congress shall make no law... abridging freedom of speech, or of the press," and nowhere in that amendment or anywhere else in the Constitution does it exempt sexual speech from that unqualified right. Therefore, wouldn't the Supreme Court have had to violate the First Amendment in order to make "obscene" speech illegal?

The answer, of course, is yes—but that's not the entire answer.

See, the First Amendment isn't the only amendment that protects sexual speech. There's also the Ninth Amendment, which reads, "The enumeration in the Constitution, of certain rights, shall not be construed to deny or disparage others retained by the people."

Think about that for a moment. What it says is that although some rights are specifically mentioned in the Constitution—for example, the right not to be searched without a warrant; the right not to be forced to allow soldiers to live in your home; the right not to have the government set up its own religion—in fact, Americans have many, many more rights that are not spelled out—"enumerated"—but which the government cannot deny or belittle—"disparage"—just because they *aren't* spelled out specifically.

During the debates about the Constitution back in the late 1780s, this was considered a major issue, since many supporters of constitutional government felt that the Constitution itself was so complete that any rights citizens might worry about losing under the new federal government were protected, because at the time, the Constitution was viewed as both a grant of some powers to the feds, but more importantly, a restriction on Congress's actions in other areas, most notably civil liberties.

But smarter (or at least more worried) heads prevailed, and a "Bill of Rights" was added to the Constitution even as the document was sent to the states for ratification—and the same argument was voiced, that even the Bill of Rights didn't sufficiently protect many citizens' activities from federal encroachment.

"If we attempt an enumeration, every thing that is not enumerated is presumed to be given [away]," said constitutional convention delegate James Wilson.[1] "The consequence is, that an imperfect enumeration would throw all implied power into the scale of the government, and the rights of the people would be rendered incomplete."

It was for that very reason that James Madison proposed adding the Ninth Amendment to the Bill of Rights: To deal with that "imperfect enumeration" by granting to the people all rights which were not specifically denied to them by the document.

However, almost from the get-go, both the Congress of the United States and its entire court system have ignored the Ninth Amendment, since one effect of recognizing it would be to diminish the power that legislators and the courts have over the ordinary citizen. Think gay people don't have the right to marry? They already do, if the government were following the dictates of the Ninth Amendment. Think recreational drug use is illegal? Not under the Ninth Amendment. Think prostitution is a valid crime? The Ninth Amendment disagrees. Think a woman can't get an abortion unless she jumps through the variety of hoops various state legislatures have laid out for her? The Ninth Amendment says, "Fuck that!" Its response would be the same if the issue were national healthcare, effective public schools or assisted suicide—or any of the hundreds of other legal restrictions on consensual human activities that harm no one except perhaps the participants.

So perhaps what's needed is a book that sets out what the Ninth Amendment is, where it came from, how it came to be included in the Constitution, and what it means for 21st century Americans.

Guess what? There is one: Daniel A. Farber's *Retained By The People.*

"Liberals (for lack of a better term) have as yet to directly embrace the Ninth," wrote Farber in the opening chapter of this seminal work. "They argue the case for rights on the basis of clauses like Due Process or give up on fundamental rights in favor of arguments based on discrimination law. I believe that's because they find the Ninth too elusive. Buried as it is in eighteenth-century ideas, in debates among the Founders as they wrote the Constitution, and in James Madison's oratory before Congress, the Ninth seems shadowy, a battle that cannot be won... It is conservatives who should fear and deny the Ninth—and many do, especially the so-called movement conservatives who make up the 'base.' ... The Ninth challenges both what they believe about the Constitution and what they publicly offer as their rationale for imposing their morality on others."

And what better example of that is there than "originalist" Justice Antonin Scalia, who stated in his dissenting opinion[2] in the case of *Troxel v. Granville* (2000) that, "the Constitution's refusal to 'deny or disparage' other rights is far removed from affirming any one of them, and even farther removed from authorizing judges to identify what they might be, and to enforce the judges' list against laws duly enacted by the people." In other words, just because the Ninth says the government can't deny unenumerated rights doesn't mean citizens actually have or can have those rights!

However, even Scalia admitted,[3] in a lecture given just this past April at USC's Gould School of Law, that "If you find what the original meaning of the Constitution is, I am handcuffed; I cannot do the nasty conservative things I would like to do to the people." He even gave examples of things he doesn't think the Constitution speaks to—"abortion, the death penalty, homosexual sodomy"—but a quick look at the Ninth Amendment would prove him wrong.

Farber has the more correct historical take on that issue.

"The Framers picked their words carefully and understood just what they were doing," he wrote. "They meant the Bill of Rights to be *illustrative*, not complete: the Ninth adds a crucial 'etc.' to the bill. This 'etc.' represents the liberties the Framers viewed as fundamental—rights that were part of their political and ethical vision, what they had fought a revolution to honor.

"Some conservatives acknowledge that the Ninth Amendment, like the Declaration of Independence, refers to innate human rights," he continued. "But they contend that these unenumerated rights lack any *legal* weight and were merely entrusted to the political process. This theory conveniently allows these conservatives to pretend belief in innate rights without ever having to do anything about them."

Farber cites several examples of how the Ninth Amendment has figured into American history, and in particular, the history of the Republican Party. It's well known that the first Republican president, Abraham Lincoln, favored abolishing slavery, and Farber argues that Lincoln, in so doing, was displaying his belief in "natural law"—exactly the sort of thing the Ninth Amendment would protect. The early Republicans' belief in natural law and the Ninth Amendment, according to Farber, led to their proposing further constitutional amendments that abolished slavery (Thirteenth), forced states to be bound by the rights and protections of the federal Constitution (Fourteenth) and gave non-whites the right to vote (Fifteenth).

Over the years, the Supremes have used the Ninth Amendment to take such actions as prohibiting courts from forcing convicted criminals to be sterilized, but rather than referencing the Ninth itself, the high court gradually folded the unenumerated rights granted by the Ninth into its conception of "substantive due process" as set forth in the Fourteenth Amendment.

Farber quotes Justice John Harlan as opining that the "full scope of the liberty guaranteed by the Due Process Clause cannot be found in or limited by the precise terms of the specific guarantees elsewhere provided in the Constitution." Moreover, Harlan believed that constitutional liberty is "a rational continuum which, broadly speaking, includes a freedom from all substantial arbitrary impositions and purposeless restraints"—a viewpoint that would invalidate many current laws that seek to punish citizens for indulging in personal pleasures that harm no one.

Justice Harlan's viewpoint still informs many contemporary court decisions, including *Roe v. Wade* (abortion) and *Griswold v. Connecticut* (access to contraception). AVN readers will recall that the Supreme Court invoked the Fourteenth Amendment in overturning laws against consensual sodomy in *Lawrence v. Texas*—though it could have found such rights much more easily in the Ninth, if the high court by then hadn't scared itself into ignoring that amendment.

But even Farber takes a step back from his own thesis in a couple of areas. For instance, he doesn't think assisted suicide is an unenumerated right under the Ninth, and also warns, "I also want to be clear that my argument for resurrecting the Ninth Amendment is emphatically not a plea for judicial activism. The biggest concern about judicial enforcement of unenumerated rights is that they can be abused by judges who simply want to pursue their own political agenda. Whether we are talking about enumerated rights like the First Amendment or the unenumerated rights of the Ninth, judicial impartiality, common sense, and humility are invaluable."

That warning notwithstanding, Farber points out that the Ninth Amendment inevitably runs up against people's prejudices and traditions. Segregation was very popular in the South and various areas of the North before it was overturned by the 1964 Civil Rights Act, which could be viewed as a congressional application of the Ninth Amendment to freedom for all humans, not just white ones. As Farber points out, the Ninth has provided good support to politicians who want to do the right thing even in the face of opposition from their own constituencies.

Farber's book goes into long discussions about the Ninth's application to *Roe*, to a person's right to die in *Cruzan v. Director*,[4] to gay rights, not just in *Lawrence* but the antidiscrimination ruling in *Romer v. Evans*,[5] to the right to a decent education in *San Antonio Independent School District v. Rodriguez*,[6] and Farber thinks the Ninth may yet come into play in the current debate over one's right to keep personal information private.

All in all, *Retained By The People* is an excellent primer for sex-positive activists who chafe at the many governmental restrictions on their rights to express themselves, to be open about their sexuality and use that openness commercially, and to be able to create sexual art forms that conservative religionists would surely find repulsive. All of those scenarios and more are simply examples of the rights most people don't know they have—but which, in the current climate, they'll have to fight tooth and nail to gain or retain. But at least they'll know that the Constitution backs them up.

Can't help but wonder whether Hawkins or Lubben is the stupider one—but the fact is, there are *some unscrupulous producers in porn, as evidenced by the massive win for the 22 women duped by the people running the GirlsDoPorn website. Fortunately, they only come along once in a decade or so. Also note: Shelley Lubben died in 2019.*

MIM CLAIMS THERE'S SEX TRAFFICKING IN THE ADULT INDUSTRY

Posted August 31, 2012

JESUSLAND—In an article[1] posted today on Morality in Media's pornharms.com website, MiM staffer Dawn Hawkins accused the adult industry of engaging in sex trafficking. Her charge is based on an article[2] which appeared on AVN.com on August 8 regarding California Ballot Proposition 35, a poorly-written attempt to increase fines and prison sentences for sex traffickers, require them to register as sex offenders, and prevent them from accessing or posting anonymously on the internet.

"Sex trafficking is happening in the porn industry," Hawkins declared in a video accompanying the article. "There's a new initiative on the ballot in California this year that extends protections to victims of human trafficking and sex trafficking... My question is, if the porn industry was not forcing and coercing, abusing, drugging its performers sometimes, getting them to perform in the production of pornography, then why are they so afraid of this? My other question is, if the porn industry really is verifying the ages of the performers, and they know that all of their performers are over the age of 18, then why are they so afraid of this?"

Of course, if Hawkins actually knew anything about the history of the porn industry, the answers would be obvious: That history is replete with minors trying and occasionally succeeding in sneaking into the industry with realistic false IDs, or real IDs that didn't belong to them. The most famous of these "practitioners" are Traci Lords and Alexandria Quinn, but there have been a few others, both straight and gay, though producers are getting a bit more savvy these days in detecting false driver's licenses, passports, etc.

Hawkins bolsters her trafficking claim by citing a handout from the thoroughly-discredited Shelley Lubben[3] of the Pink Cross Foundation,[4] which claims that "agents, porn directors, porn producers, pimps and performers who recruit and entice a woman to engage in a commercial sex act" do so by "beating, slapping and punching; beatings with objects (bats, chains, belts, hangers, whips); physical restraint e.g. forcing a woman to give oral sex by restraining her head; rape and gang rape e.g. anal sex performed on a woman without her permission; attempted rape e.g. male porn actor repeatedly attempts to insert his penis into a woman's anus and she repeatedly has to tell him no."

According to Lubben, other methods of "persuasion" allegedly include fraudulent offers of employment, money, fame; seduction; "sending women to fraudulent clinics for medical care"; and coercion, which includes threats of physical, psychological, reputational, legal or financial harm; "intense manipulation by pornographers to lure naive women into the porn business"; "intimidation and humiliation by older males to cause a woman to be fearful"; offering them drugs and alcohol "to help them get through scenes"; and of course the ever-popular "reward[ing] women by starring them on the box cover."

Sure; promise her a box cover and she'll do anything!

Needless to say, Hawkins believes all this crap, so it's not surprising to her that adult industry members would attack Prop 35 because, to her mind, they're only protecting their sex-trafficking selves.

As part of Hawkins' article, she links to a frame grab of AVN's article, underlines a couple of sentences and inserts two "word balloons" with questions. Her first underlining is of the phrase, "which would define any producer that knowingly *or unknowingly* 'causes, induces, or persuades, or attempts to cause, induce, or persuade, a person who is a minor… to engage in a commercial sex act'." Her balloon asks, "How is this a bad thing if they aren't forcing or coercing the performers to do anything??" Obviously, the several sections of the article dealing with the problem of attempting to hold producers responsible for minors who use fraud to enter the industry, which in the past have forced million-dollar recalls of product, were lost on Hawkins.

Hawkins also takes umbrage at the portion of the impending law which reads, "Mistake of fact as to the age of a victim of human trafficking who is a minor at the time of the commission of the offense is not a defense to a criminal prosecution under this section." Hawkins' question: "The porn industry uses underage kids in their films. Now they're not going to get away with it so easily. JUST CHECK THEIR AGE!" In her video, she similarly asks, "If the porn industry is not forcing women to engage in these sex acts for porn, then why are they afraid of these penalties? It [sic] won't touch them at all."

As a "true believer," Hawkins undoubtedly thinks that minors appear in adult movies all the time, and that it's pure luck or amazing subterfuge that allows the producers to get away with it. Of course, the reverse is true: Producers go out of their way to vet actresses' and actors' identities (which the federal recordkeeping and labeling law, 18 U.S.C. §2257 requires them to do anyway), so it's the rare individual who's got the craftiness to create a fake ID and manage to sneak into a movie or web scene. The most recent example was Bieyanka Moore,[5] who just last year stole the Social Security number and expired learner's permit of stripper Tyler Chanel Evans, used the permit to obtain a genuine Nevada driver's license, and managed to appear in a Reality Kings online offering.

So it's not a matter of "just check[ing] their age"; the problem is that some of these children are really good at faking their identities—and any law that puts a producer in prison because s/he was fooled by, in Moore's case, a genuine Nevada driver's license, is not a good thing... much as we're sure Hawkins would like to see every producer of (and director of and performer in) sexually explicit content put in prison for a couple of decades, if not executed.

So yes, AVN stands by its assessment that absent a rewrite, Prop 35 is a Very Bad Thing for the adult industry... and for unwary johns and teen sweethearts as well.

So keep that invective coming, Dawn. We're sure the ignorance of your supporters about nearly everything to do with the adult entertainment industry brings in those big donations.

And of course, we'll continue to be here to smack you down when you publish and publicize such horseshit.

AVN ANNOTATES MATT BARBER'S OPEN LETTER TO GAY TEENS

February 27, 2013

Periodically AVN gets missives from commentator Matt Barber[1] *with the kind offer that we are free to republish the contents. This time we took him up on his offer, reprinting his entire letter below... and adding a few footnotes. (Note: This was written before the Supreme Court case of Obergefell v. Hodges, which legalized gay marriage.)*

JESUSLAND—Who am I? I'm a husband and a father.(1) More importantly, and by the grace of God, I'm a follower of Jesus Christ.

This is what motivates me to write you.(2)

You don't have to read on, but I pray you will.(3)

What I write I write with the purest of aims and with your well-being in mind—physical, emotional and spiritual well-being, both now and for eternity.(4)

You will read truth here, not because I say it's true—I'm nobody—but, rather, because the Creator of the universe, the very God Who wove you together in your mother's womb made it true.(5)

His truths never change.(6)

I have three kids, a boy and two girls. My son will soon enter his teenage years. I've had many people ask me what I'd say to my children if one of them came to me and declared: "Dad, I'm gay."

Here's what I'd say. I'd tell them exactly what I'm about to tell you.

I love you. I neither judge you nor condemn you. I accept you and I would die for you.(7)

But you are not "gay."(8)

Yes, you may be physically attracted to people of the same sex, but how you act on those attractions is entirely your choice. Who you are—your identity—is not defined by your sexual feelings, temptations or behaviors. The difference between who you are and what you feel or do is as the difference between night and day.(9)

Here is who you are: You are a wonderful, beautiful, precious human being created in the image and likeness of the one righteous and Holy God of the universe.

You are priceless.(10)

But you are flawed—you are a sinner.

I am flawed—I am a sinner.(11)

We are all flawed sinners—corrupted beings in a corrupted world.(12) We are all tempted by sin.(13)

Those temptations manifest themselves in different ways for each of us. We are all on equal footing, however, as to how we react to those temptations.

Homosexual behavior is always wrong—demonstrably and absolutely wrong.(14)

Period.(15)

Every major world religion, thousands of years of history and uncompromising human biology declare this objective reality from the rooftops.(16)

Though your heart may deceive you, something deep within you knows this to be true. Scripture says, "The heart is deceitful above all things and beyond cure. ..." (Jeremiah 17:9)

Some say, "But Jesus never mentioned homosexuality." First, we don't know this.(17) We have no record in Scripture of Him specifically addressing homosexual sin, but neither do we have a record of His addressing incest, bestiality or other sexual sins.(18)

Jesus was clear. He condemned all sexual immorality as detailed within the moral law. He was clear that any sexual activity outside the bonds of marriage between husband and wife is sexual immorality—sin.

In fact, homosexual sin is expressly identified in both the Old and New Testaments as being among the list of sins that, if committed without repentance, will prevent you from "inheriting the kingdom of God."(19)

That is to say, yes; unrepentant homosexual behavior is disobedience to God. If we rebel against God and refuse to repent and ask His forgiveness, then we have chosen our own fate—we have chosen to disqualify ourselves from heaven.

We have chosen hell.(20)

I know, it's not easy. Temptation is not easy.

To sin, however, is easy.

Still, to endure the consequences of that sin, both here and throughout eternity, will be more difficult than our limited minds can fathom.(21)

Romans 6:23 admonishes: "For the wages of sin is death, but the gift of God is eternal life in Christ Jesus our Lord."

Sin can lead to physical death; but it also leads to emotional and spiritual death.

If you are caught up in homosexual sin, you know—intuitively you know—that such conduct is wrong, that it is both immoral and unnatural behavior.(22)

Truth is truth, even though we may deny it.(23)

God has written His law on your heart.(24) You are a physical being; but, more importantly, you are a spiritual being.(25) When we sin, we create separation between ourselves and God.(26)

God's word also says that when we sin sexually, it's particularly egregious because our bodies are the temple of Christ. This separation from God—a natural result of sexual sin—can lead to depression and even despair.(27)

If you feel such despair, know this: it is not "homophobia" causing it, as adult enablers might tell you, but, rather, it is the sin itself that causes it (or struggling alone, absent Christ, with the temptation to sin).(28)

You are being used. Adult homosexual activists with a political agenda are using you as a pawn to achieve selfish goals in a dangerous political game.(29)

You're just a means to an end.(30)

They may have convinced themselves otherwise, but they don't care about you. They don't love you.(31) They can't. Their version of "love" is built on lies. It's devoid of truth.(32)

Love without truth is hate.(33)

If you continue down this wide, empty path, make no mistake: it will not "get better."(34)

It gets much, much worse.(35)

Consider, for instance, that according to the CDC this path will lead you, boys, to a one-in-five chance of contracting HIV/AIDS. The CDC also found that 64 percent of all syphilis cases strike "gay" males and that homosexual behavior leads to astronomical risk of nearly all other forms of STD.(36)

Even more startling is the fact that, according to the International Journal of Epidemiology (IJE), "[L]ife expectancy at age 20 years for gay and bisexual men is 8 to 20 years less than for all men."(37)

Unnatural behaviors beget natural consequences. "The wages of sin is death."(38)

But there is hope.

Jesus loves you with a love that no human can fully grasp.(39) This is true not because of your so-called "sexual orientation," but, rather, it is true in spite of it.

Jesus said, "Come to me, all you who are weary and burdened, and I will give you rest." (Matthew 11:28)(40)

Kids, take your sexual confusion—your struggle with sin—to Christ.

No one else can give you rest.(41)

✡✡✡

Footnotes

1) He's also an attorney with Liberty Counsel, a reactionary right-wing legal society, not to mention an Associate Dean and Adjunct Assistant Professor of Law at the late Jerry Falwell's Liberty University School of Law, plus he has a master's degree in public policy from Pat Robertson's Regent University. Recently he has opined that allowing women to serve in military combat is "felony stupid," and he's accused the Southern Poverty Law Center of having incited some guy to shoot a security guard at Family Research Center simply because SPLC branded FRC as a "hate group" ... which it clearly is. He also wants clergy to specifically support political candidates from their pulpits, and has claimed that sex researcher Alfred Kinsey "facilitated ... the systematic sexual abuse of hundreds, if not thou-

sands, of children and infants—all in the name of science." In other words, he's a religious nutbar loon.

2) Because, y'know, "God" just hates people who have gay sex, and Barber has claimed that even the Founders hated this "crime against nature" so much that they made it a death penalty offense in the Constitution. (Do let us know if you can find that clause.)

3) Because learning how wingers express their bigotry is very educational; hence, our publishing this article.

4) Actually, he writes what he writes because he's a bigot, and clothes that bigotry in the Bible (which, BTW, is pretty good bigot clothing, what with Leviticus 20 and all.)

5) Nice to know that even "nobodys" like Barber have no trouble speaking for what he describes as "the Creator of the universe." Nice gig if you can get it! Pays well, too, we hear; just ask Robertson or Falwell's kid.

6) You mean, besides the fact that Christians have declared pretty much the entire Old Testament "inoperative," to use Nixon's term for ignoring uncomfortable things? You mean like how modern-day believers have decided that the Bible's support for slavery isn't really what God meant to say? Or that bit about how it's an "abomination" to wear clothes made of two different fabrics? Or how it's a death penalty offense ("burnt with fire") for a guy to fuck both his wife and her mother? Or how godly people should shun a guy who fucks a woman while she's having her period?

7) Really? Because once you read the rest of Barber's crap, it really doesn't sound like it ... unless the kid admits he/she is not *really* gay ...

8) We always love meeting (or reading about) people who think they know their own children's minds better than the children themselves. That *never* turns out poorly for family relationships!

9) So if you don't *act* gay, you're *not* gay—who'd'a thunk it was that simple?

10) Good thing The Lord changed Its mind about slavery, then, eh?

11) So much for "not [being] defined by your sexual feelings, temptations or behaviors"!

12) And that would be "corrupted beings in a corrupted world" made by—ooh, I bet you know this one!—God?

13) No, we're "tempted by" (as in "attracted to") other people and stuff, and you've got a book and a bunch of holier-than-thou assholes who are only too happy to define some of that attraction as "sin." But for much of humanity, attraction is just attraction; it has no theological connotation, and those who want to define those attractions as "sin" have nothing but their book and personal prejudices to base that on; that is, no *science*, or even real-world observation.

14) Well, as long as you say so. But we *would* like to see that demonstration!

15) Well, that settles it, then! YOU ASSHOLE!!!!!!!!!!!!

16) "Objective reality"? The *reality* is, there are gay people and there are straight people, and there's a whole spectrum in-between—and that doesn't even count transgenders! And during those "thousands of years of history," there have been plenty of gay people, starting with the elite of ancient Greece and Rome up to and including a few U.S. congressfolk and senators, and according to Larry Flynt's book *One Nation Under Sex*, even a few U.S. presidents, possibly even including Abraham Lincoln! And don't get me started on Catholic priests!

17) Hell, yeah! In fact, we don't even know if Jesus ever even existed! No contemporary historical texts mention him, though there are a couple—

Josephus and Tacitus—whose mentions of Jesus were added centuries after those guys died.

18) Always good to know that you can take what Jesus *didn't* say as gospel!

19) Funny thing, though: Although Barber seems to have his Jeremiah quotes at his fingertips, here he points to *no* verse of the Bible to justify his anti-sexual bigotry! C'mon, Matt; the least you could do is provide JUST ONE FUCKING CITATION where Jesus says gay sex is bad, or even extra-marital sex, couldn't you? Or maybe they just don't exist!

20) Well, you're certainly free to believe that. What you're not free to do, however, is to impose your religious anti-sexual beliefs on the rest of society, and in fact, not even on your own son.

21) Well, the "consequences of that sin ... here" seem to be that you and your fellow fundamentalists, and your lackeys in government, discriminate against gays so thoroughly that in most states, they can't marry, can't or have a hard time adopting kids, can't get spousal benefits, aren't protected from workplace or housing discrimination and are the butts (no pun intended) of millions of jocks' bad jokes. So maybe if you and your pals spent less time being bigots, gays wouldn't have such a hard time of it "here."

22) To begin with, see footnote (8). Beyond that, we're sure you *wish* that people "intuitively" knew that guys fucking other guys and women fucking other women is "wrong," but there are millions of gays out there who are perfectly happy in homosexual relationships, who feel in their own minds that it's "right," and even some who believe that, despite the bigotry of you and your buds, Jesus still loves them for who they are, gayness and all.

23) Of course, that's "truth," a *belief* based on little or no evidence, as opposed to "facts," based on scientific observation and experimentation. There's no doubt that "facts are facts," no matter how you try to deny them. But "truth" seems to be whatever you and your fellow religious fanatics

decide it is ... *today*. It might change tomorrow ... like when you and your fundie friends decided that Romney would be a bad president 'cause he's Mormon, but when he became the only game in town, somehow his Mormon "sinner" status wasn't that bad.

24) Funny; we don't recall any cardiac surgeon ever mentioning that.

25) What you call "spirit," many of the rest of us call "the rational mind."

26) Or more accurately, when people "sin," they may create a separation between themselves and their *church* (or mosque or synagogue), depending on how bigoted their clergyperson and fellow congregants are. If there is a God, the reality is, you actually have no idea what It likes or doesn't like. Maybe It doesn't like bigots ... like yourself!

27) YEAH! Because it's the *sin*, and not the fact that so many supposedly religious people *like yourself* give them "sinners" shit all the time for following their own sexual paths that *you* don't approve of!

28) Yeah; it's not the *bigots'* fault. Really. No, *really*! God said so ... somewhere. We've got a video of it ... somewhere.

29) Yeah; because *religious* activists (like Barber) would *never* use you "as a pawn to achieve selfish goals in a dangerous political game" like, oh, say, to stamp out Americans' sexual freedom like all those laws against sodomy (which the vast majority of straights also practice) tried to do before *Lawrence v. Texas*.

30) Only if you let assholes like Barber run your sex life.

31) We're back to footnote (8) again, with a bit of (29) thrown in for good measure.

32) Translation: "Nobody who doesn't believe as we believe—i.e., fundamentalist Christianity—can possibly love you, 'cause everything we say about sex is 'true' and everything they say about sex is a 'lie.'"

33) Sorry; there is no translation for this that would make any rational sense—but one thing's clear: Barber is definitely a hater, though that probably isn't how he sees himself.

34) Isn't that cute! Barber has heard of gay rights activist Dan Savage, and Savage's videos worry him: "Now listen, sonny; pay no attention to all those YouTube videos with a bunch of celebrities and others telling you that even if bigots like myself persecute and occasionally physically assault you all through elementary and high school, it *doesn't* 'get better.' You choice is to either give up all your same-gender sexual desires, join a church and become some sort of secular monk, or you might as well kill yourself."

35) Especially if me and my fundie friends get to make the laws!

36) So if you *do* engage in homosexual sex, be sure *not* to wear a condom. That way, it'll be easier for God's wrath to be visited upon you!

37) "This falsehood can be traced directly to the discredited research of Paul Cameron and his Family Research Institute, specifically a 1994 paper he co-wrote entitled, 'The Lifespan of Homosexuals.' Using obituaries collected from gay newspapers, he and his two co-authors concluded that gay men died, on average, at 43, compared to an average life expectancy at the time of around 73 for all U.S. men. On the basis of the same obituaries, Cameron also claimed that gay men are 18 times more likely to die in car accidents than heterosexuals, 22 times more likely to die of heart attacks than whites, and 11 times more likely than blacks to die of the same cause. He also concluded that lesbians are 487 times more likely to die of murder, suicide, or accidents than straight women. ... However, like virtually all of his 'research,' Cameron's methodology is egregiously flawed—most obviously because the sample he selected (the data from the obits) was not

remotely statistically representative of the LGBT population as a whole. Even Nicholas Eberstadt, a demographer at the conservative American Enterprise Institute, has called Cameron's methods 'just ridiculous.'"—Southern Poverty Law Center, "10 Anti-Gay Myths Debunked"

38) The "wages" (whatever that is) of *everything* is death!

39) So it doesn't matter if me and my buds and all the other religious lunatics around the world treat you like shit because you're gay; some imaginary Guy (Gal?) in the Sky is still in your corner ... except that He (She?) won't do anything about all the pain and suffering you'll have to endure at the hands of bigots like me.

40) Translation: "Give up all your same-sex attractions and live like a sexless monk for the rest of your life, and when you're dead, you'll finally be free of bigots like Matt Barber."

41) OR ... you could join with pro-sex activists like the Woodhull Sexual Freedom Alliance, the National Coalition for Sexual Freedom, the Center for Sex & Culture or any of several other groups that push back against antiquated ideas of sexual "normalcy," and learn to love yourself and your sexuality despite what your dad and his bigoted friends believe and how disgustingly they treat you. Give it some thought, eh?

At this writing, more than a dozen states have passed resolutions declaring porn to be a "public health crisis"—with, of course, no evidence whatsoever that porn affects "public health"—unlike, say, COVID-19—but they'd nonetheless just love *to get the CDC involved! Also noteworthy: Donny Pauling in 2015 faced 15 counts of child molestation and other child-related sexual offenses.*

CONGRATS, ADULT INDUSTRY: YOU ARE A 'PUBLIC HEALTH CRISIS'

Posted May 16, 2014

TYSONS CORNER, VA—Chances are, if you walk through the Tysons Corner Marriott this weekend, you won't be able to spit without hitting an anti-porn wacko.

Yes, the loonies—you know: the ones whose parents made sure they all slept with their hands above the covers—are out in force, shepherded by pretty much all the Usual Suspects: Gail Dines, Mary Anne Layden, Dawn Hawkins, Shelley Lubben and Donny Pauling (aka 'Donovan Phillips'), as well as "researchers, academics, legal experts, addiction professionals, nonprofit leaders, technology mavens and ministry leaders," all in town for the Coalition to End Sexual Exploitation 2014 Summit. The conference sponsors, perhaps mindful of what can result when riff-raff like actual journalists attend such events, required that all attendees first be vetted by Morality in Media's staff which, besides Hawkins, includes MiM president Patrick Trueman, a former federal obscenity prosecutor under Reagan/Bush I.

Summit sponsors are claiming that this is "the first national conference in 27 years on the harms of pornography," but apparently their memories have been dulled by too much anti-porn watching. Besides forgetting about that 2005 "Victims of Pornography Summit" which was actually held in the U.S. House of Representatives' Rayburn House Office Building, not to mention 2010's "Porn Harms: A Briefing" held in the D.C. Capitol Visitors Center, there were also the "Impact America Conference" of 2003 in Cleveland and the "National Pro-Family Conference on Pornography,

Sexually-Oriented Businesses and Material Harmful to Children" held in Lexington, KY in April of 2000, a report of which can be found elsewhere in this volume. And of course, that doesn't even count the annual Values Voter Summits which usually have anti-porn seminars and exhibitors, nor the annual Wheelock (MA) College "Stop Porn Culture" conferences run by Dines and her cronies.

But really, what would you expect? Lying comes as naturally to these people as turning off the lights before they fuck.

The Summit, which began at 7 a.m. today with a breakfast sponsored by EPIK (Empower Porn-Immune Kids.org), will last until 6 p.m. tomorrow, probably so as not to sully the Sabbath (as is so often the case, few if any of the attendees are likely to be Jewish) with sex talk. However, several of the speakers held forth at a presser at the National Press Club in D.C. yesterday, claiming that, according to Hawkins, "There's an untreated pandemic of harm from pornography" out there, and from Layden, "The earlier males are exposed to pornography, the more likely they are to engage in non-consensual sex, and for females, the more pornography they use, the more likely they are to be victims of non-consensual sex." (So, what? Guys are going to peep in through your window, see you're watching porn, and come in and rape you? Or does she think women who watch porn typically walk down the street naked wearing signs reading "Rape Me Now!"?)

But the horseshit was "piled high & deep" yesterday when Ph.D. holder Gail Dines told the crowd, "Porn is without doubt the most powerful form of sex education today, with studies showing that the average age of first viewing porn is between 11 and 14—and let me tell you, this is not your father's *Playboy*... These degrading misogynist images have become the wallpaper of our lives and they are robbing young people of an authentic healthy sexuality that is a basic right of every human being."

Indeed, it is sad that porn watching is what's passing for sex education in many quarters these days, but that's largely because the religious nuts that want to stamp out porn are the same religious nuts who oppose comprehensive sex education in the schools, and in many ways, porn is just the modern equivalent of learning about sex from your buddies on the playground.

Anyway, one who might have known what "your father's *Playboy*" was like was former skin mag photographer Pauling, who claims to have "found Jesus" and left the industry in 2005 to become yet another anti-porn zealot—and is sure that no matter what Duke University porn star Belle Knox[1] says, there's no chance she feels as "empowered" as she claims.

"I don't buy her story," he said. "I recruited more than 500 first-timers into the business and there's never been one that came back and thanked me."

(Two possibilities suggest themselves: Maybe Donny wasn't such a nice guy, or maybe the gals were making too much money to bother to stay in contact.)

But it seems that the real theme of both the press conference and the summit itself is to "work together to make pornography a widely understood public health concern," as the online membership solicitation reads—at the press conference, this quack nostrum became "public health *crisis*"—and that because the law has failed to stomp sufficiently on the First Amendment rights of adult content producers, it's time to turn to another government agency to get around the Constitution: the CDC.

"Ms. Layden suggested that if the US Centers for Disease Control and Prevention got 'interested in this as a public health issue, we can have success in the way that we had success with the issue of cigarette smoking'," News Corp's *Herald Sun* reported. ('Cause really, what's the difference between lighting up a cancer stick and slipping a DVD into the player?)

"There is going to have to be programs out there that get kids to understand how porn is manipulating them," Dines doubled down—but for her, there's just one problem: "This is a business with considerable political clout." (Cue the guffaws...)

In apparent support of Dines' new strategy, besides deeming the availability of sexually explicit material to be a "pandemic," Dawn Hawkins told the press, "There's a lot of science now proving that pornography is harmful. We know now that almost every family in America has been touched by the harm of pornography."

Of course, Hawkins is talking out of her ass once again, since the "science" she claims supports her views about the "harm" that has "touched...

almost every family in America" is almost entirely anecdotal—or as Lenny Bruce would have put it, "what kid told kid told kid"—and as one of the primary truisms of scientific research goes, "The plural of 'anecdote' is not 'data.'"

But along the way, summit attendees will apparently "learn" from Layden that "the porn industry deliberately sets out to addict users."

"It makes people anonymous," she said. "It has role models. It's sexually arousing. It's presented in pictures. And much of it is free."

And of course, Dines was there to back her up on that topic.

"Boys and men today are catapulted into a never-ending universe of images that celebrate, legitimize, and normalize sexual terrorism against women," Dines warned.

It helps to understand that pretty much any time a man "seduces" a woman in an adult movie (or, likely, vice-versa—whatever's in the *script*), Dines thinks of that as "sexual terrorism."

Anyway, check out some of the seminars and "break-out sessions" summit attendees will be subjected to, er, invited to attend:

• Panel—"Pornography and the Colonization of Childhood"

• Panel—"Links between Pornography & Sex Trafficking"

• "Pornography Addiction: A Supranormal Stimulus Considered in the Context of Neuroplasticity" (Whaaa? Maybe the anti-porn neurosurgeon Donald Hilton[2] who's giving this talk knows what it means, but it's sure opaque to everyone else!)

• "Faith-Based Prevention & Recovery Approaches"

• Panel—"Inside Porn: What is the Real Truth?" (Yeah, as if moderator Shelley Lubben knows something about *that*!)

• "The Church's Role in this War"

• Panel—"Latest Technological Delivery Systems of Pornography & Our Defenses" (Um... shut off the TV or computer?)

• "Exposing and Halting the International Sexual Rights Agenda: There is Something Everyone Can Do" (Yeah, because what's worse than people having sexual rights?)

And our favorite:

• "Making Anti-Porn Cool for Youth: How to Change the Way Youth Think about Porn" (Bet "youth" are just champing at the bit to get into that lecture!)

There's also a session scheduled for tonight, "Mock Interviews—Practice and improve skills for interviews with the press. Participants will recieve [sic] copy of their footage after the conference."

Sounds like Layden, Hawkins, Dines and Pauling could all probably have used a little of *that* before their National Press Club appearance—but then, what can you say in support of an issue like censorship that tens of millions of Americans think is just stupid... and unAmerican?

Earlier in the year this was written (2015), Morality in Media's leaders decided that it wasn't just pornography that needed eradicating; it was all forms of "sexual exploitation"—and I'm guessing that people were less willing to part with their earnings to support MiM's idea of "morality," but might be willing to monetarily bitch-slap "sexual exploitation." Also, I've redacted the real name of the former porn star rescue worker because I avoid outing people who might still suffer from discrimination because of their former profession.

MIM TOUTS FCC FINING TV STATION FOR SHOWING 3 SECONDS OF PORN

March 23, 2015

JESUSLAND—In its latest fund-raising effort, the National Center on Sexual Exploitation is rejoicing over the fact that the FCC has proposed fining TV station WDBJ-7[1] the maximum allowable—$325,000—for inadvertently airing roughly three seconds of a porn scene during a 6 p.m. newscast on July 12, 2012, during a news story about an ex-porn star turned firefighter.

"The FCC issued its first enforcement action on indecency in eight years," NCOSE claimed on its website. "The FCC unanimously voted to enforce the law against television station WDBJ, Roanoke Virginia (parent company Schurz Communications) regarding a July 12, 2012, 6 pm broadcast news clip that featured a porn video clip."

Of course, the censorship moguls at NCOSE got even that wrong: Anyone who read what the FCC actually said about the situation in their press release probably would have noticed its penultimate paragraph: "This is the *third action* the Enforcement Bureau has taken regarding the broadcast of indecent material since January 2014. In April 2014, the Enforcement Bureau settled its investigation into allegations of the broadcast of vulgar language on radio station KRXA (AM), which resulted in a payment of $15,000. In August 2014, Border Media Business Trust paid $37,500 in penalties to settle an investigation into the use of indecent sexual language during a morning show on radio station KDBR (FM)." [Emphasis added]

But facts and details have never been something NCOSE has ever worried much about.

"Today, for the first time in more than 8 years, The Federal Communications Commission began enforcing the federal law that prohibits profanity and indecency on broadcast TV," began NCOSE's fund-raising email, adding later, "Indecency on TV sexualizes our children and prepares them to become participants in the pornified world that awaits them. This is exactly why the National Center on Sexual Exploitation (NCSE), formerly Morality in Media (MIM), has been a leader in the matter of TV indecency for more than 50 years." ("Leader in the matter of TV indecency"? Awright!)

Of course, what actually happened at WDBJ—gotta love those last two letters!—isn't likely to offend anyone other than the most rabid bluenoses. Here's what the FCC's "Notice of Apparent Liability For Forfeiture" says about the situation:

"4. The materials submitted by WDBJ confirm that it broadcast a naked, erect penis and sexual manipulation thereof during an early evening news broadcast. Specifically, WDBJ submits a recording and transcript of the report at issue in the Complaints, which it acknowledges aired on its evening news, 'WDBJ7 at Six' on July 12, 2012, at approximately 6:00 p.m. The Station anchor introduces the report as the Station's 'top story [concerning] an ex-porn star' volunteer for the local rescue squad. The news report is approximately three minutes and 20 seconds in length. The recording submitted by WDBJ shows that the broadcast included images of the former adult film star. The first image is video in which only her face and shoulders can be seen. In the video, she has her finger in her mouth, moving it up and down on her tongue, with her lips partially open and then closing as she appears to suck on her finger. Just before this image appears, a reporter states: '[t]he Cave Spring rescue squad has been around for more than 60 years. In that time, it's probably never had a volunteer like [the woman].' At the time that the image is displayed, a reporter goes on to state: '[s]he's a former porn star.' The Licensee obtained the video image online from the website of a distributor of the woman's adult films. The website, which was partially displayed along with the video image, is bordered on the right side by boxes showing video clips from other films that do not appear to show the woman who is the subject of the news report.

"5. One of these video clips, displayed in a box, contains the image of sexual activity involving manipulation of an erect penis. Although the box does not show the entire body or face of the apparently nude male depicted, the image shows a hand moving up and down the length of the shaft of the erect penis. *WDBJ asserts that this image was displayed for less than three seconds.* There are also other images of the woman who is the subject of the story displayed at various times during the report, including one in which she appears to be sitting on a bed, wearing a bra." [Emphasis added]

The Notice goes on to recount what WDBJ said about the image, which is that it wasn't even visible on the station's in-house monitors and was therefore aired inadvertently, but the FCC either chose not to believe them, or decided that even an inadvertently broadcast image was worth *a third of a million dollar fine.*

"We are surprised and disappointed that the FCC has decided to propose to fine WDBJ-7 for a fleeting image on the very edge of some television screens during a news broadcast," said WDBJ-7 president and general manager Jeffrey A. Marks. "The story had gone through a review before it aired. Inclusion of the image was purely unintentional. The picture in question was small and outside the viewing area of the video editing screen. It was visible only on some televisions and for less than three seconds...

"The enormous fine proposed by the FCC is also an extraordinary burden on protected speech," Marks continued. "The FCC's largest base fine for other types of violations by broadcasters is $10,000. That is the fine for a misrepresentation to the FCC. A transfer of a license without authorization has a fine of only $8,000; use of a station to commit fraud results in a fine of $5,000; broadcast of an illegal lottery costs a station $4,000. As the FCC admits, its base forfeiture for a violation of the indecency rules is $7,000. This unprecedented proposed fine is more than 46 times higher than the FCC's own determination of the punishment for indecent speech."

Marks also said the station will appeal the proposed fine.

But the genesis of the FCC's action may go back to incoming FCC chairman Tom Wheeler's statement to the U.S. Senate Communications

Committee in a hearing in June of 2013, where *Variety* reported[2] Wheeler telling the committee that, "The FCC is in the midst of reviewing whether it should revise how it deals with complaints over indecency on broadcast television, with [outgoing chairman Julius] Genachowski's proposal to look at only 'egregious' cases."

Moreover, in the religio-conservative Parents Television Council's February 2015 newsletter, in an article titled, "FCC Should ENFORCE THE LAW!", the article's author complained that, "Unfortunately, in recent years the FCC has largely abandoned its [decency] mission. In 2013 the FCC's last chairman, Julius Genachowski, threw out more than one million indecency complaints that had been filed by members of the public, and attempted to gut indecency enforcement entirely. And since then, the networks have 'pushed the envelope' more than ever... The entertainment cartel wants there to be absolutely no restrictions whatsoever on the amount of gore, sex, nudity, and extreme content they dump into every living room in America using the airwaves owned by the American people to do so."

So it looks as though Wheeler has made his decision regarding only looking at "egregious" cases—and gone way, WAY over to censorship's "dark side."

And NCOSE couldn't be happier—well, unless someone actually sends them some money!

✲✲✲

ROANOKE'S WDBJ-7 INTENDS TO FIGHT MASSIVE FCC INDECENCY FINE

July 1, 2015

ROANOKE, Va.—Ya gotta feel sorry for Harmony Rose, the adult actress whose hand is the center of the controversy surrounding the largest indecency fine the Federal Communications Commission (FCC) has ever leveled against a broadcaster for a single incident—in part because it's the first time the FCC has attempted to fine a TV station for indecency since Congress increased the maximum fine ten-fold, to $325,000, in 2006.

The offense? As *AVN* noted earlier, during the station's July 2012 report on Rose, which cataloged some of the flack she had gotten from some residents of Cave Spring, where she had had the temerity to join the local rescue squad, WDBJ had included some photos of Rose from her former porn career: one showing her sitting on a bed clad only in a bra; one close-up of her mouth as she's sucking on her finger—and one tiny image in the corner of a background video where a hand (apparently not Rose's) can be seen jacking off a cock ... for less than three seconds.

But while the FCC filed notice of its intent to fine WDBJ (or, actually, its owner, Schurz Communications) in March of this year, the station has just filed its opposition to the levy—and although the 55-page document is not available to the public, an article on the Broadcasting & Cable website indicates that among the objections to the fine include "that the broadcast did not violate the FCC's indecency policy, that imposing the fine violates the First Amendment, that WDBJ lacked the necessary 'scienter,' a legal term for meaning to do what it did, and that even if a fine were warranted, imposing the maximum fine—the highest ever proposed for a single incident—for an inadvertent and momentary display was not warranted."

Part of the problem is that according to statements from WDBJ president/general manager Jeffrey Marks and various newsroom employees, the brief hardcore wasn't even visible on the newsroom's internal monitors, since it was along the edge of the larger video image of Rose sucking her finger, and the station denies that the airing could have been prevented if, as the FCC claims, station employees had been more attentive or had spent more time vetting the material.

Calling it a "fleeting, inadvertent, and isolated transmission," WDBJ noted that the FCC had provided no justification for levying the maximum fine, which the station described as "forty-six times the base amount" designated for such an "offense."

"While WDBJ regrets that an offensive image was inadvertently broadcast, we believe that the First Amendment does not allow the FCC to 'throw the book' at a station for unintentionally including a fleeting inappropriate image in a newscast about a legitimate story," Marks said. "WDBJ has taken steps to ensure that this kind of incident cannot be repeated. We have asked the FCC to withdraw its proposed forfeiture."

And there's good reason for the FCC to do so. For one thing, the judicial system has been particularly unfriendly to the FCC pretty much every time its indecency fines have landed it in court. For example, it lost all of its 21st-century "big name" cases like Janet Jackson's half-second tit exposure during the 2004 Super Bowl halftime show, Charlotte Ross's ass exposure in the 2003 episode "Nude Awakening" of *NYPD Blue*, Cher's responding to critics with a simple "Fuck 'em" at the 2002 Billboard Music Awards and "reality star" Nicole Richie's statement "Have you ever tried to get cow shit out of a Prada purse? It's not so fucking simple." in the same venue the following year.

Beyond that, just before he left office as the FCC chairman, Julius Genachowski asked the public to comment on the FCC's indecency policies in light of the agency's string of losses—policies that supposedly limited FCC action to "egregious" displays and continual violations rather than single "fleeting" incidents, as had been the FCC's policy since the 1978 *Pacifica* case[3] involving George Carlin's "Seven Dirty Words," until massive pressure from conservative religious groups led to the actions noted above. No word on how the public felt about the issues Genachowski raised, since the new chairman, Tom Wheeler, hasn't mentioned the subject. Indeed, as recently as March 23, FCC Enforcement Bureau chief Travis LeBlanc stated, "Our action here sends a clear signal that there are severe consequences for TV stations that air sexually explicit images when children are likely to be watching." (No shit!)

But legislators, the general public and even the mainstream media have been nearly silent on the issue, in part because as First Amendment commentator/attorney Clay Calvert recently noted, "What politician, after all, is going to pound the podium during a live televised debate and proudly proclaim, 'Fellow Americans, I'm here tonight to support your First Amendment right to receive indecent content—all day, every day, all free—on over-the-air television and radio stations. You want lurid language, nip slips, bare buttocks and Miley riding naked on a wrecking ball? Well, I say—bring them on! The more T&A on TV, the better!'"

Of course, although ~~Morality in Media~~ the National Center on Sexual Exploitation was the first to jump on the censorship-by-fine bandwagon, other holier-than-thou pressure groups weren't far behind.

"The FCC's unanimous and bipartisan ruling is a victory for families, and it serves as a powerful reminder to broadcasters who borrow the public's airwaves that they must abide by the law," said Parents Television Council (PTC) President Tim Winter,[4] later adding, "For the last several years, the FCC has failed to enforce the law—even when broadcasters have aired explicit and disgusting content, like gang rape, child molestation, and a man masturbating a horse. Hundreds of thousands of public complaints remain to be adjudicated."

(That last sentence, of course, is a lie: The FCC deep-sixed the vast majority of those complaints while Genachowski was still chairman—but since his exit, organizations like PTC have frequently encouraged their followers to file even more complaints.)

"We are grateful to FCC Chairman Tom Wheeler and all of the commissioners for this enforcement action," stated Cathy Ruse, a "Senior Legal Fellow" at Family Research Council (FRC). "This action should serve as a strong reminder to other stations and networks that there are laws in place to protect the public airways and those laws will be enforced. The fact that the FCC chose to pursue the highest possible fine is a good sign that it is taking this transgression very seriously."

One might remember that one transgression FRC *didn't* take very seriously was its employee Josh Duggar's admission that he'd sexually molested a couple of his sisters in his teens.

In any case, the battle lines have been drawn, and while it seems likely that WDBJ will cave if the FCC lowers its penalty to customary levels (say, $30,000), we just might be treated to yet another court battle over whether broadcasting three seconds of barely visible hardcore content will be considered "fleeting"—or even actionable at all.

People v. Freeman *was the decision that essentially legalized the production of porn in California, finding that performers were not prostitutes under the law, and producers were not panderers. Also, I was a panelist on the AOL Build panel that looked at* Hot Girls Wanted, *and the recording of it is worth a look if you can find it.*

AHEAD OF 2016 ELECTION, ANTI-PORN GROUP HOLDS 'CAPITOL HILL BRIEFING'

July 15, 2015

WASHINGTON, D.C.—Unfortunately, AVN was not able to attend the "Capitol Hill briefing" held by the National Center on Sexual Exploitation (NCOSE) yesterday—nor the "live abortions on display" on a Jumbo-Tron TV set up at the Lincoln Memorial—but it's not as if any new ground were broken, at least according to the several "news" stories about the event.

The Christian Broadcasting Network (CBN) seems to have published the most comprehensive coverage, and made it simple for their less discerning readers by opening with, "Porn is just prostitution with a camera—that was the message at a Capitol Hill briefing Tuesday on the ties between sex trafficking, prostitution, and pornography." (The California Supreme Court, which decided *People v. Freeman* in 1988, might have something to say about that idea.)

Present at the event were all the usual suspects—Dr. Gail Dines, Dr. Melissa Farley, Dr. Mary Anne Layden, Donna Rice Hughes and Drs. Sharon Cooper[1] and Donald Hilton (the only medical doctors in the crowd)—as well as relative newcomers Cordelia Anderson,[2] founder of the National Coalition to Prevent Child Sex Abuse and Exploitation, which "fights adult and child sexual harm," and Ed Smart, dad of world-famous kidnap victim Elizabeth Smart, now an anti-trafficking activist and sometime Mormon missionary. And since the event was put together by NCOSE, current and former executive directors Dawn Hawkins and Patrick Trueman filled out the bill.

And Anderson was more than ready with the falsehoods.

"This is supposed to be a sex enhancer, but instead it's harmful. It's the same lies the tobacco industry used, that this would help you with your anxiety, make you look sexy," she told the crowd. "Now we're still hearing that to be hip, if you want to show you're hip sexually and cool and show you're tolerant and 'with it,' then you're supposed to be okay with your partner using porn or using it yourself."

Well, that's certainly the first time we've seen it implied that porn will give you lung cancer...

For her part, Dines repeated almost word-for-word the same claims she made during the AOL Build panel[3] on the "documentary" *Hot Girls Wanted*,[4] saying, "When they studied 50 of the top-selling, top-watched scenes in porn, 90 percent had some form of sexual, physical, or emotional violence against women," Dines told the standing-room-only crowd. "This is the peer-reviewed literature. Those who argue that pornography is not violent are basically lying, or what they say is not based on peer-reviewed literature."

Bear in mind that for Dines, "violence in porn" includes one partner slapping the other on the ass during the heat of intercourse, or having his/her hand on the neck of that partner. It's a bit unclear what Dines means by "emotional violence" since she provided no examples—nor to what "peer-reviewed literature" she's referring.

Anti-porn/prostitution crusader Melissa Farley[5] made similar bogus claims, including, "The same things happen to women who are pornographized, trafficked, and prostituted. They're recruited in many of the same ways. The same kind of violence and coercion channel them into the sex industry. ... If you understand what sexual abuse is, what humiliation is, what rape and intimate partner violence are, then imagine if people get paid and are generating profits from those activities. That's what the sex industry is. Just because there's money thrown at acts of violence and coercion and sexual assault of children, it doesn't mean it's any different."

Farley apparently has some trouble understanding the difference between people who are forced to do something against their will, and people who do things, even sexual things they're paid to do on movie sets—*not* real life!—with eyes wide open, with agents, friends and other performers looking out for them, and with the ability to walk away from whatever activity they're asked to engage in and not look back.

And of course, if one listens to these jackasses, porn is the biggest boner killer around.

"We're seeing increased sexual dysfunction among young men these days," Hawkins claimed. "We're seeing increased demand for prostituted and trafficked women and children and increased child sexual abuse. Our courts and our jails are overwhelmed with predators right now and we would argue that pornography has played a role in that."

Of course, the target of all this bullshit was whichever Capitol Hill politicians and aides they could get to attend the briefing, though the only actual legislator mentioned in any of the news stories was California Rep. Jackie Speier, who told[6] *USA Today* that she plans to introduce a bill to make "revenge porn" a federal crime.

One "legislative advisor," Eleanor Kennelly Gaetan of the Coalition Against Trafficking in Women, told *USA Today* that the Centers for Disease Control and Prevention should conduct research assessing the connection between pornography, sex trafficking and prostitution.

"Until CDC identifies a phenomenon as harmful to the public, then from that identification can flow policy," she said. "To date there's no research by the federal government."

But, of course, there's plenty of research by non-governmental entities, and all of it that's been peer-reviewed has found that porn is enjoyable and harmless, and in some cases even beneficial to relationships.

Ah, well; another day, another porn-bashing seminar. Expect many more of them as the 2016 presidential election draws near.

It was at about this time that organizations like NCOSE began to focus on the fallacy that there's a lot of sex trafficking going on in the adult industry. Sure, they'd mentioned it before, but by this time, they'd settled on the idea that by talking enough about this alleged "sex trafficking," it'd be easier to rally their supporters against any sexually explicit content. Also, I think it's important to make the distinction "recognized U.S. adult movie industry" to distinguish the industry I worked in from the amateur producers in the U.S. and any producers in foreign lands. And "W", of course, refers to George W. Bush. And in terms of who's doing sex work, I should probably point out that a good friend of mine, who was a fellow court reporter, started hooking on the side when her "official" business flagged—and she's hardly the only one.

IT'S NOT TOO SOON BEFORE THE 2016 ELECTION TO TALK ABOUT PORN, IS IT?

Morality in Media doesn't think so!

Posted November 17, 2015

JESUSLAND—For those of you who've watched the Republican presidential debates so far, didn't you get the sinking feeling that something was missing? Sure, things like cutting Social Security benefits, repealing the Affordable Care Act ("Obamacare"), keeping the minimum wage at the low, low $7.25/hour, abolishing the IRS, making sure everybody can get (and keep) as many guns as they want, making abortion illegal again, defunding Planned Parenthood and figuring out how to make same-sex marriage illegal again are all important topics—but *how about* ***porn****?!?!?*

Fortunately, the "good" folks at the National Center on Sexual Exploitation (NCOSE) are on top of that issue. In fact, they've composed a cute little questionnaire that they'd like all the presidential candidates—even Democrats!—to answer so the Right-Wing NutJob (RWNJ) segment of the public can get a better idea of the most censorship-friendly candidate to support in the primaries, and even the national election a year from now.

There are only ten questions, so it's pretty simple—but they probably actually only need one: "Will you promise to scrub (with lye) every bookstore, video store, 'love boutique,' magazine rack and the World Wide

Web of its pornography, and imprison anyone who's ever created, sold, posted, owned or looked at a sexually explicit (including simple nudity) DVD, book, magazine, photo or Web page?" (That should decrease the size of the electorate pretty significantly!) (Including some of the candidates themselves!)

But for some reason, NCOSE has decided it needs to parse its request for ~~prejudice~~ information a little bit more, so here's the full list, with commentary, of the questions they'd undoubtedly like the moderators of the next Republican debate to ask each candidate—and which NCOSE themselves will be asking through e- and snail-mail:

1) "If elected president will your administration redirect research resources to determine all factors contributing to sex trafficking, as well as allocate the law enforcement resources necessary to aggressively combat the demand for commercial sex?"

Comment: Hopefully, those "factors" to be "determined" will include America's insane prostitution laws, which prevent women (and men) who choose prostitution from reporting abusive pimps and clients to police because they'd be busted for practicing their profession; laws which make certain addictive drugs illegal and therefore so expensive that people will rent (not "sell"!) their bodies for sex to support their habits; outdated religious ideals of "staying pure until marriage" that cause teens (and younger!) to sneak around to have sex, often with no protection against STIs and/or pregnancy, because their parents would disown them if they found out; and comprehensive sex education classes in public schools that show kids that sex can be fun and pleasurable if they choose the right partner and take the proper precautions? (And of course, as we all know, thanks to NCOSE, one of the prime causes of a "demand for commercial sex" is pornography—which, of course, *is* in itself a form of "commercial sex"!)

2) "If elected president will you ensure the continuation of National Security Presidential Directive 22[1] preserving the federal government's abolitionist approach to combating sex trafficking?"

Comment: Gosh, we'd forgotten about that relic from the early W era. We mean, who even remembers a "Cabinet-level Interagency Task Force to Monitor and Combat Trafficking in Persons"? Was it ever even created?

(Let's face it: if Cheney and Rumsfeld weren't on board with it, it probably never happened during W's tenure.) And as for the part of that directive that states, "According to some estimates, each year at least 700,000 and possibly as many as 4 million people, primarily women and children, are trafficked around the world, including thousands into the United States," estimates from people who actually *know* something about human trafficking put the numbers at far less—and "sex trafficking" at far less than that. For example, the Federation of American Scientists, in a 2013 report, found that a total of 17,500 people were trafficked in the U.S. in 2004, the year after Directive 22 was published, and that the vast majority of those people were trafficked for "domestic servitude, agriculture, manufacturing, janitorial services, hotel services, construction, health and elder care, [and] hair and nail salons"—and *none* in the adult movie business, though some were caught dancing at strip clubs.

3) "If elected president will you nominate to the position of Ambassador-at-Large for Trafficking in Persons at the U. S. Department of State an individual who is committed to combating all forms of human trafficking (sex and labor trafficking), who will emphasize the role of demand for commercial sex in the sex trafficking phenomenon, and who will vigorously support National Security Presidential Directive 22?"

Comment: As we noted above, sex trafficking in the U.S. is practically non-existent, though there are undoubtedly some underage boys and girls who begin hooking on their own to earn extra money—but we can't help but suspect that when NCOSE talks about "demand for commercial sex in the sex trafficking phenomenon," they're really talking about trafficked men and women in *porn*—which in the recognized U.S. adult movie industry is non-existent. Also, seems that the current "Ambassador-at-Large for Trafficking in Persons" is former Assistant U.S. Attorney Susan Coppedge of Georgia, appointed by President Obama last month(!)—so of course, NCOSE will want a change, because how could *anyone* appointed by Obama really want to fight trafficking?

4) "If elected president will you support the efforts of the National Association of Attorneys General in their call for Congress to amend the Communications Decency Act of 1996, which, as some courts interpret, allows companies such as Backpage.com to profit from the child and adult sex trade?"

Comment: Oh, yeah; we forgot: Republicans are all about supporting U.S. businesses—unless, of course, they have anything at all to do with sex! Trouble is, the vast majority of people placing ads for "adult services" on Backpage.com, Craigslist and similar spaces are people who, in just about any other business, would be considered entrepreneurs: People who create their own business models and then apply their own intellect and sweat to make a success of them. There'd be no problem if NCOSE had limited their call to investigation of *minors* selling sex, but being incredibly religiously hung up on anything to do with sex (as was Congress when it passed the CDA), NCOSE wants to target even adults who know exactly what services they're advertising and are doing it of their own free will.

5) "If elected president will you direct the U. S. Department of Health and Human Services to undertake a major effort to abate the effects of pornography addiction?"

Comment: Ah, now we get to the good stuff: PORNOGRAPHY!!! And after all, why would NCOSE let a little thing like the fact that ***there is no such thing as pornography addiction*** get in the way of its politicking? Now, there *is* "obsessive compulsive disorder" (OCD), which *Psychology Today* defines as "an anxiety disorder in which people have unwanted and repeated thoughts, feelings, ideas, sensations (obsessions), or behaviors that make them feel driven to do something (compulsions). Often the person carries out the behaviors to get rid of the obsessive thoughts, but this only provides temporary relief. Not performing the obsessive rituals can cause great anxiety. A person's level of OCD can be anywhere from mild to severe, but if severe and left untreated, it can destroy a person's capacity to function at work, at school or even to lead a comfortable existence in the home." (Gee; sort of like how NCOSE spends so much of its time trying to get rid of porn!)

6) "If elected president will you direct the U.S. Department of Justice to vigorously enforce federal obscenity laws, which prohibit distribution of hardcore pornography on the Internet, on cable/satellite TV, on hotel/motel TV, in retail shops, and by common carrier[?]"

Comment: Morality in Media was formed in 1962, and it's pretty clear that time moves a lot slower for them than it does for most of the rest of the population. See, over the past 40+ years, most people have come to realize that even if they themselves may not want to look at people having sex, other people do, and Americans generally being "live and let live" types (except, of course, religious fundamentalists like NCOSE supporters), the number of obscenity prosecutions over the past decade or so have nose-dived. There have been few local obscenity prosecutions, mostly in conservative areas—Polk County, Florida, Alabama, South Carolina, Virginia and a couple of others made the grade there; the vast majority have been based on FBI stings—of Max Hardcore, Evil Angel, Rob Black, Barry Goldman, James Schaeffer and Jeffrey Killbride, JM Productions, Adult DVD Empire... even Ira Isaacs, whose material was substantially different than that released by those other defendants. The point is, the vast majority of Americans now understand that wanting to see how other people have sex is pretty natural, and they don't want to see the people who make that sexually explicit content thrown in the hoosegow. Crazy religionists and RWNJs do.

7) "Internet service providers in the United Kingdom block pornography to user accounts unless users specifically opt in to receive pornography. If elected president will you use your leadership position to encourage U. S. Internet service providers to adopt the UK 'opt in' model and thus protect children and families from unwanted pornography?"

Comment: Oooh; sorry to report, NCOSE, but the European Parliament has ruled that UK Prime Minister David Cameron's edict that ISPs have to block porn automatically until the user decides to "opt in" is illegal (though Cameron has announced that he intends to try to thwart that edict and keep forcing Britains to make that embarrassing phone call). Of course, in the United States of America, we have this thing called the "First Amendment," and since "pornography" is one of the categories of speech that the Supreme Court is unwilling to find legally actionable, an edict from a Republican U.S. president (because, of course, no Democrat would be that stupid) would run afoul of that First Amendment pretty quickly. Beyond that, there are plenty of religiously-based ISPs and filtering programs out there that if a person really wants to avoid all porn showing up on his/her computer, it's pretty easy to subscribe and voilà: No more porn!

8) "If elected president will you insist that the FCC vigorously enforce the federal indecency law designed to protect children from damaging sexual content and appoint commissioners committed to fulfilling this mission?"

Comment: "Damaging sexual content"—that's pretty funny! They say that as if it were actually possible for a person to be "damaged" by seeing a bare tit or cock, hearing someone say "shit" or "fuck," or watching "reality show" contestants walking around naked[2] except for their genitals being obscured by computer masking. Apparently, NCOSE still has a problem with the fact that real people use real vulgarity (and occasionally profanity) in their personal lives—even sometimes when they're interviewed on TV. So whether it's Nicole Richie asking exasperatedly/rhetorically, "Does anybody know how hard it is to get cowshit out of a Prada purse? It's not so fucking simple," or Cher saying "Fuck 'em" to critics of her music, or Bono exclaiming, "Fucking brilliant!" after receiving a Billboard Music award, NCOSE is against it—"it" being "human nature." And rest assured, NCOSE definitely wants a candidate who *will* target human nature through his (we're pretty sure they can't imagine a woman president) appointments, just like all the other conservative politicians have done.

9) "A federal statute (18 U.S.C. §2259) requires that, in child sexual exploitation cases, a defendant must pay restitution for 'the full amount of the victim's losses.' That works for crimes in which a defendant directly causes specific harm to a victim, but child pornography crimes are different. 'Amy' and 'Vicky' are the victims in two of the most widely-distributed child pornography series in the world. On April 23, 2014, in *Paroline v. United States*,[3] which reviewed Amy's case, the Supreme Court found that the existing restitution statute is not suited for cases like theirs. The Amy and Vicky Act[4] creates a restitution process for victims of child pornography. If elected president will your administration encourage Congress to pass this bill as quickly as possible so that you can sign it into law?"

Comment: This might seem like one of the more innocuous questions NCOSE would ask, since it wouldn't have any significant impact on the adult entertainment industry, but generally speaking, this whole concept of "child porn victim restitution" is a major can of worms. For instance, kid porn victim "Amy Unknown" (as she's usually referred to) has already received about $1.8 million from 182 child porn defendants, one of whom contributed $1.2 million but most of whom were assessed figures between $1,000 and $530,000—and her uncle, who made the porn in the first place, put in $6,000 and had to spend a decade in the clink. It's not known how much Vicky Unknown, a similar victim, has received. Interestingly, the Amy and Vicky Child Pornography Victim Restitution Improvement Act of 2015, which would clarify that child porn victims can collect every penny they can squeeze out of anybody who's ever downloaded one of their photos/videos, passed the U.S. Senate in January, but as of March, the House had done nothing with it, preferring to spend its time demonizing Obamacare, blasting the IRS for doing its job in denying tax-exempt status to activist political groups, harassing Hillary Clinton on Benghazi and her emails, and other valuable endeavors.

10) "If elected president will your Departments of Justice and State give guidance to the U.S. states and foreign governments advising against the full decriminalization of prostitution and against the normalization of prostitution as 'sex work'?"

Comment: Understanding that most people don't give a fuck about porn, Morality in Media changed its name to the National Center on Sexual Exploitation, at least in part because fighting prostitution and "sex trafficking" is where the Big Money is these days—so of course, they were a little upset that Amnesty International, the international human rights group, voted[5] to support decriminalization of that sort of employment, recognizing that "sex work" is *work*—something to which post-worldwide-recession populations are more and more turning. Understand, in 2003, the W administration put a rule in place[6] that any agency or group receiving federal funding for international HIV/AIDS prevention or similar sex-related services was required to affirm that it would officially oppose both prostitution and sex trafficking. Calling "bullshit" on that, several organizations sued the federal government, charging that the requirement violated their First Amendment speech rights—and in June of 2013, the Supreme Court agreed.[7] NCOSE would dearly love to try to reverse that decision through legislation or even presidential edict. The simple fact is, prostitution is a job like most others, and the people who practice (or have practiced) that art come from pretty much all walks of life: actresses, attorneys, housewives, clergy, musicians, clerks, secretaries, court reporters... the list goes on. But NCOSE would like to throw all those folks in prison simply for bringing a little pleasure into their clients' otherwise all-too-often drab lives. "Killjoy" barely begins to cover it.

Anyway, the full list of questions NCOSE intends to pose is no longer available. And rest assured, since Republicans have nothing else of substance to run on in the coming year, expect to see a lot more anti-porn/anti-sex-work pandering to groups like NCOSE as the right-wing "pretenders to the throne" see the general public rejecting more and more of their heartless ideology.

It continues to fascinate me that Some People can't get it through their heads that some other people like it when others cause them pain in pre-agreed sex play—outmoded U.N. definitions of "torture" notwithstanding. Also, one actress told me personally that her preferred word for "stop the current action" was "Scalia"!

COMMENTARY: YOU SAY 'TOH-MAY-TOH'; I SAY 'WHAT THE HELL ARE YOU TALKING ABOUT?'

Morality in Media is at it again, conflating porn with torture

Posted March 3, 2016

JESUSLAND—Some people like pain. Scratch that; some people *love* pain—and fortunately for them, producers like Kink.com, Severe Sex, Venus Girls, Taboo Dream Studios, and producers Glenn King, Aiden Starr and the like are only too happy to make content to appeal to that fetish. Never mind that such content is usually shot in exceptionally controlled environments, the action is discussed beforehand in minute detail so there are no (well, few) surprises once the cameras roll, safe words are *de rigeur* ("Scalia!"), and most importantly, nobody who has an objection to being tied up, whipped, gagged or made to wear ultra-tight-fitting corsets is forced to do so... and most performers don't.

So we found it a little off-putting to read, in the first paragraph of the National Center on Sexual Exploitation's *Report: The Gender-Based Torture Found in the Pornography Industry*,[1] which they were kind enough to send to the United Nations' Rapporteur on Torture Juan Méndez recently, that "the pornography industry—and for the purposes of this report specifically hardcore or obscene Internet pornography—intentionally causes severe physical and mental suffering to the women filmed or photographed, and that it should therefore be recognized as torture." (Apparently, Méndez is busy preparing an official report on just that topic!)

And rest assured, NCOSE isn't just talking about BDSM movies; they mean just about every production this industry puts out!

See, according to the definition used by the United Nations, torture is "any act by which severe pain or suffering, whether physical or mental, is intentionally inflicted on a person for such purposes as obtaining from him or a third person information or a confession, punishing him for an act he or a third person has committed or is suspected of having committed, or intimidating or coercing him or a third person, or for any reason based on discrimination of any kind." Of course, it's usually governments that are committing torture—you know; like the CIA did in Iraq's Abu Ghraib[2] or our own Guantanamo Bay prison[3]—but there are also such entities as "non-state torturers," some of whom are noted to be "multinational companies, familial relations [and] human traffickers."

Perhaps you see where this is going. If "human traffickers" are "non-state torturers," and since it's NCOSE's position that pretty much all actresses in the adult industry have been trafficked into it, it only stands to reason that every sex act in which an actress engages is, by that definition, "torture"!

But actually, it's apparently worse than that.

"Unlike theatrical movies, where punches are faked and sexual penetration is merely implied, the pornography industry is built upon explicit and real violence," the report's author, Haley Halverson, claims. "Women are not 'acting' as though they are being punched, choked, spit on, electrically shocked, or violated sexually in a multitude of painful and degrading ways, they *are* actually experiencing these abuses."

Of course, Halverson is hobbled by the fact that she's never been on a porn set (or, we're guessing, a Hollywood one either), so she's apparently ignorant of the fact that the Hollywood stuntmen and -women often do take actual punches (which they have learned to roll with), and that actors in late-night "Skinemax" fare sometimes do engage in sexual penetration that isn't explicitly shown in the finished product. (We know because we *have* been on such sets.) And just because porn performers aren't usually described as "stunt people" doesn't mean that that isn't exactly what they are: They engage in more physical activity to make adult content than most Hollywood actors will ever do on-screen in their entire lives. But except in very rare instances, porn performers aren't actually punched, aren't actually choked (though some actresses say they like it), aren't spit upon unless they've agreed beforehand that it's okay, ditto for electrical shocks—but we're pretty sure that as far as NCOSE is concerned, *every* sex act a performer engages in is a "sexual violation."

The "report" (is something really a "report" if it has no factual basis?) goes on to quote from some UN conferences from as far back as the early '90s, that were attended by people at least as clueless about porn as NCOSE itself—not to mention the "team of researchers" (*ghod*, how easily that phrase is thrown around!) which "randomly selected and analyzed 50 of the [most bought/rented] films, which contained a sum of 304 scenes," and "found" that "88% of these scenes contained physical violence, and 49% contained verbal aggression, and 94% of the time the violence and aggression was directed toward the woman. The typical scene averaged 12 physical or verbal attacks."

Anyone who's kept up with the latest adult releases—even the ones from 2010 when this "study" was made—knows what utter horseshit it is that anywhere near 88 percent of them contain physical violence—until you understand that virtually anything that isn't pure, man-on-top, whitebread sex can be "found" to have "physical violence." Some of those "violent" acts include when one partner slaps the other one's ass in the heat of fucking; when the man holds the woman's head while she's giving head; when one partner puts a hand on the other's throat in missionary or doggie—the list goes on and on.

In fact, perhaps the most telling sentence in the entire "report" occurs on page 7, where Halverson lets slip the incredible concept that, "Because there is no valid consent to sexual exploitation, all of the acts in pornography ought to be considered torture." And of course, since *all* acts in porn are considered by NCOSE to be "sexual exploitation," 88 percent must represent the lowest estimate they thought they could come up with for "sexual violence."

And what "report" would be complete without "researcher" Gail Dines, who "found" that the "most common themes in mainstream Internet pornography" are triple penetration, double anal, double vag, deep-throat with gagging, and ass-to-mouth. And people actually think this woman knows something about porn!

Next up are the "true life tales," beginning with a quote from a Max Hardcore interview in 2005 in which he claims to have invented having actresses drink cum from their asses, and throat-fucking them until they puke. Three guesses as to whether the "Rapporteur on Torture" will figure out that Hardcore is one of the outermost outliers in the field of porn production.

The "report" also finds space for something moronic that Bill Margold said in '95, claiming that what men "really" want to see is "violence against women," and how anti-porn Prof. Robert Jensen is convinced that porn producers "offer men sexual gymnastics and circus acts that are saturated with cruelty toward women; they sexualize the degradation of women."

Perhaps Halverson's single valid point involves the titles of some adult videos, like *Anally Ripped Whores*, *Teen Dirty Slut* and *White Sluts on Black Snakes*—but what the hell is wrong with a title like *Horny Black Pussy*? And the fact that despite the derogatory language, the action in many of these movies doesn't live up (or down) to their titles isn't something Halverson sees fit to include. The "report" also includes a list of other titles and categories Halverson finds offensive, all of which are drawn from descriptions on the Kink.com and Pornhub websites—and none of which are seen in mainstream porn.

The final section of the "report" is devoted to single paragraphs by six unidentified women who claim to have had bad experiences on porn sets, which as far as Halverson is concerned, all meet the definition of "victim" found in the United Nations Committee Against Torture's Comment No. 3.[4] This exercise is tantamount to reporting on the number of unarmed black civilians who've been shot dead by police, and using that to generalize that all police are racist killers.

Seems the whacked-out politicians in Utah never give up trying to deprive their citizens of a little harmless sexual entertainment, which in Utah-speak is the genesis of a "public health crisis."

UTAH POLS DECLARE PORN A 'PUBLIC HEALTH CRISIS'! UM ... HOORAY?

March 11, 2016

JESUSLAND—According to the National Center on Sexual Exploitation (NCOSE), **"The Utah House of Representatives passed the Utah state resolution declaring pornography a public health crisis last night!** Soon it will be presented to Governor Gary Herbert for his signature." [Emphasis in original, here and below]

Yep, the state with the highest per capita number of subscribers to adult websites,[1] the state whose favorite adult search term is "Lesbian," the state that many years ago gave up one of its own religious principles and buckled under pressure from the federal government to declare polygamy unMormon, has a legislature that wants to go on record to proclaim, among other incredibly stupid ideas, that "pornography is contributing to the hypersexualization of teens, and even prepubescent children, in our society"; "exposure to pornography often serves as childrens' [sic] and youths' sex education and shapes their sexual templates" (sadly, in too many areas—including, we're sure, Utah—that one's true) (but no less stupid); "pornography treats women and children as objects and often depicts rape and abuse as if they are harmless"; and "pornography equates violence towards women and children with sex and pain with pleasure, which increases the demand for sex trafficking, prostitution, child sexual abuse images, and child pornography."

Well, as one might expect from NCOSE Executive Director Dawn "Terrifying Porn Flight" Hawkins, "We were on pins and needles yesterday, waiting to hear if the resolution would make it on the docket before the midnight deadline to be voted on this session. In a dramatic turn of events, the resolution passed 75-0 at 10:40 p.m. last night!"

We can just imagine the conversation: "Say, honey, it's almost bedtime; wanna go in the bedroom and have a quick fuck?" "Sorry, dear, I've got to go to the House of Representatives chambers and vote on an anti-porn resolution in a dramatic turn of events, so sex will *just have to wait!*"

And in case you were afraid that NCOSE had just been sitting around, twiddling its thumbs as most Americans become more and more comfortable with their sexuality, both in their personal lives and in their media (yes, we're thinking of you, Parents Television Council and the inaptly named 1 Million Moms), fear no longer:

"**The National Center on Sexual Exploitation is honored to have written this resolution**, which was proposed by State Senator Todd Weiler. We wrote the resolution because **we believe it is vital for the government to formally recognize the harms of pornography**."

And rest assured, if that government is headed up next year by one of the "Usual Gang of Idiots" (apologies, Bill Gaines[2]), it's a sure bet that it will. Thankfully, as things stand now, porn prosecution is what one might call "low priority" at the Department of Justice, and we're guessing that Sanders (definitely) or Clinton (likely) won't change that ... which is good, because:

"YOU CAN TAKE ACTION:

1) Propose this resolution in your state! We have already heard from several supporters around the nation who are going to ask their representatives to follow Utah's example. If legislators recognize the harms of pornography on children, families, and society it will educate and inform the public, along with future policy decisions!"

Yes, despite the fact that no presidential candidate except Rick Santorum was willing to answer NCOSE's bullshit "survey" (read "push poll") about "sexual exploitation," one question of which reads, "As a result of the failure of previous administrations to enforce federal adult obscenity laws, the United States is being inundated with pornography, much of which normalizes sex with children and which is increasingly violent and abhorrent. Federal obscenity laws prohibit distribution of hardcore pornography on the Internet, on cable/satellite TV, on hotel/motel TV, in retail shops, and by common carrier. If elected president will you direct the U.S. Department of Justice to vigorously enforce federal obscenity laws?", it seems highly likely that the eventual Republican presidential candidate will "ace this exam"—even Donald Drumpf. And rest assured that when that happens, NCOSE will be on hand to say, as they end their recent press release, "Thank you for your support and passion for these issues. Together, we are making history!"

Section 230 is pretty much the only thing keeping the internet alive nowadays... so of course anybody who's anybody wants to destroy it. How sad(!) that even in an administration as fucked up as Trump's was, NCOSE couldn't get much of its agenda enacted.

NCOSE RELEASES ITS ANTI-FREEDOM 'FREEDOM FROM SEXPLOITATION' AGENDA

March 23, 2017

TRUMPINGTON, D.C.—With the Religious Right firmly in power in the nation's capital, the National Center on Sexual Exploitation (NCOSE) figured it'd be a good time to roll out its legislative agenda for the next four years, and who knows? With the Sociopath-In-Chief generally delegating such "domestic" matters to his underlings, there's little doubt that once Congress is done destroying healthcare, the environment, the schools, gay/trans rights, immigrants' rights and the rights of "certain religions," it might look favorably upon NCOSE's anti-sex agenda—or at least use it as a distraction from whatever the administration doesn't want to get too much attention at the time.

In fact, it's surprising that NCOSE waited until this past Monday to hold a press conference touting the release of its "Freedom From Sexual Exploitation Agenda,"[1] whose opening paragraph states, "America is suffering from a sexual exploitation crisis. Sex trafficking, sexual assault, child sexual abuse, pornography, and more, are issues significantly impacting American citizens, families, and communities. This necessitates that our federal government address the full spectrum of sexual harm. ... We also know that pornography is often made of sex trafficked women and children, and increases the demand for buying sex. Further, females who consume pornography are at greater risk of being a victim of sexual harassment or sexual assault." (Where *do* they get this crap?)

"Crisis" is the Religious Right's (and conservatives') current favorite word. Whether it's an "immigration crisis" that requires that Muslims be banned from entering the country (or building mosques somewhere) or a "healthcare crisis" that requires stripping millions of citizens of their health insurance ... or that familiar "pornography is a public health crisis" that legislatures across the country are now passing resolutions in agreement, without having any idea what they're talking about—but it's a *CRISIS*, damnit, and we have to DO SOMETHING about it!

And rest assured, NCOSE has plenty of ideas about what to do—16 of them, in fact, all laid out in their "Policy & Legislative Recommendations to Curb Sexual Exploitation"—and of course, since "sexual exploitation" is in their name, objective #1 is to get rid of sites like Backpage.com, which recently took down its adult listings after its owners were browbeaten in congressional hearings. But where one falls, another is sure to rise, so NCOSE wants Congress to "Amend Section 230 of the Communications Decency Act (CDA) of 1996 to allow prosecution of those who facilitate illegal commercial sex acts via the Internet."

"Ironically, courts have recently interpreted section 230 of the CDA as shielding sex trafficking and prostitution websites from criminal and civil liabilities in cases involving the facilitation of sex trafficking via the Internet," the agenda states. "As a result, sex trafficking is flourishing on the Internet, and those profiting from the sexual exploitation of countless individuals have repeatedly escaped justice."

In fact, the vast majority of "adult services" ads on sites like Backpage involve adults offering their *consensual* sexual services to other adults—and if prostitution were legal, as a variety of organizations including Amnesty International have championed, it would be easier to weed out the few ads from traffickers from those of legitimate sex workers.

But don't worry; NCOSE also has agenda item #6, which begins, "As the *2013 Trafficking in Persons Report* observed, 'If there were no demand for commercial sex, sex trafficking would not exist in the form it does today. This reality underscores the need for continued strong efforts to enact policies that prohibit paying for sex.' **Thus, it is imperative that DOJ, under the provisions of the Justice for Victims of Trafficking Act, prosecute those who 'solicit or patronize' victims of human trafficking for the purpose of commercial sex acts."** [Emphasis in original]

Now, what's stated above would likely not be a problem for anyone, assuming it were clear which sex workers were trafficked and which weren't—except NCOSE then goes on to say, "DOJ should also work with its federally funded anti-trafficking task forces to ensure the investigation, arrest, and prosecution of persons who purchase sexual acts, as part of a concerted effort to combat the demand for sex trafficking." In other words, for NCOSE, it doesn't actually matter if the person providing the sex is trafficked or not; they want *everyone* who "purchase[s] sexual acts" to be arrested and prosecuted. It's called the "Nordic model"[2] and it's failed in every country that's tried it.

What's more, they also want (item #7) for the U.S. to maintain its "abolitionist approach to combating human trafficking by recognizing that activities such as prostitution, pimping, pandering, and maintaining of brothels contribute to the phenomenon of trafficking in persons; and formalizes the U.S. government's opposition to prostitution and related activities as inherently harmful and dehumanizing," and (item #8) "Immediately nominate an individual to the position of Ambassador-at-Large for Trafficking in Persons at the U. S. Department of State who is committed to combating all forms of human trafficking (sex and labor trafficking), and who will address the role of demand for commercial sex in the crime of sex trafficking."

From all this, it's pretty clear that NCOSE will never understand that the best way to combat sex trafficking is through legalizing sex work and monitoring the workers to make sure they're free from disease and, as importantly, coercion—but religio-conservatives have always been fucked up about sex, so really, no surprises here. Just sadness.

Perhaps even sadder is that NCOSE wants the U.S. government to penalize other countries who don't toe the line when it comes to prostitution legalization (items #9 & 10)—and even agencies within our own country, like the Office on Violence Against Women and the U.S. Department of Education (item #11), which should "review their institutional policies and practices for ways in which they can share research, provide educational materials, and institute policies, regarding *pornography's role in exacerbating sexual violence*." [Emphasis added] That horseshit is based upon a 2015 "meta-analysis" of 22 studies from seven countries which supposedly "provides clear evidence confirming that pornography exposure is significantly associated with sexual aggression"—except, of course, it doesn't, since for several of the studies that were "meta-analyzed," the researchers couldn't even identify how many participants took part in the study, and several other earlier, more comprehensive studies, most notably by researcher Dr. Neil Malamuth,[3] found exactly the opposite.

Of course, since NCOSE's predecessor organization was founded to rid the country of sexually explicit books, magazines and films, the agenda's #2 objective is, "Instruct the U.S. Attorney General to vigorously enforce current federal obscenity laws 18 U.S.C. §1460 to 18 U.S.C. §1470." Those sections of the United States Code prohibit doing pretty much anything with material deemed to be "obscene"—making it, selling it, importing it, mailing it, transporting it across state lines, broadcasting it, showing it to kids, etc.—though we suspect that the section that gets NCOSE members the wettest is §1467, "Criminal Forfeiture," where the government can seize from anyone convicted of trafficking in obscenity "any property, real or personal, constituting or traceable to gross profits or other proceeds obtained from such offense."

There's just one problem: Americans like their sexual material. DVD and magazine sales may be down somewhat, but online porn sites are booming, and it's been estimated that porn is a $97 billion business worldwide—and American juries pretty much anywhere except the Deep South (and often, not even there) have no interest in putting someone in prison for selling the material that at least some members of the jury and their pals are getting off to.

There's also one agenda item devoted specifically to 18 U.S.C. §1464, "Broadcasting obscene language," where NCOSE wants the Federal Communications Commission to "vigorously enforce" that section "to protect children from damaging sexual content on television," and it also wants Dear Leader to "appoint FCC commissioners committed to fulfilling this mission." Of course, no one has any real idea what "damaging sexual content on television" is, especially since it exists only in the minds of would-be censors.

But the agenda is hardly done with media, both adult and mainstream. Agenda item #14 wants Congress to "Disband the current TV Parental Guidelines Oversight Monitoring Board (TVOMB)" because, you know, it's "a sham composed of broadcast television insiders, and is utterly lacking in congressional oversight and public transparency" that has "enabled and sheltered a flawed content ratings system" because shows like *The Simpsons*, *Family Guy*, *Last Man On Earth*, *The Mick*, *Law & Order: SVU*, and all the *NCIS*es "may include gratuitous sex, explicit dialogue, violent content, or obscene language" but are rated something other than TV-MA.

NCOSE also wants Congress to expand the Family Movie Act of 2005,[4] which allowed the development of technology that would edit cable and even DVD movies (mainstream and otherwise) to remove "bad" language and images "on the fly." Trouble is, according to NCOSE, "Today the preferred method for viewing movies has shifted from DVD to streaming," and NCOSE wants the law updated so that movies streaming on Netflix or Hulu or AppleTV can also be censored. So far, such censorship is voluntary, but since censorship is NCOSE's business model, we can't help but worry what such laws might mean for adult.

The agenda also targets the U.S. military in a couple of points. It wants to require (item #3) that soldiers, sailors, etc. be "informed" about the so-called "harms of pornography," and (item #4) that all military personnel be forbidden from entering strip clubs *anywhere in the world*! Because, after all, "Military personnel participating in the consumption of commercial sex at strip clubs fuel the demand for sex trafficking." (*Whaaa?*)

Oh; and let's not forget other government employees, because NCOSE didn't. That's item #12, "Pass H.R. 680 'Eliminating Pornography from Agencies Act'," [5] which would prohibit any government employee from watching porn on his (or her!) computer at work.

But the most potentially dangerous recommendation in this whole agenda may be item #5, which calls on the U.S. Surgeon General and the Department of Health and Human Services to create a study "into the public health harms of pornography," which should include "a nationally representative survey of pornography use among adolescents and adults; a meta-analysis of the neurological studies linking pornography use to compulsive behaviors; the association between adult pornography use and child sexual exploitation; the association between pornography consumption and sexual violence generally, and violence against women in particular; the association between pornography use and sex buying behaviors; the association between pornography use and child-on-child sexual abuse; pornography's impacts on other sexual behaviors and attitudes among adolescents and adults; the impacts of pornography use on intimate relationships; the link to erectile and sexual dysfunctions; transmission of STDs; and detrimental impacts on brain health; etc." (*Whew!*)

Trouble is, as anyone who's spent any time reading the studies that have *already* been done *ad nauseam* of these same claims knows that a lot of them are crap; there's nothing to them. There *is no* "neurological link" between porn use and compulsive behavior." There *is no* "association between adult pornography use and child sexual exploitation"—child predators aren't interested in *adult* porn! There *is no* link between porn and not being able to get a hard-on. There *is no* link between using porn and getting or giving an STD. And Judith Reisman's fantasies aside, there are no "detrimental impacts" of porn use on "brain health"—"erototoxins" (or whatever they're calling them these days) don't exist!

Now, after all that, believe it or not, there is one recommendation we can get behind: #16, "Pass S.534 'Protecting Young Victims from Sexual Abuse Act of 2017'."[6] This would "require amateur athletics governing bodies to immediately report sex-abuse allegations to local or federal law enforcement, or a child-welfare agency designated by the Justice Department," and ensure that those who do report such allegations don't suffer any blowback from the school because of such reporting. That's a damned good idea—and it's too bad that it's surrounded by such a ration of shit.

The full NCOSE report can be found on its website. (**UPDATE**: Lotsa luck finding it.) Read it and weep.

It's always fun to listen to two ignoramuses talk about a subject of which both are pretty much ignorant. Also, NCOSE took Dines' advice and has filed several lawsuits against MindGeek, most charging that the company allowed child porn and non-consensual rape videos on its site—material that MindGeek has since done its best to eradicate.

GAIL DINES: IF MINDGEEK DISAPPEARS, SO DOES PORN

April 11, 2017

JESUSLAND—The National Center on Sexual Exploitation has something called "The Sexploitation Podcast,"[1] and this week's guest is Gail Dines, a professor at Wheelock College in Massachusetts and a real whackadoodle when it comes to porn, which she hates with a passion.

The topic of the podcast is "Is Pornography a Big Business?"[2]—a puzzling question since NCOSE has spent millions opposing porn, and Dines has made it her life's work to get rid of it in every form imaginable—because she's a "feminist" and she once saw a slide show and "When I saw those images, I absolutely couldn't believe it. I just could not believe what I was seeing. I couldn't believe that men made those images and I couldn't believe that men found them arousing." Of course, the slide show was created by Andrea Dworkin's group Women Against Pornography, so there's a chance that the images Dines saw weren't exactly representative of mainstream porn.

After some blah-blah about how anti-porn groups like NCOSE and Dines' latest group Culture Reframed should work together to get rid of sexually explicit material, the podcast hostess Haley Halverson asked, "You used the phrase, 'pornography industry.' Do you think that this really is an industry? Do you think there's a business model or marketing model behind what's going on, what's being hyped into so many young boys' and girls' homes?"

Ooh, ooh; we know this one! People like to watch other people having sex, and some companies have been formed to hire people to have sex on camera so other people can watch! Sounds like a "business model" to us!

Dines, interestingly, agrees—sort of: "It is absolutely an industry, which is what makes it a problem," she stated. "It's not a group of a few guys in the Valley in L.A. making porn. In fact, the porn production is less industrialized than is the distribution side of the industry. So what we know is, it holds its own trade shows, it interfaces with venture capitalists, it works with all the major corporations all over the world and banks. It's a global industry, not just an industry—and it has a very sophisticated business plan."

Um ... Gail? It's true that some porn studios have investors, but "all the major corporations all over the world and banks"? Are you nuts? (Don't answer that.)

"For example, the free porn, which is now the only way you get into the porn world for most people, was developed very cleverly," Dines went on to claim, "and one of the reasons was as a way to bring in boys at that developmental stage when their brain is absolutely ready for novelty and risk-taking. It was a brilliant business plan, terrible for the culture, terrible for the boys, terrible for girls, terrible for everybody else, but for the porn industry, it's a massive money-maker, because what you're doing is, it's like giving out free alcohol to 14-year-olds; it's like giving out free cigarettes to 14-year-olds. You've got the time when the brain is especially primed, when they're developing their masculine identity and their sexual templates."

Okay; she is nuts. Free (aka tube) porn was invented as a way of getting eyes on a website so the webmaster's advertisers could sell the viewers something—and guess what? Whatever they were selling, 14-year-olds couldn't buy it—no credit cards, don'tcha know—so the idea that tube sites were targeting under-18s is simply ludicrous.

"Now, that didn't come about by accident," Dines opined before dropping her "blockbuster," "just as the mobile phone didn't come about by accident. *The porn industry put a ton of money into developing the actual screen of the mobile phone because they realized this was how kids would eventually get access to their pornography, and they could do it quietly, away from their parents, because it's mobile; exactly.*" [Emphasis added.]

Okay; that's just crazy. If she can provide one shred of evidence that any adult entertainment company put one thin dime into the development of mobile phone screens, we'll make it the cover story in *AVN*. It just didn't happen.

"So is this an industry? Not only is it an industry, it's an extremely sophisticated industry," she stated, and not as a compliment. "It is what they call in business lingo a 'maturing industry,' which means that it keeps evolving in new ways, and the next thing that we're going to have to deal with is virtual reality. And I was at the porn expo in Las Vegas in January and you should see where they're going with virtual reality. I mean, it's just absolutely astounding, and you're going to have a full-body experience soon, so I mean, I think, if this continues, women are going to become absolutely obsolete in the eyes of men."

Y'know, we at *AVN* like porn as much as the next person, but the idea that most men would prefer a VR porn experience to fucking an actual woman is, again, ludicrous.

Halverson, of course, agreed with Dines, adding that porn is helping the development of VR in general—which got Dines off on another tech rant.

"[Porn] drove the VCR, it drove the internet, it's driving virtual reality," she agreed. "See, one of the reasons for that is that when a new technology comes out—let's take for example the VCR. It was very expensive. So who are the first people most likely to invest in something expensive? People who want their porn privately. So we know, for example, that for every one regular video that was bought, four were pornographic in the beginning. Then it switched, of course. We also know that in the war between Betamax and VHS, VHS won, and the reason they won is that Betamax wouldn't carry pornography. So when you look back at the history of the technology, pornography is front and center, absolutely. So the two work symbiotically: Porn drives technology, technology drives porn."

Dines is probably correct that a lot of people bought their first VCR to watch porn, but the idea that you couldn't buy porn on Beta is simply wrong—it was available widely, and *AVN* even used to review some porn movies on Beta. The reason the industry went with VHS is simply because you could record more higher-quality material on a VHS tape than on a Beta one (2 to 4 hours versus 1 to 2 hours), plus the VHS's loading mechanism was less prone to eating the tape than was the Betamax. On the other hand, it's undeniable that porn does drive technology—and some people who aren't Dines actually think that's a good thing, since it gets that new tech out to the public that much quicker. But considering that pretty much all Boomers and Gen Xers know the correct history, it's tough to understand why Wheelock College keeps letting this obvious ignoramus teach its students.

But as the podcast draws to a close, Halverson finally gets to the real point she wanted to discuss.

"Do you think that this industry of pornography, is this a multi-headed Hydra, that there are so many pornography businesses out there that it's impossible to really pinpoint who the top dog is?" she asked.

"No, it's actually extremely easy," Dines responded. "The top dog, without question, is MindGeek, that is based in Luxembourg with offices in Miami, in Los Angeles, in Montreal—it looks like it's moving its main businesses to Montreal. I would say it distributes anything from 70 to 90 percent of the most viewed pornography in the world."

No doubt MindGeek will be happy for the plug, but to say that it distributes 70 to 90 percent of the most viewed porn has to be referring to its PornHub business, which over the past couple of years has tried to reform its rep as a tube site full of pirated content to a business that actually pays for its content, though much of it comes from other MindGeek entities like Brazzers, Reality Kings, etc., as well as licensing from other producers.

"So if we're thinking as activists now, about how do we go after the pornography industry, there's no point in going after the hundreds of thousands of producers [!!!!!!!] from the Valley in L.A. right through to eastern Europe, all over the world," Dines prescribed. "First of all, they haven't got much money. Secondly, they make a film and close up shop; you can't find them. So if we want a legal recourse in a civil court, you go after the top dog. The top dog without doubt is MindGeek; was originally called Manwin ... and this is a very good way to think about activism: If we had a thousand producers and a thousand distributors, we'd be like a chicken with our head cut off, right? But we've got one group to go after. You go after MindGeek; we sue them, for example, for violation of civil rights, we sue them for all the injuries that have done to women and men on the porn set; we sue them for the child pornography that's often on their websites, which people don't realize is they do carry—some of it's accidental; I'm not saying they do this purposely, but there is so much content uploaded onto their porn sites, they can't control it all, so some of them are in violation of 2257, which is a law that says you're not allowed to have anyone under 18 on the porn set—they're in violation of that. They also are in violation of the law that says you can't distribute child porn. There's many, many ways we could get MindGeek, and that makes our job a lot easier."

So much fun stuff there to unpack, like the idea that most producers don't have much money, and do one movie and then disappear (hee-hee), or that the performers working for MindGeek routinely get injured on porn sets—or that they have child porn "often" on their websites, or that people under 18 are *ever* on a MindGeek set! If we're talking about lawsuits, seems MindGeek is in a great position to sue NCOSE and Dines for defamation! (In fact, we'll send a URL of this article to their attorneys.)

But then Halverson gets down to the real meat of the matter.

"What do you think would happen to the pornography industry as it exists now if MindGeek were sort of taken down with these civil lawsuits?" she asked.

"They would collapse, absolutely collapse," Dines opined, "because ... they set the business model and they are the center of it. I mean, it would take time to regroup, and meanwhile, we'd be coming after every group that was regrouping, so this is the way to do it. That's one way. The other way, which my group Culture Reframed does, is the public health model. What we do is, we're building programs for parents and for professionals in how to build resilience and resistance in youth to the porn culture, so we can help them develop capacity in their children not to get into trouble with pornography. There's many ways to tie the monster down ... you've got to go after it as many ways as you can."

Well, you heard them, MindGeek: Better start suing them for defamation before they start suing you for their bullshit delusions!

Seems pretty obvious to me that so-called "religious people" who want to discriminate against gays, transgender people, sex workers, etc., ought to quit their jobs, close their businesses, apply to be preachers and go work in their church. Of course, their lifestyle might suffer a bit, but it's all worth it, eh? And even with Trump now out of office, the IRS appears still to be ignoring the law (aka the Johnson Amendment) and letting preachers endorse whichever candidates they want (just about all Republican, natch!)

FAMILY RESEARCH COUNCIL SEEKS PRO-DISCRIMINATION TRUMP EXEC ORDER

May 2, 2017

TRUMPINGTON, D.C.—In a live webcast today, Tony Perkins, former Congressman and current head of the reactionary Family Research Council, called for Pr*sident Tr*mp to sign an executive order permitting businesses and social organizations to discriminate against their employees, members and customers who may be gay, trans, or who simply hold different religious views than the organization's owners/leaders.

The proposed executive order seems simple enough:

"Dear President Trump:

"Under the Obama era's anti-religious policies, people and groups across America have either suffered religious freedom violations or are about to suffer them. We need protections that you can grant in an executive order. I urge you to take executive action to ensure their freedom to believe and live out those beliefs is protected."

"In the last few years, we have seen an increase in government-imposed restrictions on the ability of Christians and other religious people to fully live out their faith in all aspects of their lives," Perkins began his webcast. "Many of these restrictions are falling on those who are most public with their lives: Business people, those running Christian organizations and those in places of high visibility within our own government, including our nation's military. The beliefs which are making them targets for government hostility and even prosecution in some cases are the same beliefs held by millions of Americans across this country... This government-sponsored hostility will only expand until we stand together and demand the government respect the Constitution's guarantee of our fundamental first freedom of religion. That is the only way—the only way—any of us will ultimately remain free."

Perkins went on to claim that the government's attempts to have all citizens treated equally and fairly in the public sector somehow infringes on religious adherents' ability to practice their religion—but as became abundantly clear during the webcast, such "freedom of religion" is simply a disguise to allow businesses and religious organizations to make their employees and members live by the same pseudo-religious tenets as those leaders. And as government agencies have stepped in to enforce the rights of those employees and members not to be bound by the prejudices of their bosses/leaders, organizations like Family Research Council and religious law firms like Alliance Defending Freedom and First Liberty Institute have sued to allow such discrimination to take place.

"It's not right that nuns trying to serve the poor are required to compromise their beliefs regarding human life in order to continue their work," Perkins intoned. "It's not right that a Christian organization working hard to assist victims of human trafficking should be forced out of doing that work because they don't want to adopt someone else's view on the issue of human sexuality... Our beliefs, quite frankly, are not something we can simply give up, they're not something we can negotiate away; they're fixed; they are ingrained in who we are as individuals and quite frankly as a nation."

Of course, once Perkins started presenting "witnesses" and "victims" to back up his case, the charade became clear—beginning with Archbishop William E. Lori of the Archdiocese of Baltimore,[1] who gave examples of "how religious freedom in this country, the exercise of that freedom has been inhibited in recent years," including regarding "health insurance plans, where we are in those ministries being forced in some way to insure for contraception and in some places even abortion, and where we are being driven out of adoption agency and the work of placing children with families through adoption because of our support for traditional marriage, and many other examples as well."

His "prime example" was the case of the Little Sisters of the Poor,[2] an organization of nuns who refused to provide their (non-nun) employees with access to contraception under the Affordable Care Act mandates, and when the government essentially said, "No problem; just sign this affidavit saying you have religious objections to doing this," the nuns refused to sign, saying that doing so would somehow be giving their permission for the birth control in violation of the nuns' religious beliefs. (The Supreme Court vacated circuit court rulings in favor of the government on this issue and required the circuits to reconsider their prior rulings in light of supplemental briefing which the high court had requested.)

"No one's saying that we don't have the right to worship in our church," Perkins summarized, "but as you pointed out, it's when we take that faith that we're taught on Sundays and the sermons that we hear or the mass that we participate in and we go out and we live according to that; that's where the conflict has begun, when we're actually living our faith out in the marketplace." In other words, as far as Perkins is concerned, religious people never actually leave their church; they take it with them outside and anyone who comes in contact with them is automatically sucked into and required to follow that religious doctrine.

Perkins' next guests were Rev. Wesley Modder[3] and his attorney Mike Berry. Those who've been following the news may remember that Modder used to be a chaplain at the Naval Nuclear Power Training Command—until he was reassigned for, among other things, telling a cadet that she was "shaming herself in the eyes of God" for having premarital sex; telling another that "the penis was meant for the vagina and not for the anus," while making what ThinkProgress's Zack Ford described as "an inappropriate hand gesture"; and telling others that homosexuality was wrong and insinuating that he had the ability to "save" gay people.

Of course, that's not the way Modder sees it.

"I was shocked; I felt betrayed by my country and by the Navy," Modder told Perkins. "I think the issue was, the government was not invited into my conscience, and as an ordained minister, I'm going to give that biblical worldview." In other words, didn't matter what religious beliefs the people at the training command center had; Modder was going to browbeat and attempt to intimidate them for holding/practicing whatever beliefs didn't correspond with his own—and he wants Trump to support and approve that sort of conduct by executive order.

Next up was Dr. Everett Piper,[4] president of Oklahoma Wesleyan University, and his attorney, Greg Baylor. Piper was called out in January of 2016 by the Human Rights Campaign (HRC) for attempting to get a waiver from the government under Title IX of the Civil Rights Act of 1964 for his ultraconservative Christian school so he would not have to admit any applicant who was gay or transgender.

"We refuse to comply with the misogyny endemic to the transgender agenda," Piper told the HRC. "We recognize the ontological and biological dignity of the female. We believe in science and we believe in facts and there is little more empirically obvious than one's sex. Being a female is an objective reality and we refuse to insult women by ignoring such self-evident truth... we believe that sexual identity is a scientific fact, not a human fabrication, and we refuse to degrade men and women by suggesting otherwise."

Guess what? Piper hasn't changed his views in the slightest—and he's added a new cause: Refusing to provide birth control to any of his female employees, despite the ACA mandate.

"We're pro-life," he claimed. "By definition, you don't get hired at Oklahoma Wesleyan University unless you are pro-life, so whether you're on the staff, the faculty, the president or a professor, you must subscribe to the idea that God defines life and you don't. As a result of that, the federal government is crossing swords with us and telling us that we have to provide abortifacient drugs in our healthcare... to a bunch of pro-life women that work for us that don't want the drug, won't use the drug, and are smart enough, quite frankly, to know what kind of healthcare they want in their healthcare package."

Guess what, Piper? Even women who don't believe in abortion use birth control, in part to make sure they're never put in a position where they are pregnant and don't want to be—and the drugs the ACA mandates are not "abortifacient"—they don't medically abort a fetus; they prevent the fertilized egg from being implanted in the uterus so a fetus (or what the religious would call a "person") never develops.

"We are pro-women as well as pro-religious freedom," Piper claimed. "We believe that women should be given the dignity to choose what they want and don't want in their healthcare." Except apparently some of those women whose dignity he claims to support *do* want birth control in their health plan; otherwise, how would the government have found out that Wesleyan doesn't offer it short of one of them complaining about that deficit?

Perkins' final "civilian" guest was Donald Vander Boon,[5] co-owner of the West Michigan Beef Company—and despite his demure appearance, a dedicated anti-gay bigot. But let's let him tell it:

"A couple of years ago, around the time of the same-sex marriage decision, I had seen quite a few articles in the newspaper and we have a break room with a couple of tables where people sit and eat and it got to be the practice that people could bring in magazines, newspapers to share with others," he said. "So around the time of this decision, I noticed a lot of the newspaper articles were very supportive of same-sex marriage and a lot of articles were kind of encouraging it, so when I saw an article on the internet that was giving more of a biblical idea of what marriage is and what family is and what I believe is God's plan for the family, I printed it out and put it on my break room table and didn't think too much of it, but within a few hours, I was told there were people there to see me in my office."

To make a long story somewhat shorter, those "people" were the USDA inspectors who inspect meat at the plant and their boss, and the inspectors objected to being proselytized against same-sex marriage by Vander Boon in the company break room—and stated that they'd refuse to work in the plant as long as that literature was in the break room, thereby effectively shutting down Vander Boon's business.

Of course, faced with that ultimatum, a more rational person might have decided, "Gee, if my religious views on marriage offend people in my workplace, maybe I'll just keep those views to myself and out of the workplace." And though no one on the webcast mentioned it, Vander Boon apparently *did* remove the offending article—and promptly filed a complaint with the USDA, which the agency is still considering.

"This is incredible," Perkins assessed. "His own business, his own building, his own break table and if he puts information that says—if you've got the government coming in, thumbing through his mail to see what he's reading and sharing with his employees and threatening to shut down his business... This sounds like something out of Orwell."

Somehow, we don't recall Big Brother being too keen on protecting anybody's rights, much less those of gay people—or, for that matter, religious ones.

The final two guests were U.S. Reps. Jody Hice (R-GA),[6] a former Baptist pastor, and Mike Johnson (R-LA),[7] formerly an attorney for Alliance Defending Freedom.

"We've been in this battle for well over ten years, probably closer to 15 at this point," Hice intoned, "and we've watching the continual demise of religious liberties in our country, and there's the appetite now in the movement to take a stand and turn this around, and I'm grateful that we have a president who's willing to take a stand with us."

Hice expressed his support not only for FRC's proposed "religious freedom" executive order, but also for repealing the "Johnson Amendment"—that portion of the Internal Revenue code that prohibits religious organizations and other tax-exempt entities from endorsing political candidates.

"In every aspect of our society right now, when people are taking a stand for their faith, are being outspoken about their faith, particularly in the areas of life or marriage, we're watching those freedoms be taken away," Hice claimed. "And so we are talking now of the need, the necessity to be able to broaden our understanding of religious liberties, that it's not isolated just to the four walls of a church building, but it's something the First Amendment protects [for] everyone, in every walk of life."

Except, of course, when those so-called "liberties" infringe on the liberties of others who don't share the same viewpoint—a point that hopefully other people on the House's Oversight & Government Reform Committee will understand when Hice brings up the topic, as he said he would.

Johnson echoed much of what Hice said, claiming, "We—First Liberty Institute and others and FRC—over the years have begun to catalog and count the increasing attacks on religious freedom that we've seen. You know, sometimes the media tries to whitewash that, and it doesn't always make the evening news, but it's happening every day at a local level, a state level, impacting individuals and small business owners and professionals in every single field, and if we don't get on top of it now, we're going to have a problem that we simply can't overcome. Our fundamental freedoms are being taken away from us, and that's why these steps are necessary now."

Simply put: Bullshit. These people want the ability to discriminate against people whose beliefs and lifestyles they don't agree with, and they want an executive order allowing them to do it. And of course, Trump being Trump, they're likely to get it.

✡✡✡

OP-ED: TRUMP SIGNS 'RELIGIOUS FREEDOM' EXECUTIVE ORDER, ENDING DEMOCRACY AS WE KNOW IT

May 4, 2017

TRUMPINGTON, D.C.—This morning, President Donald Trump signed an executive order supposedly protecting "religious freedom" in the U.S., but which in fact is the first step toward guaranteeing that conservatives—and likely the subset of religious conservatives—will remain in power in the federal government far into the future—and as a sidelight, will probably signal the end of the adult entertainment industry in a few years.

The text of the executive order was only made public at about 3 p.m. Eastern time, and it's a masterpiece of obfuscation. For example, it states, "The Founders envisioned a Nation in which religious voices and views were integral to a vibrant public square, and in which religious people and institutions were free to practice their faith without fear of discrimination or retaliation by the Federal Government." That's true only to the extent that those "religious ... institutions" didn't attempt to involve themselves in direct political action, a caveat that's well analyzed in Geoffrey Stone's recent book *Sex and the Constitution*. It's one of the reasons that Article VI of the Constitution states, "no religious Test shall ever be required as a Qualification to any Office or public Trust under the United States."

But it gets worse. Under "Sec. 2. Respecting Religious and Political Speech," it states, "the Secretary of the Treasury shall ensure, to the extent permitted by law, that the Department of the Treasury does not take any adverse action against any individual, house of worship, or other religious organization on the basis that such individual or organization speaks or has spoken about moral or political issues from a religious perspective, where speech of similar character has, consistent with law, not ordinarily been treated as participation or intervention in a political campaign on behalf of (or in opposition to) a candidate for public office by the Department of the Treasury. As used in this section, the term 'adverse action' means the imposition of any tax or tax penalty; the delay or denial of tax-exempt status; the disallowance of tax deductions for contributions made to entities exempted from taxation under section 501(c)(3) of title 26, United States Code; or any other action that makes unavailable or denies any tax deduction, exemption, credit, or benefit."

To put it more simply, and as Trump explained this section when he signed the order, it calls on (aka requires) the Internal Revenue Service to "exercise maximum enforcement discretion to alleviate the burden of the Johnson Amendment"; in other words, to ignore, almost entirely, churches and clergy who meddle in politics by endorsing political candidates and specific pieces of legislation, in direct violation of the IRS Code—and no matter what this order says about "to the extent permitted by law."

Or as the *Washington Post* reported earlier today: "For too long the federal government has used the state as a weapon against people of faith," Trump said,[8] later telling the religious leaders gathered for the event that "you're now in a position to say what you want to say ... No one should be censoring sermons or targeting pastors."

Back in February, at the White House's National Prayer Breakfast, Trump told his religious supporters that, "I will get rid of and totally destroy the Johnson Amendment and allow our representatives of faith to speak freely and without fear of retribution." He essentially reiterated that promise when he told the audience present for the signing of today's order that, "We will not allow people of faith to be targeted, bullied or silenced ever again."

The Johnson Amendment was added to the IRS Code in 1954 at the instigation of then-Sen. Lyndon Johnson, and it makes perfect sense. Anyone reading this article, whether they are religious or not, certainly knows someone (and probably lots of someones) who are religious, often devoutly so. There are in fact tens of millions of people in the U.S. who regularly attend a church, synagogue, mosque or other religious gathering, who engage in prayer to a "supreme being" of some sort, and most importantly for this point, believe that what their clergyperson is conveying to them through his/her words are the *commands of the supreme being* they worship—and that to disobey such commands is tantamount to rebelling against that supreme being and, for Christians in particular, a sure path to eternal damnation.

Now, as bad as that political action on the part of religious groups might be, this is, after all, the United States, and its supreme law is the U.S. Constitution, whose First Amendment says, in pertinent part, that "Congress shall make no law respecting an establishment of religion, or prohibiting the free exercise thereof; or abridging the freedom of speech." But what the Johnson Amendment recognizes is that some religious institutions—most notably in the U.S., Christian churches—are enormously powerful, in part because they claim to be preaching the "will of God," but also because as a whole, they are massively wealthy, owning vast amounts of untaxed property in every state and paying no income taxes whatsoever on contributions made to them—many of which funds, if they wanted, they could put towards political campaigns, far outstripping the amounts that ordinary, non-affiliated candidates would be able to raise on their own. Because to the extent that any institution is tax exempt, all of the public goods and services it uses, like firefighters, police, public hospitals, roads, libraries (and on and on and on) it *doesn't pay for*; people who *do* pay taxes, aka taxpayers, do!

So the Johnson Amendment is, in a sense, a necessary compromise. It basically says, "Sure, all you priests, rabbis, ministers, imams, bishops, prelates, et cetera, you can say whatever you want, condemn anyone or anything you want, support or disparage any political candidate or piece of legislation you want—but if you do so, you lose that status that allows you to avoid paying taxes on your properties, on your clergy's salaries, on your monasteries, your rescue missions, your whatever, and puts you in the same position as every tax*payer* in the country, unable to put your *untaxed* wealth toward political activities."

Now, it's sad but true that since the Johnson Amendment was enacted, it has almost never been enforced. Exactly one church has been stripped of its tax-exempt status: the Church at Pierce Creek, in Binghamton, N.Y., which took out newspaper ads in 1992 warning Christians not to vote for then-candidate Bill Clinton. But the amendment did make churches and the like more cautious in their public statements for a number of years, thanks to reminders from Americans United for Separation of Church and State—until religiously-oriented law groups like the well-funded Alliance Defending Freedom (total revenue of $61.9 million for the fiscal year ending June 30, 2015) began exhorting clergy to take part in "Pulpit Freedom Sundays," where those clergy were encouraged to endorse religiously conservative candidates (all Republicans, don'tcha know) for office and/or warn their flocks not to vote for Democrats—and last year, 450 of them did exactly that, with no action at all taken against them by the IRS.

But the sea change brought about by Trump's executive order is that ***for the first time ever***, a U.S. president has essentially said that neither the U.S. Department of Justice nor the U.S. Department of the Treasury (of which the IRS is a part) will be enforcing the law which prohibits candidate endorsements by clergy—and those who don't think that churches in some parts of America won't be taking the pulpit this Sunday and telling their congregants not to vote for candidates such as Jon Ossoff for U.S. Rep. from Georgia, Rob Quist for U.S. Rep. from Montana, Phil Murphy or one of the other Democratic candidates for Governor in New Jersey, or any of dozens of others running for office, are just fooling themselves.

And that's where the American experiment in "democracy" comes to an end. The path is simple, really: 1) Conservative candidate announces that he (or, less likely, she) will be running for such-and-such an office. 2)

Said candidate begins making the round of churches and other religious institutions to give speeches to parishioners, possibly coupled with direct endorsements of the candidate by the presiding clergyperson (or possibly that endorsement will come later—and in any case, liberal candidates will not be permitted to speak). 3) Clergyperson makes literature supporting the candidate available at the church and on the church's website; maybe holds rallies for the candidate. 4) As the election draws nearer, the clergyperson makes stronger and stronger pleas for the candidate's election, possibly (likely?) telling the parishioners that God supports the candidate and/or that God condemns his/her opponent—and that to vote for anyone other than the candidate is a sin. 5) Candidate is elected by a huge majority.

Picture that happening at every level of federal, state and local government. The result? A religious dictatorship voted in by the very people who claim to support the "religious freedom" guaranteed by the Constitution.

Now, the above scenario obviously won't happen in every parish; there are still some churches and other religious institutions that are liberal-leaning or just don't care about politics at all. But let's remember that at present, the overwhelming majority of U.S. Representatives are conservative, most religiously so, and about half of the U.S. Senate is the same way. And let's not forget that it's Trump who will be appointing new Supreme Court justices for the foreseeable future, pretty much guaranteeing that his policies won't face many challenges from the high court.

But it's probably not necessary to add that in due time, making sexually explicit content will be made illegal, and those who do so will be sentenced to long prison terms.

Just thought you'd want to know.

"We're a nation of believers. Faith is deeply embedded in the history of our country," Trump said today. "No American should be forced to choose between the dictates of the American government and the tenets of their faith."

And pretty soon, if things go according to plan, they won't even have a choice.

UPDATE: The Freedom From Religion Foundation is already mounting a lawsuit against this.

Woodrocket was a fairly popular adult production company whose politically aware owners liked to produce hardcore parodies of mainstream events—and most were pretty damned funny, not to mention sexy. The "Cambria list" refers to First Amendment attorney Paul Cambria who, back in 2001, at the request of prominent adult video company Vivid Entertainment, put together a list of acts which he felt stood the greatest chance of getting busted if they appeared in a company's production. Also, Trueman talks about "videotape" sales as if anyone in 2017 was still producing videotapes; they'd all switched to DVD at least 15 years before, and that's what stores have carried ever since.

NO, NCOSE: PORN IS BOTH A CONSTITUTIONAL RIGHT AND A HUMAN RIGHT

June 15, 2017

TRUMPINGTON, D.C.—On Tuesday, the National Center on Sexual Exploitation (NCOSE) held a seminar at its offices titled "Today's Pornography: Not a Constitutional Right, Not a Human Right," and the sole explainer of this was former Justice Department prosecutor and NCOSE CEO Patrick A. Trueman, who also headed NCOSE's predecessor, Morality in Media. With those credentials, is it any wonder that nearly everything he said was wrong?

Briefly introduced by staffer Madison Darling, it took Trueman less than one minute to make his first boo-boo—and it involved *AVN*, no less!

"In his Senate confirmation hearings this year, Senator Jeff Sessions was asked about federal obscenity laws, and it was Senator Orrin Hatch of Utah that raised the question," Trueman began. "He pointed out that in the previous eight years, the last administration, these federal laws were not enforced, and he asked Senator Sessions this direct question: 'If you are confirmed as the next attorney general, will you vigorously enforce federal obscenity laws?' Senator Jeff Sessions said he would. Now, that promise by Mr. Sessions did not go unnoticed by the porn industry. They've written about it. In fact, the porn industry, in their trade journal, *Adult Video News*, has advised pornographers that producers who want to produce pornography, said in so many words, 'Tone it down because you'll get convicted if you don't.'"

Can we just say: BULLSHIT!!! Perhaps Trueman missed this post[1] on AVN.com, in which industry leader Larry Flynt takes issue with the idea that successful porn prosecutions are even possible in this day and age, and stated, "Obscenity laws are antiquated. Sessions can talk all he wants, but it's very, very difficult to get 12 people on a jury to vote to convict someone on pornography. Pornography is the purest form of art there is."

Flynt went on to distinguish mainstream porn from "defecation and urination and ... the fringe aspects, scatological behavior and stuff like that," but absolutely nothing was said about "toning down" mainstream porn. In fact, what Flynt did do was to warn *Hollywood* producers that Washington's "new conservatism" could cause *them* problems "because nobody wants to produce a film they can't get distributed because of the rating [NC-17]. It does have a chilling effect on filmmakers and the First Amendment in general."

Not even AVN's legal columnist Clyde DeWitt suggested toning anything down, though in his column for our March issue, he did suggest that producers have an attorney on retainer, and warned that, "If you are a target of prosecution, unless you are a huge company, you will be bankrupted by a federal obscenity charge."

Trueman then moved on to try to explain what porn is, what the porn industry is and what the current laws are—and again, he pretty much failed.

Regarding the industry, he said, "It was once very easy to define the porn industry. It was a producer who would hire a camera crew—most of this took place in the Los Angeles area—so they would hire very cheaply these students at UCLA who were studying film and theater, and they could produce films by renting a home or renting a warehouse where they could set up a studio. Then there were also a group of bigger companies that might own their own building with several studio sets and act just like a Hollywood producer and they would produce and then distribute that material to 50 states."

Of course, in fact, the majority of porn camera operators in L.A. have been "moonlighters" who came from mainstream Hollywood, not UCLA, as was the case with much of the tech crew including lighting techs and makeup artists, and Trueman for some reason ignores the then-thriving adult industry in New York City—Morality In Media's base of operations back then! And while some adult companies did have production studios in their office buildings, most didn't—but they did have the budgets to rent better houses to shoot in.

Trueman then went on to note that several European companies have gotten into the American porn market, but his biggest example? MindGeek!

"Today you might have an overseas producer or distributor, something like MindGeek, which is the biggest in the world. They're operating out of Luxembourg and Montreal, and they own most all the free so-called 'tube sites' on the internet, where individuals can produce their own sex films and upload them to YouTube and other similar companies owned by MindGeek."

We're guessing that MindGeek will be surprised to learn that they own YouTube, though probably not the concept that they're "the biggest in the world." And no matter where the company's home offices may be, a lot of what MindGeek distributes is shot right here in the good ol' U.S. of A.

Trueman went on to claim that it's only a "handful of companies" that own the porn tube sites, "and that's important because as we talk about prosecution, this is not an intractable problem. We can prosecute the industry and put them out of business."

That's a strange statement to make, since he followed it up immediately with, "The porn industry is also the college cam girl who sets up a studio in her own dorm room and is on the internet and for a price, will perform sex acts for an individual internet audience. It's also the cam website that might have several cam girls independently employed, doing the same thing that the cam company will set them up in the industry with their own website connected to the main website and providing advertising so that they're guaranteed a good income." So, what? They're going to bust every cam girl and every cam aggregator in the country? That shouldn't tie up the courts for more than, say, 20 years or so!

But then Trueman went full bore into cloud-cookooland: "The porn industry today is also the sex trafficker that forces women to perform sex acts on the internet and sells those acts, again, to an internet audience, and it's much more than that." No one doubts that there's one hell of a lot of XXX material on the internet, but to accuse what everyone today knows as "the porn industry" of putting videos of trafficked women (or anyone) on the internet is ludicrous. Are there some videos with trafficked women? Undoubtedly—but they're not being made by the *real* porn industry—the one that's the subject of laws like 2257.

Trueman then launched into a discussion of whether porn is protected by the First Amendment, and of course, as far as he's concerned, it isn't.

After reading the "freedom of speech" portion of the First Amendment, Trueman noted that courts have held that not all speech is protected, citing slander and libel as two prohibited types.

"The United States Supreme Court as well as state courts have devoted over 200-and-something years to trying to decide what that language means, and they've said it means many, many things. ... But one thing the First Amendment has never been thought to protect, the court has never said it protects, is obscene material. You do not have a right to distribute obscene material."

He then proceeded to quote from *Miller v. California* that, "To equate the free and robust exchange of ideas and political debate with commercial exploitation of obscene material demeans the grand conception of the First Amendment and its high purposes in the historic struggle for freedom. It is a misuse of the great guarantees of free speech and press. Such obscene material simply is not protected."

Talk about your judicial activism (which the Right routinely rails against)! In fact, one need only read Geoffrey Stone's seminal work, *Sex and the Constitution*, to learn how randy our Founders actually were, to the point that there's the distinct possibility that the word "Happiness" in the phrase "Life, Liberty and the pursuit of Happiness" may refer to the right to "pursue" sexual intercourse! In fact, up to 1820, only one state had a law targeting sexual material, which seems a bit strange if the Founders were so against it as to intend to exclude it from freedom of speech—and rest assured, tons and tons of written and drawn/painted porn was available in the colonies, much of it imported from Europe.

"The Court has freely said in case after case that legislatures and Congress can find that obscene material is harmful; harmful to the public and harmful to individuals—and that is true even if the material is distributed to consenting adults," he continued. Trouble is, of course, that *no* peer-reviewed scientific study of porn has come to that conclusion—though of course, NCOSE's website is replete with pseudo-scientific "analyses" that *do* say that despite overwhelming evidence to the contrary.

Trueman then quoted from Justice Warren Burger's opinion in *Paris Adult Theatre v. Slaton*[2] that, "The sum of experience, including that of the past two decades, affords an ample basis for legislatures to conclude that a sensitive, key relationship of human existence, central to family life, community welfare, and the development of human personality, can be debased and distorted by crass commercial exploitation of sex... The States have the power to make a morally neutral judgment that public exhibition of obscene material [can] endanger the public safety, or ... jeopardize ... [a State's] 'right ... to maintain a decent society.'"

What's particularly interesting about that slightly misquoted quote is what he leaves out of it: After the words "crass commercial exploitation of sex," Burger's very next sentence was, "Nothing in the Constitution prohibits a State from reaching such a conclusion and acting on it legislatively *simply because there is no conclusive evidence or empirical data*." [Emphasis added]

In other words, fuck the science; states should be allowed to criminalize porn based on their gut. And everyone who's tried to find that so-called "conclusive evidence or empirical data" has failed miserably. But that minor detail didn't stop Trueman from running with the concept.

"Now that's a very important right: The right to maintain a decent society," he opined, both failing to define "decent" and adding, "You get people saying, 'Look, if I look at pornography in the privacy of my home, how does that hurt you?' It harms the overall community and the right to maintain a decent society." Again, despite the myriad modern cries of "porn is a public health crisis," there's absolutely no evidence to back that up.

Trueman then displayed on the screen what he called the "porn triangle," which has as its base "hardcore pornography," and going upwards from there, such concepts as "promiscuity," "addiction," "adultery," "divorce" and "prostitution"—"It's common sense!" he claimed, that porn causes all those things.

He elaborated on that concept, claiming that it's people who watch porn that patronize prostitutes—obviously some do and most don't—but then he dredges up the old saw that porn leads to watching kiddie porn because "people who are engaged in the consumption of pornography always move to harder and more deviant material, and many of them will actually move to child pornography. They go through many different genres before they get to the point where they can enjoy child pornography, but many of them will get there." Again, BULLSHIT! Most adults enjoy porn featuring adults and are repulsed by porn made with children; it's that simple. Unless one already has pedophilic tendencies, one doesn't "move" from adult porn to kiddie porn.

"Child pornography was virtually wiped out in the United States 20 years ago," he lied, noting that it's (more) available now thanks to the internet and because "people are always looking for what the brain demands, and that is something new, and they end up here. ... All forms of sexual acts of exploitation are in one way or another connected."

Trueman then gave his "own personal definition" of porn, which oddly enough leaves out such things as nudity in medical books, Michelangelo's statue of David and the like; apparently, porn isn't porn unless it "excites" you or makes you "lust."

"That does not mean that every item of pornography is illegal," he stated, then promptly contradicted himself, continuing, "So what we have to determine is what is illegal and what is not illegal. ... The court uses the term 'hardcore pornography' synonymously with the term 'obscenity,' so we look to say, 'What is obscene? How do you determine whether something is obscene because only what is obscene can be determined to be illegal." In fact, the Supreme Court does *not* use "hardcore porn" and "obscenity" interchangeably, but even so, according to Trueman, apparently the only material that isn't "obscene" is simple nudity.

But in attempting to answer his own question, Trueman began citing the history of obscenity law since about 1957 (which saw the *Roth* decision) but quickly segued to *Miller* in 1973.

"*Miller v. California* settled on this test: The material has to appeal to a prurient interest, it has to be patently offensive and it has to lack serious value," he stated, then went on to try to explain what each of those terms mean—and of course, he did a shitty job of it.

Obscenity, it turns out, is a thought-crime, according to Trueman.

"We had cases when I was at the Justice Department where the pornographers would produce—I don't even want to describe the material but it was bodily function—they call them 'scat films'—in connection with sex, and the defense attorneys would argue to the jury, 'None of you are turned on by this. This doesn't appeal to your lustful interest.' No, it doesn't have to. The pornographer *intended* that it appeal to a lustful interest to somebody. Again, it's the *intent* of the material that's critical."

Trueman has similar delusions about the meaning of the concept of "patently offensive."

"The test is not whether the adult buyer of the pornography would find that the work is 'patently offensive,'" he claimed. "Why is that? Because who's buying this? People who like hardcore pornography and they watch it in their home. So the defense attorney cannot argue to the jury, 'Well, if it wasn't patently offensive to the buyer—he's not offended by it; he enjoys it!' That's not the test. A better question for the test is not whether the buyer found it offensive. A better question is whether that pornography would be shown, for example, on a city bus. If you had your computer and you were sitting on a bus with people standing around you or sitting around you, would you watch this porn film? No, you wouldn't? Why? Because it would be patently offensive to people."

Well, aside from the fact that most people would not try to watch hardcore porn on a city bus, and if they did, could properly be prosecuted for doing so ("disturbing the peace" or "creating a public nuisance"), especially if minors were present, the real question is what stake the government has in banning porn that *nobody sees but the buyer*? And if he/she doesn't like it for some reason, he/she can try to get his/her money back, not send the maker to prison for being "patently offensive"!

Finally, Trueman tackled the "serious value" prong of the *Miller* decision.

"The pornography defense attorneys always argue that that porn film is a work of art," he claimed. "But the prosecutor's job is to say, 'Well, what art museum, ladies and gentlemen, have you ever been in where they're playing movies like this? No, they don't play that, because it's not art. They play it in a porn theater."

How about this: "Well, ladies and gentlemen, what art museum have you been in where they're playing movies like Lars von Trier's *Nymph() maniac*? How about Stanley Kubrick's *Eyes Wide Shut*? No, they don't play that, because it's not art. They play it in a movie theater." Who'd be stupid enough to make that argument, and who'd be stupid enough to believe it?

But Trueman doubled down: "Some cases that we've been involved in, the defense attorneys have said, 'Well, as you saw, ladies and gentlemen, this film, we had a caricature of the president and other political figures. This is a political work.' Well, it wasn't intended to add to the political dialog; it was intended by the pornographer to be porn, and that's about all you have to say to the jury because they get it." Again, thought-crime. It's about what the producer *thought*.

And that's been one of the problems with porn prosecution since its beginning: Self-styled art critics like Trueman think they get to decide what's good, *constitutionally protected* satire and what isn't. Anyone see any of those short politically oriented films that Woodrocket turns out? Does anyone think a jury that wasn't entirely made up of the Deeply Religious would say those aren't political satire?

And then, of course, there's the "contemporary community standards" fallacy.

"If we found a work to be obscene here in Washington, D.C., it doesn't mean that that same work would be found obscene in New York City," he correctly stated. "So a jury in New York City can decide what they think is obscene based on this three-part test. Now this protects the public, because what we don't want is the standards of Manhattan in New York City to be imposed on Manhattan, Kansas. In other words, the pornographer is distributing porn movies in Manhattan and they're distributing them all around the country including in Kansas, and they're prosecuted in Kansas. They can't come into court and say, 'Well, we were tried on this case, the same film, in Manhattan, New York, and we were found innocent, so you can't bring the case here.' No, the same film can be found obscene in one community and the next community over, non-obscene, and the next community over, obscene. So this protects the pornographer's First Amendment right because not all pornography is obscene—has to be the three-part test and community standards come into play—but it also protects the communities, so that you can't have—mostly, porn films are produced in the Los Angeles area, California, and those pornographers always used to argue in court that we should be allowed to distribute our material anywhere in the country, and of course people on the jury in Harrisburg, Virginia, or Tampa, Florida, want to be able to say, 'No, you don't get to decide what the community standards are in our community; we'll decide that.' So that jury looks at the film, applies that three-part test—does it appeal to a lustful interest, is it patently offensive, without value—and they can make that determination for themselves."

Think about that: In what other situations do we allow government or juries to decide, say, what TV shows will play on local TV channels, or what Hollywood movies can play in local theaters? Suppose someone gets the idea that *The Real O'Neals*, which deals with adolescent homosexuality, shouldn't be played on the local NBC channel in Salt Lake City? Or that BBC's cable show *Versailles*, which has plenty of nudity and "sexual situations," is too hot for Birmingham, Alabama? Or that Showtime's *Masters of Sex*, which features simulated hardcore sex, should be blocked from cable subscribers in, say, Manhattan, Kansas? Or that the movie *Hysteria*, all about the invention of the vibrator, isn't fit for movie houses in Waco, Texas?

And then there's the question of how 12 people who, to use a common meme, weren't smart enough to get out of jury duty, are somehow intelligent and outgoing enough to have discussed with their neighbors (i.e., "the community") what their sexual preferences are when it comes to media? Can Juror #7 truly say that he or she has asked next door neighbor Bob, or Betty down the street, what type of porn they like to watch? (The possibility that Bob and Betty don't watch any porn is, after all, fairly small.) Of course not; thanks to their religious "moral" upbringing, which they don't even have to attend religious services to be affected by, it's not considered "proper" to ask such questions—so how the hell can they sit on a jury and decide what "community standards" are? In fact, in modern society, it should be clear that in any decently large city, even in the so-called "Bible Belt," "community standards" are a complete fiction.

So then the question arises, how do those facts fit with Trueman's immediately following statement that, "One thing else that I would point out is that your personal opinion does not count, so when a case goes to the jury, the judge will instruct the jury, 'Don't put your personal opinion about what's patently offensive or what appeals to a prurient interest. This is by community standards, so you have to decide, does an average person in our community think that this work would be patently offensive in the way I talked about earlier; would the average person in our community think that this work appeals to a prurient and lustful interest? And this protects the pornographer, again, because the court does not want a sensitive juror, someone who is—I hate to use the term—a little old lady who finds that any mention of sex is obscene. She doesn't get to impose her values on the community. She like all the others has to decide, what does the average person in our community think is obscene?"

The "little old lady" reference, of course, is a red herring: NO ONE is able to speak for "the average person in our community" when it comes to one's taste in pornography, because no one—and definitely not the jurors in the case—has ASKED a significant portion of other community members what their tastes in porn are.

But as Trueman's talk drew to a close, he revealed his true feelings about porn: That it should all be illegal—and he bolstered that by again quoting from the 1973 *Miller* decision (so much for *contemporary* community standards!)

"The Court said it's possible to give a few plain examples of what could be found obscene," he said, quoting, "'Patently offensive representations or descriptions of ultimate sexual acts,' like sexual intercourse, 'normal or perverted'—Now notice that; it's a direct quote. It could be normal sex acts. It could be a couple having sex on camera, because what we're not finding to be illegal—in other words, it isn't the portrayal of illegal sex acts, it's the illegal portrayal of sex acts. What the Court is concerned about, what legislatures are concerned about is sexual exploitation; that's at the root of all the pornography laws. Are we exploiting sex? Because if we are, it has a detrimental effect on the person and on the community. That's the sum and substance of what the courts have said is what obscenity laws are concerned with, so it could be normal acts or perverted acts; it could be actual sex acts or simulated. Yes, it's true that a couple having pretend sex under the covers of a film can be found to be obscene. Maybe that's not going to be found obscene in Manhattan, but it might be found obscene in a community in Ohio, in Minnesota, in Florida, in Pennsylvania. So it doesn't have to be actual sex, and it doesn't even have to be sex at all; it could be just simulated."

Ain't that a kicker: This jackass wants the courts not only to go after the adult industry, he wants them to go after half of Hollywood! And anyone who can parse the meaning of the sentence, "it isn't the portrayal of illegal sex acts, it's the illegal portrayal of sex acts," is a better person than this author, or Trueman, or any judge on any American court. If a sex act itself isn't illegal, how can portraying it be illegal?

And Trueman wasn't yet done quoting *Miller.*

"'Patently offensive representations or descriptions of masturbation, excretory functions, and lewd exhibition of the genitals.' It doesn't have to be a sex act at all. It could be just lewd exhibition of the genitals or pubic area of an individual that may be found to be obscene. It might not be found to be obscene in your community but it could be found to be obscene in other communities."

Now, let's remember that we're not talking about someone walking down the street waving his dick around, or bouncing her tits in anyone's face; we're talking about something that's on a DVD or website that NO ONE other than the buyer has to look at!

"So in a legal sense, obscenity may involve simulated sex or involve explicit actual sex and either type may be found to be obscene in any given community in any given year," he summarized, adding, "So what does federal law prohibit then? The current federal law, upheld by the United States Supreme Court, prohibits distribution of hardcore pornography on the internet. A lot of people don't know that because there's hardcore pornography all over the internet, but that's a violation of federal law, and most of the material, in my judgment, is likely to be found obscene in most communities in the country."

Of course, the reason "a lot of people don't know that" is because it's BULLSHIT! What Trueman has done is take the Supreme Court's decision in *Reno v. ACLU, et al* (1997),[3] where the court struck down the Communication Decency Act's prohibition on "transmission" of "indecent" material on the internet and decided that because the ACLU and its co-respondents had challenged only the prohibition on "*indecent* transmission" and hadn't bothered to challenge the prohibition on "*obscene*" transmission (because the Supremes were not about to strike that down and the ACLU knew it), and decided that that meant that "hardcore pornography," the *entirety* of which Trueman equates with "obscenity," has therefore been ruled out on the internet by the Supreme Court. (Thanks to attorney Reed Lee for pointing out this "sleight of hand.")

But Trueman wasn't done: "It's a violation of federal law to distribute hardcore pornography on cable or satellite TV. Comcast, Verizon, all those companies have their hardcore porn channels. They're all illegal. They'll tell you they're not but their general counsels for those companies know very well they are." Again, bullshit, for the exact same reason.

And why isn't all of this stuff being prosecuted right now? Of course, Pat has the answer: "The only reason they have those [porn channels] is because of lack of enforcement by the federal government. If the Attorney General of the United States would stand up in a press conference and say, 'We're going to prosecute illegal pornography under our federal obscenity laws, and whether you're on the internet or a cable company or in a hotel or motel... we're going to prosecute you,' do you think Comcast would stay in the porn business a minute longer? No, they would clean up that system immediately because they know that it's possible prosecution."

And hey, retailers and distributors: You aren't safe either!

"It's a violation of federal law to be in the retail business—just being in the business of the retail distribution, so that mom-and-pop video shop that's down the street from you that has the back room where they're selling porn videos or renting them, just being in that business is a violation of federal obscenity laws, and if you're in the wholesale business, the same."

BULLSHIT!!!

But he pressed on: "It's a violation of federal law to distribute hardcore pornography by mail or common carrier like UPS. Now, as a practical matter, the federal government doesn't prosecute individuals, so if you were to send a porn video to a friend of yours, it's not likely the federal government would come after you. I say it's not likely; it's possible. They're not looking for you, but the reason it would be possible is that maybe you've committed some other crime. They can't convict you of the rape you've committed, but you took a film of it and you sent that. If the only evidence of the rape they have [is] your computer fingerprints on the distribution, they'll prosecute you for that. But the norm is, they prosecute the major producers and distributors of hardcore pornography."

Equating porn producers with rapists; that's a good one! And in fact, over the years, the feds have prosecuted plenty of individuals for sending porn through the mails.

But after admitting that it's completely legal to possess "obscene material in the privacy of your own home," he noted that "you don't have a right to distribute it from your home, and you don't even have the right to receive it in your home. So what good is that right if you don't have a right to receive it? See, because if you're receiving it, someone used the mail or common carrier or the internet to get it to you. And what the federal law prohibits is the interstate distribution of the material, regardless of the means."

Of course, Trueman thinks no one should be allowed to possess porn, but he slipped up by pointing out the logical fallacy of *Stanley v. Georgia*,[4] which legalized possession of obscenity, by drawing attention to the fact that you may legally possess it but there's no legal way to get it to you. And let's face it: A right you can't exercise is no right at all!

Trueman then noted that the last federal obscenity trial was in 2012, and the defendant was Ira Isaacs, "who's quite prominent in the porn industry." No offense to Ira, but the porn industry had barely heard of Isaacs when he was busted—but since he was convicted of movies featuring bestiality and defecation, it's no wonder Trueman wants to tie him in with regular porn producers. Or as Trueman put it, "I always say, if you can win a case in Los Angeles, you can win a case anywhere."

Trueman then laid out three reasons why someone would want to prosecute porn because "This is very important to us because we have tried here very hard to get our federal laws enforced again. They were vigorously enforced just eight or nine years ago."

"Number one, the law is a great teacher." And what does it teach? That *revenge porn* can be prosecuted! But guess what? *No company is producing or selling revenge porn!!!* Also, "it causes pornographers to self-regulate by changing the nature of the material. It gets softer." I know what you're thinking: He's kidding, right? Sadly, no; he's just completely out of the loop. Know how we know? Because he cites the so-called "Cambria list," even though pretty much every item on there nowadays can be found somewhere, if it's not already common, in commercially produced porn.

But Trueman notes that, wonder of wonders, a lot of adult distributors won't send their material to states where obscenity cases have been brought—because what company wants to spend hundreds of thousands if not millions of dollars defending an obscenity charge when the citizens of the state where the prosecution would be brought aren't brave and savvy enough to change their state's laws or the prosecutors who bring such cases?

Finally, in a tribute to circular reasoning, Trueman's third reason for prosecuting porn is, "It helps to establish community standards. If you prosecute a case in your community, and let's say you have maybe ten *videotapes* in your prosecution, that you're prosecuting this pornographer for. Some *tapes* depict group sex, some *tapes* depict oral sex, some *tapes* depict some other kind of sex, and you get convictions on all of those, that establishes your community standards, because then the porn industry says, well, we can't send you anything that's got this kind of sex, that kind of sex, et cetera, because they've been convicted of it." [Emphasis added] So watch out, retailers, and get all those bad *videotapes* off your shelves!

And what NCOSE lecture would be complete without a little bashing of the Obama administration, with Trueman claiming that because Attorney General Holder didn't mount any obscenity prosecutions, "anything goes—

and the porn industry reads them; they know they're protected because there's not going to be a conviction and they can send anything. This is why the internet is what it is today: Because we haven't been prosecuting them."

That's pretty much it, except for the commercials for NCOSE's pet projects. Anyone who's interested can watch the whole thing (if you can find it) on NCOSE's Facebook page—and considering who the new attorney general is, and despite the fact that he stated in his confirmation hearing that he didn't know the Obscenity Prosecution Task Force had been disbanded, Trueman and his cronies once again have a friendly ear in the administration, and they're going to run with it as hard and as fast as they can.

If you're interested, just search the Web for "Bob Dole" and "Viagra" to see his 1998 boner pill ad. Also, former talent agent Bill Margold is lauded by many early porn performers whom he helped in one way or another, but reading his testimony before the Meese Commission as well as various articles he's written and interviews he's given should put such adulation in the grave with him where it belongs.

OP-ED: NCOSE EXPLAINS 'PUBLIC HEALTH HARMS OF PORN'

Ain't that great?

June 27, 2017

TRUMPINGTON, D.C.—The National Center on Sexual Exploitation webcast another of its online video seminars on Facebook earlier today, this one titled "The Public Health Harms of Pornography Explained"—and unsurprisingly, their lecturer, NCOSE Director of Communications Haley Halverson, got pretty much everything wrong.

Halverson began by asking her audience to "imagine a world where cigarettes are completely normal, where celebrities talk about how cool it is to smoke, where doctors say that is actually healthy for you, and where children are regularly given cigarettes, sometimes even in school." You know where this is going, right? Just substitute "porn" for "cigarettes" and you're in a world where you and even your kids can get lung cancer from sexually explicit content!

From there, Halverson expresses her problems with the accepted definitions of "public health crisis" that have already been laid down by the Centers for Disease Control ("a problem that is cause for immediate concern and action") and the World Health Organization ("a serious problem that needs to be addressed"), calling them "very vague"—so she supplies one of her own: "A serious, harmful problem that affects individuals or groups beyond their capacity alone to correct." Nothing vague there! But she's not talking about rampant poverty, the nuclear arms build-up or even Donald Trump; she's talking about ... porn! And who does she quote to support her (re)definition? Why, anti-porn zealot Dr. Gail Dines, of course!

"We need to recognize that the pornography industry is not in this business to empower women, it's not in this business to be a champion of free speech; it's in this business to make money, and they're very good at it," Halverson said, apparently not understanding that the industry can do all three almost simultaneously.

But apparently, the fact that an unnamed porn site (we're gonna guess PornHub) had "over 87 billion video views" in 2015 to her means that "this is a global problem in that pornography production is pervasive" and "harming people at an alarming rate." (You may not see the connection between the two, but then again, you're probably not an anti-porn zealot.)

From there, we get the first of a series of anecdotes about how some mom was looking on the internet for something innocuous—"age-appropriate video games for her daughter"—and wouldn't ya know it? "... she was still exposed to pornography." (Funny; when we searched for "age-appropriate video games," all we got were ... links to age-appropriate video games—and how to avoid violent ones!)

"This mother was doing everything right," Halverson claimed. "She was trying to take an active part in her child's online experience and she was looking for age-appropriate materials but she couldn't stop them from being exposed." (Apparently, mom's never heard of web filters ...)

Then, after revealing that she attended a conference of clergymen where all but one admitted to having had a "problem with pornography"—the one who didn't was raised in Africa and didn't have internet access until his early 20s—Halverson got to the real meat of her talk: The harms porn does to "the brain, the body and sexual violence[?], and recognizing the fact that anecdotal research and peer-reviewed research is showing that these are serious harms."

Of course, one could go to one of the NCOSE-related sites like FightTheNewDrug.com, EndSexualExploitation.org or PornHarmsResearch.com to look for that "peer-reviewed research," but what's there, if it's in fact "peer-reviewed" in some legitimate medical journal at all, falls into basically two categories: Studies that don't say what NCOSE says they say, or studies that could apply as easily to eating a hearty dinner or watching an exciting sports event as they could to watching porn—such as, to quote

Halverson, porn's "addictive qualities, and it has negative impacts on users' brain structure and function... Pornography changes the brain, pornography conditions the brain and pornography makes the brain susceptible to addiction or compulsive use." (Yeah! How about them Red Sox, eh?) (**UPDATE**: And let's not forget how Trump's Big Lie has done exactly that to his supporters' brains!)

Take Halverson's report of a "study" involving female rats which were sprayed with "cadavorine, which is the smell of rotting flesh, and rats really don't like this smell; they usually run away from it." Well, turns out that when the researchers dumped a bunch of "young male virgin rats" into the same cage, lo and behold, the males didn't have a problem mating with the corpse-smelling females. But when they took those same corpse-smelling females and virgin males, and put them in with regular-smelling females and more virgin males, turns out the virgin males who'd previously had the "corpse" experience would fuck any females no matter what they smelled like, while the new virgin males who hadn't been previously exposed wouldn't fuck the corpse-smelling females! You can easily see how that relates to porn viewers, right? Right?

Halverson's takeaway from that experiment? "We see that pornography is conditioning the brain to very violent material." Hunh?

She also claimed that some other bullshit "study" found that "the user needs more extreme content over time in order to achieve the same level of arousal," which she said is "a hallmark of addiction, this escalating need for more extreme content or larger quantities of the content." Why? Because porn stimulates the production of the pleasure hormone dopamine—just like eating your favorite food, engaging in a stimulating workout (for those so inclined), or watching your favorite sports team at play, though of course she didn't make that addendum.

But see, the "problem" is that there's so much porn available on the internet that users can click around a porn site all day and not see the same video twice—which somehow means they're "addicted"!

"There have been brain scans of people who are compulsively using pornography and they show that they have increased pleasure stimulation in their pleasure centers when watching pornography than controls, than people who don't have compulsive pornography problems, and this is similar to drug addicts," Halverson claimed. "This is almost directly similar to heroin addicts in the ways that they have an increased anticipation as their dopamine spikes are conditioned to pornography and they're looking for what they know will come as they watch."

Note how Halverson sneaks in the word "compulsive" in describing the porn users, as if all people who watch a decent amount of porn are "compulsive." In fact, someone who "compulsively" watches porn suffers from a condition known as "obsessive-compulsive disorder," or OCD. It's the *condition* that creates the *action*, not the other way around—and anyone who knew anything about psychology would know that.

But no; according to Halverson, porn is "linked to negative body image, sexually transmitted diseases and pornography-induced sexual dysfunctions"—and she's got the "studies" to prove it! Apparently, again according to "studies," there are some assholes out there who look at porn and criticize their partners for not looking like porn stars—though it's unclear if that criticism extends to women who might be described as BBWs or MILFs or GILFs or who have as many tats as Janine Lindemulder or who haven't had their tits surgically "enhanced"—the list of popular niche porn performer body types goes on.

And of course, porn induces erectile dysfunction, especially among "millennials"—just ask anybody selling boner pills on cable TV or the web ... like former presidential candidate Bob Dole.[1] And for those who aren't among the "26 percent [who] have problems with erectile function," there's the problem, again caused by all that porn on the web, of "higher sexual desire but lower sexual satisfaction," which is "a hallmark of pornography, where you have a craving but a dislike of what you're engaged in. ... We hear so often that pornography is what's liberating about sexuality, it's empowering, it's a way to engage in sexuality, to learn more, but what we're finding is not only is it harming individuals' body image or desire to engage romantically with a partner but it's also actually stopping the ability for so many people to even have sexual encounters and it's ultimately sex-negative." That might be true of the sexual repressives, deviates and eunuchs who populate the anti-porn movement, but most normal people, when they're having sex, like it—and want to have more, whether they watch porn or not—and they also don't expect their partners to look like porn stars.

But Halverson saves the most outrageous charges for last, that porn is "very much linked to sexual violence in a variety of ways."

"Pornography teaches that women enjoy sexual violence," she lied. "There's one study done a few years ago on popular pornography of the time, that found that 88 percent of pornographic scenes featured violence against women, and [in] 95 percent of those scenes, the women responded either neutrally or with pleasure, which is literally sending a message to anyone who watches it that women enjoy sexual violence."

The anti-porn crowd has been quoting this "study," conducted by Gail Dines herself, for several years now, and anyone who's seen even a little bit of porn knows what crap that claim is. Sure, several videos will show the guy (or sometimes even the gal) slapping their partner's ass in the middle of fucking, and some performers like to put their hand on their partner's throat, both of which acts Dines considers to be "violent," but even in regular porn—not talking BDSM or other fetish porn—that's not uncommon—and yes, the partners generally *do* like that being done to them because for many people, that's a part of their sexual enjoyment and feels quite natural to them. But no way in hell is that or anything like it present in 88 percent of scenes!

Yet, supposedly all this "violence in porn" makes its viewers violent as well, because, you know, "monkey see, monkey do"—and apparently these anti-porners like Halverson aren't much more evolved than apes—or they think porn viewers aren't. This also goes for their claim that people who watch porn are more accepting of rape because, you know, there's so much "rape" in porn.

"Ultimately, pornography lies," Halverson lied. "It says that women are tools to be used and that men are inevitable predators that naturally, if you are a man, you must want to act this way towards a woman. ... Pornography is linked to increased verbal and physical aggression." No one who's ever seen even a little bit of porn could possibly come away with that impression—but putting forth such lies is how Halverson and her cronies fund their paychecks, so what do you expect?

Ironically, Halverson makes a good point when she talks about how too many 9- or 10- or 11-year-olds are getting their sex education from internet porn, but the problem there isn't the porn; it's that these kids' parents and/or schools and/or churches are too uptight and/or chicken-shit (and/or ignorant) to give them a *real* sex education, so the kids pick up their "knowledge" wherever they can. Take a hard look at yourself and your buddies, Haley, for the solution to that "problem."

Oh; and guess what? "Studies show" that men who patronize (or in Halverson's term, "buy") prostitutes also watch porn! Ain't that a kick in the ass? Halverson also claims that hookers are seeing more violent johns, thanks to porn; that sex traffickers are shooting porn of their kidnapees and selling those scenes "over and over and over again"; and that the traffickers use those scenes to keep their slaves in line, threatening to show those videos to—who? (Halverson doesn't say)—if the trafficked women give them any trouble. But while it's true that some tube sites allow their users to post pretty much any sexual content, including videos of non-consensual sex, that's not something the actual adult industry engages in, and companies like Pornhub have promised to take down such videos as soon as they can find them.

And finally, Halverson claims that "women and men are exploited in the pornography industry itself." And how does she know this? Why, it's all right there in a New York Academy of Medicine "in-depth survey and interviews with pornography performers in Los Angeles [which] found that so many of them had experienced physical trauma while on set, that they frequently left the industry with [sic] fiscally insecure without making a lot of money, and that they were regularly exposed to substance abuse and other harms as well." (The study is apparently the National Institutes of Health one which interviewed a whole 28 performers in 2008, so thanks again, Bill Margold; your legacy continues.)

And guess what one alleged male performer allegedly told them? "If the women were completely sober, no alcohol, no drugs, I can guarantee you, most of them would probably have mental breakdowns." Wow! It's like holding up a mirror, isn't it?

Bottom line, according to this idiot Halverson, "So it's important to recognize that even if one person is watching it and they're okay with their own sexual templates being distorted because they think they might not go out and harm someone else, by even watching these videos, they're engaging in and promoting the profiting from another person's sexual exploitation, who is vulnerable and could be looking for help or some kind of livelihood."

And what's the solution to those "problems"? Why, join and donate to anti-porn organizations like hers, of course; browbeat elected officials into declaring that "porn is a public health crisis"; and don't patronize any company on NCOSE's "Dirty Dozen list,"[2] which includes such villains as the American Library Association, Amnesty International, YouTube, HBO, Amazon, *Cosmopolitan* magazine and ... the U.S. Department of Justice?

If your reaction to this is, "These people are fucking nuts!"—join the crowd!

'SEX AND THE CONSTITUTION': A REVIEW

July 11, 2017

Sex and the Constitution: Sex, Religion and Law From America's Origins to the Twenty-First Century, by Geoffrey R. Stone; Liveright Publishing Corp., 500 Fifth Avenue, New York, NY 10110; 669 pgs. including end notes; $35 list price.

There are only a few books that are "must-haves" for the library of any progressive person who's interested in how sex and related topics are treated in the United States. The first is *America's War on Sex* by Dr. Marty Klein, which deals with the ongoing "war" between conservative religious activists, modern sex-positive culture and the adult industry. The other is *Girls Lean Back Everywhere* by Edward de Grazia,[1] which traces the development of obscenity law in the U.S. from its beginnings in the late 1800s with the persecution of James Joyce's *Ulysses* through the 1990 Cincinnati Mapplethorpe bust and conservatives' attempts to defund arts considered (by them) to be too risqué.

But now there's a new mandatory read for sex-positive activists: Attorney Geoffrey Stone's examination of how secular law has been subverted over the centuries by religious activists to create the "sex crimes" of publishing/selling/transporting/reading erotic literature and films, being and/or patronizing a sex worker; prescribing and/or providing contraception or abortion services; having sex with and/or marrying the "wrong person"; and more.

The value of Stone's work is easily seen from the beginnings of the first chapter, where Stone states, "Perhaps surprisingly, the pre-Christian world generally thought of sex as a natural and positive part of the human experience. It did not see sex as predominantly bound up with questions of sin, shame, or religion." He follows that statement with examples from Greek culture as early as 500 B.C., where "*eros* was a primal force which permeated all facets of life." This included Aphrodite's priestesses frequently having sex with strangers "as a form of worship"; Greek architecture, vases and terra-cottas featuring "explicit scenes of vaginal and anal intercourse, masturbation, and fellatio"; and Greek playwrights dealing easily with such subjects as "masturbation, fellatio and male-male anal sex," and women masturbating by hand or by use of primitive sex toys. The Greeks even had their own forms of birth control, and practiced abortion "as long as it occurred prior to quickening"—a position supported, interestingly enough, even by the Catholic Church until fairly recently.

In fact, before the Christians came along, western culture generally considered sex in most of its manifestations as close to divinity. Even the early Romans, who had little love for the Greeks, used phalluses in religious iconography and even jewelry, and Stone reports that "Prostitution also flourished in Rome," and that "there were as many as thirty-four brothels in Pompeii" alone, or about one for every 300 inhabitants.

Skipping forward a few centuries to the Middle Ages, Stone reports that, "It was in this setting that the Church implanted in Western culture its judgments about sex and sin. Sexual desire gradually became linked to guilt, humiliation, failure and shame," and Stone goes into much detail regarding the Church's thoughts on all subjects sexual, including masturbation, sex outside of marriage, homosexuality, etc.—but still, secular law took little notice until the late 13th century, when "Criminal statutes against same-sex sex were suddenly enacted throughout Europe," thanks to Church-spread rumors that "same-sex sexual conduct was rampant." Roughly two centuries later, during the Reformation, Martin Luther "encouraged the state to prohibit and punish prostitution, fornication, adultery and other sexual immoralities, explaining that if the State 'wishes to be Christian' it should punish such behavior in order to maintain an orderly society." Guess what? Over time, that's exactly what governments did! And guess how orderly society has become!

And it was in part due to religious repression, sexual and otherwise, that Europeans took their lives in their hands to cross the Atlantic and colonize the "New World"—and guess what? Aside from the Puritans, who largely remained in Massachusetts, the colonists were a fairly randy bunch.

"[C]olonial bookstores in the eighteenth century contained an 'amazing variety of erotica'," Stone reports, adding that "Americans could find pretty much whatever they wanted. Cultural and political leaders like Thomas Jefferson and Benjamin Franklin collected many of these works. Jefferson counted among his library Boccaccio's *The Decameron*, several bawdy Restoration plays, and Charles Johnstone's *Chrystal*, which portrayed vivid scenes of sexuality, lust, and sexual scandal ... In a less literary vein, a broad range of bawdy humor was sold by hawkers throughout the colonies, and sexually-explicit anti-papist tracts were especially popular ... There were no prosecutions for obscenity during the entire colonial era... The first true obscenity prosecution in the United States did not occur until well into the nineteenth century. Throughout the colonial era, the distribution, exhibition, and possession of pornographic material was not thought to be any of the state's business."

Of course, not everyone thought this way, and early in the 19th century, the country experienced a religiously-based "Second Great Awakening," which pushed religious views on sexuality onto many state law books—but one phrase that Stone mentions several times in regard to the fledgling Americans' sexual rights is "pursuit of Happiness," which those who are familiar with their Declaration of Independence will recall is part of the phrase "all men ... are endowed by their Creator with certain unalienable Rights, that among these are Life, Liberty and the pursuit of Happiness." Without actually stating it outright, Stone definitely implies that the use of the word "happiness" in that phrase was meant to refer to Americans' right to pursue sexual intercourse! Take *that*, Jefferson Beauregard Sessions III!

It's impossible for this review to catalog all of the excellent points Stone makes about the "war on sex" that's even now taking place in this country, even though he does go into great detail regarding the 1873 Comstock Act,[2] which prohibited the mailing of "obscene literature," of which birth control information was considered a part; the persecution of sex researcher Alfred Kinsey; the Supreme Court's decision in *Miller v. California* regarding obscenity; the high court's *FCC v. Pacifica Foundation* "seven filthy words" and *Barnes v. Glen Theatre* nude dancing cases; the persecution of adult entrepreneur Reuben Sturman; the Extreme Associates case; and many, many more—and that's just the sections on sexual speech! He gives equally incisive dissections of the cultural and legal issues surrounding religious conservatives' fight against the legalization of contraception, abortion, gay rights and same-sex marriage.

In short, *Sex and the Constitution* belongs on the bookshelf of every person who's even the least bit interested in how sex has been treated by American laws, and the impacts of religion on that treatment.

Sadly, Preacher *wasn't a terribly good TV show, but one episode did catch my eye as being superior to just about any sexual depiction one could see on mainstream TV.*

IN AMC'S 'PREACHER,' JESUS HAS SEX. LATER, RELIGIONISTS GO NUTS.

August 30, 2017

It's not unlike something one would see in a softcore porn movie: a reasonably good-looking guy (Tyson Ritter) with a man-bun and a beard having sex with a not beautiful but not unattractive woman (Carrie Lazar) in a bare, dimly lit room.

"JESUS!" she cries out in ecstasy. "I'm getting close!"

"I'm so happy!" he answers.

"Could you just stick your finger in my...," she trails off.

"Like this?" he responds.

"Yes! Oh, yes!" she screams. "Don't stop!"

But they do stop for a moment as the guy thinks he hears a noise outside, but she tries to put his fears to rest: "I told you my husband's not gonna be back till Sunday," she whispers. And then it's back to fucking, with the fireplace light continually casting the shadows of the couple's different sexual positions on the wall, and the pair bouncing so hard that they knock a clay pitcher off of the side table by the bed. The background music barely masks her cries of delight.

Afterwards, as they're lying in post-coital quiet, holding each other, she admits, "You know, I never really do this."

"Me neither," he agrees.

"Come on," she jibes, unbelieving.

"For real," he says. "You're the only one."

"Like, ever? (pause) That's crazy. You could have any girl you wanted," she challenges.

"I wanted you," he says sheepishly.

"I wanted you too, since the first moment I saw you in the market hanging out with your friends," she admits. "I knew you were special."

She invites him to stay for supper, but he demurs, saying, "I have to do something for my dad."

"In the middle of the night?" she questions.

"I made him a promise," he states, adding gently, "Tonight meant a lot to me, and no matter what happens, I want you to remember one thing: I love you. Also, you can never, ever tell anyone about this. Cool?"

"Cool," she replies hesitantly.

He steps away, releasing his shoulder-length hair from its constraint and shaking it to its fullness.

Almost immediately, there's a pounding on the door: "Jesus! Jesus! Are you in there?"

And so the game of "*What?* Really? *No way!* Are you kidding?" comes to an end as Jesus opens the door to confront his followers and explain that since they were all passed out in the garden when he left them, "I came here to bless this ailing woman"—a woman who helpfully lets fly a couple of slight, sheepish coughs.

And that's just the opening five minutes of the August 21 episode of the AMC series *Preacher*, titled "Dirty Little Secret"[1]—an understatement if there ever was one.

For those who aren't familiar with the series, now in its second season, it's based on a DC/Vertigo comic book series[2] by Garth Ennis and Steve Dillon, revolving around a preacher, Jesse Custer (Dominic Cooper), his sort-of girlfriend Tulip (Ruth Negga) and their vampire buddy Cassidy (Joseph Gilgun), all of whom, at the end of Season 1, go on a road trip to search for God.

Oh; and also at the end of Season 1, Jesse's been granted the "Genesis power": Whenever he says something while invoking it, whoever his words are directed at must obey whatever he wants them to do. (Last season, he used it to [inadvertently] send someone to hell.)

Now, considering what censorious busybodies conservative religionists are, one might expect that they'd have already had something to say about this series that's been coming into American homes for the past year and a half... but no; not even the ultra-nitty-picky Parents Television Council has mentioned it on their website, much less reviewed any of the 24 episodes that have aired so far.

But some little church-y minion must have tuned across the "Dirty Little Secret" episode, because both Glenn Beck's bloated organ *The Blaze* as well as the American Family Association offshoot One Million Moms have posted articles blasting the show, and not just for the part about Jesus—you know: the Son of God, made in the image of Man, and put on earth to walk in his shoes—having sex, much less adulterous sex. But more on that in a moment.

"Catholic League President Bill Donohue in a statement to Fox News expressed his outrage at the television show and warned that Christians will 'rally' against the production should offenses continue in this lurid manner," reported *The Blaze*'s Sarah Taylor. "'Depicting Jesus in a grotesque sex scene is an assault on the sensibilities of all Christians, as well as people of good will who are not Christians,' Donohue said. 'We have been treated to this kind of fare from some pay-per-view channels, but we are not accustomed to AMC getting into the mud. If this is a signal of what it aspires to become, we will rally Christians against it.'"

"The AMC series 'Preacher' is advertised as gory good fun and airs during primetime," wrote[3] One Million Moms' Monica Cole in an email. "The 'preacher' in the show is far from it, and the program blasphemes Jesus in the latest episode with the Son of God depicted as a lying s-x p-rvert. The show opens with extremely graphic Jesus s-x scene and closes with an inbred Messiah. (A dash '-' is used to bypass internet filters.) AMC continues to air the anti-Christian program 'Preacher' on Monday evenings at 9:00 p.m. ET/ 8:00 p.m. CT." (We're guessing they included that last bit just in case any of their devout readership wants to check the show out.) (Heh-heh...)

Of course, since Cole is religious and this author isn't, she kindly provides a bit of context for the Jesus sex scene.

"The show decides to spend its first five minutes depicting Jesus Christ having gratuitous s-x with a married woman the night he is arrested in the Garden of Gethsemane," Cole explains. "They are shown moaning and screaming in multiple positions during this extremely graphic scene. In a long series of shadow silhouettes[,] the Son of God is depicted engaging in every s-xual act and position imaginable accompanied by groans and moans. The woman he is with tells the Jesus character not to worry as her 'husband will not be home for days.' After the marathon s-x session, Jesus admits he was a virgin and then gets ready to leave, subtly referencing the Last Supper and upcoming crucifixion. He is then caught by his disciples so he lies his way out of the situation, but not every disciple believes him."

That unbelieving disciple is Thaddeus, and his only words to Jesus' paramour are, "Don't worry, your secret's safe with me." Little does the audience realize how important those words will be.

See, let's not forget that Season 2 has been devoted to Jesse's search for God, and his tight-knit group is currently in New Orleans because he'd heard that God is a big fan of jazz. But there's a shadowy religious group called The Grail, headed by the one-eyed Herr Starr, that's been busy putting obstructions in Jesse's way—until "Dirty Little Secret," when Herr Starr offers to take Jesse, blindfolded, to see God's son—who turns out to be Tyson Ritter once again, but this time playing what Cole refers to as an "inbred Messiah." This requires Jesse to first pass through a metal detector and then have a brief meeting with the Pope and the Archbishop of Canterbury, both of whom Herr Starr just happens to have sitting in his office.

"Are you sure you want to know?" asks the Archbishop. "Some things cannot be unheard."

But Jesse wants to see him, and thanks to the Genesis power, Herr Starr is forced to show him what is essentially Jesus Christ XXV, the last descendent of the child born to Jesus' paramour—and it turns out that "the Messiah" is a nearly illiterate, wall-eyed idiot named Humperdoo, whose first act, as Jesse kneels before him, is to pee on Jesse. He also likes to raise his robe and show people his genitals—and rub up against them till he cums. The interview kind of goes downhill from there.

Before the episode aired, co-producer Seth Rogen (yes, that Seth Rogen) tweeted, "Tonight's episode of #Preacher has some stuff I've been excited to bring to life for years and I'm SHOCKED they let us do it. Please watch."

Perhaps the point to be taken away from all this is that if mainstream cable can air this, even though a couple of adult companies have recently put out features with religious themes, there's little chance that any of their future endeavors will come anywhere close to the "blasphemous heat" of this *Preacher* episode.

UPDATE: One Million Moms, as they so often do, wants its readers to "Hold Sponsors Of 'Preacher' Accountable." The email is basically a repeat of their original, part of which is quoted above, with the addition of the final paragraph: "Take Action: Please use the information we have provided on our website to contact Febreze (owned by Procter & Gamble) and ask that they pull their financial support from "Preacher'."

This author's recommendation? Buy as much Febreze as you can afford!

UPDATE #2: We won't tell you just which *Preacher* sponsor One Million Moms is mad about this time, but feel free to switch your phone/internet service to Verizon anytime.

UPDATE #3: Guess who also doesn't like Cricket Wireless's sponsorship of this show? (More to come, we're sure...)

UPDATE #4 (7/10/18): Like several states, Louisiana has passed a law giving tax incentives to movie and TV production companies to film in the state—with, of course, the usual exemption for any production that's required to keep 2257 records—better known as porn. But guess what?

"State Sen. John Milkovich and two Baptist preachers, Larry Pridmore and Edward Roberts, have recently urged 'the Louisiana Office of Economic Development to flatly reject [a] request for a $16.2 million tax refund check' for the AMC show *Preacher*," noted the Freedom From Religion Foundation in its April newsletter. "The complainants have stated their case plainly in the last sentence of their letter: '[T]he larger truth is that there is never a good time to reward production companies that trash our Louisiana values, mock our beliefs—and dishonor Christ.'" Guess which episode they were referring to!?!

For those who've been living a sheltered life for the past 20 years or so, AVN puts on (pre-pandemic) expos in January of each year: The Adult Entertainment Expo (AEE), the Adult Novelty Expo (ANE) and for a few years, the GayVN Expo. The following covers one of the more interesting ANE panels from 2018, since it dealt with religion's suppression of sexuality.

ANE PANEL EXPLORES SPEAKING SEXUAL TRUTH TO THE FAITHFUL

January 24, 2018

LAS VEGAS—The first AVN Novelty Expo (ANE) seminar for January 24 tackled a subject that many retailers and other adult-oriented vendors face: How to talk to religious customers and others whose faiths may create conflicts with their quests for sexual enjoyment.

The panelists included ShaRonda Parker,[1] a Louisiana retailer who said that she doesn't run a "sex shop," but rather a "sexual health and wellness" store; Kim Airs,[2] the legendary owner of the Cambridge, Mass., store Grand Opening and a 25-year veteran of the pleasure products industry; and Dr. Nikki Goldstein,[3] a sexologist and sex educator from Australia who's worked with religious leaders in her home territory.

Parker, whom moderator Sherri L. Shaulis described as the inspiration for the current panel, began by noting that the Deep South is the heart of the Bible Belt, and that everything is steeped in religion, including sex, and that many sexual practices that others consider completely normal are thought of as wrong, sinful or unclean. A former school teacher, Parker sees her task as one of "freeing people" from some of their sexual preconceptions, in part by opening her retail outlet and also by partnering with churches to educate them on sexual issues in a way that respects their religious sensibilities.

For her part, Airs noted that she'd opened her store outside of Boston in a very Catholic area, and that as part of her business, she saw it as her duty to help her customers overcome some of the unfortunate sexual attitudes they'd picked up from the religion, their parents and other societal influences.

"Everybody's doing the exact same thing as anywhere else," Airs said she responded when others questioned her choice of retail location. "And it just depends on how tight they pull that bedroom door."

Goldstein, who doesn't have a retail outlet ("Yet," she noted), told of how more orthodox Jews tend to be more conservative sexually than more liberal believers, and that her home territory, the Gold Coast, was not overly religious, but that in her travels, she had come across all levels of religiosity, and had to learn to deal with them.

"I spoke to this [Jewish] philosopher who told me it was kosher to have anal sex as long as the man finished off inside the woman," she reported.

She also stated that her own (rather liberal) rabbi acknowledged that there is a relative lack of education regarding sex toys, and that "when it comes to a religious couple, everything to do with sex is about increasing intimacy ... how you can reconnect together and increase intimacy." She saw that as an important goal in sex education generally.

All of the participants agreed that the best way to approach getting religious conservatives to consider adding sex toys to their bedroom activities was to "think small."

"Especially if you're talking to a woman with all the same issues and everything, if she goes home with a realistic one like this," Airs said with her hands spread wide apart, "it's going to be grounds for divorce."

Parker noted she had done "tasteful" presentations to local parishioners in church, with the aim of increasing marital intimacy, using such words as "stimulator" or "massager" rather than "vibrator," but observed that as long as "the marital bed is undefiled," religious people are fairly open about what they'll consider doing. She also handed out candy kisses and coupon books at a church holiday party that netted her 15 new couples customers. "That little coupon book opened them up to so much other stuff," she said, adding that "they are a very sensitive group."

"You have to give people your permission and let them know it's okay," she summarized, "because what I've found is, the church uses guilt and sin and they basically play on people's emotions. It's a form of social control, and they're like, 'We're doing it for their own good because if we don't put boundaries on people, they're going to wonder about this, this and the other, and what they have to learn is, it's okay to walk in your freedom."

She also approaches the issue of birth control with some of them, having told them, "If you know that your family's complete, then there are different things that you can do to not have to take birth control, but to still be able to not have another baby."

Airs stated that another taboo subject she sometimes comes across is ED—erectile dysfunction—which she said men are afraid to discuss but about which they are hungry for advice. "People will tell you their most intimate secrets within two minutes," she said, "so you need to have that compassion and knowledge to let them know it's okay."

For Goldstein, the three most important concepts in getting the religious to overcome their fear of sexual topics are "Educate, normalize and collaborate—get people to talk about things like desire, intimacy." She gave the example of a woman who doesn't have orgasms blaming her husband's penis for the lack, when according to Goldstein, what she really needs is the right sex toy.

"Get yourself into the mainstream to normalize yourself," she advised. "If you can jump on TV, radio, podcasts—and I'm not talking specifically about things with the word 'sex' in them—really mainstream stuff, and this is where you can change your language. If you're a pleasure product provider, you are an intimacy enhancer expert, and take the word 'sex' out of it. People can get very fearful when they go, 'Oh, you're the girl who sells rubber dicks.' "I'm not selling rubber dicks; I am helping couples enhance intimacy.'"

Airs suggested that most of what the panelists have said regarding educating religious people could also be applied to the medical community, which often is ignorant about sexuality. She said that giving them samples of sexual products could help.

Shaulis then opened the floor for questions, and Beth Liebling, owner of Darling Way Boutique in Houston, suggested referring to toys as "romantic props."

"I tell everybody, when you shut the bedroom door, you should be able to see a different show in your bedroom in your real life just like on your TV," she said, "and when I talk about props that can be kept in a prop closet, it helps them realize that those are extras, and for men who sometimes are afraid and they say, 'Oh, she's gonna like that better than me,' I tell them, 'Nobody ever goes to the theater to see the props. The props are there to make the stars shine and make the show come to life.'"

Much of the discussion centered around how to reach people who, because of upbringing or philosophy, can't quite seem to grasp the idea that sexual pleasure is okay, especially within marriage.

"Sometimes when you're dealing with people who are closed-minded, sometimes you just can't change certain people, what they feel, how they feel," said Parker. "Don't let that have any bearing on you and what you have to offer to the next person. Don't let them discourage you, because I've learned over the years, some people are just set in their ways, but you have a new generation of young people who want to be set free, want to be liberated, so you be that person for them."

In response to a questioner who said she lived in a very conservative area, Parker noted that her store doesn't carry any explicit DVDs, just toys and lingerie and other more benign merchandise. Goldstein advised carrying items in the store that are not explicitly sexual, but rather "sensual and beautiful." Parker also added the concept of starting small, saying that a bullet vibe is most women's first toy, and the fact that they use and enjoy that may allow them to consider other, perhaps bigger toys.

All in all, the audience appeared to have heard advice that would stand them in good stead in their communities, and might even allow them to help people of faith gain new insights and pleasures in their own sexuality.

After this article was written, several states opened investigations into clergy pedophilia, and in every case, found multiple offenders, many of whom were still performing clerical duties. There were also several scandals involving religious institutions, perhaps the most high-profile of which was the revelation that then-Liberty University President Jerry Falwell Jr. enjoyed watching his wife being fucked by the pool boy (shades of porn plots!) and that several women had charged that they were raped on campus and that the university failed to do anything substantial about it.

ENOUGH WITH THE RELIGIOUS KETTLE CALLING THE PORN POT BLACK

"Thoughts and prayers" are even more meaningless for these victims than many others

August 17, 2018

> *"Everybody knows that you love me baby*
> *"Everybody knows that you really do*
> *"Everybody knows that you've been faithful*
> *"Give or take a night or two*
> *"Everybody knows you've been discreet*
> *"But there were so many people you just had to meet*
> *"Without your clothes*
> *"And everybody knows"*
> —Leonard Cohen, *Everybody Knows*

At least in the United States, adult content—porn—has been branded by the world's top religions—Christianity, Judaism, Islam—as one of the most sinful—that is, bad—activities a human being can engage in. Doesn't matter if people buy it, look at it, talk favorably about it or, "God forbid," make it, sell it or act in it, the prescription from those religions is that such indulgers are going to Hell, to burn for eternity in a fiery pit.

And the reason those people are so against porn is that for the most part, it paints sex as an enjoyable and relatively consequence-free activity. You look at it, you get off on it, you wipe up the fluids and you're all good.

But as all good Christians and Jews know, once Adam and Eve took a bite out of the fruit of the Tree of Knowledge (!) and saw that they were naked, whose nakedness apparently didn't mean anything till they took that bite, that was the ballgame as far as sex was concerned. From then on (except for King Solomon, of course), sex was something you did only when married, to create babies—and if possible, you did it in the dark, undressing in the closet before climbing into bed under the covers with the lights off for a missionary-position romp.

And as pretty much everyone in the adult entertainment community knows, as do many of its fans, that's just sick. In fact, sex is pleasurable, looking at (some) naked people is pleasurable, getting off by looking at people having sex, naked or otherwise, is pleasurable, and there's exactly zero evidence that anyone pays a price after they're dead for indulging in such pleasure.

But for the moment, that's beside the point. What *is* to the point is that within the last week, it's become internationally known that the very people who've spent the most time criticizing and deploring porn, both verbally and in writing; who've passed and supported laws making it illegal to buy and sell porn; and who've defamed pretty much anyone connected with the adult industry, have behaved far worse, sexually speaking, than virtually anyone who does make or sell porn. I'm referring, of course, to evangelicals in general, but here specifically to Catholic priests and church hierarchy, the subjects of a far-reaching report[1] put together by a Pennsylvania grand jury which describes in some detail how some 300 predatory priests in Pennsylvania's six largest dioceses—Allentown, Erie, Greensburg, Harrisburg, Pittsburgh, and Scranton—molested more than (likely many, *many* more than, considering how retraumatizing it could be to admit the abuse) 1,000 children over the past 70 years—and their superiors did their best to hide that fact, to provide cover for the priests that did it, and who went out of their way to minimize the problem in the press.

"Despite some institutional reform, individual leaders of the church have largely escaped public accountability," the grand jury wrote. "Priests were raping little boys and girls, and the men of God who were responsible for them not only did nothing; they hid it all. For decades."

Want some examples? How about Father Chester Gawronski, who fondled and masturbated at least 12 different children by saying he was just showing them "how to check for cancer." How about Father Thomas D. Skotek, who raped an underage girl, got her pregnant, then paid for her abortion. His Bishop later wrote in a letter—to Skotek!—"This is a very difficult time in your life, and I realize how upset you are. I too share your grief." How about Father Edmond Parrakow, who admitted to molesting "approximately thirty-five male children" because sex with girls was "sinful" and raping boys didn't "violate" them. One altar boy said Parrakow told them to go naked under their cassocks during Mass because God didn't want "man-made clothes" touching their skin during services. (Parrakow now works in a shopping mall.)

(Many more examples can be found in the *New York Times* article,[2] an article by Hemant Mehta,[3] or the full grand jury report. And BTW, there are currently a total of just 849 priests "practicing" in Pennsylvania, though it's unclear how many of those figure in the grand jury's report.)

But the problem isn't just the rampant molestation; there's also the attempts by bishops and other church officials to cover the whole thing up. According to the grand jury, such church officials used "a playbook for concealing the truth," as *The New York Times*' Scott Dodd reported. Among the clergy's tactics were (are!) making sure to use euphemisms rather than real words to describe the sexual assaults in diocese documents. For instance, never say "rape"; say "inappropriate contact" or "boundary issues." Then, after failing to conduct genuine investigations with properly trained personnel, church hierarchy in an effort to appear to act with integrity would send priests for "evaluation" at church-run "psychiatric treatment centers," where "experts" would "diagnose" whether the priest was a pedophile, based largely on the priest's "self-reports"—and regardless of whether the priest had actually engaged in sexual contact with a child. Perhaps worse, bishops and cardinals allowed priest-rapists to continue to live in church housing rent-free, and in several cases, when their molestations became known, transferred them to distant dioceses to continue their illegal activities. And of course, "above all, don't tell the police." Child sexual abuse, even short of actual penetration, is and has for all relevant times been a crime. But don't treat it that way; handle it like a personnel matter, "in house."

But since Catholicism is a religion, it isn't treated like a secular organization whose members committed the same offenses would have been.

"They would have been arrested under the RICO federal laws already and they would have been considered organized crime," Pennsylvania State Rep. Mark Rozzi, a Democrat and molestation survivor, told Salon.com.

Surely, at this point, many members of the adult entertainment community reading this are feeling a bit nauseous. Wanna know who isn't? How about Haley Halverson (aka McNamara), Vice President of Advocacy and Outreach at the (virulently anti-porn) National Center on Sexual Exploitation, who wrote[4] on Townhall.com, "The heartbreaking reality is wherever there are people—especially when some have greater power or authority than others or where an institution desires self-preservation—there is the possibility of sexual abuse. Sometimes the power differential is in the boardroom at work. Sometimes the institution seeking self-preservation is a Hollywood production company. And sometimes, the scene of sexual abuse is the church." YEAH! Why should a priest be held to a higher standard than, say, Harvey Weinstein or Republican National Committee finance chairman Steve Wynn? And I can't help but notice that nowhere in Halverson's "apologetic" is there any suggestion that the priests' "toxic" religion might have impelled them to have committed these horrendous acts, in contrast to the frequent claim by her and her ilk that "toxic" porn inspires people to rape.

Or how about Dr. Jennifer Roback Morse, president and founder of the anti-gay Ruth Institute? "Some news stories give the impression that 'sexual orientation' played no role in past or current clergy abuse scandals," she wrote.[5] "However, two studies by the John Jay College of Criminal Justice (commissioned by the U.S. Conference of Catholic Bishops) in 2004 and 2011 found that over 80% of those abused were victims of male-on-male predation by priests against under-age (pre-teen and teenaged) boys. ... There has been an active homosexual subculture in the Catholic Church, which operates in seminaries and dioceses." Imagine that: an institution that tells its employees that they can't marry or have heterosexual sexual relationships somehow attracts a number of gay/pedophile employees! As if that were an excuse for them to molest children—some of whom, let's recall, were little *girls*! (Pedophilia knows no gender bias, either in the perps or the victims.)

But my favorite has to be Bill Donohue, president of the Catholic League for Religious and Civil Rights, who's put out an 11-page report on what he thinks the Pennsylvania grand jury got wrong. Here are a couple of examples:

"*Myth*: The grand jury report was initiated to make the guilty pay. *Fact*: False. It has nothing to do with punishing the guilty. Pennsylvania Attorney General Josh 'Salacious' Shapiro admitted on August 14 that 'Almost every instance of child abuse (the grand jury) found was too old to be prosecuted.' He's right. But he knew that from the get-go, so why did he pursue this dead end? Why did he waste millions of taxpayer dollars in pursuit of alleged offenders when he knew he couldn't do anything about it? Because he ... wanted to shame the Catholic Church." YEAH! It had *nothing* to do with exposing a vast group of religious pedophiles, many of whom still molest kids and whose superiors are still covering it up!

"*Myth*: The priests 'raped' their victims. ... *Fact*: This is an obscene lie. Most of the alleged victims were not raped: they were groped or otherwise abused, but not penetrated, which is what the word 'rape' means." BIG difference! Gee, Bill, thanks for pointing that out! Not to mention pointing out that most of the kids who were molested were 15 rather than 5 years old, which for Donohue means that the priests who did it weren't "pedophiles"—a legally incorrect stance which Hemant Mehta described as "a new low bar for Catholic Church defenders."

But here's an important point to take away from this situation: This is a study of the molestations and cover-ups committed by Catholic clergy in major cities in just one state. There are 49 others to go, a couple of which have done their own investigations, though few as thorough as Pennsylvania's, and there are plenty of other clergy from other religious sects—Baptists, Lutherans, Methodists, Mormons, Seventh Day Adventists, Rabbis, Imams—the list is long—who haven't yet been investigated. Guaranteed, it's not just Catholic clergy who are molesting kids.

My advice? Print out a copy of the 1,356-page Pennsylvania grand jury report and be prepared to drop it at the feet of the next religious asshole who tries to tell you that you'll be going to Hell for making or watching porn!

Of course, The Faithful don't believe there is such a thing as a transgender person. As far as they're concerned, people who identify as such are either crazy or con artists.

'THE FAITHFUL' NOTICE THAT 'SUPERGIRL' FEATURES A TRANS ACTRESS

OMG!OMG!OMG!OMG!OMG!OMG!OMG!

May 2, 2019

If there's one thing that distinguishes *Supergirl* and its star Melissa Benoist[1] from pretty much all other TV superheroes ever, it's the show's and the star's willingness to get out in front of societal issues and deal with them in a progressive way—and the show's latest season has jumped into the political fray headlong and feet first.

Benoist has long been recognized as at least a liberal. Just a couple of months after President Grab 'Em By The Pussy took office, Benoist was part of the Women's March on Washington, holding a handmade sign that read, "Hey Donald, don't try to grab my pussy—It's made of steel." She's also tweeted such thoughts as, "Support survivors, share your story, take a stand against and help raise awareness about domestic violence and the epidemic it is," and "Proud to stand in solidarity with sisters for equity, parity and a better future and proud of..."

And while Benoist doesn't have any screenwriting credits on her show, it's getting more and more reflective of her values—most notably the current season, where the President of the United States (Bruce Boxleitner) has rescinded the "Alien Amnesty Act" signed into law by his predecessor (Lynda Carter) and set Agent Liberty (Sam Witwer) on a mission to round up and imprison every alien in the country. And, this being a comic book-based show, we're not talking about Mexicans; we're talking about immigrants from other planets—and yet, it's just possible to come away from each episode with the sinking feeling that the plotline *is* about human immigrants and the violence perpetrated on them by ICE and other "law enforcers."

One of those aliens that Supergirl befriends is Nia Nal, born on Earth but the daughter of a human father and a mother from the planet Naltor. Nia is played by Nicole Maines,[2] and in real life, Nicole is transgender, a fact that was reported by several news organizations when she debuted on the show in 2018, but which had escaped the attention of everyone on the Religious Right—except one Lindsay Kornick,[3] who's published a couple of rants on the fundamentalist "news" site Newsbusters, most recently with the "ironic" headline, "'Supergirl' Trangender Hero Preaches 'Sharing Our Truth' on 'Authentic Selves',"[4] which begins, "Let's face it, CW's *Supergirl* has always been preachy. But there's preachy, and then there's obnoxiously, sycophantically preachy. The superhero series flies towards the latter in yet another episode proclaiming how being trans is being 'strong' and 'authentic' nowadays."

The inspiration for the rant that follows was last Sunday's episode, "American Dreamer," a title with a double meaning all its own: Maines' character on the show has the secret identity of "Dreamer," who has the power to see the future in her dreams, and of course, Nia Nal considers herself an American, having been born here, though Agent Liberty can only see the alien blood coursing through her veins.

As part of her effort to thwart Agent Liberty's pogrom against alien residents, Supergirl uses her secret identity as news reporter Kara Danvers to interview Dreamer on her company's TV show, where she asks at one point, "So you are both human and alien?"

"Yes," Dreamer replies. "My parents believed that humans and aliens could co-exist. And I'm living proof of that. But growing up wasn't easy. **I am also a trans woman. I'm different, Miss Danvers, but so is everybody. And I don't know when that became such a bad thing. The greatest gift we can give each other is our authentic selves and sharing that. Sharing our truth is what will make us strong. So, here I am. I am both human and alien. And I am a trans woman.** S'mores are my favorite dessert. But I will always choose salty over sweet. I broke my nose when I was 15 during a game of kickball. My mother was my heart. And since I lost her, it's felt like a piece of me is missing. But my father is my spine... **And I am proud of all that I am.**"

To which Kara adds, **"You should be."** [All emphasis courtesy of Newsbusters]

Kornick's reaction? "The other characters predictably hail her words as brave and inspiring instead of the preachy and cringey mess they really are. They act like we've never heard these words before in the media or even on this very show. We didn't believe it then, and we don't believe it now."

Indeed; the first time Kornick heard those words was back in January, during an episode where Supergirl accompanies Nia back to her hometown, and Kornick's bigotry toward transgender people is clear in her opening paragraph: "CW's *Supergirl* has promised to debut the first transgender superhero on television, and now we've reached the cusp of that character's origin story. To absolutely no one's surprise, it's deluded, self-righteous, and more than a little confusing. But that's what you get when pretending a man has the superpower to transform into a woman."

To be clear, "transforming" from a man to a woman isn't Nia's/Maines' power. She *is* a woman; her *power* is to dream the future, which she inherited from her mother. But pretty much no one who writes for religio-conservative websites is willing to admit that there's actually such a thing as a transgender person; as far as they're concerned, they're all men *pretending* to be women (or women pretending to be men). It's an article of faith among The Faithful.

And that's part of the reason why Kornick is so bent out of shape when Nia tells her sister Maeve, who believed that she would be the recipient of her mother's predictive power rather than Nia.

Kornick quotes this bit of Maeve's dialog from the January episode: "How did you, of all people, get the powers? They're supposed to be passed down from mother to daughter. So how did someone like you get them? You're not even a real woman."

Of course, Kornick is all over that: "This is supposed to be a personal blow, but the thing is... Nia isn't a woman. And she'll never really be one. She wasn't born with an XX chromosome, so she isn't genetically a daughter. The series could in theory explain that biology works differently on Naltor than Earth, but then she couldn't be the accurate transgender representation everyone wants her to be. Even if this episode wasn't chock full of liberal nonsense, it would still be confusing."

Only to people who don't accept the fact that some people's gender doesn't match up with their genitalia, asshole!

But *Supergirl* deserves major props for not only casting a transgender woman as a transgender character on the show, but making her a major superhero—and in the process, infuriating people who can't get over the fact that some women have dicks.

There are actually several sexually explicit movies that belong in the National Film Registry, but it'll take much more enlightened federal government employees to get them there.

OP-ED: CNN IGNORES ONE OF THE '70S TOP GROSSING FILMS: 'DEEP THROAT'

Isn't it time—in fact, way past time—to put the world's most famous XXX film into the National Film Registry?

August 5, 2019

TVLAND—In a precedent-setting move for the channel, in early July, CNN began running a new series titled simply "The Movies," a six-part look at some of the greatest Hollywood productions of all time. Interestingly, though, the first two-hour episode dealt with the 1980s, Part 2 covered the '90s, and Part 3 dealt with productions from 2000 on. Strangely, however, Part 4, which aired last week, was all about the 1970s—and the reason that time sequence was strange was because it was clear that some of the best movies of the last 70 or 80 years were made during that decade—but the show had at least one important omission.

Of course, some of these '70s classics include *The Godfather*, *Shaft*, *Annie Hall*, *Lenny*, *Jaws*, *Close Encounters of the Third Kind*, *Alien*, *M*A*S*H*, *Network*, *The Exorcist*, *All That Jazz*, *Star Wars* and *A Clockwork Orange*, but several were of particular interest because of how they attempted to deal with sexual subjects: *Taxi Driver*, whose second lead (Jodie Foster) is a hooker; *Cabaret*, with Liza Minelli as a nightclub dancer in 1931 Berlin, and one of whose plotlines involves gay sex; *Shampoo*, where Warren Beatty gets blown under a table by Julie Christie and later fucks her on the kitchen floor; *Carrie*, where star Sissy Spacek gets her period—*nude!*—in the high school shower(!) and all the "good girls" throw tampons at her; and *Grease*, where at least a couple of the "Pink Ladies" are sexually liberated, and Olivia Newton-John decides she has to "slut it up" to land John Travolta.

A few '70s films, though, went a bit further, like *Animal House*, with John Belushi famously peeping in windows in the girls' dorm, Sarah Holcomb getting devirginated at the frat and Mary Louise Weller getting her clothes ripped off during the big parade; *Saturday Night Fever*, where "loose women" continually throw themselves at "stud" John Travolta; *American Graffiti*, where "loose woman" Candy Clark spends most of the movie seducing "nerd" Charles Martin Smith—and, of course, *The Rocky Horror Picture Show*, which glorifies transvestism and sexual exploration—and after nearly 40 years, still plays midnight venues across the country.

But two '70s classics deserve special mention. First, there's *Carnal Knowledge*, the sexual "coming of age" dramedy that got busted for "obscenity" in Georgia in 1972, the manager of the theater where it was shown convicted, which conviction was upheld by the Georgia Supreme Court until overturned by the U.S. Supreme Court, which wrote, "Our own viewing of the film satisfies us that *Carnal Knowledge* could not be found ... to depict sexual conduct in a patently offensive way. Nothing in the movie falls within ... material which may constitutionally be found ... "patently offensive" ... While the subject matter of the picture is, in a broader sense, sex... There is no exhibition whatever of the actors' genitals, lewd or otherwise, during these scenes. There are occasional scenes of nudity, but nudity alone is not enough to make material legally obscene..."

And then there's *Rocky*, the world-famous boxing drama starring Sylvester Stallone, a statue of whom still graces the steps of the Philadelphia Museum of Art in PA—pretty impressive, considering that Stallone began his film career in 1970's *The Party at Kitty and Stud's*,[1] a softcore porn film later reedited and renamed *Italian Stallion* and now no longer available, that apparently had Stallone "seeing naked women wherever he goes."

But guess what? Somehow, CNN didn't manage to cover the one '70s film that pretty much every adult in the world knows about, and many have seen, often more than once: *Deep Throat*.[2]

Deep Throat premiered at the World Theater in Times Square on June 12, 1972, and played off and on in that area for more than 20 years, even though Judge Joel J. Tyler found the movie to be obscene[3] less than a year later, on March 1, 1973. (We can't say the judge was religiously motivated, but he did describe the film as "this feast of carrion and squalor," "a nadir of decadence" and "a Sodom and Gomorrah gone wild before the fire.")

Nevertheless, the public liked the film, depositing $1 million in the theater's coffers in just the first seven weeks after it opened, and another $2 million by the end of six months. Altogether, that's about $18 million in 2019 dollars, making it one of the ten top-grossing films of all time up to that point. Since then, between theatrical and videotape/DVD sales, the film has earned at least $100 million, according to the FBI, though other knowledgeable sources put the figure as high as $600 million, and Randy Barbato and Fenton Bailey, writers/directors/producers of the documentary *Inside Deep Throat*, suggest the figure could be even higher.

In terms of historical significance, *Deep Throat* was the first hardcore movie to play multiple mainstream venues in major cities throughout the country, and is consistently either at or close to the top of nearly every list of the major sexually explicit movies of all time, placing #28 in the Internet Movie Database's list, and is the first film mentioned in the documentary *X-Rated: The Greatest Adult Movies of All Time*.

In terms of cultural significance, consider this partial list of celebrities and other famous people who acknowledge having seen the film: Roger Ebert, Martin Scorsese, Brian De Palma, Truman Capote, Jack Nicholson, Johnny Carson, Barbara Walters, Doris Day, Warren Beatty, Richard Dreyfuss, Spiro Agnew, Nora Ephron, Pauline Kael, former Gov. (and current presidential candidate) John Hickenlooper (who took his mom also[4]), Brian Grazer, John Waters, Hugh Hefner, Gore Vidal, Bill Maher, Dr. Ruth Westheimer, Larry Flynt, Erica Jong, Xaviera Hollander, Dick Cavett, Helen Gurley Brown, Camille Paglia, Norman Mailer—the list goes on. But perhaps most importantly, Bob Woodward, half of the reporting team that covered the Watergate scandal for *The Washington Post*, has also seen it, and may have been the one who suggested to FBI agent W. Mark Felt that he use "Deep Throat" as his cover name when providing Woodward and partner Carl Bernstein with inside information about how the Watergate investigation was going.

Besides *Inside Deep Throat*, the movie also inspired the stage play *The Deep Throat Sex Scandal*, which played briefly in New York City and for about ten weeks in Los Angeles, and featured several adult stars in the cast during that run.

So, there's no question that CNN missed a bet by not including this blockbuster in its greatest '70s films episode—but you know who else has missed that same bet? The National Film Registry[5]—and *that* problem is continuing.

See, each year, the National Film Registry inducts 25 films that are "culturally, historically or aesthetically significant," and *Deep Throat* (as well as several other XXX films) easily meet those criteria, as well as being more than ten years old, another requirement. The FAQ for the Registry also states, "These films are not selected as the 'best' American films of all time, but rather as works of enduring importance to American culture. They reflect who we are as a people and as a nation." Well, according to an article on Medium.com, "The porn industry makes... close to $15 billion in profit... more money than Major League Baseball, The NFL and The NBA combined." Seems to us that that clearly "reflect[s] who we are as a people and as a nation"—and *Deep Throat* is the best-known example of that.

Fact is, the National Film Registry doesn't have a single XXX movie in its list—*not one* out of the 1,000 films that have been added to the Registry since it began in 1989.

But the deadline for nominating films for inclusion in 2019 is September 15, and this author's list of 2019 nominees has already been submitted.

On the nomination form,[6] it asks nominators to "tell [the Registry] more about the films you've nominated today." This response was given:

"Can't help but notice that there is not a single sexually explicit film nominated for or already inducted into the Registry, and some of those such as *Deep Throat*, *The Devil In Miss Jones*, *Behind the Green Door* and *Debbie Does Dallas* are well-known to the majority of the American (if not the world) public, are still popular after more than 45 years of existence, and are clearly culturally and historically (and possibly even aesthetically, since tastes vary) significant. Hell, the FBI source in the Watergate hearings was called 'Deep Throat'!"

One person saying such things might not make that much of a difference... but 100,000 or a million porn fans writing similar thoughts just might!

In my opinion (which probably isn't shared by most), if people were more enlightened sexually, so-called "revenge porn" wouldn't be such a big deal. So what if someone is shown nude or mid-coitus, even if they didn't know they were being photographed/ videoed? But people aren't so enlightened, so revenge porn continues to be a problem.

REP. KATIE HILL: THE MOST IMPORTANT 'REVENGE PORN' CASE?

October 29, 2019

Rep. Katie Hill of California's 25th District wasn't supposed to win the 2018 election. After all, the seat had been held by Republicans since the 1992 elections, first by Howard McKeon, then Steve Knight did a four year stint. He's the one Hill defeated, in part because of her election platform which included reforming healthcare, rebuilding the middle class, addressing income inequality and affordable housing, and getting big money out of politics. On that last note, she ran her entire campaign without accepting a dime from corporate PACs, amassing a little over $1 million from 5,100 individual donors.

And of course, the other reason Hill won was that her district, which includes the northern San Fernando Valley and parts of Santa Barbara and San Bernardino Counties, not to mention Californians in general, had become sick of Donald Trump and his cronies screwing everyone from the working poor to veterans to immigrants to environmentalists... the list goes on.

Of course, Hill is just 32 years old, so one might almost expect that she'd done a bit of sexual experimentation—she's admitted to being bisexual—and of course, that's part of what did her in, politically. But according to most political commentators, what actually forced her resignation this past Sunday was the fact that nude photos of her and one of her 2018 campaign staffers surfaced on the far-right-wing website RedState.com, as well as in the UK's *The Daily Mail*,[1] all thanks to her soon-to-be ex-husband Kenny Heslep, who'd joined the women for a threeway or two—and those who think religio-conservative media in the U.S. aren't making bales of hay out of this just haven't been keeping up with the news for the past decade or so.

Or as *The Guardian*'s (UK) Moira Donegan[2] puts it, "Hill's own conduct—tacky, unprofessional, and ill-advised as it was—pales in comparison to what is being done to her, which amounts to a misogynist rightwing smear campaign. The publication of the nude photograph belies any claim RedState and other Republicans may make to being concerned about the ethics of Hill's conduct."

After all, a picture's worth a thousand words, right?

"Revenge porn, an increasingly common tactic of misogynist rancor, is ... a particularly hateful gesture, meant to humiliate and degrade its target," Donegan continued. "The very point of revenge porn is to discredit its victims, because in the misogynist logic that propels it, for a woman to have sex is to surrender her claims to privacy, authority, or the belief or sympathy of others. What Hill's attackers want us to think is that if she were worthy of being a congressperson, she wouldn't be having sex at all."

And of course, there was no need for RedState and others to publish the nude photos. After all, they'd already published some intimate text messages between Hill and the staffer... but a picture's worth a thousand words, right?

"The use of certain images, while holding back on more scandalous ones, showed editorial restraint many outlets seem to have forgotten—that you can post enough to show something happened without posting too much and losing the point of the story," RedState[3] senior editor Joe Cunningham laughably claimed, implying that there were more sexually explicit photos of Hill out there to whet the appetite of the ravenous, anti-sex conservative hordes.

(By the way, RedState is part of Townhall Media, which sends out Townhall Daily, a collection of conservatives' writings. Townhall Media, in turn, is an affiliate of the Salem Media Group, which according to Right Wing Watch claims to have "successfully reached audiences interested in Christian and family-themed content and conservative values" for over 40 years. And what's more "family-themed" and "conservative" than nude photos of a female Democratic politician?)

So let's be as clear about this as was sex-positive feminist journalist Jessica Valenti, who wrote[4] on Medium.com, "Revenge porn is a form of domestic and sexual abuse. It's a way to control, humiliate, and punish. ... Make no mistake: Hill was the victim of a crime, but she's the only person being punished."

Make that "punished in spades." Just today, Newsbusters.org, formerly the Christian News Service, published three—count 'em, *three*—articles on Hill, mostly dealing with how the major TV networks have been handling the news, terming it a "bizarre sex scandal"—and mostly claiming that those mainstream sources haven't spent enough time "examining" (that is, bashing) Hill's behavior. Altogether, Newsbusters has published six screeds on Hill since RedState broke the original story.

And while a couple of news outlets have made mention of Hill being the victim of a "double standard," that point was driven home by Jezebel.com's Esther Wang,[5] who noted, "California Representative Duncan Hunter, after all, is alleged[6] to have had numerous affairs in recent years, including with a member of his staff, the aide of another Republican member of Congress, and several lobbyists. These romantic and sexual relationships came to light when the Justice Department charged Hunter with illegally using campaign funds to pay for everything from his vacations to his boozing habits and found that he had spent thousands to finance his affairs. Yet despite these both ethical and criminal violations, Hunter, whose federal trial[7] will begin next January, remains in office."

As for Hill herself, she's planning to sue *The Daily Mail* for claiming that Hill has a Nazi symbol, an iron cross, tattooed somewhere on her body, but her political career has at least been put on hold—if not deep-sixed entirely. California Gov. Gavin Newsom is empowered to choose a replacement for Hill until a special election can be held, and considering that the same collection of proto-fascists remains in power in Washington, it seems likely that another Democrat will be chosen to replace her, though just when that election will take place is unknown.

UPDATE: Here's a shocker: The reporter who supplied the nude photos of Hill to RedState.com, *The Daily Mail* and others, Jennifer Van Laar,[8] used to work for—surprise, surprise!—her Repugnican opponents.

"After publishing the photos and shortly before Hill's resignation, Van Laar posted a tweet urging followers to 'help us flip' Hill's seat by backing Republican candidate Mike Garcia," Salon.com reported. "In a later tweet, Van Laar promoted former Rep. Steve Knight, R-Calif., who lost to Hill in 2018, in hopes that he would run for the seat again."

Religious prejudice against the sexually sane creeps in pretty much everywhere, but to deny a legitimate, legal *business the same tide-over loans that have been approved for every other business should be illegal—and probably is. And guess what? That's exactly what the SBA did—until some courts (but sadly, not others) stopped them.*

GOOD NEWS: ADULT BUSINESSES CAN APPLY FOR SBA DISASTER LOANS!

April 3, 2020

Earlier this week, *AVN* called the adult industry's attention to the sex-negative prejudices[1] built into the Small Business Administration's Economic Injury Disaster Loan Program, whose application states that a business is barred from applying for such a loan if it "present[s] live performances of a prurient sexual nature or derive[s] directly or indirectly more than de minimis gross revenue through the sale of products or services, or the presentation of any depictions or displays, of a prurient sexual nature."

In explaining that clause of the application, *AVN* looked to a mainstream dictionary's definition of the word "prurient"—and that was wrong. It's the *legal* definition of "prurient" that's applicable here, and several First Amendment attorneys called that fact to our attention.

"It is true that the application form does require that the applicant state that they are not involved with prurient sexually-oriented activities," noted prominent First Amendment attorney Lawrence Walters. "However, I believe a valid argument can be made that adult businesses are not involved with prurient sexual activities because prurience has been defined in case law to mean a 'shameful or morbid interest in sexuality,' and I believe adult businesses could validly take the position that they're involved with a *healthy* interest in human sexuality and not a shameful or morbid interest. So ultimately, it may come down to a court interpreting, first off, whether the exclusion applies to a particular adult business, and secondly, if the loan was denied based on this exclusion, whether that is constitutional, and I believe that denying a loan based on the content of entertainment or speech would be an unconstitutional conditioning of a government benefit."

It's important to note that every obscenity case involving adult content—tapes, DVDs, magazines, websites—has hinged on whether the material was "prurient" in nature.

"It is critical to recognize that that the U.S. Supreme Court has equated 'prurient interest' to a 'shameful or morbid interest in sex, nudity, or excretion'," explained adult defense attorney and legal scholar Reed Lee. "This goes back at least to the *Memoirs* case[2] in the mid-1960s. It was the primary vehicle for narrowing the category of the legally obscene to almost nothing. When I was doing obscenity defenses 25-30 years ago, we had quick acquittals when the jury got this definition of 'prurient' (and particularly when they heard that 'morbid' means 'of or pertaining to disease') And those cases involved what would still pass for fairly edgy hardcore today."

"Both Free Speech Coalition and the First Amendment Lawyers Association are looking at this problem," Lee continued. "For myself, I am inclined to think that a well-advised adult business can legitimately check the box disclaiming prurience (because its wares are not 'shameful or morbid') and perhaps fly under the radar and get what others are getting by way of relief."

Indeed, it's the "flying under the radar" that worries the attorneys.

"Ultimately, it will come down to some loan processor at the SBA or potentially their legal department deciding whether or not the prurient exclusion applies to any particular adult business," Walters predicted, "and that is inherently the problem: You are allowing government agents to make decisions on critical disaster relief based on the content of speech, which flies in the face of the First Amendment."

Interestingly, the prohibition against businesses of a "prurient sexual nature" being unable to receive SBA loans dates back to the regulation's entry into the Code of Federal Regulations back in 1996, found at 13 C.F.R. §120.110. Subsection (p) of that section has language mirroring the prohibition in the eligibility requirements for the Economic Injury Disaster Loan program—but as First Amendment attorney J. Michael Murray (who's still waiting for the Third Circuit's decision in the 2257 lawsuit he's been prosecuting) points out, that particular section has been ignored in the eligibility requirements for small businesses to the Payroll Protection

Program just rolled out in the $2 trillion CARES Act which was just signed into law by President Trump.

"If you go to the SBA's website and look at their Payroll Protection Program, they've got a sample of an application form that does not include that question, and that's the program that they're trying to finalize to go into effect on April 3. That's based on the bill that Congress passed about a week ago, the $2 trillion stimulus bill... Now, with the COVID-19 bill, I think small businesses can get a disaster loan, [and] I think a few adult businesses may have applied, and yes, that appears to still be on that form, but the other program that they're going to start to implement, which is that you can borrow up to two-and-a-half months' worth of your payroll, and if you use it for your payroll, at the end of the period—you can use it for like eight weeks, and at the end of the period, you can apply for loan forgiveness, and the principal amount of that loan will be forgiven.

"You actually go through the bank; the SBA guarantees it," he continued, "and on that program, if you go to their website, you'll see that there's a sample application form for that program, which is the one that I think a lot of adult businesses currently might be trying to use, and it looks like that 'prurient sexual nature' exclusion won't apply to that program at all, and that makes sense, because if you read the statute that was passed, it would suggest that there shouldn't be an exclusion. In fact, there's a bunch of exclusions that would probably not apply to that."

But regarding the Economic Injury Disaster Loan program, however, Murray is in total agreement with his First Amendment litigator colleagues.

"As far as we First Amendment lawyers are concerned, the 'prurient' of a 'prurient sexual nature' is really a legal term of art that goes back to the legal definition of obscenity," Murray told *AVN*, "and remember, 'prurient' is a 'shameful or morbid or unhealthy interest in sex,' and the adult industry, their materials don't appeal to a shameful or morbid interest in sex; they appeal to a normal, healthy interest in sex and they're perfectly accepted by contemporary community standards. So the adult industry takes the position that none of its materials would be of a prurient sexual nature because that's a legal term of art going way back to the definition of obscenity, which the U.S. Supreme Court talked about way back in 1954 in *Roth v. United States*, and then of course it was incorporated in the first part of the three-part test for obscenity in *Miller v. California* in 1973. So if the government were to use that criterion as an exclusion and attempt to apply it to adult businesses, first of all, there would be an argument that it doesn't apply because it doesn't meet the prurient sexual nature test but if the government were to take that position, then you've got a content-based regulation that we would argue is unconstitutional under the First Amendment because it's a content-based distinction that can't meet the test for strict scrutiny, or even intermediate scrutiny if that were the test, and the argument would be that it doesn't meet it."

But if there's one thing that all of the First Amendment attorneys *AVN* consulted agreed upon, it's that adult businesses of any type that want to apply for either an Economic Injury Disaster Loan or the Payroll Protection Program should first discuss the idea with their attorneys, who may be able to help craft the application so that adheres to all the guidelines set forth in the law.

Netflix, being essentially a cable channel, isn't subject to the same restrictions as a mainstream TV channel—but that hasn't stopped The Godly from trying to make them toe the censorship line.

RUH-ROH! PTC DISCOVERS THEY SAY 'SHIT' ON NETFLIX. CHAOS ENSUES

April 30, 2020

JESUSLAND—Anyone who spends any appreciable amount of time around teens and pre-teens, say 11 years of age and up, has likely heard the kid at one time or other utter the magic satanic words "shit" and/or "fuck." There's a pretty good reason for that: Everyone shits, and a fair number of people aged 16 and up fuck, and even a few younger kids are aware of that. Life doesn't exist without shitting and fucking.

One would think that even the censor-happy crowd at the ultra-conservative Parents Television Council would have tipped to those truisms, but no. Rather, they've just released a "report" titled "Teen-Targeted Broadcast TV Can Be Vulgar...But *Stranger Things* Are Happening On Netflix,"[1] where apparently PTC supporters sat down and watched 255 episodes found in 23 Netflix categories rated TV-14 or TV-MA by the company—via VidAngel,[2] of course, the company that automatically censors content for its viewers—and wouldn't'cha know it? "*[E]very single program* **contained multiple uses of the "s-word" and almost every Netflix original program rated as appropriate for teens (TV-14) had at least one use of the "f-word."** [Emphasis in original]

"Our findings clearly demonstrate that Netflix is marketing explicit content to children," charged PTC President Tim Winter. "Explicit profanity like the 'f-word' and 's-word' are nearly ubiquitous on Netflix's Teen programming, revealing an apparent disconnect between what Netflix deems appropriate for teen viewers and what the average parent might consider appropriate."

"Shit" and "fuck" utterances are "explicit programming"? What world do these people live in? (Word of warning: Don't click on any website that has "hub" as part of its name.)

PTC has a problem with the fact that 25.9 percent of the "teen" titles offered on Netflix have a TV-14 rating, while 40.8 percent are rated TV-MA (as in "mature audiences"—and who says a modern-day teen can't be reasonably "mature," at least when it comes to the TV fare he or she watches?) Worse, though, are the "Netflix Originals" series, where 31.3 percent are TV-14 and a whopping 55.2 percent are TV-MA. Among the worst offenders in that category are the sci-fi/drama/horror series *Stranger Things*, with 257 mentions of "shit" and 11 "fuck"s (yes, apparently someone counted all those naughty words); *Atypical*, a coming-of-age series featuring an autistic teen looking for romance, with 58 shits and 3 fucks; low-rated sci-fi drama *Rim of the World* with 44 shits and 5 fucks; supernatural-themed drama *Locke & Key*, with 52 shits and 2 fucks; and the one season of high school-centered comedy/drama *On My Block* that VidAngel had available, which had 48 shits and 4 fucks.

"Words like 'f*ck' and '"sh*t' were once unthinkable for dialogue on programs rated as appropriate for 13- and 14-year old children; but on Netflix they are becoming ubiquitous," the PTC report claims. "Either the content is being rated inaccurately, or there has been considerable 'ratings creep' with the criteria used to determine an age-based rating. Neither option allows parents to do their job effectively."

The question is, what's "effective" or worthwhile about shielding kids from hearing the words "shit" or "fuck"? If a kid is 13 years old or older, he or she needs to know what "fuck" means lest the (presumably hetero) kid starts fooling around, a penis goes into a vulva and there's a surprise nine months later. And as for "shit," what possible harm is there for a kid to learn one of the words commonly used for what comes out of his/her ass?

If all of that is "ratings creep," it's high time for it—and although PTC makes the bulk of its money scaring parents into trying to protect their kids from everyday words and images that, short of living in a cave on a mountainside, they are bound to see as they go through life, the company must be getting pretty desperate if they're targeting "shit" and "fuck."

So... which high school course is most likely to do mainstream students the most good in the long run? Physics? Woodshop? Home Ec? Or Sex Ed, where they learn how not to get pregnant/be a father?

OP-ED: SEX ED IN PUBLIC SCHOOLS? NOT IF FRC CAN HELP IT!

May 27, 2020

WASHINGTON, D.C.—Adult performers come from a variety of backgrounds. Some were raised by the modern-day equivalent of hippies, learning early on that sex is no biggie, while others come from incredibly strict religious upbringings, and for them, having sex on camera is a form of rebellion—and then, of course, there's the majority who simply like sex, aren't afraid of it, and see no reason why others shouldn't enjoy such pleasures as well, even if vicariously, by watching them Do It on camera. But if the Religious Right has its way, expect the adult industry to become overrun with the rebellious ones—who very possibly may also be supporting a family because they got poor contraceptive training in their early teens.

Enter Cathy Ruse, who has what passes for a distinguished CV in Religious Right circles. She's an attorney, a senior fellow at the ultra-religiously conservative Family Research Council (FRC) and director of the organization's "Human Dignity" wing, and in the waning days of the Clinton presidency, she was Chief Counsel to the Constitution Subcommittee in the (Republican majority) U.S. House of Representatives, where she had "oversight of civil rights and human rights issues" as well as "religious freedom and free speech matters." And now, Cathy has authored (or at least oversaw the creation of) a new FRC brochure, "Sex Education In Public Schools: Sexualization of Children and LGBT Indoctrination"[1]! (The .pdf may be downloaded from FRC's website.)

The brochure definitely starts off with a bang:

"Did you know that...

• "Some public schools teach children they could be born in the wrong body?

• "Young teens are shown videos with techniques to pleasure their sex partners?

• "Students are told how to get secret abortions without telling their parents?"

Translation:

• Some public school teachers are aware of the fact that not every kid feels that their gender identity corresponds with their genitalia at birth, and actually talk to them about it.

• Some sex ed courses actually teach that sex can not only be enjoyable but that there are techniques to help bring that enjoyment about.

• Some parents are so whacked in the head that if they found out their daughter was pregnant, they'd make sure she carries the child to term, no matter how the girl herself feels about it. (Sound familiar, some stars of my acquaintance?)

But Cathy knows her audience for this crap: "Most of us remember what sex education was like when we were in school. A couple of uncomfortable hours. Line drawings showing human growth and development. Admonitions to be careful, respect others, and save sex for marriage... Talking to children about sexuality... is emotionally charged, even under the best of circumstances."

No, it isn't—unless you make it so by being so afraid of sex and any discussion of it that you make the kids crazy by osmosis—and to an extent, Ruse understands this: "Frankly, most parents really don't want to have these awkward conversations with their children. Parents instinctively don't want to disturb the natural innocence and sexual latency period before puberty." Yeah! Why discuss sex with kids until just as their hormones have begun coursing through their veins and they're noticing that the opposite sex (or even the same sex) seems attractive—and before anyone's told them what could happen if they decide to experiment with those attractive partners?

But Ruse's real target is what's called "Comprehensive Sexuality Education" (CSE), which she claims has "failure rates as high as 87 percent for school-based sex ed programs." And where does that stat come from?

The Utah-based Institute for Research & Evaluation,[2] a pro-abstinence organization!

"Year after year, sex ed programs push the limits on what is appropriate, both in terms of the material presented to students and the age at which it is presented," Ruse claims. "In many school districts today, lessons introduce sexual concepts to very young children and promote risky sexual behavior to vulnerable teens and pre-teens."

Leaving aside the question of which teens and pre-teens are "vulnerable," probably from their having been indoctrinated by ignorant parents and clergy, Ruse clearly conflates "risky sexual behavior" with simply explaining to teens how sex actually works—something they likely aren't getting anywhere else except maybe on the proverbial playground.

And sure enough, the very next paragraph states, "What was once simply imparting science-based information and skills to save sex until marriage has now become creating young radical sexual ideologues with the desire to exercise their 'sexual rights.' Preparing children to have sex with multiple partners over the course of a lifetime seems to be a basic assumption underlying much of sexual education content. Needless to say, this is not in line with Christian and other faith views on sexuality and marriage."

No shit! Of course, "science-based information and skills to save sex until marriage" is just a disguised term for abstinence education, a form of sex ed that study after study have shown is entirely useless in preventing teen pregnancies and sexually transmitted diseases—not to mention, *real* sex ed hardly "prepar[es] children to have sex with multiple partners"; it just lets them know that sometimes finding the person (or persons) you'd like to share the rest of your life with may take some experimentation—you know; like *science*!

And all that is in just the first six pages of this 56-page screed! Topics that follow include bashing sex ed programs in California, Texas, Indiana and Virginia—but the overriding target is Planned Parenthood's "Get Real" sex ed curriculum, where Ruse has a problem with what one "Get Real" trainer told teens in Massachusetts: "Building skills around consent means moving beyond the 'how to say no' model of teaching refusal skills to also *teach young people how to ask for consent...*" [Emphasis courtesy of Ruse]

Yeah! "Heaven" forbid that a guy (or gal) actually ask a potential lover for consent! Better to just pick them up at a bar and get them too drunk to know what's being done to them!

"Consenting to a sex act does not make that act healthy, acceptable, or safe," Ruse claims. Maybe not, but it does make it *consensual*!

Ruse is a big fan of abstinence "education," and not only do some states make abstinence ed the only approved form of sex ed, but recent federal legislation has provided millions of dollars for it. But Ruse saves her gravest ire for what she calls "LGBTQ Indoctrination."

"Lessons can be highly manipulative—carefully designed to get children to approve of the concept of sexual rights and fluid sexual 'identities,' and to reject their religious beliefs, the authority of their parents, and even physical reality itself," Ruse claims. "The LGBTQ movement demands that homosexual relationships be presented to children as good, healthy, and equal in every way to heterosexuality within man-woman marriage. Many sex ed developers and providers are all too happy to comply... Can you define 'consensual non-monogamy' or use 'polyamory' in a sentence? Your children might soon be able to... Have you heard of PrEP? Most parents haven't. But it is being promoted to children in public schools today."

YEAH! After all, it wouldn't be right to teach kids how to avoid contracting a deadly disease from their sin!

But of course, the worst are transsexuals:

"Many public schools are beginning to teach the radical, anti-science proposition that biological sex is meaningless, that some kids are born in the wrong body, and that some girls have penises, too. The American College of Pediatricians calls this psychological child abuse." (According to the Southern Poverty Law Center,[3] "The American College of Pediatricians is a fringe anti-LGBT hate group that masquerades as the premier U.S. association of pediatricians to push anti-LGBT junk science, primarily via far-right conservative media and filing amicus briefs in cases related to gay adoption and marriage equality.")

Ruse clearly has a real hard-on (sorry) for anything transgender, devoting several pages of the pamphlet to the subject. After castigating schools for "opening girls' bathrooms to biological male students who identify as girls," she lists what she calls "model transgender school policies," about which she has just as much enthusiasm as she does for actual sex ed. They include:

- School-wide affirmation of a student's trans-gender identity
- Forced use of false pronouns
- Opening of private spaces and sports teams to the opposite sex
- Adding "born in the wrong body" lessons to sex ed

And "god" forbid that the schools teach "LGBTQ history"!

Worse, "Every October, the public schools in Evanston, Illinois go all out for LGBTQ+ Equity Week. Kindergarten children get story time with books like *My Princess Boy* and *I Am Jazz* about Jazz Jennings, breakout star of the transgender movement. First-graders are tasked with making 'pride' flags and practicing gender-fluid pronouns. Sixth graders learn about various LGBTQ+ activists and their strategies."

The horror! THE HORROR!!!

Ruse also has a list of some of the things she considers sex ed no-nos. She's really upset that many actual sex ed curricula include, retaining her numbering: 2) "Teach[ing] children to consent to sex" (what the hell is it with her and consent???); 3) "Normal[izing] anal and oral sex" (how sad that she's never blown her husband or allowed him to fuck her ass); 5) "Promot[ing] sexual pleasure" (YEAH! Because sex should never be "fun"!); 6) "Promot[ing] solo and/or mutual masturbation" (because kids shouldn't have alternatives to fucking and getting pregnant); 7) "Promot[ing] condom use in inappropriate ways" (she *really* doesn't like them on bananas—or penis models); 10) "Promot[ing] transgender ideology" (otherwise known as telling kids trans people exist and they're not spawns of Satan); and of course the biggie, 13) "Undermin[ing] traditional values and beliefs" (because as we all know, whatever sex stuff happened yesterday needs to happen tomorrow as well.)

Truth is, Ruse is just following a long Christian tradition of misinforming people about sex and relationships—indeed, she described her work with FRC as "almost like working for the church"—and she's hardly the only one.

Take, for instance, Lori Alexander, who writes a sexual advice column called "The Transformed Wife"[4]—and boy, does she have lessons for women!

"Sex was created for marriage," she wrote on May 14. "Sex was created for child bearing. Sex was created for pleasure ONLY in marriage. Sex was created to build families and nations, but the way sex is being used today, it is tearing all of these down and destroying our nation." (Must be why we have a pandemic going on right now...)

Not to mention, "Once sex enters into a relationship, the emotions take over and all sense of reason is gone. It distorts the relationship and turns it far from God's intended purpose."

And then there's this bit of marital wisdom regarding how ready wives should be for their husbands to fuck them: "We live our lives by doing what's right, by obeying God, even when we don't feel like it. Yes, and that even includes sex. You know, how long does it take?! Got it, ladies? *It'll just take two minutes. What are you so damn upset about?!*" [Emphasis courtesy of Alexander]

The point is, there's no shortage of "experts" out there who'll be only too happy to tell you how to handle every aspect of your sex life—and they start by getting the youngest among us "in line." After all, it was Aristotle who said, "Give me a child until he is 7 and I will show you the man"—so think what these assholes could do with a few *more* years!

Guess what? Prostitution has been around since the beginning of civilization, and most countries didn't give a shit about it for a very long time!

NINTH CIRCUIT DEEP-SIXES NEVADA ANTI-BROTHEL LAWSUIT

December 11, 2020

SAN FRANCISCO—The appeal of the long-running lawsuit[1] filed by the National Center on Sexual Exploitation (NCOSE) on behalf of three women who claim they were forced into prostitution in Nevada brothels, and that those brothels, which are legal in several Nevada counties, should be shut down as both violations of the federal Mann Act and the anti-slavery amendment to the U.S. Constitution, has just been dismissed[2] by a three-judge panel of the Ninth Circuit Court of Appeals, which agreed with a lower court that the plaintiffs all lack standing to sue.

The prime mover behind the suit was Rebekah Charleston,[3] who claimed that not only was she held captive by a man acting as a pimp and forced to supply sexual services in "one of Nevada's most famous brothels," but that because such brothels continue to exist, she and her fellow appellants are "under threat of an actual and imminent injury" and suffer an "exponentially higher risk of revictimization" because, according to them, "people typically re-enter commercial sexual exploitation multiple times before permanently leaving."

Trouble was, the appeals court noted that it must be the appellants themselves who suffer that "higher risk of revictimization" and are "at risk of 'actual and imminent' harm" in order to have standing in the case, not random women working in the brothels for whatever reason.

Moreover, the court dismissed the appellants' claim that they suffer ongoing injury (which would be one basis of standing) because "the physical and psychological effects of sex trafficking and prostitution endure long after victims escape from their... exploitation," because the U.S. Supreme Court has previously ruled that "[t]he emotional consequences of a prior act simply are not a sufficient basis for an injunction absent a real and immediate threat of future injury by the defendant"—and it's clear that none of these appellants are in any danger of future harm by the mere existence of legal brothels.

The appeals panel also declined to recognize the appellants as representatives of any third parties (presumably, the prostitutes who continue to work in Nevada's brothels), since although attorney Neal Kuman Katyal argued in a 1993 Yale Law Journal that, "Third-party standing may be the only practical way to assert the rights of enslaved human beings," the court declined to read the appellants' arguments as invoking third-party standing "because they neither expressly do so nor cite any relevant cases."

Curiously, a footnote to the opinion reads, "This disposition is not appropriate for publication and is not precedent except as provided by Ninth Circuit Rule 36-3," which states that "Unpublished dispositions and orders of this Court are not precedent, except when relevant under the doctrine of law of the case or rules of claim preclusion or issue preclusion," though such dispositions issued after January 1, 2007 "may be cited to the courts of this circuit in accordance with [Federal Rules of Appellate Procedure] 32.1." What that likely means is that the disposition dismissing the Charleston, et al case is not likely to be cited in any subsequent case of a similar nature unless the same claims or issues are presented.

All the information in this article was available within days after the shooting, but for some reason, no one put it together quite like this. BTW, Tiesto is a Dutch DJ quite popular in dance clubs.

WHAT WERE THE ATLANTA MASSAGE PARLOR MURDERS REALLY ABOUT?

(Hint: Sex work)

March 17, 2021

ATLANTA, Ga.—On Tuesday, March 16, Robert Aaron Long, 21, using a gun he'd purchased *that day*, went to three massage parlors in the Atlanta area and opened fire, killing eight people and wounding another, most of whom were Asian—and that last fact became the headline that most news reports ran with: "Man Goes On Anti-Asian Rampage."

Only later was that "gimme" conclusion challenged, and from everything that's come out since then, there's good reason to believe that whether Long's victims were Asian played a much lesser role in his spree than the fact that most of them were sex workers.

Let's consider the facts:

• The Cherokee County Sheriff's Office identified those killed in the first shooting as Delaina Ashley Yaun, age 33; Paul Andre Michels, age 54; Xiaojie Yan, age 49; and Daoyou Feng, age 44—three of four were Asian—while all of the rest were Asian as well: Soon Chung Park age 74; Hyun Jung Grant age 51; Sun Cha Kim age 69; and Yong Ae Yue, age 63—none of whom would be described as "spring chickens." But as anyone familiar with the adult industry is well aware, age rarely prevents an adult actress (sex worker) from appearing in an adult movie—in fact, several actresses of our acquaintance are in their 50s, and even a few are over 60—with "Mothers I'd Like to Fuck" (MILFs) being one of the industry's most popular genres. And not only can MILFs appear in porn, they can also ply their sexual trade in massage parlors, bordellos, swing clubs, dungeons, etc. Unfortunately for these victims, massage parlors are the only such businesses that advertise openly—and in the case of the three parlors targeted here, all displayed plenty of neon outside their doors so it'd be hard to miss them in any case.

Randy Park, son of victim Hyun Jung Grant, 51, told[1] *The Daily Beast* that, "She loved 'dancing and partying,' She would always try to convince me to go out. She loved going to clubs. She loved Tiesto. She was like a teenager."

• As Elizabeth Nolan Brown reported[2] on the Reason.com website, "Long allegedly told police he had been a customer of at least two of the businesses, that he was addicted to sex, and that he wanted to eradicate his temptation."

• According to his former roommate Tyler Bayless, Long was treated at least twice at an evangelical "sex addiction" clinic named HopeQuest,[3] which advertises its treatment of "sex addiction" and "pornography addiction" in addition to drugs, alcohol and gambling, located about a mile from Young's Asian Massage, the first spa that Long shot up.

• As *The New York Times* noted, "'Sex addiction' is not an established psychiatric diagnosis, and there is a debate in the mental health community about how to define and treat compulsive sexual behavior." In fact, so-called "sex addiction" is likely a manifestation of obsessive-compulsive disorder, where the sufferer spends an inordinate amount of time thinking about the object of their obsession, and may act out compulsively regarding that obsession. Such obsessions may present themselves in such activities as avoiding stepping on cracks in the sidewalk, compulsively washing one's hands, even praying—or much, much worse, as was the case here.

• According to the *New York Post*,[4] "Nico Straughan, who went to high school with Long, described him as 'super nice, super Christian' and 'very quiet,' adding that Long walked around the school with a Bible."

• Long grew up in a fundamentalist Christian family and attended Crabapple First Baptist Church from a young age. The church, where Long had been baptized, had posted a celebratory video of Long explaining his "journey to finding Jesus," only to take it down once his crimes became known.

"The Long family have been members of our church for many years," Crabapple posted on its website. "We watched Aaron grow up and accepted him into church membership when he made his own profession of faith in Jesus Christ."

• According to an interview[5] with Samuel Perry, an associate professor of sociology at Oklahoma University who studies sex, race, gender and faith, "The subculture of evangelical purity culture says, 'This is an addiction like heroin is an addiction. You need to be so serious about this violation in your life that you're willing to go to extremes to avoid it.' And that's where it gets a little bit worrisome. When the New Testament talks about gouging out your eye and cutting off your hand in order to avoid lust, the implication is 'I need to be willing to do anything to avoid this kind of sin'."

• According to researcher Kelsey Burke, "Young white Protestant men like Long are indeed the most likely group to perceive themselves to be addicted to pornography, even though they use it less frequently than their secular counterparts. These 'addictions' may not be traditionally diagnosable, but the system that pushes them—and in some cases profits from them—is very real. Many of the people behind this system are deeply rooted in the church and believe not only that young men's sexual desires are pathological but that porn and sex work are an evil temptation that must be criminalized."

• According to sex-positive activist Jessica Valenti's recent column[6] in *The New York Times*, Long "told the police that the women murdered were 'temptations' he needed to 'eliminate'."

• And perhaps most tellingly, according to *Newsweek* magazine,[7] "The suspect in the Atlanta massage parlor shootings was arrested while he was on his way to Florida to target 'some type of porn industry,' officials have said."

• Of note: Asshole reactionary columnist Ann Coulter ended her latest diatribe with the following "thought" on Long's killing spree: "We don't have a lot of women mass shooters, so it's hard to flip the script. But maybe, in the future, whenever a white man is falsely accused of rape (Steven Pagones, the Duke lacrosse players, a fraternity at the University of Virginia) or murder (Darren Wilson, Jake Gardner, Staten Island police officers), white men should fan out across the airwaves to talk about how damn sexy they are."

So it seems pretty clear at this point that the fact that almost all the women Long killed were Asian was less important to him than that they were sex workers... leading to the San Francisco-based Erotic Service Providers Legal Education and Research Project (ESPLERP)[8] and The Sex Workers Outreach Project Sacramento (SWOPSac)[9] to issue a press release condemning "sex addiction" as a justification for the murders. Portions of that press release are as follows:

"The Erotic Service Providers Legal Education and Research Project (ESPLERP) and The Sex Workers Outreach Project Sacramento (SWOP-Sac) today reject law enforcement's excuse that the Atlanta Massage Parlor Murders were because Aaron Long, the shooter, 'was pretty much fed up and kind of at the end of his rope' due to 'sex addiction.'

"Not only does such rhetoric excuse and dismiss murders of sex workers and those close to the sex work community, it also excuses hate crimes against the Asian population, and the targeting of women.

"For law enforcement and the media to allow Aaron Long to use 'sex addiction' as a justification for violence is simply unacceptable. Such rationalization allows Long to evade responsibility and promotes the idea that the perpetrator is just too 'turned on' to control themselves—as if sex workers possess some magical power that renders the assailant irresponsible for their actions. This idea is couched in moral supremacy, and victim-blaming, and perpetuates the belief that the person engaging in sex work is somehow responsible for the violence done to them... In the past year alone, over fifty sex workers were murdered, according to SWOP.

"ESPLERP calls on Congress to immediately pass a national ban on the criminalization of prostitution and reform the immigration laws so as not to leave so many people's lives outside of equal protection."

How nice of the porn haters to try to get "justice" for the alleged "thousands" of women appearing in online videos who they're so sure aren't there because they want to be!

NCOSE BACKS ANOTHER 'JANE DOE' LAWSUIT AGAINST AN ADULT WEBSITE

March 19, 2021

LOS ANGELES—For nearly a decade, the National Center on Sexual Exploitation (NCOSE) has been railing against the presence of sexually explicit material in society, and as far as they're concerned, many (if not all) of the women who appear in such explicit material have either been tricked into appearing in it, or have been sex-trafficked into it by boyfriends, husbands or pimps.

Trouble is, one need only look at the material released by the LA-based legal adult entertainment industry to see what kind of horseshit that claim is—so over the past year or so, NCOSE has turned its attention to tube sites, filing lawsuits for various "Jane Does" who claim that photos and videos of them either nude or engaging in sex acts were posted on the sites, and that at the time the images were recorded, the women/girls were either underage, being forced to participate (what NCOSE calls "sex trafficked") or both.

NCOSE filed its first suit against MindGeek and its corporate parents in February,[1] and that got so much media attention that the organization moved quickly to stay in the headlines, filing another "Jane Doe" suit yesterday in federal court in California against WebGroup Czech Republic (WGCR) and related companies, operators of the tube site XVideos.

Wait a minute, you may say: How could a California court have jurisdiction over an adult company based in the Czech Republic? Shouldn't they have filed the case in the Czech Republic, or the World Court at the Hague?

"The [California] Court may properly exercise personal jurisdiction over all Defendants," the lawsuit claims. "Each of the Defendants maintains minimum contacts with California, such that maintaining this lawsuit does not offend traditional notions of fair play and substantial justice." Seems the plaintiff claims that WGCR and its affiliated companies have "ownership and control" over various Penthouse entities, and since Penthouse's offices are in the Los Angeles area, WGCR is fair game. Also, Defendant VS Media Inc is located in Westlake Village and "manages the XVideos webcam model platform from their California headquarters," and "XVideos directs all those interested in becoming an 'XVideos webcam model' to the California VS Media team stating, 'Once you click submit, a member of our Los Angeles-based staff will contact you to help you complete the setup process for new live cam models.'"

Also implicated are other alleged WGCZ properties, Xnxx.com, Xvideosdaily.com, and Xvideostoday.net.

Finally, on page 8 of the complaint, the plaintiff reveals her claims, that "The Defendants conspired, facilitated, and financially benefited from participating in what they knew or should have known were sex trafficking ventures. In these ventures, Jane Doe and other minors were trafficked and commercially exploited for sex, in violation of law, including but not limited to, the TVPRA, 18 U.S.C. § 1591, et seq.," and that, "Sex traffickers and the Defendants worked together to earn a profit from commercial sex acts and child pornography involving the Plaintiff and Class members."

Sorry; did we forget to mention that Jane Doe claims to be suing "on behalf of herself and all others similarly situated"? What that means is that anyone who's appeared in an explicit video on XVideos might be ripe for joining this lawsuit's "class"—however many thousands of women that might be.

One of NCOSE's/Jane Doe's problems with XVideos is its "download button" which allows for "transferring images and videos, including the child sexual abuse material appearing on the WGCZ Defendants' websites, from their servers to an undisclosed number of child pornographers, child sex traffickers, and pedophiles"—and considering that the site currently offers just over nine and a half million videos, and allows members to "grab our 'embed code' to display any video on another website," if there were a problem with any particular video, it would be difficult for the company to police not just its own site but any site which embedded XVideo videos.

That's a problem MindGeek recently dealt with regarding its Pornhub site, by prohibiting anyone but known entities to upload videos to the site, and attempting to go through its own millions of videos to determine if any performers are underage or appeared to be performing unwillingly. However, at this point, XVideos has not reportedly taken such steps, although the site does have a "content partner program" which allows "verified" users to post videos as long as they have made a video of themselves "that shows that you are a real XVideos viewer."

"The WGCZ communication system combined with the enormous reach and popularity of its website, allowed sex traffickers to market sex trafficking victims, including minors, and connect illegal sex providers and buyers in an anonymous fashion," the complaint claims, adding later, "WGCZ makes it easy for traffickers, rapists, or other would-be criminals to go undetected as account holders who control and recover any associated compensation. WGCZ completely fails to control the torrent of videos available on its sites depicting children being molested, rapes of children and adults, persons who are incapacitated and otherwise unwilling participants."

The complaint also claims that, "Minor victims of sex trafficking and their representatives have contacted WGCZ to remove videos of them from its websites, but WGCZ has refused to do so."

There are a lot more allegations about how WGCZ and its affiliates, most notably ServerStack, which hosts XVideos, do business—although the plaintiff admits that, "In the last two years, Digital Ocean [ServerStack's owner] reported more than 75 instances of child pornography to the National Center for Missing & Exploited Children."

Finally, on page 29 of the complaint, NCOSE gets around to revealing what it claims XVideos did to Jane Doe: That she "was trafficked when she was just fourteen (14) years old"; that "a sex trafficker forced Jane Doe to participate in the creation of videos of adults engaging in sex acts with her" and also "sold her for sex, and some of the sex acts forced upon Jane Doe were recorded on video and uploaded to the xVideos website."

"At least four videos that included Jane Doe being trafficked as a minor have been identified on WGCZ sites," the complaint claims, and that, "Neither XVideos, nor any other website, owned or operated by WGCZ

Defendants undertook any measure to verify Jane Doe's identity or age." Also according to the complaint, "The broad dissemination of child sex abuse material depicting Jane Doe has severely harmed Jane Doe, including financial, physical, emotional, and reputational harm."

Interestingly, the first "Cause of Action" listed in the complaint is that XVideos made money by providing explicit videos—or as the complaint puts it, "Defendants knowingly benefited from participation in what they knew or should have known was a sex trafficking venture." It also claims that XVideos "knowingly received, possessed, and distributed child pornography depicting Class members including Plaintiff... in or affect[ing] interstate or foreign commerce," and that the company should have policed the material on its site more carefully, which lack of age verification caused them to violate... California's Unfair Competition Law?!?!?2 (Don't ask.)

Finally, the complaint gets around to the "class" aspect of the suit, with the claim that Jane Doe is bringing the action "on behalf of All persons residing in California who were under eighteen years of age at the time they were depicted in any video or image, (1) in any commercial sex act as defined under 18 U.S.C. §§ 1591 and 1595, or (2) in any child pornography as defined under 18 U.S.C. § 2252A, or (3) engaging in sexually explicit conduct as defined under 18 U.S.C. § 2260, that has been made available for viewing on any website owned or operated by the Defendants. (the "California Subclass")," later noting that "The Class consists of thousands of people" even though NCOSE and Doe haven't yet been able to identify any of them, or else they'd be (pseudo)named plaintiffs. Doe/NCOSE is basically counting on the idea that since there are so many videos on XVideos, there must be *some* other "abuse victims."

And what is Doe looking for in this complaint? Basically, she/NCOSE want the defendants to limit who can upload videos to the site, require government-issued IDs for all participants and send such IDs to the FBI and the National Center for Missing and Exploited Children to see if anyone claims they're underage, use facial recognition software to ferret out any underage performers, remove all of Jane Doe's images from the site and "archive them for use in this litigation"; "timely respond to all reports of child pornography, and proactively disable the streaming or downloading of reported videos without a human moderator"; stop allowing videos to be downloaded and use "video fingerprinting" to make sure the vids aren't uploaded again; use human moderators to screen all videos, using "standards for screening for child pornography"; ban people who have uploaded child porn or "trafficking videos"...and fire any employee who has "failed to fairly moderate material."

Oh; and of course, Doe/NCOSE is also looking for "all available damages including but not limited to compensatory and punitive damages in favor of Plaintiff and the Class" not to mention "restitution and disgorgement of all profits and unjust enrichment obtained as a result of Defendants' unlawful conduct."

Heck, that shouldn't amount to much more than a few hundred billion dollars!

AFTERWORD

There are just SO MANY people I would like to thank for making this book possible, including (in no particular order) some of my favorite women in porn like Nina Hartley, Veronica Hart, Sharon Mitchell, Chanel, Kylie Ireland, Stormy Daniels, Alexandra Silk, RayVeness, Christi Lake, Nikki Charm, Nikita Denise, Katie Morgan, Aiden Starr, Joanna Angel, Penny Flame, Georgina Spelvin, Candida Royalle, Linda Lovelace, Lola, Angela White, Annika Albrite, Chanel Preston, Dee, Lucky Starr, Phoenix Marie, Alexis Fawx, Sunny Lane, Jewel De'Nyle, Jeanna Fine, Patricia Kennedy, Melanie Moore, Britt Morgan, Kelly O'Dell, Nicole London, Sharon Kane, Dru Berrymore, T.J. Hart, Wendy Divine, Lana Sands, Bionca, Cherokee, Jessie James, Tiffany Mynx, Felecia, Aria, Kelly Nichols, Anna Malle, Sindee Coxx, Melissa Hill, Jill Kelly, Kiss, Marylin Starr, Nici Sterling, Caressa Savage, Roxanne Hall, Shanna McCullough, Francesca Lé, Alex Dane, Tricia Devereaux, Stephanie Swift, Johnni Black, Tina Tyler, Mila, Rebecca Bardoux, Sydnee Steele, Inari Vachs, Shayla LaVeaux, Liza Harper, Ava Vincent, Bunny Luv, Kaylynn, Holly Hollywood, Brooke Hunter, Aurora Snow, Kim Chambers, Kimberly Kane, Nicki Hunter, and of course, Jenna Jameson.

Also well worth mentioning is Raymond Pistol, owner of Showgirl Video in Las Vegas, who yearly would host Bill Margold's Legends of Erotica show, where famous porn stars would memorialize their hands and tits in cement, not unlike what exists in front of Graumann's Chinese Theater in Hollywood.

Finally, I'd also like to pay homage to some of the real freedom fighters in the adult industry past and present, including Hal Freeman, owner of Hollywood Video, whose film *Caught From Behind Part II* was the center of a California Supreme Court case that essentially legalized the production of sexually explicit media, as well as the late retailers/distributors Reuben Sturman and Eddie Wedelstedt, who were known to restock adult stores for free that had been busted for obscenity, Mel Kamins (now 80 and still going strong at this writing), and others.

END NOTES:

(Note: Since many of the articles referenced in this volume are no longer available on the internet, some of the links below point to other statements/activities of the person/organization mentioned in the news story.)

Chapter 2
1. https://www.ep.tc/realist/16/

Chapter 3
1. https://www.nytimes.com/1996/09/26/nyregion/at-the-peale-center-in-pawling-ny-quiet-efficiency-meets-positive-thinking.html

Chapter 4
1. https://en.wikipedia.org/wiki/Mark_Foley_scandal
2. https://transcripts.thedealr.net/script.php/a-fine-madness-1966-FiQ
3. https://nationalpost.com/holy-post/child-abuse-is-a-sin-files-on-36-pedophile-priests-show-how-chicago-archdiocese-hid-sex-assault-allegations
4. https://en.wikipedia.org/wiki/United_States_v._X-Citement_Video,_Inc.
5. https://www.northstarnews.com/
6. https://positivepsychology.com/harlow-experiment/
7. https://www.congress.gov/bill/104th-congress/house-bill/4123
8. https://supreme.justia.com/cases/federal/us/535/234/
9. https://www.nytimes.com/1997/08/13/us/court-upholds-law-covering-pornography.htm
10. https://www.latimes.com/archives/la-xpm-1997-06-27-mn-7342-story.html
11. https://www.law.cornell.edu/supremecourt/text/00-795
12. https://www.dga.org/
13. https://www.imdb.com/event/ev0000687/overview/
14. https://www.frc.org/
15. https://www.afa.net/

16. https://aclj.org/
17. https://supreme.justia.com/cases/federal/us/458/747/
18. https://ncsfreedom.org/
19. https://cc.org/

Chapter 5
1. https://www.christianitytoday.com/ct/1989/december-15/awareness-week-pornography-foes-urge-renewed-awareness.html
2. https://en.wikipedia.org/wiki/American_Family_Association
3. https://www.ccv.org/

Chapter 6
1. https://www.rame.net/reviews/misc/torridtl.html
2. https://en.wikipedia.org/wiki/I_know_it_when_I_see_it
3. https://en.wikipedia.org/wiki/People_v._Freeman
4. https://en.wikipedia.org/wiki/John_Gotti#1992_conviction
5. https://www.washingtonpost.com/archive/lifestyle/2006/01/09/expert-witness-span-classbankheadactivist-lawyer-jan-larue-is-carrying-a-banner-for-sam-alito-in-a-battle-thats-as-personal-as-it-is-politicalspan/6425d203-7917-432f-92df-de13bfce4748/
6. https://avn.com/business/articles/legal/adult-industry-pioneer-eddie-wedelstedt-has-died-886429.html
7. http://www.nostatusquo.com/ACLU/dworkin/other/ordinance/newday/AppD .htm
8. https://www.amazon.com/Protecting-communities-sexually-oriented-businesses/dp/0962546410/ref=sr_1_4?qid=1665946820&refinements=p_27%3ALen+Munsil&s=books&sr=1-4
9. https://www.instagram.com/officialangelyne/?hl=en
10. https://jamanetwork.com/journals/jama/article-abstract/379036
11. https://en.wikipedia.org/wiki/Donna_Rice_Hughes
12. https://www.mtsu.edu/first-amendment/article/22/city-of-renton-v-playtime-theatres-inc
13. https://www.mtsu.edu/first-amendment/article/20/city-of-erie-v-pap-s-a-m

14. https://en.wikipedia.org/wiki/Charles_Keating
15. https://en.wikipedia.org/wiki/Peter_Popoff
16. https://en.wikipedia.org/wiki/Oral_Roberts
17. https://en.wikipedia.org/wiki/Jimmy_Swaggart
18. https://www.nytimes.com/2000/04/30/weekinreview/holy-cow-ohio-has-a-motto-problem.html
19. https://www.history.com/this-day-in-history/the-victim-of-an-anti-gay-assault-dies
20. https://endsexualexploitation.org/articles/interview-with-paula-houston-utah-obscenity-and-pornography-complaints-ombudsman-state-attorney-generals-office/
21. https://avn.com/business/articles/video/apocalypse-now-at-evil-angel-35739.html
22. https://en.wikipedia.org/wiki/John_Paulk
23. https://en.wikipedia.org/wiki/Antonin_Scalia
24. http://cleanhotels.com/

Chapter 7

1. https://www.theglobeandmail.com/arts/dr-laura-the-queen-of-mean/article767776/
2. https://avn.com/business/articles/video/anti-porn-adelphia-founder-son-convicted-of-conspiracy-avn-39497.html
3. http://news.bbc.co.uk/2/hi/1788845.stm
4. https://xxxchurch.com/
5. https://en.wikipedia.org/wiki/Phil_Harvey
6. https://www.amazon.com/Government-Vs-Erotica-Siege-Adam/dp/157392881X
7. https://cbldf.org/
8. https://firefightingnews.com/hazmat-response-team-dispatched-to-the-cafe-risque-adult-supercenter/dscf7595-jpg/
9. https://epublications.marquette.edu/lnq/vol74/iss4/2/
10. https://archive.nytimes.com/www.nytimes.com/library/cyber/week/021198 porn.html
11. https://www.wired.com/1998/11/the-perils-of-cda-ii/

Chapter 8
1. https://www.law.cornell.edu/supct/html/03-218.ZO.html
2. https://www.aclu.org/other/supreme-court-and-copa
3. https://www.fcc.gov/consumers/guides/childrens-internet-protection-act
4. https://www.dwt.com/insights/2003/03/federal-appeals-court-again-finds-child-online-pro
5. https://supreme.justia.com/cases/federal/us/529/803/
6. https://www.dwt.com/insights/2008/07/3rd-circuit-invalidates-child-online-protection-ac
7. https://www.britannica.com/topic/Communications-Decency-Act

Chapter 9
1. https://aclj.org/
2. https://www.mtsu.edu/first-amendment/article/793/attorney-general-s-commission-on-pornography
3. https://lc.org/
4. https://americandecency.org/
5. https://www.congress.gov/bill/107th-congress/senate-bill/2886?s=1&r=8
6. https://www.sourcewatch.org/index.php/Talk:Institute_for_Media_Education

Chapter 10
1. https://en.wikipedia.org/wiki/Joe_Redner

Chapter 11
1. https://www.priestsforlife.org/elections/voterguide.aspx
2. https://en.wikipedia.org/wiki/Sam_Harris

Chapter 12
1. https://www.imdb.com/title/tt0335345/?ref_=nv_sr_srsg_0

Chapter 13
1. https://vimeo.com/723860813
2. https://oxbowacademy.net/educationalarticles/senate_hearing_porn4/
3. https://avn.com/business/articles/video/extreme-associates-case-dismissed-obscenity-laws-ruled-unconstitutional-41913.html
4. https://en.wikipedia.org/wiki/Jeffrey_Satinover
5. https://avn.com/business/articles/video/feds-indict-goalie-entertainment-owner-others-42619.html
6. https://www.law.cornell.edu/supremecourt/text/413/15%26amp#writing-USSC_CR_0413_0015_ZD1
7. https://en.wikipedia.org/wiki/Mike_Pence

Chapter 14
1. https://www.forbes.com/sites/beltway/2017/06/07/the-great-kansas-tax-cut-experiment-crashes-and-burns/
2. https://www.govinfo.gov/content/pkg/CHRG-109shrg44825/html/CHRG-109shrg44825.htm
3. https://scholarship.law.unc.edu/falr/vol9/iss1/3/
4. https://www.lifeissues.net/writers/reis/reis_89picturepoison.html
5. https://reason.com/2021/12/06/rip-phil-harvey-entrepreneur-and-philanthropist-who-expanded-human-pleasure-and-human-choice/
6. https://www.law.virginia.edu/faculty/profile/fs7t/1206076
7. https://avn.com/business/articles/video/feds-indict-goalie-entertainment-owner-others-42619.html

Chapter 15
1. https://www.law.cornell.edu/uscode/text/18/2257
2. https://avn.com/business/articles/video/mary-carey-a-hit-at-bush-fundraiser-44186.html

Chapter 16
1. https://avn.com/business/articles/video/adult-freedom-foundation-launches-site-43384.html

2. https://avn.com/business/articles/video/adult-freedom-foundation-requests-witnesses-for-new-obscenity-hearing-42557.html
3. https://www.woodhullfoundation.org/
4. https://www.nytimes.com/2005/09/11/books/review/pornified-dirty-minds.html
5. https://www.judithcoche.com/services-all
6. https://drjillmanning.com/
7. https://cdt.org/staff/leslie-harris/
8. https://en.wikipedia.org/wiki/Rodney_A._Smolla

Chapter 17
1. https://www.congress.gov/bill/109th-congress/senate-bill/616/text
2. https://avn.com/business/articles/video/bush-signs-anti-indecency-bill-49734.html
3. https://ballotpedia.org/Mark_Pryor
4. https://www.fcc.gov/biography-kevin-j-martin
5. https://en.wikipedia.org/wiki/L._Brent_Bozell_III
6. https://en.wikipedia.org/wiki/Kyle_E._McSlarrow
7. https://www.theofficialboard.com/biography/jessica-marventano-e5685
8. https://www.fiercewireless.com/person/preston-padden
9. https://www.ocregister.com/2017/06/13/trinity-on-hook-for-entire-2-million-judgment-judge-says/
10. https://www.businessinsider.com/nbc-exec-says-watching-tv-linearly-is-the-way-god-intended-and-takes-shots-at-netflix-and-you-tube-2016-1
11. https://www.c-span.org/person/?1011030/JimDyke
12. https://www.nytimes.com/2007/04/27/movies/27valenti.html
13. https://en.wikipedia.org/wiki/Desperate_Housewives
14. https://avn.com/business/articles/legal/court-overturns-fcc-fine-for-janet-jackson-broadcast-53845.html
15. https://www.nytimes.com/1974/06/25/archives/high-court-up-holds-carnal-knowledge-but-rules-ad-for-us-report.html

Chapter 18
1. https://en.wikipedia.org/wiki/George_Lakoff
2. https://www.firstthings.com/article/2002/05/gods-justice-and-ours
3. https://en.wikipedia.org/wiki/Ferris_Alexander_trial
4. https://en.wikipedia.org/wiki/VCA_Pictures
5. https://medium.com/authority-magazine/5-things-i-wish-someone-told-me-before-i-became-a-ceo-with-susan-colvin-of-calexotics-4f7bc-321cb0e
6. https://avn.com/business/articles/video/the-adult-industry-remem-bers-christian-mann-1961-2014-568317.html
7. https://avn.com/business/articles/legal/georgia-woman-sues-city-because-she-can-t-legally-buy-vibrator-561783.html
8. https://bigthink.com/people/samharris/
9. https://en.wikipedia.org/wiki/Jerry_Falwell
10. https://en.wikipedia.org/wiki/Pat_Robertson
11. https://en.wikipedia.org/wiki/Donald_Wildmon
12. https://en.wikipedia.org/wiki/Tom%C3%A1s_de_Torquemada
13. https://en.wikipedia.org/wiki/Robert_A._Heinlein

Chapter 19
1. https://www.parentstv.org/leadership/robert-w-peters
2. https://en.wikipedia.org/wiki/Victor_Cline
3. https://www.scribd.com/doc/20282510/Dr-Victor-Cline-Pornogra-phy-s-Effects-on-Adults-and-Children
4. https://en.wikipedia.org/wiki/Gary_Ridgway
5. https://en.wikipedia.org/wiki/Dennis_Rader

Chapter 20
1. https://casetext.com/case/on-command-video-v-lodgenet-entertain-ment-corp
2. https://www.facebook.com/398775493518126/posts/dr-mary-anne-layden-co-director-of-the-sexual-trauma-and-psychopathology-program/1196784293717238/

3. https://www.catholicnewsagency.com/resource/56076/interview-with-roger-young-a-retired-fbi-agent-who-specialized-in-child-pornography-and-obscenity-cases
4. https://www.law.cornell.edu/supct/html/02-102.ZS.html
5. https://www.thelocal.se/20050406/1235-2/
6. https://www.roks.se/about-roks
7. https://archive.ph/iZQKw

Chapter 21
1. https://www.martyklein.com/

Chapter 22
1. https://avn.com/business/articles/video/night-of-the-stars-nominees-announced-44152.html
2. https://www.frc.org/
3. https://www.drjamesdobson.org/bio/dr-james-dobson
4. https://en.wikipedia.org/wiki/Ted_Baehr
5. https://en.wikipedia.org/wiki/Gary_Bauer
6. https://anncoulter.com/
7. https://religionnews.com/2017/06/14/barry-lynn-looks-back-on-25-years-of-separating-church-and-state/
8. https://politics.princeton.edu/people/robert-p-george
9. https://en.wikipedia.org/wiki/Marilyn_Musgrave
10. https://en.wikipedia.org/wiki/Maggie_Gallagher
11. https://en.wikipedia.org/wiki/Mike_Huckabee
12. https://en.wikipedia.org/wiki/Tony_Snow
13. https://en.wikipedia.org/wiki/Don_Feder
14. https://www.lifesitenews.com/news/the-phill-kline-saga-planned-parenthood-protected-children-forgotten-the-pr/
15. https://www.wellingtonboone.com/
16. https://www.congress.gov/bill/109th-congress/house-bill/235
17. https://en.wikipedia.org/wiki/Richard_Land
18. https://en.wikipedia.org/wiki/Jim_Inhofe
19. https://en.wikipedia.org/wiki/Charles_W._Pickering

20. https://generationnext.me/about/
21. https://www.leadershipinstitute.org/training/contact.cfm?FacultyID=41322

Chapter 23
1. http://www.jamesllambert.com/
2. https://janetfolgerporter.com/about-janet/
3. https://www.christianitytoday.com/news/2022/june/kennedy-coral-ridge-media-hate-group-splc-thomas-defamation.html
4. https://adflegal.org/

Chapter 24
1. https://enough.org/news-57
2. https://patch.com/pennsylvania/southwhitehall/parkland-students-may-be-involved-in-sexting-case
3. https://www.sourcewatch.org/index.php/Robert_Knight
4. https://www.bmj.com/content/334/7599/867.1.short
5. https://www.amazon.com/Forbidden-Fruit-Religion-American-Teenagers/dp/0195395859

Chapter 25
1. https://en.wikipedia.org/wiki/Expelled:_No_Intelligence_Allowed
2. https://en.wikipedia.org/wiki/Albert_Mohler
3. https://www.congress.gov/bill/110th-congress/senate-bill/1810/text
4. https://www.mathematica.org/publications/impacts-of-four-title-v-section-510-abstinence-education-programs
5. https://en.wikipedia.org/wiki/Wendy_Wright
6. https://en.wikipedia.org/wiki/Ted_Haggard
7. https://avn.com/business/articles/legal/analysis-deconstructing-dines-404545.html
8. https://robertwjensen.org/articles/why-porn-why-this-porn-why-so-little-concern/

Chapter 26
1. https://www.asacp.org/page.php
2. http://abcnews.go.com/TheLaw/FedCrimes/
story?id=4712725&page=1
3. https://www.ojp.gov/ncjrs/virtual-library/abstracts/child-molesters-
behavioral-analysis-professional-investigating

Chapter 27
1. https://www.glaad.org/gap/cathy-ruse
2. https://casetext.com/case/phe-inc-v-department-of-justice-2

Chapter 28
1. https://avn.com/galleries/adultcon-15-1074
2. https://www.comm.ucsb.edu/people/daniel-linz
3. https://www.dianarussell.com/index.html
4. https://xxxchurch.com/
5. https://en.wikipedia.org/wiki/President%27s_Commission_on_Ob-
scenity_and_Pornography

Chapter 29
1. https://www.lifesitenews.com/news/hardcore-adult-porn-contrib-
utes-to-child-sexual-abuse-mim-report/
2. http://www.searsarchives.com/catalogs/history.htm
3. https://en.wikipedia.org/wiki/Dolf_Zillmann
4. https://journals.sagepub.com/doi/10.1177/019251388009004006
5. https://www.researchgate.net/figure/Estimated-Prevalence-of-Chil-
dren-under-12-years-with-Sexual-Behaviour-Problems_fig1_237114117

Chapter 30
1. https://en.wikipedia.org/wiki/North_American_Man/Boy_Love_
Association
2. https://avn.com/business/articles/legal/commentary-pornography-
and-the-problem-with-history-45518.html
3. https://en.wikipedia.org/wiki/Conservatives_without_Conscience

4. https://www.reuters.com/article/us-usa-senator-prostitution/u-s-senator-apologizes-for-sex-scandal-idUSN1634565120070716

Chapter 31

1. https://ballotpedia.org/Mark_Shurtleff
2. https://www.nytimes.com/2000/03/16/us/utah-law-creates-first-pornography-czar.html

Chapter 32

1. https://www.firstthings.com/article/2010/06/the-weight-of-smut
2. https://marjorieheins.academia.edu/
3. https://archive.nytimes.com/cityroom.blogs.nytimes.com/2007/07/10/times-square-ad-with-naked-derrieres-faces-a-judges-scrutiny/
4. https://avn.com/business/articles/legal/dawn-hawkins-terrifying-porn-flight-updated-465580.html
5. https://www.smartrecovery.org/the-brain-that-changes-itself/
6. https://www.nationalreview.com/corner/sex-kathryn-jean-lopez/
7. https://www.nationalreview.com/corner/pornography-some-e-mails-kathryn-jean-lopez/

Chapter 33

1. https://tavistockandportman.nhs.uk/care-and-treatment/our-clinical-services/portman-clinic/
2. https://www.theguardian.com/media/2009/oct/12/louise-chunn-to-edit-phsychologies
3. https://avn.com/business/articles/legal/review-the-porn-report-455972.html
4. https://iqfy.com/the-profound-effects-of-porn-on-children-teenagers/
5. https://www.drpatrickcarnes.com/
6. https://www.valsampson.co.uk/

7. http://www.nydailynews.com/lifestyle/2010/06/07/2010-06-07_young_children_have_more_access_to_online_pornography_study.html

Chapter 34
1. https://www.culpa.info/prof/2592

Chapter 35
1. http://www.youtube.com/watch?v=NjuWn32pzLM&context=C34d7ae8ADOEgsToPDskL7lmyerhDPU_ZiREbmKx3x
2. https://www.youtube.com/watch?v=yQYtcsx2F-U

Chapter 36
1. https://www.mountvernon.org/library/digitalhistory/digital-encyclopedia/article/james-wilson-1742-1798/
2. http://www.law.cornell.edu/supct/html/99-138.ZD1.html
3. http://dailytrojan.com/2012/04/10/justice-scalia-defends-view-of-the-constitution/
4. https://www.oyez.org/cases/1989/88-1503
5. https://www.oyez.org/cases/1995/94-1039
6. https://www.oyez.org/cases/1972/71-1332

Chapter 37
1. https://endsexualexploitation.org/articles/evidence-of-sex-trafficking-in-porn-industry/
2. https://avn.com/business/articles/legal/another-california-ballot-initiative-to-be-wary-of-484953.html
3. https://www.iafd.com/person.rme/perfid=roxy/gender=f/roxy.htm
4. https://en.wikipedia.org/wiki/Shelley_Lubben#Pink_Cross_Foundation
5. https://avn.com/business/articles/legal/rk-seeks-to-dismiss-lawsuit-alleging-minor-was-knowigly-filmed-432153.html

Chapter 38
1. https://www.glaad.org/gap/matt-barber?response_type=embed

Chapter 39
1. https://avn.com/business/articles/video/blue-devil-unmasked-meet-duke-porn-star-belle-knox-551136.html
2. https://truthaboutporn.org/media/dr-donald-hilton-m-d/

Chapter 40
1. https://www.facebook.com/wdbj7/posts/328879030533487/?comment_id=329189160502474&comment_tracking=%7B%22tn%22%3A%22R%22%7D&paipv=0&eav=Afa6eHA5m_0SPbnuTV73LHP_xd-wSx498jmNRsN1VEuYN0AFJD-FEOK_xyT67eBONlsQ&_rdr
2. http://variety.com/2013/tv/news/tom-wheeler-grilled-on-backdoor-regulations-1200498360/
3. https://cbldf.org/about-us/case-files/obscenity-case-files/obscenity-case-files-fcc-v-pacifica-foundation-george-carlins-seven-dirty-words/
4. https://www.parentstv.org/leadership/tim-winter-1

Chapter 41
1. https://endsexualexploitation.org/articles/pornography-harms-children/
2. https://endsexualexploitation.org/articles/solutions-work-cordelia-anderson-speaks-pornography-public-health/
3. https://avn.com/business/articles/legal/op-ed-jousting-with-the-insane-on-aol-build-598936.html
4. https://avn.com/business/articles/video/hot-girls-wanted-the-bullshit-continues-587800.html
5. https://avn.com/business/articles/legal/op-ed-jousting-with-the-insane-on-aol-build-598936.html
6. http://www.usatoday.com/story/news/nation/2015/07/14/pornography-public-health-crisis/30152095/

Chapter 42
1. https://www.hsdl.org/?abstract&did=470299
2. https://www.vh1.com/shows/dating-naked
3. https://www.oyez.org/cases/2013/12-8561
4. https://www.congress.gov/bill/115th-congress/senate-bill/2152/text
5. https://www.amnesty.org/en/latest/news/2016/05/amnesty-international-publishes-policy-and-research-on-protection-of-sex-workers-rights/
6. https://en.wikipedia.org/wiki/Anti-prostitution_pledge
7. https://en.wikipedia.org/wiki/USAID_v._Alliance_for_Open_Society_(2013)

Chapter 43
1. https://endsexualexploitation.org/articles/united-nations-torture-report/
2. https://www.newyorker.com/magazine/2004/05/10/torture-at-abu-ghraib
3. https://www.esquire.com/news-politics/politics/a39369449/guantanamo-bay-torture-program/
4. https://digitallibrary.un.org/record/732217?ln=en

Chapter 44
1. https://www.cnbc.com/2009/07/14/Top-US-States-For-Online-Pornography.html
2. https://www.tumblr.com/usualgangofidiots/659970248854913024/the-usual-gang-of-idiots-published-wednesday

Chapter 45
1. https://endsexualexploitation.org/freedomagenda/
2. https://nordicmodelnow.org/what-is-the-nordic-model/
3. https://onlinelibrary.wiley.com/doi/abs/10.1002/1098-2337%281986%2912%3A3%3C225%3A%3AAID-AB2480120310%3E3.0.CO%3B2-B
4. https://www.congress.gov/bill/109th-congress/house-bill/357

5. https://www.congress.gov/bill/115th-congress/house-bill/680
6. https://www.congress.gov/bill/115th-congress/senate-bill/534/text

Chapter 46
1. https://endsexualexploitation.org/articles/category/podcast/
2. https://endsexualexploitation.org/articles/podcast-pornography-really-industry/

Chapter 47
1. https://catholicreview.org/archbishop-lori-among-bishops-saying-hhs-proposal-violates-religious-freedom-and-is-bad-medicine/
2. https://www.oyez.org/cases/2019/19-431
3. https://blog.acton.org/archives/76744-navy-chaplain-allegedly-removed-from-unit-for-teaching-christian-view-of-sexuality.html
4. https://www.hrc.org/press-releases/oklahoma-wesleyan-university-president-is-proud-to-discriminate-against-tra
5. https://www.freetobelieve.com/donald-vander-boon
6. https://en.wikipedia.org/wiki/Jody_Hice
7. https://www.dailykos.com/stories/2022/10/18/2129842/-Rep-Mike-Johnson-R-proposes-nationwide-version-of-Florida-s-infamous-Don-t-Say-Gay-law
8. https://www.washingtonpost.com/news/acts-of-faith/wp/2017/02/02/trump-said-hell-totally-destroy-the-johnson-amendment-what-is-it-and-why-do-people-care/

Chapter 48
1. https://avn.com/business/articles/legal/larry-flynt-talks-trump-sessions-with-the-hollywood-reporter-708475.html
2. https://www.oyez.org/cases/1972/71-1051
3. https://www.oyez.org/cases/1996/96-511
4. https://www.oyez.org/cases/1968/293

Chapter 49
1. https://www.youtube.com/watch?v=oMeulTWdqiY

2. http://endsexualexploitation.org/dirtydozen-2016/

Chapter 50
1. https://www.nytimes.com/1992/08/30/books/l-girls-lean-back-everywhere-360792.html
2. https://www.mtsu.edu/first-amendment/article/1038/comstock-act-of-1873

Chapter 51
1. https://www.imdb.com/title/tt5943660/?ref_=ttep_ep10
2. https://en.wikipedia.org/wiki/Preacher_(comics)
3. https://bleedingcool.com/movies/one-million-moms-verizon-preacher/

Chapter 52
1. https://theppgstore.com/sharonda-parker-2/
2. https://www.bostonmagazine.com/best-of-boston-archive/1999/grand-opening/
3. https://drnikki.com.au/

Chapter 53
1. https://www.attorneygeneral.gov/report/
2. https://www.nytimes.com/2018/08/14/us/pennsylvania-child-abuse-catholic-church.html
3. https://friendlyatheist.patheos.com/2018/08/15/here-are-the-worst-abuses-by-catholic-priests-from-the-pa-grand-jurys-report/
4. https://townhall.com/columnists/haleyhalverson/2018/08/16/when-churches-become-scenes-of-sexual-abuse-n2510153
5. http://www.christiannewswire.com/news/3265681513.html

Chapter 54
1. http://www.celebritybeliefs.com/melissa-benoist/
2. https://www.ted.com/speakers/nicole_maines

3. https://www.newsbusters.org/blogs/culture/lindsay-kornick/2020/03/15/supergirl-protects-vulnerable-trans-community-those-who
4. https://www.newsbusters.org/blogs/culture/lindsay-kornick/2019/04/29/supergirl-transgender-hero-preaches-sharing-our-truth

Chapter 55
1. https://www.imdb.com/title/tt0065904/
2. https://www.iafd.com/title.rme/title=deep+throat/year=1972/deep-throat.htm
3. https://www.nytimes.com/1973/01/04/archives/obscenity-trial-of-throat-ends-ruling-expected-in-a-monthboth.html
4. https://www.cnn.com/2019/03/20/politics/john-hickenlooper-x-rated-movie/index.html
5. https://www.loc.gov/programs/national-film-preservation-board/film-registry/
6. https://www.loc.gov/programs/national-film-preservation-board/film-registry/nominate/

Chapter 56
1. https://www.dailymail.co.uk/news/article-7609835/Katie-Hill-seen-showing-Nazi-era-tattoo-smoking-BONG-NAKED.html
2. https://www.theguardian.com/commentisfree/2019/oct/25/katie-hill-democrats-politics-
3. https://redstate.com/tags/katie-hill
4. https://gen.medium.com/katie-hill-was-brought-down-by-the-same-forces-that-enable-weinstein-e46ea59d7493
5. https://theslot.jezebel.com/katie-hills-resignation-is-an-ugly-mess-1839411503
6. https://www.nytimes.com/2019/06/25/us/duncan-hunter-affair-wife.html
7. https://www.latimes.com/california/story/2019-10-07/duncan-hunter-criminal-trial-delayed

8. https://redstate.com/author/jenvanlaar

Chapter 57
1. https://avn.com/business/articles/legal/congrats-adult-industryy-oure-officially-second-class-citizens-878133.html
2. https://www.mtsu.edu/first-amendment/article/400/memoirs-v-massachusetts

Chapter 58
1. https://www.parentstv.org/Teen-Report.pdf
2. https://avn.com/business/articles/legal/religious-video-pirate-vidangel-owes-disney-et-al-624-million-875124.html

Chapter 59
1. https://www.frc.org/brochure/sex-education-in-public-schools-sexualization-of-children-and-lgbt-indoctrination
2. https://institute-research.com/
3. https://www.splcenter.org/fighting-hate/extremist-files/group/american-college-pediatricians
4. https://thetransformedwife.com/

Chapter 60
1. https://casetext.com/case/charleston-v-nevada-1
2. https://law.justia.com/cases/federal/appellate-courts/ca9/19-17423/19-17423-2020-12-10.html
3. https://www.rebekahspeaksout.com/

Chapter 61
1. https://www.thedailybeast.com/son-of-atlanta-shooting-victim-hyun-jung-grant-calls-bullshit-on-robert-aaron-long-sex-addiction-claim
2. https://reason.com/2021/03/23/sex-trafficking-panic-and-victim-blaming-follow-atlanta-massage-parlor-murders/
3. https://hopequestgroup.org/

4. https://nypost.com/2021/03/18/atlanta-spa-shooting-suspect-expressed-shame-for-porn-addiction/
5. https://www.newyorker.com/culture/q-and-a/a-sociologist-of-religion-on-protestants-porn-and-the-purity-industrial-complex
6. https://www.nytimes.com/2021/03/22/opinion/atlanta-shooting-women-violence.html
7. https://www.newsweek.com/robert-aaron-long-pleads-guilty-atlanta-spa-killings-1613499
8. https://esplerp.org/
9. https://sacramentoswop.org/

Chapter 62
1. https://endsexualexploitation.org/articles/statement-class-action-lawsuit-filed-against-pornhub-by-two-survivors-of-childhood-sex-trafficking/
2. https://www.winston.com/en/legal-glossary/california-unfair-competition-law.html

CPSIA information can be obtained
at www.ICGtesting.com
Printed in the USA
BVHW060337120123
656153BV00023B/281